A Customized Version of Introduction to

Social Psychology

Designed Specifically for Dr. Robert Short
at Arizona State University

Jennifer Feenstra
Northwestern College

Kendall Hunt
publishing company

Pages xvii–xx, 1–36, 41–64, 79–102, 121–250, and 255–314 from *Introduction to Social Psychology*
by Jennifer Feenstra. Copyright © 2011 by Bridgepoint Education.

Cover image provided by the author.

Kendall Hunt
publishing company

www.kendallhunt.com
Send all inquiries to:
4050 Westmark Drive
Dubuque, IA 52004-1840

Copyright © 2013 by Robert A. Short

ISBN 978-1-4652-2177-3

Printed in the United States of America
10 9 8 7 6 5 4 3 2 1

Brief Contents

Contents

chapter 2
Studying the Self *19*

chapter 5
Making Judgments *79*

chapter 6
Prejudice *91*

chapter 8
Persuasion Techniques *139*

chapter 9
Persuasion by a Group: Conformity *151*

chapter 10
Persuasion by an Individual: Obedience   *161*

chapter 13
Attraction   *203*

About the Author

Jennifer S. Feenstra is an associate professor of psychology at Northwestern College, Orange City Iowa. She earned her Ph.D. in social psychology as well as a master's degree in college teaching from the University of New Hampshire.

Preface

Social psychologists investigate how we view ourselves and others, how we interact with others, how we influence others, and how we act when we are part of a group. Given the amount of time each of us spend thinking about and interacting with the people we encounter every day, much of our lives are spent with the subject matter of social psychology. You encounter social psychology in your day-to-day life, and a textbook on social psychology should reflect that.

This book draws on experiences we might encounter to enhance learning of social psychological theories and concepts. After the first module each section begins with a description of an experience one might come across, like a job interview or an infomercial. Within each section connections are made between aspects of that experience and social psychological terms, concepts, and theories.

The text covers the wide variety of topics studied by social psychologists. The stage is set in the first module with an introduction to the field, including some of the history of social psychology and research methodology. The first section includes this introduction and then begins with the smallest unit of study for social psychologists, the self. The text then slowly expands the viewpoint. The second section moves from the self to thinking about others. Thinking about others includes attributions, attitudes, judgments, and prejudice. In the third section the text offers an investigation of influence. Persuasive messages and persuasive techniques are examined, as well as the impact of conformity and obedience on our lives. The fourth section examines our interactions with others, both the good interactions and the bad, with an exploration of aggression and helping behaviors. This section also covers what attracts us to one another and how we engage in, maintain, and end relationships. The final section focuses in on the group's impact on the individual, in both behavior and judgment, as well as the dilemmas groups face in working together.

Features

Highlighted Terms

Given the importance of terminology in social psychology important terms are highlighted when defined in the text and a glossary provides definitions of each term.

Social Psychology in Depth

In each module is a box that provides more depth on a topic from the module. The boxes focus on specific studies, researchers, or topics.

Critical Thinking Questions

Knowledge of social psychology has a variety of implications for our lives. To encourage application of social psychological concepts, each module ends with several critical thinking questions.

Links to Additional Material

If a particular topic sparks some interest, links to additional material are provided at the end of each module to allow for further investigation. These links might go to a blog post on a topic from the module, a video clip, a research article, a survey, or other material.

PART I

Discovering Social Psychology and the Self

"There is one thing even more vital to science than intelligent methods; and that is, the sincere desire to find out the truth, whatever, that may be."

—Charles Sanders Peirce

1 Discovering Social Psychology

Learning Objectives

By the end of the chapter you should be able to:

- Define social psychology
- Describe the history of social psychology
- Describe the scientific method
- Discuss the observational method and explain when that method is most appropriate to the research question
- Discuss the correlational method and explain when that method is most appropriate to the research question
- Discuss the experimental method and explain when that method is most appropriate to the research question
- Understand the dangers of hindsight bias

1.1 What Is Social Psychology?

As of 2011 Facebook had over 500 million users, each user with an average of 130 friends (Facebook, 2011). By the end of 2010 there were 152 million blogs on the Internet (Pingdom, 2011). In 2010 Twitter boasted 190 million visitors per month. Twitter users generate about 65 million tweets a day (Schonfeld, 2010), with 100 million new accounts added in 2010 (Pingdom, 2011). Human beings, it seems, are intensely interested in and seek out interaction with other human beings. If you are one of those people who is interested in other people, you've come to the right place. Social psychology is a field that studies people, in particular people interacting with one another.

Social psychology is the scientific study of human thoughts, feelings, and behavior as they relate to and are influenced by others. Many academic disciplines are interested in human thoughts, feelings, or behavior. If you were to take a literature course you would find yourself contemplating the thoughts of Ishmael in *Moby Dick* or the actions of Lady Macbeth in *Macbeth*. In an art course you might work on translating a particular feeling into a sculpture or a painting. In a biology course you might learn how the heart works to pump blood around the human body. Social psychology is different in the method it uses to study humans. Social psychology involves the scientific study of people. Social psychologists use a particular method in their work, the scientific method. We will think more about this method a little later in this section.

Most people consider social psychology a branch of psychology, although some social psychologists come from a sociological perspective. The difference is that psychology is concerned with the individual, whereas sociology looks at the group or social system. Therefore social psychology as a branch of psychology focuses on how individuals are affected by others; social psychology from a sociological perspective pays more attention to the social setting and the person's place within the dynamics of the social system.

Social psychology studies how humans interact with one another.

Social psychology is often paired with another branch of psychology, personality psychology. For example, one of the largest organizations for social psychologists is one that also includes personality psychology, the Society for Personality and Social Psychology. These two fields are like two sides of a coin. Social psychologists emphasize how different people act in similar ways in similar situations, documenting how outside forces affect behavior.

Personality psychologists focus on differentiating people from one another, observing how forces inside the person affect behavior. For example, in explaining why Stuart joined a cult, a social psychologist might look at the persuasive techniques the cult used to convince all of its converts to join. A personality psychologist would, instead, focus on how Stuart's tendency toward following those in authority makes him, but not someone else, particularly vulnerable to cults.

Social psychologists study a wide variety of topics, including views of the self, persuasion, attraction, and group processes. In general social psychologists are interested how people relate to and influence one another, but throughout this course you may find topics that do not seem to fit this definition. Don't be surprised. Social psychology is a large, unwieldy, and largely disjointed field of study. In a history of the field of psychology, science writer Morton Hunt (1983) does a good job of summarizing the issue. "The problem" he writes, " is that social psychology has no unifying concept; it did not develop from the seed of a theoretical construct . . . but grew like crabgrass in uncultivated regions of the social sciences" (p. 397). Welcome to the study of crabgrass.

Large, unwieldy, and disjointed it may be, but social psychology offers the student and the scientist a way of answering the questions that haunt our daily lives. How do I understand who I am and my capabilities? What should I do in this new situation? Is that person interested in dating me? Does that infomercial really convince anyone to buy the product? How do I get my school or work group to work better together? The diversity of topics found in social psychology also allows for wonderful interconnections with other areas of psychology. Both social psychologists and cognitive psychologists are interested in decision making and attributions. Social psychologists and developmental psychologists are both interested in attachment and romantic relationships. The special expertise and focus of the different areas means we know more about these topics than we might if they were studied in only one area.

1.2 Where Did Social Psychology Come From?

The Beginning

It all began with a bicycle. Several bicycles actually. And the people on them, of course. In 1898 Norman Triplett published an article where he asked a question about bicyclists. He wondered why cyclists seemed to race faster when in the presence of other cyclists than when racing against the clock alone. He proposed some reasons and then tested these using the scientific method. Because he explored the effect of others on individual action using the scientific method, Triplett is considered by many social psychologists to have conducted the first social psychological research study (Allport, 1954; Jones, 1998;

It is thought that the first social psychology experiment examined why cyclists raced faster in the presence of others than when they were alone.

though there is some disagreement, see Danziger, 2000, and Haines & Vaughan, 1979). Triplett found that in general, participants in his study were able to perform actions more quickly when in the presence of others. We will come back to his study in Chapter 15.

If we date the start of social psychology to 1898, we realize that the field is not very old, at least not for a scientific discipline. Social psychology is technically a little over 110 years old, but looking more deeply into its history we discover that the field is even younger. A few important social psychologists and their theories were developed in the first 50 years of the 20th century, but it was not until after World War II that the field of social psychology took off.

Social Psychology Before 1950

One important early social psychologist was a refugee from Nazi Germany who moved to the United States in 1933. Kurt Lewin (1890–1947) had a large effect on the field of social psychology; yet in most social psychology textbooks, including this one, you will find his name only in the section on the history of social psychology. Lewin believed that outside forces affect the behavior of the individual. For example, he theorized that the actions and decisions of the individual are constrained by what he described as fields of force, like the planets in our solar system are constrained in their movement by the pull of gravity from the bodies that surround them. Lewin's contributions were primarily in the realm of theory and method. It was the *way* he did social psychology that people emulated. For more on what Lewin did and how he did it, see the *Social Psychology in Depth* box.

Other researchers were also active in the early days of social psychology. Research on attitudes was prominent, research that continues to today. In 1934 a researcher by the name of Richard T. LaPiere published a study involving travel. For two years he and two of his friends traveled in the United States and LaPiere recorded the welcome they received at the restaurants and lodgings they visited. Before you consider writing about your next road trip, consider what was unique about his study. The friends LaPiere traveled with were from China, and in 1934 in the United States attitudes toward Chinese people were quite negative. Despite this prejudice, LaPiere and his friends received a warm welcome from all but one place they visited on their journey. Strangely, when LaPiere later collected surveys from these establishments nearly all responded they would not serve Chinese. Why the vast difference between actions and attitudes? This is one question about attitudes LaPiere and other researchers have since sought to answer.

Social Psychology Since 1950

In the 1950s and 1960s social psychological research took off. A number of factors contributed to this explosion of interest in the field. One desire of a number of social psychologists, and therefore a topic of study in this period, was to explain the violent events leading up to and taking place during World War II. Researchers looked into the causes of aggression. They focused on group actions like conformity and social facilitation and on individual actions like obedience. Many of the topics you will read about throughout this text began to be studied seriously in these decades. These concepts, researchers, and their major findings are summarized in Table 1.1. Many of the names and concepts in the table will be new to you; however, skim through and note the dates. As we explore social psychology throughout the coming weeks, keep this table in mind.

Social Psychology in Depth: Lewin's Contributions

The psychologist finds himself in the midst of a rich and vast land full of strange happenings: There are men killing themselves; a child playing; a person who, having fallen in love and being caught in an unhappy situation, is not willing or not able to find a way out; . . . there is the reaching out for higher and more difficult goals; loyalty to a group; dreaming; planning; exploring the world; and so on without end.

It is an immense continent full of fascination and power and full of stretches of land where no one ever has set foot.

Psychology is out to conquer this continent, to find out where its treasures are hidden, to investigate its danger spots, to master its vast forces, to utilize its energies. How can one reach this goal? (Lewin, 1940, cited in Marrow, 1969, p. 3)

As a young science, social psychology struggled to find its direction and focus. Kurt Lewin helped the field find its way, while also making great contributions to child development and industrial/organizational psychology (Ash, 1992). Lewin explained that behavior (B) was a function (f) of both the person (P) and the environment (E), resulting in an equation written as $B = f(P, E)$. For human beings, the environment (E) most often includes other people, so Lewin was intensely interested in the effect we have on one another. In fact, Lewin was the person who coined the term *group dynamics* (Berscheid, 2003).

Lewin saw the importance of studying the person outside the laboratory, in everyday situations. He also wanted to study the important issues of the day, focusing psychological study on the particular social issues that needed to be solved. The study that initially put him on the map in the United States was one of leadership styles. Lewin and his colleagues (Lewin, Lippitt, & White, 1939) compared the behavior of children assigned to groups led by those using an authoritarian and laissez-faire style with the behavior of children led by those using a more democratic style. They found that hostile behavior was usually higher in the groups when led using an authoritarian or laissez-faire style than when led using a democratic style.

Though this research may not seem revolutionary now, at the time social psychology was dealing with some growing pains. Lewin believed that groups could be studied experimentally and did so in studies like the one on leadership styles. Another prominent psychologist, Floyd Allport (1924), argued that only the individual could be the subject of study. Psychology studies the individual, Allport argued, so extending psychology to groups goes against the definition of the field. Allport also believed that social psychologists should focus on laboratory studies. It was Allport who pointed to Triplett's 1898 study as the first in the history of social psychology, not because Triplett himself saw it as a social psychological study but because it fit Allport's model of what a study in social psychology should be (Berscheid, 2003). Allport was a good salesman. The section on history in this text began with a review of Triplett.

Thanks to Allport's efforts, Triplett may have won the battle of "who conducted the first social psychological research study," but Lewin won the war. Social psychologists study the interaction of the person and environment. Social psychologists also study groups, both large groups and very small groups, those made up of two people. The Society for the Psychological Study of Social Issues, an organization Lewin helped start, is alive and well. Lewin's ideas continue to be used in the area of action research. Action research focuses on making improvements to difficult situations while advancing scientific knowledge (Bargal, 2008; Sommer, 2009). Given the big issues we face in the world today—war, poverty, and discrimination, to name a few—one can hope for Lewin's tradition to continue.

Table 1.1 Social Psychological Topics and Researchers of the 1950s and 1960s

Topic	Researcher, Date, and Work	Major Finding
Aggression	Berkowitz, L., & LePage, A. (1967). Weapons as aggression-eliciting stimuli. In the *Journal of Personality and Social Psychology*.	The presence of a weapon elicited greater aggression than the presence of a neutral stimulus or no object.
Attraction	Walster, E., Aronson, V., Abrahams, D., & Rottmann, L. (1966). Importance of physical attractiveness in dating behavior. In the *Journal of Personality and Social Psychology*.	Attractive individuals were liked more, more likely to be pursued for a later date, and rated their dates more harshly.
Cognitive dissonance	Festinger, L., & Carlsmith, J. M. (1959). Cognitive consequences of forced compliance. In the *Journal of Abnormal and Social Psychology*.	Participants receiving a small reward to lie to another participant were more likely to report they enjoyed the boring study and would participate in a similar study in the future than those who received a large reward.
Conformity	Asch, S. E. (1956). Studies of interdependence and conformity: A minority of one against the unanimous majority. In *Psychological Monographs*.	Even when an answer is obviously wrong, individuals will conform to a unanimous group at least some of the time.
Helping	Latane, B., & Darley, J. M. (1968). Group inhibition of bystander intervention in emergencies. In the *Journal of Personality and Social Psychology*.	Participants sought help more quickly when alone than when in the presence of unresponsive others or other naïve participants.
Obedience	Milgram, S. (1963). Behavioral study of obedience. In the *Journal of Abnormal and Social Psychology*.	Commands of obedience are obeyed, even when the commands appear to harm another individual.
Social facilitation	Zajonc, R. B., Heingartner, A., & Herman, E. M. (1969). Social enhancement and impairment of performance in the cockroach. In the *Journal of Personality and Social Psychology*.	Cockroaches running a difficult maze took a shorter time when they were alone than when they were observed by other cockroaches. Cockroaches running an easy maze took a longer time when they were alone than when they were observed.

With this explosion of research also came an explosion of debate about the ethics of research methods. At the heart of many of these debates were the rights of research participants. In doing research, social psychologists have a difficult problem to solve. Researchers want to know how a normal person in a normal situation might act, but simply having a researcher watch the action can change the action. For example, if you knew someone was watching you in a public restroom you might spend more time washing your hands than you normally do.

To get away from this problem, researchers have disguised the purpose of their studies, disguised the identity of the researchers, or, at times, not told research participants that they were partici-pating in research. If you were a research partici-pant, how would you feel if you were lied to or not told you were being observed? Most of us do not like the idea. A number of studies included someone trained by the experimenter to appear to be a naïve part of the situation, usually pretending to be another participant. Although very useful in studies because this individual, called a **confed-erate**, could help create a situation that would be

Some researchers enlist the help of a "confederate"—someone privy to the study's true intent. This can be consid-ered ethically questionable.

otherwise impossible to set up, the practice is ethically questionable because it involves deceiving the participant. By not revealing the true nature of the study, that is, by deceiv-ing the participant, the researcher introduces a number of issues to the research. One obvi-ous problem is that most of us do not like being lied to and may be angry or upset when we find out we have been duped. This could cause distress in the short term but could also affect how individuals feel about themselves over the long term. Dealing with people who are angry or upset may be a problem for the researcher who did the deception, but these reactions may cause larger problems for research in general. Knowing they may be deceived, participants may be less likely to volunteer to participate and more suspicious during a study, leading to behavior that is not as natural as a researcher might desire. If researchers become known as liars, the results they are reporting might be questioned as well. If they were willing to lie to research participants, why not lie about the results as well? Deception is a potentially dangerous practice in research for all of these reasons.

Since the 1960s the field of psychology as a whole has paid more attention to issues of the rights of participants and the ethics of research methods. Studies involving human participants must go through an **institutional review board**, a committee at a university, college, or other organization where research is done that evaluates the ethics of a research study. For most studies researchers must obtain informed consent from participants. With **informed consent**, researchers tell the participants what they can expect within their par-ticipation and their rights as participants, including the right to discontinue participation. Research participants can then be part of the research knowing what is expected of them or decline to participate. Deception is still used in some social psychological research, but only when deemed absolutely necessary. Researchers who use deception are also care-ful to talk to participants afterward and address any feelings of anger or upset. Almost all research in social psychology now includes an explanation to participants about the nature of the study, whether or not that study included deception. This explanation is called a **debriefing**. A major goal in debriefing is to identify and address any distress a research participant might have experienced in the course of the study.

Since the 1960s psychology as a whole has put more emphasis on cognition, which is the thinking process of the person, and neuroscience, which studies the brain mechanisms at work. This has trickled down to social psychology. In Part 2 we will explore social cognition—how we think about others. In Chapter 5, for example, we examine how our cognitive processes impact the judgments we make. Neuroscience is a more recent focus of psychology, so less has been done in making connections between neuroscience and social psychology. In more recent decades social psychologists have also paid more attention to the impact of cultural differences on the person (e.g., Markus & Kityama, 1991). People may think differently about themselves and their relationships and interact with one another differently depending on culture. For example, people in the United States place more emphasis and importance on romantic relationships than people in South Korea do. When we look at how young adults experience romantic relationships in the United States and in South Korea, we see how this plays out in real life. When not in a romantic relationship, Korean young adults do not experience as much romantic loneliness as young adults in the United States do. Within relationships, young adults in the United States report greater closeness to their partner than young adults in Korea do (Seepersad, Choi, & Shin, 2008).

Social psychologists have also been using evolutionary theories to explain some psychological findings. According to evolutionary theory, those characteristics of an organism that allow it to survive and reproduce within its environment are most likely to appear in later generations. Evolutionary theory is often used in biology and other sciences, but within psychology our focus is more often on adaptive behaviors (being afraid of strangers) than on adaptive biological characteristics (opposable thumbs). Evolutionary psychology can act as a metatheory, a theory that explains other theories (Duntley & Buss, 2008). For example, on the theme of romantic relationships, evolutionary psychologists would suggest that a man who is able to identify a fertile woman and keep that woman away from other men will be more successful in passing down his genes to future generations. A woman, on the other hand, would want to identify a man who is willing and able to invest in her and her offspring, given the long investment she has in pregnancy and a dependent infant. We find exactly these kinds of patterns across cultures (Buss, Larsen, Westen, & Semmelroth, 1992; Buss & Schmitt, 1993; Kaighobadi, Shackelford, & Buss, 2010). Men report greater interest in physical attractiveness, desire more sexual partners, and are more jealous of sexual infidelity than emotional infidelity. Women, on the other hand, show more interest in status and income and are more jealous when a partner becomes emotionally close to another woman, which could potentially lead him to stop investing in her and their offspring.

1.3 How Do We Do Social Psychology?

The image many people have of science or scientists is of a lab filled with test tubes and petri dishes and a person in a white lab coat. Social psychology rarely involves test tubes or white lab coats, so what is it that makes it a science? The common theme among the chemist in the lab, the physicist at the Large Hadron Collider, the ecologist out in the forest, and a psychologist is the method all use to explore the subject matter. It is also the method you may have used for your fourth-grade science fair project: the scientific method.

Within the scientific method we begin with a testable prediction, a **hypothesis**. This prediction may come from your experience in the world. For example, if you were watching an infomercial, one of those half-hour to hour-long commercials that you often find on late-night television, you might find yourself asking: Does giving me a set of knives along with my food dehydrator make me more likely to respond to that infomercial? A hypothesis can also come from a **theory**, which is a set of principles or a framework for a set of observations, sometimes based on previous research. Once you have a hypothesis, you will want to actually test your prediction. There are three basic methods for testing hypotheses: the **observational method**, the **correlational method**, and the **experimental method**. Which one to use depends on the question asked.

Observational Method: What Is Happening?

When a researcher simply wants to know what is happening within a situation or with a particular phenomenon, observational methods are most appropriate. Your interest in infomercials might begin with wondering how many include a "free bonus gift." To answer this you might employ an observational method. Consider for a minute how you might answer this research question.

Observational methods are useful in answering questions about if and how often something might happen.

Did your solution involve watching a lot of late-night television? If so, you're on the right track. When using observational methods, a researcher observes a behavior or situation. Note that you are not doing anything to the infomercials or the people watching them. You are not attempting to change anything; you are simply observing and recording what is happening. Depending on your research question, observational research might take you to very different places to observe. If you were interested in children's aggressive behavior, you might go to a day care to observe. If you were interested in actions of people waiting in waiting rooms, you might visit your local dentist.

Observational methods are helpful in predicting *if* or *how often* something might happen. Many observational studies take place in naturalistic settings, so people's behaviors are generally the same as in their everyday lives. One drawback of this method is that relatively rare or private behaviors, such as sexual activity, are difficult to observe. Scientists using this method also need to be careful to not allow their presence to affect the behavior being observed.

Correlational Method: What Might Happen?

Researchers often want to be able to predict if one behavior (or feeling or thought) will occur based on another behavior. In these cases they use the correlational method. If you were interested in whether the age of people affects their likelihood of buying an infomercial product, you might use the correlational method. Consider for a minute how you could answer the question of whether age and purchasing behavior are related.

Using the correlational method, you would need to find out two things from the people in your study. First you would need to find out their age. Second, you would need

A: Positive correlation

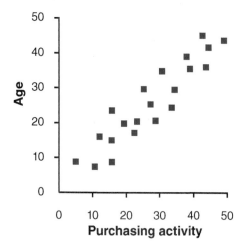

B: Negative correlation

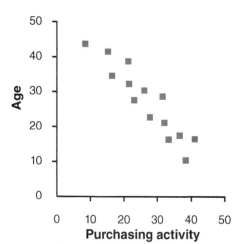

C: No correlation

Figure 1.1 Scatterplot of a Positive Correlation, Negative Correlation, and No Correlation

In a positive correlation (a), when scores on one variable increase, so do scores on the other. For a negative correlation (b), as scores on one variable increase, scores on the other decrease. When there is no correlation (c), no discernable pattern exists.

to find out how many infomercial products they had purchased within a specified time period, for instance within the last month. In research, the entities you assess when using a correlational method are your variables; in this study you have two variables, age and purchases. A **variable** is literally something that varies or can vary. You are interested in whether there is a relation between the two variables you have asked about. Does knowing a person's age tell you anything about the number of advertised products they bought last month? Are they co-related?

Most of the time researchers use the results of a statistical test to describe any potential relation between variables, called a **correlation** (technically a Pearson Product-moment correlation). A correlation coefficient is a number that describes a relationship between two variables. There are three possibilities for a correlation. The first possibility is that as one variable increases, the other variable increases as well. If the older people in your study bought more than the younger people, and the older they were the more they bought, you would have a **positive correlation**. The second possibility is that as one variable increases, the other variable decreases. If the older that people are, the less they buy—that is, if buying goes down as age goes up—you would have a **negative correlation**. The final possibility is that the two variables are not related to one another. In this instance age would have no relationship to buying, no correlation. Figure 1.1 shows what this might look like graphically.

The correlational method can be very useful and illuminating, but we must use it with caution. If knowledge of one variable (age) helps us predict another (buying), does that mean that one causes the other? Not necessarily. It is possible that the first variable caused the second, that the second variable caused the first, or that some other variable caused both variables. Without further research, we cannot know which. For example, a researcher might find a negative correlation in schools between the number of teachers monitoring hallway behavior and the number of acts of aggression in the hallway. It is possible that more teachers in the hallway caused lower aggression, but it is also possible that teachers fled the hallway because of the aggression. Knowing that there is a correlation between two events does not tell us which, if either, is the cause.

In fact, it is quite common to have a third variable cause a correlation between two other variables. For example, sunburn and outdoor temperature are correlated. Does this mean that hot weather causes sunburn, or that sunburn causes hot weather? Of course not. The summer sun causes both sunburn and hot weather. Correlation is not causation.

Experimental Method: What Causes That?

A researcher who is interested in causality uses the experimental method. If you were interested in whether offering a free gift makes people more likely to buy things, you would need to do an experiment. Experiments can be very complex, but we will look at them in their most basic form.

In our research question we want to know if free gifts cause increased buying. To look at this we might get a group of people and randomly assign half of them to see an infomercial where a free gift is offered at the end and the other half to see an identical infomercial but without reference to a free gift. We would then assess how many in each group wanted to buy the product.

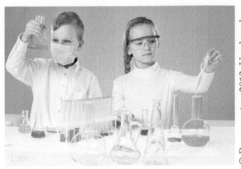

Researchers use similar terms for various parts of an experiment. To understand a study it is helpful to know these terms. The variable we manipulate in an experiment, in this case the presence or

Social psychology experiments study people and their behaviors rather than chemical reactions in the lab.

absence of a free gift offer, is called the **independent variable**. The variable we measure in an experiment, in this case buying behavior, is the **dependent variable**. In an experiment we are testing whether the independent and dependent variable have a cause and effect relationship. If the presence or absence of a gift, the independent variable, changes buying behavior, the dependent variable, we make the assumption that gifts cause buying. Many experiments involve random assignment. **Random assignment** means that each individual in the sample has an equal chance of being in each of the groups (levels of the independent variable). For our study we might flip a coin and assign those who got heads to the free gift group and those who got tails to be offered no free gift. Random assignment is important because it lessens the possibility of extraneous variables affecting our study. **Extraneous variables** are things that are outside of our interest but may affect the results of the study. For example, if we assigned the first half of the people who came to be part of the study to watch the infomercial with the free gift, they may be more likely to buy because they are eager people rather than because of the free gift. Random assignment allows preexisting differences within our participants to be randomly distributed among the groups in our study.

Extraneous variables can sneak into a study in other ways. Notice that we showed our participants the same infomercial except for the offer of free gifts. Consider for a moment why we would have done that. If we want to know how the offer of free gifts affects buying, we want to be sure it is actually the free gift and not something else causing the buying. If we had shown the participants different infomercials it could be that those in the free gift group wanted to buy because their infomercial was better in some way, not because of the offer of a free gift. In experiments we strive to keep everything the same in the environment except the variable we're interested in, the independent variable.

Experiments are helpful in determining when one variable causes another variable. A problem we can run into with experiments is an inability to manipulate or use random assignment for a particular variable. For example, a researcher cannot manipulate age. If participants were recruited to be part of a study of age and buying behavior, the researcher could not randomly assign half of them to the 60 years old group and the other half to the 20 years old group. Age is a pre-existing characteristic of participants that cannot be manipulated. The problem with variables like age is that a group of 60 year olds might act differently than a group of 20 year olds not just because of age but also because of history, ability level, and a host of other extraneous variables. If we find a difference in buying behavior at the end of a study comparing a group of 60 and 20 year olds we cannot be sure if the difference is because of age or because of an extraneous variable like ability level. Experimenters also want to be sure that participants are acting naturally. If participants act differently in a research lab than they do in everyday life, a researcher can only predict what happens in research labs, not in the real world where most of us spend our time. This issue is one of **generalizability**. A study that is generalizable is one whose results can be applied in a variety of situations.

Hindsight Bias

If you had a medical emergency, would you be more likely to receive help if you were in the presence of a crowd of people or a single person? You can probably think of reasons why a crowd of people would be helpful. There are more people to give help. The crowd could work together, one person giving you first aid while another person makes sure the area is safe and yet another person calls for an ambulance. Even if one person in the crowd did not want to help, you should receive help because of the sheer number of people. It seems clear that a crowd would be more likely to provide you with help than a single person.

Does the answer seem obvious? **Hindsight bias** is our tendency to believe something was obvious after the fact (Bernstein, Atance, Loftus, & Meltzoff, 2004; Werth & Strack, 2003). This is also called the I-knew-it-all-along phenomenon. One problem many students of social psychology face is hindsight bias. As you read about the research of social psychologists you may think that the conclusion was obvious, so much so that it seemed like a silly study to do in the first place. The problem comes when you are later asked to recall this obvious conclusion. Suddenly you no longer remember what was so clear before. And what is obvious is not always right. Contrary to what you may have thought, social psychologists have found that in an emergency a person is more likely to get help in the presence of a single observer than a crowd (Latane & Darley, 1970). In a crowd, responsibility for providing help is spread out across many people, so each person feels only a small sense of responsibility. When a single person observes an emergency, responsibility rests solely with him or her. Until the researchers did the studies, the answer was not so clear. As you study social psychology be sure to pay attention to all findings, even the seemingly obvious ones.

Conclusion

Social psychology is a broad field, covering a variety of topics. At the heart of social psychology is an interest in people as they relate to others. Although not a very old field, it is one of much richness and diversity.

Summary

What Is Social Psychology?

Social psychology is all about people. Social psychologists use the scientific method to study how others affect our thinking, actions, and feelings.

Where Did Social Psychology Come From?

Most date the beginning of social psychology to 1898 with Norman Triplett's study on the effects of the presence of others on bicyclists' speeds. After World War II social psychology took off as a field and now covers a wide range of topics. A great deal of debate about the ethics of research accompanied the increased interest in the field. Researchers now pay more attention to potential ethical issues. They have their research plans checked by an institutional review board, and participants provide informed consent.

How Do We Do Social Psychology?

Social psychologists use the scientific method. A hypothesis, or testable prediction, is developed and then tested using observational, correlational, or experimental methods. These different methods answer different kinds of questions. Observational methods answer questions relating to what is happening. Correlational methods look at relationships between variables, enabling prediction. Correlation, however, does not allow us to determine causation. With the experimental method researchers manipulate one variable, the independent variable, and measure the effect of that manipulation, through assessment of the dependent variable. At times, once one knows the results of a research study those results may seem obvious, but people tend to fall short when truly predicting results beforehand. This sense that you knew it all along is hindsight bias.

Critical Thinking Questions

1. What makes social psychology different from other academic disciplines?
2. What makes social psychology different from other areas of psychology?
3. Consider a topic such as infomercials. What research questions might a social psychologist ask about this topic? For these questions, what research method might you use to answer them?
4. If two things are correlated, why is this correlation not evidence of causation?
5. Experiments are designed to investigate causality. How do they do that?
6. Why is hindsight bias dangerous?

Key Terms

Confederate

Correlation

Correlational method

Debriefing

Dependent variable

Experimental method

Extraneous variables

Generalizability

Hindsight bias

Hypothesis

Independent variable

Informed consent

Institutional review board

Negative correlation

Observational method

Positive correlation

Random assignment

Social psychology

Theory

Variable

Expanding Your Knowledge: Links to Additional Material

Participate in Research

Want to see what social psychological research is really like? Participate in online research. One clearinghouse for studies can be found at the Social Psychology Network website: http://www.socialpsychology.org/expts.htm.

Another source for psychological experiments can be found at http://www.psych.uni.edu/psychexps/index.html. Click on Participate in Experiments.

What Do Social Psychologists Do?

If you are interested in what social psychologists do, visit the Society for Personality and Social Psychology (SPSP) website. SPSP is an organization for social and personality psychologists with over 7,000 members. The SPSP website provides a brief introduction to what social and personality psychologists do. Check out the SPSP site: http://www.spsp.org/what.htm.

For information on what social psychologists do and the education and types of careers social psychologists engage in, look at the frequently asked questions page of the Social Psychology Network at http://www.socialpsychology.org/facq.htm.

Unethical Research

One of the most famous unethical studies in the history of social psychology was conducted in the early 1960s by Stanley Milgram (covered in Chapter 10). The purpose of this study was to investigate obedience, although the participants were deceived about its purpose. Find a clip of this study (search YouTube for "Milgram experiment") and consider the following questions:

1. Participants experienced extreme stress during the study. Is it ethical to put participants in a situation that will elicit such extreme stress?
2. The experimenter in the study insisted the participants continue even when they protested. An ethical study is one that participants can leave if they desire to do so. Is it ethical to place participants in a situation where they feel as though they cannot escape?
3. Participants were deceived about the true nature of the study and the identity of the other participant, the confederate who played the role of learner. When, if ever, is it ethical to lie within a study?
4. The majority of participants in the initial study continued to the end of the shock generator, potentially harming or even killing their supposed fellow participant. After completing the study participants knew they could and would engage in such behavior. In the long term these participants needed to live with that knowledge, knowledge they might have been happier to not know. Is it ethical for a study to provide participants information about the dark side of their own personalities?

Hindsight Bias

As noted in the text above, hindsight bias can be a problem for students of social psychology. Research findings may seem obvious after the fact. Before reading any farther in the textbook, take the quiz found at http://jfmueller.faculty.noctrl.edu/crow/commonsenseno .htm. Hang on to your results and discover whether you were right as you continue in the course, or follow the link at the end of the quiz for the answers.

Looking for More?

In-Mind is a site with interesting, accessible articles on social psychology for the general public. If you would like to learn more about current findings in the field from respected researchers, take a look at http://beta.in-mind.org/.

2 | Studying the Self

Learning Objectives

By the end of the chapter you should be able to:

- Define self-schema and identify how self-schemas influence memory and behavior
- Describe what self-esteem is and what we know about it.
- Define self-efficacy
- Compare public self-awareness and private self-awareness
- Explain the concept of self-serving bias
- Identify why impression management is important
- Describe why people might engage in behaviors that are self-defeating
- Understand the power of roles
- Discuss how self-regulation occurs
- Describe how the self influences actions

Chapter Outline

Think back to your last job interview. What did the interviewer ask you? If you have been through a number of interviewers, have you noticed any common questions? Job applicants are often asked to describe themselves in a job interview (Kennedy, 2008). Describing one's strengths and weaknesses is also common (Powers, 2010). What do you think a job interviewer is trying to find out by asking these questions?

2.1 Who Am I?

"Tell us about yourself" is a popular interviewer request. If you were asked to answer the question "Who are you?," how would you answer it? Psychologists have long explored our views of our self and how we come to those views (James, 1890). **Self-concept** is the collection of things you know about yourself—such as your overall cognitive understanding (learned beliefs, attitudes, and opinions) about yourself. When you answer the question "Who am I?," you are describing your self-concept.

Self-Schema

Job interviewers obviously think a question about applicants' views of themselves is important or they would not ask. Social psychologists agree that someone's description of the self is important. The collection of things we know about ourselves are not just a random collection of facts and beliefs. Human beings (or at least the brains of human beings) like organization and pattern. We naturally categorize and organize information that comes into our environment (Markus, 1977; Macrae, Milne, & Bodenhausen, 1994). Schemas are organized packages of information. You may recognize this term if you have taken a developmental psychology course. For example,

Self-schema refers to how you describe yourself.

you know that dogs are furry, have four legs, and bark. Your schema of a dog is a barking, four-legged, furry animal.

We have schemas about ourselves as well. **Self-schemas** are knowledge structures about the self. Although sometimes the terms *self-schema* and *self-concept* are used interchangeably, self-schemas organize and help us use the vast amounts of information within the self-concept. Because they organize and help us use the information about ourselves, self-schemas affect how we view the world (Markus, 1977). For example, would you describe yourself as an exerciser? Do you like to keep in shape, stay physically active, and work out regularly? If so, you have an exercise self-schema. Researchers consider schemas to be on a continuum, so if your responses to the above questions were "absolutely not," you would have a nonexercise self-schema. For those of you in the middle, researchers would call you aschematic in regards to a self-schema for exercise. *Aschematic* simply means without schema.

In general, individuals who have a self-schema for exercise are quicker to respond to stimuli that pertains to their schema (energetic), are able to provide more examples of behaviors that relate to their schema, and are more likely to choose and do behaviors in accord with that schema (participate in an exercise program) (Kendzierski, 1990). Reacting to things related to the self in this way leads to the **self-reference effect**, our tendency to remember better those things we have related to ourselves (Rogers, Kuiper, & Kirker, 1977). For example, you might remember that Joelle has a blue car like yours, but not remember what color car Shana drives because it is different from yours. We often think about ourselves and relate things to ourselves, and this appears to be a good strategy for memory (Symons & Johnson, 1997). As you study, keeping the self-reference effect in mind may be helpful. Relate new material to your life and when it is time to remember it later, you will be more likely to be able to come up with it.

Cultural Influences

How do you know what to say when asked by an interviewer to describe yourself? Where does our self-knowledge come from? Our sense of self is something we develop. This sense of self continues to change over our lifetimes (Greve, Rothermund, & Wentura, 2005). One large impact on the development of our self-concepts is our culture. Cultures vary greatly in a variety of ways, but one large difference is in the way cultures view the self and connections with others. In **independent cultures**, people are viewed as separate, unique individuals whose qualities are independent of their social connections. In **interdependent** (or collectivistic) **cultures**, people are viewed as enmeshed within social connections such that the person cannot be described adequately without social context and connections (Markus & Kitayama, 1991). Some of the differences between these cultures are summarized in Table 2.1.

When individuals from an interdependent culture are asked to write down statements in response to the question "Who am I?" they tend to include more role-specific and concrete information (Cousins, 1989). For example, a Korean student might write that she is silly when with friends. People from independent cultures respond with more trait or attribute characterizations. An American might write that he is artistic. Notice how the individual from an interdependent culture included context (with friends) when describing herself but the person from an independent culture did not.

Table 2.1 Characteristics of Independent and Interdependent Cultures		
	Independent	Interdependent
Tend to be found in . . .	United States, Western Europe	Asia (e.g., Japan, Korea, China), Central and South America
The self is seen as . . .	Unique, not dependent on social context	Flexible, varies with context
Internal attributes are . . .	Expressed through interactions with others; others allow for an expression of internal attributes	Meaningful and complete only in interactions with others
Behavior is . . .	Largely determined by the self and one's internal attributes	A result of the situation and social roles; internal attributes of the self are not powerful in regulating behavior

2.2 Thinking About the Self

In a job interview someone might ask you to describe your strengths and weaknesses (Powers, 2010). Along with knowing who you are, interviewers want to know how you evaluate yourself. Like interviewers, researchers are also interested in our evaluations of ourselves, both qualities we believe we have and actions we believe we can do. How much focus we place on these aspects of ourselves, our awareness, does vary. In this section we will investigate our evaluations of the self and our awareness of various aspects of the self.

Self-Esteem

If you answered the question "Who am I?," it is likely you listed some things about yourself that you liked (I am helpful) and some things you didn't like (I get angry easily). Your overall evaluation of these qualities or how you emotionally feel or value yourself is your **self-esteem**. Self-esteem, at least theoretically, is on a continuum from very high, individuals who think very well of themselves, to very low, individuals who think very poorly of

People with high self-esteem are often more confident, happier, and more successful. But high self-esteem can have dark side.

themselves. When we look at our actual self-esteem scores, however, most people feel pretty good about themselves. Low self-esteem usually manifests itself as feeling OK about oneself rather than feeling terrible (Baumeister, Campbell, Krueger, & Vohs, 2003).

Self-esteem is related to confidence and happiness. People with high self-esteem are more likely to take initiative, speak up in social situations, make friends, and take risks (Baumeister et al., 2003). There is a dark side to high self-esteem. Those with high self-esteem may take more risks and therefore get better jobs or have more adventuresome travel experiences, but risks also include experimentation with drugs and risky sexual practices.

People with high self-esteem are happier than those with low self-esteem (Diener & Diener, 1995). Individuals with low self-esteem are more vulnerable to depression (Orth, Robins, Trzesniewski, Maes, & Schmitt, 2009). This vulnerability seems to be independent of the stressful events one experiences. It appears that how you view the qualities your possess, how you value your self, affects your tendency toward depression (Orth, Robins, & Meier, 2009). People with high self-esteem also report a number of things people with low self-esteem do not. For example, those with high self-esteem report being smarter, better liked by others, and better looking. Yet researchers find that when people with high self-esteem are given IQ tests, their friends are surveyed, and their attractiveness is judged by others, none of these hold true. People with high self-esteem believe these things to be true of themselves, but objectively they are not (Adams, Ryan, Ketsetzis, & Keating, 2000; Bowles, 1999; Gabriel, Critelli, & Ee, 1994).

Self-esteem is related to academic success. Individuals with high self-esteem tend to have higher grades than those with lower self-esteem (Bachman & O'Malley, 1986). As you read this, keep in mind what we talked about in the first chapter about correlation. Does having a high self-esteem help one get better grades, or does getting better grades help raise one's self-esteem? Correlation is not causation. Just because self-esteem is related to academic success does not mean that raising self-esteem causes a rise in grades. When researchers looked more deeply into this relationship and did some experiments to sort out causality, they found that activities to raise self-esteem, like giving children prizes for nothing in particular, are unlikely to affect grades. A blue ribbon for simply being in the classroom will not necessarily raise self-esteem. It seems that the relationship between self-esteem and academic success exists because higher grades give self-esteem a boost rather than the other way around. Given this, it would be a better idea to hire a tutor for your child to raise his or her grades and thus self-esteem, than to attempt to raise the child's self-esteem with the hopes of raising grades.

Our self-esteem levels are attuned to our social standing. According to the sociometer theory of self-esteem, one's level of self-esteem rises and falls with feelings of acceptance and rejection from those in that person's social world (Leary, Tambor, Terdal, & Downs, 1995). For example, if you searched for a job and were unsuccessful, it is likely your self-esteem fell. Starting a new job would likely provide a self-esteem boost.

Although self-esteem is a global evaluation of oneself, in this context all aspects of the person are not created equal. Our self-esteem is more closely related to the things on which social acceptance is based. Researchers have found that outward qualities like popularity and attractiveness are more important to social acceptance, and therefore self-esteem, than communal qualities like kindness, supportiveness, and honesty. So people who view themselves as popular would have higher self-esteem than if they believe they are unpopular, no matter what they believe about their kindness and honesty. This holds true generally, but not always. For those in roles or cultures where communal qualities are more valued, honesty, supportiveness, and kindness tend to rise in importance in determining self-esteem (Anthony, Holmes, & Woods, 2007).

Self-Efficacy

While self-esteem deals with your evaluation of the qualities you possess, another concept focuses on your evaluation of your abilities. If you have been interviewed it is likely that you were asked whether you could work as a team or complete assignments on time or do any number of other activities. Your evaluation of your ability to perform particular tasks is called **self-efficacy** (Bandura, 1977, 2000). Have you ever read the children's book *The Little Engine That Could* (Piper & Long, 2005)? In this book a small train engine pulling a train loaded with animals attempts to climb a mountain. As the engine puffs up the hill she says "I think I can, I think I can, I think I can." This mantra is the essence of self-efficacy.

A belief that we can do something is generally good for us. Individuals with higher self-efficacy are more persistent, more productive, and less depressed (Chemers, Hu, & Garcia, 2001; Cheung & Sun, 2000; Huang, 1998). Self-efficacy beliefs vary depending on the behavior. Someone might have high self-efficacy for academics but low self-efficacy for athletics. Because we have a sense of self-efficacy for any behavior we might engage in, self-efficacy can get pretty specific. Researchers have studied everything from leadership self-efficacy (Ng, Ang, & Chan, 2008) to bicultural self-efficacy (David, Okazaki, & Saw, 2009), harm reduction self-efficacy in drug abusers (Phillips & Rosenberg, 2008), and driver competence self-efficacy (Sundstrom, 2008). In a job search it is likely that your job-search self-efficacy would come into play (Brown, Cober, Kane, Levy, & Shalhoop, 2006).

Self-Awareness

The degree to which we are aware of ourselves, or particular aspects of ourselves, can vary. Your awareness of your internal states, for example your thoughts, feelings, or desires, is your **private self-awareness**. Awareness of how you appear to others is your **public self-awareness**.

© Mast3r, 2013. Used under license from Shutterstock, Inc.

Due to heightened public self-awareness, people are more likely to wash their hands if someone else is in the restroom.

Private self-awareness can make us more aware of our attitudes and values (Fejfar & Hoyle, 2000; Wiekens & Stapel, 2010). When our behaviors do not match our attitudes or values (our standards) a discrepancy is created. Because we do not like discrepancies, we usually seek to change our behavior or avoid being self-aware (Gibbons, 1990; Silval & Duval, 2001). A discrepancy could lead people to act in a more positive way, striving to live up to their values. Private self-awareness can also lead to destructive behaviors. In an attempt to escape self-awareness, someone might engage in binge eating, drug use, or suicidal thoughts (Tassava, & Ruderman, 1999).

Public self-awareness is higher when we believe we are being observed (Wiekens & Stapel, 2010). In research studies an experimenter who wishes to increase public self-awareness might inform participants that they are being videotaped. Public self-awareness generally makes individuals act in ways that satisfy social norms. One set of researchers measured how often women in a public restroom washed their hands (Munger & Harris, 1989). When someone else was in the restroom, increasing public self-awareness, 24 of the 31 women (77%) washed their hands. When the women believed they were alone in the rest-room, so public self-awareness was relatively low, 11 of the 28 women (39%) washed their hands. Public self-awareness may not always have a positive effect on behavior. In a study on cheating on an academic task and self-awareness, researchers found that participants with high public self-awareness were more likely to cheat, because they were concerned about how their performance on a task would be viewed (Malcolm & Ng, 1989).

Self-Serving Bias

When we think about ourselves our overall desire is to view ourselves positively. We may, therefore, distort reality, noticing only the good things and largely ignoring the bad (Heider, 1976). This bias toward the positive when it comes to ourselves is called the **self-serving bias**. The self-serving bias means that when we succeed at something we attribute that success to something about us or something we did, whereas we more often attribute failure to things outside of ourselves. If you got an A on your last chemistry test it was because you are smart, but if you got an F on your history test it was because the teacher was unreasonable and the test impossible. Although we have this tendency to attribute success to something about the self, there is some evidence that when self-awareness is high and we see our failure as something we can improve on, we may attribute that failure to ourselves (Duval & Silvia, 2002). For example, if you misunderstood what you would be tested on for your history test, you could attribute the failure to yourself knowing that next time you will do better. The next time we do the task we would, presumably, improve, providing us with a boost in our positive sense of self.

The self-serving bias is more likely to occur when we are thinking about and aware of ourselves (Duval & Silvia, 2002). As noted in the section on self-awareness, we are uncomfortable when there is a discrepancy between our behavior and attitudes. Being mindful of the discrepancy between our bad test score and our view of ourselves as good students may lead to more self-serving bias. The self-serving bias is also more likely when we feel a threat to our sense of self (Campbell & Sedikides, 1999). If someone were to question whether you are a good student you would want to find evidence of your academic prowess in that good chemistry test and find an excuse for your failure in history.

Although one might think that viewing reality as it really is would be best for one's mental health, the research results suggest otherwise. Fully functioning self-serving bias is related to greater happiness and less depression (Abramson & Alloy, 1981; Kuiper, 1978; Rizley, 1978). When the self-serving bias is not at work, people are much more likely to show symptoms of depression (Greenberg, Pyszczynski, Burling, & Tibbs, 1992; Sweeney, Anderson, & Bailey, 1986). Self-serving bias can go too far. Narcissistic individuals show a particularly strong self-serving bias (McAllister, Baker, Mannes, Stewart, & Sutherland, 2002). Self-serving bias is common across cultures, though its strength can vary. The effect is not as strong in Asian samples as it is in samples of individuals from Western cultures (Mezulis, Abramson, Hyde, & Hankin, 2004).

2.3 The Acting Self

From the previous section you know that this thing we call the self is something we think about and evaluate. But does the self affect our actions? The self may affect how we act so that we present an image of ourselves that we want others to have. The roles we play may affect our actions. Applying self-regulation within situations has an effect on our future abilities to engage in actions. The self may also affect where we live and the profession we pursue, sometimes in surprising ways.

Impression Management

When going on a job interview, attending a party, or starting something new (new job, new school) we often pay special attention to our appearance. Why? In our interactions with others we are interested in presenting a certain image of ourselves. Given the self-serving bias, we would expect that image of ourselves we are trying to project to be positive, and it is. In a job interview, for example, people want to present a favorable image with the hopes that the employer will give them a job. If you think back to the sociometer theory of self-esteem you know that how others view you affects your self-esteem.

In interactions we use a variety of tactics to influence the impressions others have of us. We might make excuses, justifications, or apologies for our actions. We might attempt to ingratiate ourselves with someone of greater power. **Ingratiation** involves some form of flattery. For example, one might compliment the boss on a new tie, agree with a supervisor about the likelihood of a sports team to win, or offer to get coffee for a project manager. In an attempt to influence others we may also attempt to appear more attractive or professional. Manipulating the impression of our prestige, power, or credibility can influence a person's view of us (Tedeschi & Melburg, 1984). You might engage in some impression management during a job search—hopefully with positive results.

The image a person projects does matter. Inter-viewers need to make relatively quick decisions about hiring based on limited information. Despite the hopes of many to the contrary, physical appearance affects the rating of the interviewer for a job candidate more than other things a job candidate might have or do, such as agreeing with the interviewer (Barrick, Shaffer, & DeGrassi, 2009).

© Wavebreakmedia, 2013. Used under license from Shutterstock, Inc.

Wanting to make a good impression is a significant part of social life—as well as the job interview—but it can be taken too far.

Self-presentation is a necessary part of social life, but it can create problems. Women might take diet pills, smoke, or yo-yo diet to try to control weight, seriously damaging their health (Camp, Klesges, & Relyea, 1993; Gritz & Crane, 1991; Wang, Houshyar, & Prinstein, 2006). These same women may avoid the gym or even the local jogging trails because of concerns of how they would look to others (Leary, Tchividjian, & Kraxberger, 1994). Some men might use steroids to assist in gaining or maintaining a muscular body, despite medical issues like heart problems and stunted growth and psychological problems like depression and increased aggressiveness (Leary et al., 1994; Galli & Reel, 2009).

A clever study that investigated how far people would go to make sure that another person had a favorable impression of them was done by Martin and Leary (1999). A confederate offered to allow the participant to drink out of his water bottle after the participant had tasted something unpleasant. Although the researchers used clean water bottles, it appeared to the participant that the confederate had already drunk out of the bottle, presumably making the transfer of germs a distinct possibility. Some of the participants were challenged by the confederate with the phrase "if you're not worried about drinking out of the same bottle as me" (p. 1095). The challenge brought up self-presentation concerns in the participant; they did not want to be seen as overly cautious. The researchers found that those participants who were challenged by the confederate drank more than those who were offered the water but not challenged. For these participants, concern about how they might look to others caused them to engage in a potentially risky behavior.

Self-Handicapping

In the 2010 season of *The Biggest Loser*, one of the contestants, Daris, gained two pounds at the last weigh-in before the final episode. During his time at home before the weigh-in, he would engage in binge-eating late at night (Barile, 2010). Knowing that the weigh-in was coming, why would he engage in such self-destructive behavior? There are a large number of factors at work here, but one is **self-handicapping**. With self-handicapping, people create an excuse for a later failure by doing something that is likely to hinder their success. Public performance is particularly vulnerable. If you really tried your hardest to lose weight and failed, you have no excuses to offer those watching. If you sabotage your own success, then failure is expected, and you can maintain, to yourself and for others, that if you had really tried you would have succeeded. When others are more confident in your success than you are, self-handicapping allows you to maintain that positive image others hold (Lupien, Seery, & Almonte, 2010). A student might play a card game late into the night before a big final or an employee might work on other projects and not prepare adequately for an important presentation. When the student fails the final or the employee does not get the account they can point to the game or other projects as the problem. This allows for maintenance of one's self-image in the eyes of others. If each of these individuals worked their hardest and still failed to lose weight, do well on the final, or get the big account, it might affect self-esteem or public image (Bailis, 2001). If they do well despite the handicapping their success is even more remarkable (Tice, 1991). See table 2.2 for a summary of terms related to the self.

Table 2.2 Self Related Terms: Definitions and Examples

Term	Definition	Example
Self-awareness	Self-awareness involves being aware of particular aspects of one's self-concept. There are two types: Private self-awareness is awareness of one's internal states such as thoughts, feelings, or desires. Public self-awareness is awareness of how one appears to others.	Having been asked what she hopes to do after college, Brittany has an increase in private self-awareness. Standing in front of her colleagues at work, ready to give a speech, Selena has an increase in public self-awareness.
Self-concept	The collection of things one knows about the self. This collection is large and diverse.	Elaine likes the color yellow, is good at math, can run a mile in 8 minutes, enjoys jazz, is a mother of two children, and wants to be a teacher.
Self-efficacy	One's evaluation of one's ability to perform a particular task.	If Andy believes he can do differential calculus, he would be described as high in self-efficacy for differential calculus.
Self-esteem	One's evaluation of the qualities one possesses; how one values oneself.	Trina has an overall positive evaluation of herself, she has high self-esteem.
Self-handicapping	Creating an excuse for later poor performance by doing something that hinders success.	Shawna stays up late playing video games before taking the Scholastic Aptitude Test (SAT), creating an excuse for her low scores.
Self-reference effect	The tendency to remember better those things related to the self.	Cindy remembers that her date takes his coffee with cream, like she does, but forgets that he told her he likes rock climbing, something she has no interest in.
Self-schemas	Knowledge structures about the self. Self-schemas organize the information within our self-concept and affect our processing of information and our ability to remember information.	Music is very important to Ed. He thinks of himself as a musician and a music lover.
Self-serving bias	A bias toward viewing successes as something we can attribute to the self and failures as owing to something outside the self, such as a difficult situation. The self-serving bias helps us maintain our self-schema and self-efficacy and influences our tendency to self-handicap and use impression management strategies.	Devon believes his success at selling used cars is due to his intelligence and charm. He blames his failure in his marriage on his ex-wife's unreasonable demands and unpleasant personality.

Roles

Have you ever started a new job and felt out of place and awkward? This is not unusual. As we move from one role to another role there is a period of transition (Morrison, 1993). As we enter a new role it is as if we are actors learning a new part. We learn our lines and what is expected of us. Erving Goffman's (1959) classic theory proposes that in everyday life we engage in a drama. It is as if we are on stage and must play a part. This approach to describing how we present ourselves is called the *dramaturgical approach*. The power of roles and the transition we must go through as we enter these roles was dramatically demonstrated in a study by Philip Zimbardo.

Describing ourselves in terms of the roles we play is known as the dramaturgical approach.

In 1973 Zimbardo and colleagues (Haney, Banks, & Zimbardo, 1973) recruited 24 college men to participate in a simulated prison for two weeks. Half were randomly assigned the role of guard and half the role of prisoner. The prisoners were picked up by the local police, fingerprinted, and brought to a makeshift prison in the basement of the psychology building on campus. The guards were asked to maintain order but were not allowed to use physical force. Each participant wore a uniform appropriate for his role. Both prisoners and guards quickly became engrossed in their roles. Guards were controlling and manipulative of the prisoners; some became verbally abusive. Prisoners acted in a passive way. Some prisoners became so distressed about their lack of power and control over their own situation that they exhibited extreme emotional reactions, including depression, crying, anxiety, and rage. Conditions deteriorated and prisoners were in such misery that the experiment was stopped after 6 days. This study demonstrates just how powerful roles can be in affecting our behavior.

Self-Regulation

Imagine you've signed up to be part of a study on taste perception. To prepare you were asked not to eat anything for 3 hours. When you enter the room where the study will take place, you smell baking chocolate chip cookies. A plate of warm cookies and other chocolates sits on the table alongside a bowl of radishes. The researcher explains to you that for this study you will be eating one of two distinctive foods, radishes or chocolate. You have been assigned to the radish condition. You are asked to eat two or three radishes within the next 5 minutes. The experimenter leaves the room. Even though you would probably prefer the chocolate chip cookies, you dutifully eat three radishes before the researcher returns. While (supposedly) waiting for the sensory memory of the radishes to diminish, you are asked to do a task that the researcher presents as unrelated to the taste perception study. You are asked to work as long as you can on a task requiring you to trace a geometric figure without lifting your pencil. Frustrated by your lack of success, you quit after only a couple minutes.

If you had just spent an hour being bored on the phone, you might be less willing to do another distasteful task. This is ego depletion.

© Johan Larson, 2013. Used under license from Shutterstock, Inc.

Unbeknownst to you, the researchers were very interested in how long you worked on those geometric figures. The geometric figures were unsolvable and the researchers wanted to know how long you would persist without success. They believed you would work for a shorter period of time because you ate radishes rather than the chocolate (Baumeister, Bratslavsky, Mauraven, & Tice, 1998). Any ideas on why that might be? Take a minute to think about it before reading on. For more on self-regulation, see the *Social Psychology in Depth* box.

The researchers were studying something called **ego depletion**. In this context, ego refers to a resource that each of us have for volitional (chosen) action. The idea is that when you choose to do something you use some of this resource, leaving less for future actions (Hagger, Wood, Stiff, & Chatzisarantis, 2010). When you engage in self-regulation to do something you would rather not do, like eating radishes in the presence of chocolate, you use a lot of this resource, depleting it. Because you've depleted the ego you are less able to work on other difficult tasks. Think of the ego like a muscle. After lifting something very light you have plenty of strength left for lifting again. If you lift something very heavy the muscle gets tired and you no longer have the strength to help your friend move that refrigerator.

Unless you are on a diet you are not likely to spend a lot of time eating radishes instead of chocolate. It is also unlikely you would subject yourself to tracing geometric figures that are actually untraceable, so why does this matter? Baumeister and colleagues (1998) believe that we encounter such situations every day. When you are studying for social psychology rather than watching TV, you are depleting your ego. Ego depletion will make other tasks (mowing the lawn, cooking dinner) more difficult for you to get the energy up to complete.

If you are on a diet, in school, have a tough job, or have household chores this sounds like bad news. But there is good news. It is our perception of depletion more than actual depletion of this resource that seems to have the largest effect. When individuals engaged in a lot of self-regulation but perceived the task as not using much, they did better on later tasks (Clarkson, Hirt, Jia, & Alexander, 2010). Encouragement can also help us out when we are depleted. Students who wrote about a personal quality that was very important to them after they engaged in an ego-depleting activity did better at a later task than if they wrote about something that was not important to them and was therefore not self-affirming (Schmeichel & Vohs, 2009). Theoretically you should also be able to work on increasing your ability to self-regulate by strengthening the ego. If the ego is like a muscle, the more you use it the more you will have in the future. You might exhaust the ego today, but day after day as you work and go to school and build relationships with friends and family, you will be building up strength for the future.

Social Psychology in Depth: Testing Our Self-Regulation

Is our capacity for self-regulation like a muscle or is it a skill we develop? If self-regulation is a muscle, it would tire as we use it. If self-regulation is a skill, using it should not affect later performance. A study by Baumeister, Bratslavsky, Mauraven, and Tice (1998) involving chocolate chip cookies and radishes cleverly pitted these two possibilities against each other. After controlling their urge for freshly baked chocolate chip cookies and forcing themselves to eat radishes instead, research participants were less able to continue working on a frustrating task. Self-regulation, then, appears to work more like a muscle than skill set. When we engage in self-regulation we deplete the ego, consume our limited store of self-regulatory strength, and have difficulty in the short term with tasks requiring more self-regulation.

Ego depletion can affect a number of behaviors. Ego depletion is related to greater aggression. With ego depletion we are less able to inhibit our tendencies toward aggression (Stucke & Baumeister, 2006). Dieters asked to exhibit self-regulation in making a choice later ate more than dieters who were not asked to exhibit self-regulation (Kahan, Polivy, & Herman, 2003). Complex intellectual tasks and decision making also suffer with ego depletion. Tasks that require a great deal of mental energy and self-regulation such as logic, reasoning, decision making, and reading comprehension suffer when we are depleted while tasks requiring less from our systems such as simple memorization do not suffer (Schmeichel, Vohs, & Baumeister, 2003; Zyphur, Warren, Landis, & Thoresen, 2007).

The effects of ego depletion are not irreversible and a number of techniques can be used to avoid the effects. Ego depletion is short term. After a rest period people regain their capacity for self-regulation.

Distraction can be an effective counterstrategy. Even when ego is depleted, distracting someone from what they are doing will lessen the decline in strength (Alberts, Martijn, Nievelstein, Jansen, & DeVries, 2008). Individuals who engaged in self-affirmation, focusing on a value that was important to them, showed more self-regulation after ego depletion than those who did not engage in self-affirmation (Schmeichel & Vohs, 2009). Inducing a positive emotion or reminding people of a persistent person also has positive effects for performance in the face of ego depletion (Martijn et al., 2007; Ren, Hu, Zhang, & Huang, 2010). Positions of leadership can motivate people to expend resources even when depleted. Leadership, it seems, induces people to engage in self-regulation, sometimes even beyond their capacities (DeWall, Baumeister, Mead, & Vohs, 2011). Above all, it is important to remember that practice can increase capacity for self-regulation (Hagger, Wood, Stiff, & Chatzisarantis, 2010). As with physical activity, if you want to avoid straining a muscle in the short term it is best to pace yourself in behavior involving self-regulation, but if you want to build up muscle over the long term, engaging in ego-depleting activities is good for your future strength.

Implicit Egotism

Throughout this section you have seen that your "self" is more active and important than you may have realized before. Researchers have found evidence that the effect of the self on decisions goes farther than most people realize. Does your name have any relationship to where you live? Pelham, Mirenberg, and Jones (2002) argue that it does. The researchers looked at people's first names and the city they lived in. They found that statistically we would expect 288 people with the name of Jack in Jacksonville, but 436 Jacks call this city home. Similar results were found for surnames.

Personalized mugs. Social psychologists suggest that the self may affect our decisions, even subconsciously.

We would expect 760 people with a surnames beginning with the letters Cali to be living in California, but 929 were in the telephone directory. Similarly, although we would expect only seven entries for someone with a surname beginning with Texa in Texas, 34 are listed. This holds true for first names as well. There are more Florences in Florida, Georgias in Georgia, Louises in Louisiana, and Virginias in Virginia than we would expect by chance. Lest you think all the parents in Georgia have the brilliant idea to name their child Georgia after the state they live in, the researchers also found that Georgias move to Georgia in a greater rate than one would expect by chance.

Beyond location, Hodson and Olson (2005) showed that a person may be more attracted to certain brand names when they match one's name. A person's name can even affect choice of profession (Pelham et al. 2002). Women with a first name beginning with Den (e.g., Denise or Denna) were more likely to become dentists than we would expect by chance. Lauras (and those with similar La names) were more likely to become lawyers. The same held true for men. Now you know why your dentist is named Denny but your lawyer is named Lauren. Similarly you are more likely to find Harry owning a hardware story, while Ralph will be in roofing.

Implicit egotism does interact with self-esteem. Individuals with low self-esteem sat farther from other people sharing their initials than those with high self-esteem. When participants with high self-esteem met someone who shared their initials, they sat closer (Kocan & Curtis, 2009). All of this is done without our conscious awareness. We are not being egocentric or selfish; our sense of self seems to compel us to respond in particular ways. Implicit egotism shows us just how important the self is, even to aspects of our lives we would never suspect being influenced by the self. Few Lauras would likely claim that their name helped attract them to the study of law, but the evidence is that this is so. If we unconsciously make choices in line with our self, how much more might our conscious sense of self influence our lives?

Conclusion

Social psychologists are interested in who we are. Our sense of self is affected by what we know about the self and by the people around us. The self is a powerful force. The self affects how we feel, what we think we can do, and what we in fact do.

Summary

Who Am I?

Self-concepts are the collection of things one knows about oneself. Self-schemas organize this information, affecting how one views the world and takes in information. A sense of self is affected by one's cultures. Cultures can be divided into those that emphasize independence of the self from others, such as those found in the United States and Western Europe, and those that focus on context and social roles as important, such as those found in Asia and Central and South America.

Thinking About the Self

Evaluating the qualities we associate with ourselves provides us with self-esteem. As a global evaluation of the self, self-esteem can influence our confidence and happiness. Individuals with high self-esteem report being better in many areas (e.g., they may believe they are smarter than their peers), but this belief seems to be a result of self-esteem, not a cause. According to the sociometer theory of self-esteem, our self-esteem is based in our social standing, so qualities that are related to social acceptance tend to have a more powerful impact on self-esteem than hidden qualities do. People evaluate their own abilities. Our belief about our ability to do particular actions or tasks makes up our self-efficacy. Self-efficacy can be measured for very specific behaviors and tends to be related to persistence and performance of tasks related to those behaviors. We vary in our awareness of aspects of ourselves. Private self-awareness is our focus on our internal thoughts, feelings, and desires, while public self-awareness is our awareness of how we appear to others.

The Acting Self

People attempt to present certain images of themselves to others. We most often do this through presenting a positive side of ourselves (e.g., appearing more powerful or credible) and it does affect the judgments others make of us. Occasionally we do something that is self-defeating. In self-handicapping we engage in behaviors that hinder our success, allowing us an excuse when things don't turn out well or greater accolades when we succeed. Although it takes us a bit to enter into new social roles, these roles have a powerful impact on our behaviors. In Zimbardo's famous prison study, normal college men were quickly turned into defeated prisoners and power-hungry guards. When we have engaged in actions involving self-regulation, we find it more difficult to do other, seemingly unrelated, actions. Ego depletion describes what happens when we've used self-regulation and no longer have the willpower to perform other actions. We can avoid ego depletion by perceiving that an action took less self-regulation, by engaging in self-affirmation, or by building up the ego through long-term use of self-regulation. Our self can have an impact we are not even aware of. Researchers have found that people live in places resembling their names at higher rates than would be expected by chance.

Critical Thinking Questions

1. Throughout the chapter, job interviews were used as an example of how we think about and encounter the self on a day to day basis. Are there other aspects of job interviews that you might apply to concepts from the chapter?
2. If a friend of yours said that how she feels about herself is not important, that it has no effect on her actions, how would you respond? Does the self affect everyday life?
3. How might high academic self-efficacy affect you?
4. Is impression management and self-handicapping positive or negative for an individual?
5. How might your knowledge of ego depletion affect how you structure your activities?

Key Terms

Ego depletion	Public self-awareness	Self-reference effect
Independent cultures	Self-concept	Self-schemas
Ingratiation	Self-efficacy	Self-serving bias
Interdependent cultures	Self-esteem	
Private self-awareness	Self-handicapping	

Expanding Your Knowledge: Links to Additional Material

Where Does It Come From?

Children learn to live within a culture from their parents and others they encounter. To study this, researchers looked at how children in isolated villages in Nepal handled emotions. These villages differed in the way caretakers dealt with the negative emotions of children (specifically anger), so the children responded to negative events differently. This blog post, which describes the Nepal study, illustrates the origins of cultural differences as well as how different individuals within a particular culture can be: http://scienceblogs.com/cognitivedaily/2006/11/insight_into_how_children_lear.php.

Goals, Well-Being, and Culture

Given the different views of the self and different values within independent and interdependent cultures, what makes people happy in these cultures may also be different. In a study by Oishi and Diener (2001), the researchers found that pursuing a goal to please parents and friends increased subjective well-being in Asian Americans but not in European Americans, while pursuing goals related to fun and enjoyment increased subjective well-being for European Americans but not Asian Americans. Follow the link to read the original study: http://www.corwin.com/upm-data/2954_12Pspb01.pdf#page=111.

Test Your Self-Esteem

Wondering where you fall on the continuum of self-esteem? The Rosenberg Self-Esteem Scale is a short measure of self-esteem and is widely used by researchers. Rosenberg originally tested the scale on high school juniors and seniors, but it has been used with a variety of populations since its development. It tends to have good reliability and validity.

The Rosenberg Self-Esteem Scale can be found at http://www.yorku.ca/rokada/psyctest/.

Self-Efficacy

Intrigued by the concept of self-efficacy? A large amount of information on self-efficacy can be found at the site linked below. You can read a short description of self-efficacy from Albert Bandura, a leading researcher in the field, and learn more about him and his work. You can explore a variety of readings on the topic of self-efficacy, and be inspired by quotations or amused by self-efficacy cartoons. Links to some self-efficacy scales can be found on the site as well (click on Information on Self-Efficacy Instruments).

Self-efficacy site: http://www.des.emory.edu/mfp/self-efficacy.html.

Self-Regulation

Expand on your knowledge of self-regulation and learn about the brain structures responsible for our willpower by watching Dr. Sam Wang's TED presentation on willpower and the brain. Dr. Wang describes myths that exist about the brain and then focuses in on the brain structures that are responsible for our self-regulation. He discusses how to increase willpower as well as the implications for willpower we can draw from our knowledge of brain development.

Link to the talk: http://www.livestream.com/tedxsf/video?dirId=7d0daac8-63a8-427b-960c-586ebe6f2960&clipId=pla_4aae6081-bc07-4885-a05e-3263ee66646b.

INDIVIDUALISM COLLECTIVISM

Four kinds of social patterns have been identified across cultures:

1. Community Sharing: Pattern in which people know each other extremely well. Intimacy, cooperation, and self-sacrifice within the group (e.g., family, tribe) are emphasized.
2. Authority Ranking: Pattern in which obedience, admiration, and giving and following orders without questioning are typical behaviors.
3. Equality Matching: Involves equal-status friendship characterized by reciprocity. Taking turns and dividing gains equally are common practice.
4. Market Pricing: Involves the exchange of money for goods; friendship is instrumental and continues only as long as the benefits outweigh the costs.
*   Every culture emphasizes and shares these four orientations of social patterns.
*   "Traditional" societies (esp. East Asia) tend to emphasize the first two; cultures in northwestern Europe and North America emphasize the last two;
*   These emphases illustrate the difference between individualists and collectivists and contrast between simple, homogeneous cultures and complex, heterogeneous cultures.

People in Homogeneous Cultures
*   Have relatively few choices in the groups to which they may belong: extended family and/or a few friends.
*   As such, groups are very important; therefore, people do what the group expects,i.e., ingroup norms.
*   Success is attributed to the help of others and failure to individual's own lack of ability.

==> Collectivism

People in Hterogeneous Cultures
*   Many group affiliations, personal choice determine belonging (e.g., relationship with God "Born Again" versus "Catholicism").
*   Joins if it pays to, leaves if it's too costly (e.g., marriage?).
*   Behavior is characterized more by personal attitude rather than ingroup norms.
*   Success = Personal intelligence; Failure = Difficulty of the task or bad luck

==> Individualism

1. *How do you think individualists and collectivists differ in their value systems?*
Triandis: Individualists associated with freedom, independence, autonomy, achievement, exciting life, winning in competition, and fair exchange.

Collectivists associated with security, obedience, duty, interdependence, ingroup harmony, and self-restraint.

2. *How do you think differences in individualism/collectivism are likely to affect patterns of interaction and relationships within family, work group, college or community, classroom?*

<u>Collectivists</u>: Worst thing is to be excluded from the group (e.g., chimp research and social chastisement).

- Therefore, more likely to sacrifice individual rights for the group.
- More value on harmony, allowing others to save face.
- Direct confrontation and blunt honesty are rare.
- Elders and superiors demand respect.
- Within family, children are taught interdependence, cooperation, and communal sensitivity.
- Live with parents until married (go away to college?); and older parents live with children until death (nursing homes?).
- Work groups: Relationships are long-term; employer loyalties are strong.
- Classroom: Cooperation rather than competition is more likely.

3. *How do you think differences in individuals/collectivism are likely to influence the judgments made of other groups and relationships between them? Which orientation is more likely to promote ethnocentrism? Altruism?*

<u>Individualists</u>

- Differences are expressed openly and honestly.
- Family: Children are to be independent, self-reliant, and show good judgment.
- Children decide their own restaurant orders, open their own mail, choose their own friends, and chart own goals.
- Work and school: Competition prevails.

<u>Collectivists</u>

- Distinguish between groups, more polite toward in-groups, hostile toward out-groups.
- More likely to help in-group and expect help in time of need from fellow group members.

4. *What factors shape our becoming individualist or collectivist? How do gender, religious convictions, and political attitudes influence these orientations?*

Triandis:
- Income
- Hunters more individualistic than gatherers
- Migrated populations more individualist than sedentary populations
- Movement from rural to urban correlated positively with individualism

5. *How do these orientations affect our personal and social well-being? Should present emphases be changed? Are there ways of capturing the best of both individualism and collectivism?*

<u>Individualists</u>

- Enjoy personal freedom, take greater pride in their achievements, enjoy more privacy, live with greater spontaneity, and are more creative.

Extreme: greater loneliness, higher divorce rates, more homicide, and increased vulnerability to stress-related disease.

Empirical Summary of Individualism/Collectivism

- **Individualism**: Complex behavior based on concern for oneself and one's immediate family or primary group.
- **Collectivism**: Behavior based on concerns for others and care for traditions and values.
- In **collective** cultures, group norms, above anything else, are likely to direct individual behavior.
- In **collective** cultures, people tend to prefer harmony-enhancing strategies of conflict resolution.
- In **individualistic** cultures, people tend to prefer competitive strategies.
- Typically, **collectivism** is high in Asian countries, in more traditional societies, and in the former communist countries.
- Typically, **individualism** is high in Western countries.
- United States is highest, scoring 91; Spain is moderate at 51; and Guatemala scores the lowest at 6.

At least two dimensions to this continuum: **Horizontal** and **Vertical**

- **Vertical**: People refer to each other from power and achievement standpoints; they communicate with each other as employees and employers, leaders and the led.
- **Horizontal**: Benevolence and equality
    - E.g., Totalitarian regimes emphasize equality (horizontal) but not freedom.
    - E.g., Western democracies emphasize freedom (vertical) but not necessarily equality.

Examples:
- India (traditional culture): **Vertical collectivists**
- United States: **Vertical individualists**
- Sweden: **Horizontal collectivists**
- Why?

Americans tolerate inequality to a greater extent than Swedes (e.g., economic inequality between the top 10% and the bottom 10% of the population is three times lower in Sweden than in the United States)
- Fijeman et al. (1996)

College students from Hong Kong, Turkey, Greece, the Netherlands, and the United States asked to express opinions regarding eight hypothetical scenarios of psychological and economic need.

They were also asked to indicate their readiness to help others with money, goods, or personal hospitality.

Results
- **Collectivists** not only expect to contribute to others, they expect others to support them back.
- **Individualists** not only expect to contribute less to others, but also tend not to expect others to help or support them, thus reducing their own expectations of entitlement.

Possible Selves

- Ideas about what we may be in the future

<u>Discrepancies</u>

<u>Actual self</u>: What you or another think you are currently.

<u>Ideal self</u>: Mental representation of the attributes that either you or another would like you to be or wishes you could be.

<u>Ought self</u>: That which you or others believe you should be.

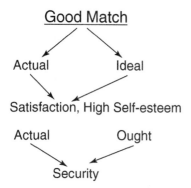

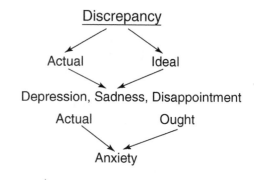

PART II | Thinking About Others

"Let no man pull you low enough to hate him."

—*Martin Luther King Jr.*

3 | Making Attributions

Learning Objectives

By the end of the chapter you should be able to:

- Describe what an attribution is
- Differentiate between internal and external attributions
- Define the fundamental attribution error
- Explain how explanatory style works
- Differentiate between optimistic and pessimistic explanatory style
- Describe the hostile attribution of intent

Chapter Outline

If you have ever tried online dating, you are in good company. A 2009–2010 study funded by Match.com reported that about 20% of single people dated someone they met online. A similar percentage of those in newly committed relationships (such as marriage) met their partner online (Chadwick Martin Bailey, 2010).

Most online dating sites involve profiles, where potential daters post information about themselves. Others then access that information and decide whether they would like to communicate with or date the person profiled. As we know from the previous chapter, people try to present particular impressions of themselves, and online daters are no different (Whitty, 2007). In meeting new people, online or face to face, we all try to figure out who the other person is.

Attributions are important in all areas of life. At work you might want to know if your boss intended his behavior as encouragement to pursue a raise or as a clue that your job might be in danger. Attributing your friend's late-night phone call to concern will affect the relationship differently than attributing it to rudeness. In deciding the proper punishment of a child or a criminal we make attributions about their intentions and reprimand accordingly. While you are walking, the attributions you make for a driver's behavior may affect whether you step out to cross the street or stay safely on the sidewalk. Attributions touch us and affect our lives every day.

3.1 Internal and External Attributions

What would you think if an online profile you read on a dating site said that the person had recently taken a trip to Turkey? How would you interpret a situation where you asked to communicate with someone but that person never responded to your request? What if you set up a date and the person showed up late? Our daily lives present us with situations where we need to explain the behaviors of others. Social psychologists have studied how we make those judgments.

Attributions

In our everyday social interactions we need to make judgments about why others act the way they do (Ross, Greene, & House, 1977). In doing so we are making attributions. **Attributions** are our explanations of the behavior of ourselves and others. Attributions have been of interest to psychologists for a long time. Fritz Heider (1958) wrote a book about how we make judgments about one another. According to Heider, and others who came after him, we generally explain others' behavior as due either to something internal to the person or to something external to the person.

Imagine you are sitting in a coffee shop waiting for a date you met online. Your date is late. If you decide that your date is inconsiderate, you have made an internal attribution. When you make an **internal attribution** you blame personality, attitudes, or some other dispositional factor for the action. If, on the other hand, you think your date is late because of the traffic or some emergency at work, you have made an external attribution. When you make an **external attribution** you attribute situational factors for the action. We do find differences in the patterns of attributions in different cultures. In independent cultures, such as that found in the United States, salespeople tend to attribute their performance to internal factors. In more interdependent cultures, such as that found in India, attributions tend to be more external (DeCarlo, Agarwal, & Vyas, 2007).

Fundamental Attribution Error

Sitting in a coffee shop, watching the rain come down on thick traffic, you conclude your late date is a jerk. Is that an appropriate attribution? There are potential situational forces at work here. Perhaps your date can not find a taxi in the rain or is being held up in the heavy traffic or could not find an umbrella. When people attribute behavior to dispositional factors when there are clear situational factors at work, they are engaging in correspondence bias, also known as **fundamental attribution error** (Gilbert & Malone, 1995; Gilbert, Pelham, & Krull, 1988; Jones & Harris, 1967; Ross, Amabile, & Steinmetz, 1977). This phenomenon came to be known as the fundamental attribution error because so many researchers found similar results over a number of years (Jones, 1998).

There are certainly times when late behavior is due to rudeness, so your decision that your date is a jerk could be appropriate. The fundamental attribution error is an error because we make these kinds of decisions about someone's disposition when there are situational factors that we are not taking into account. You don't make this error, do you? Most people believe themselves to be less vulnerable to the fundamental attribution error than others, even though we are generally similar in our tendency to make the error, at least within a particular culture (Van Boven, Kamada, & Gilovich, 1999; Van Boven, White, Kamada, & Gilovich, 2003).

The fundamental attribution error got the "fundamental" part of its name because social psychologists assumed it was common in all people, in all cultures. Later work has not shown this to be true. Researchers have found that in comparison with European Americans, East Asians are more aware of situational constraints on behavior. When situations are powerful or easily recognized, East Asians are more likely to attribute behavior to those situational factors (Choi, Nisbett, & Norenzayan, 1999; Miyamoto & Kitayama, 2002; Morris & Peng, 1994). East Asians also think more holistically about the person (Choi, Nisbett, & Norenzayan, 1999). Even if a person's behavior is blamed on internal factors, these internal factors are explained situationally. For example, a person is rude because his parents never taught him manners. It turns out the fundamental attribution error is not as fundamental as we thought.

When someone is late, what is your first assumption? Do you think you're prone to fundamental attribution error?

3.2 Other Attributions

As we make attributions day after day we may develop patterns for making these judgments. Two of the major patterns investigated by researchers are those surrounding whether we make internal attributions for the events that occur to us (that happened because of something about me) or external attributions for those events (that happened because of chance or some other outside force). Another pattern involves the extent to which we expect hostility from others in our interactions.

How would you interpret being laid off? Would you blame it on yourself, or on the economy? This is your explanatory style.

Explanatory Style

As we go through our days we interpret not only the actions of others but also the events that occur to us. As we interpret actions and events we may fall into a certain pattern of explanation. Consider how you would explain the following: someone complimenting you on your appearance, and your not being able to find a job.

According to researchers you have three decisions to make as you interpret those events (Seligman & Nolen-Hoeksema, 1987; Seligman & Schulman, 1986). When you are explaining a compliment you receive, you could assume the other person was just having a good day and complimented everyone. On the other hand, you could assume that the compliment was prompted by your own appearance. In this case you are attributing the compliment to either an external cause, something about the other person or the circumstance, or an internal cause, something about you. Your second choice involves whether you consider the compliment to be an event that will likely never or rarely happen again, say a free make-over you just had, or something that will always be around—your attractive face. In this case you are making an attribution that is either unstable, meaning that the cause is there rarely or only some of the time, or stable, meaning that the cause is always there. Finally, you decide whether the compliment just applies to your present appearance at the mall where you got the make-over, or whether you will likely get compliments in all situations in your life. In this case you are making a decision of whether the cause is specific, applying only in this particular situation, or global, applying to all situations. All together then, when you decide on the cause for a behavior or event you decide whether it is external or internal, unstable or stable, and specific or global.

People tend to have relatively stable patterns in making such decisions. The pattern is that person's **explanatory style**. If you received a compliment, what kind of attribution do you think would make you feel the best? If you consider the cause of the compliment to be internal (something about you), stable (something that will always be there), and global (something that will be found in all situations), you are likely to feel better about yourself.

Would the same be true in explaining long-term unemployment? If you think about a negative event like long-term unemployment, an explanation that will make you feel best about yourself is one that says the cause is external (something about the job market), unstable (a job market that will change), and specific (applies only to the job market). People with an **optimistic explanatory style** show exactly this pattern. Someone who is optimistic will explain positive events as internal, stable, and global. Negative events, on the other hand, will be explained as external, unstable, and

Is the glass half empty or half full? Having an optimistic or pessimistic explanatory style might explain a person's approach to different situations.

specific. Individuals with a **pessimistic explanatory style** have exactly the opposite pattern. Someone with a pessimistic explanatory style explains positive events as external, unstable, and specific, and negative events as internal, stable, and global.

Negative explanatory styles have been linked to depression and suicide (Hirsch, Wolford, LaLonde, Brunk, & Parker-Morris, 2009; Peterson & Seligman, 1984).When people with negative explanatory styles encounter bad events, like losing a job, they are likely to explain it as due to something about them, such as having unmarketable skills; something that will always be there, such as no one will ever hire someone with their skills; and something that is global, such as that all of their skills are useless. With an explanation like that for losing a job, you can probably see how quickly one would start to feel bad. Negative explanatory styles are also linked to poorer academic performance (Peterson & Barrett, 1987). Researchers found that first-year university students who interpreted negative events as internal, stable, and global received lower grades. These lower grades seemed to be due to a reluctance to seek help when struggling (why do so if you believe your poor performance is due to your lack of intelligence?) and a lack of academic goal setting. For more on attributions and depression, see the *Social Psychology in Depth* box.

Individuals with optimistic explanatory styles are more likely to persist in the face of failure. One professional group that experiences a lot of failure is life insurance sales agents. The majority of potential clients they approach say no to their product. Researchers assessed the explanatory style of beginning life insurance agents and followed them to see how much life insurance they would sell and how long they would remain in their jobs (Seligman & Schulman, 1986). Those agents who were most optimistic sold the most insurance. At the end of the first year those who were in the top half of the scale for optimism were twice as likely to still be selling insurance. Those in the uppermost quarter of agents for optimism were 3 times as likely to still be in their jobs.

Hostile Attribution of Intent

Some individuals see the world as a hostile place. Imagine you are on the bus and someone steps on your toes, or you are headed for the checkout line in the supermarket with just a gallon of milk and someone with a cart loaded with groceries cuts in front of you. How do you interpret those actions? Did the person on the bus not like you and stepped

---

Social Psychology in Depth: Attribution, Story, and Depression

Our explanations for behavior influence the feelings we have about ourselves. Might we see these tendencies in the stories we tell? Adler, Kissel, and McAdams (2006) interviewed adults within the community, asking them to tell about eight different episodes in their life (e.g., childhood memory, high point, low point), as well as themes they saw in their life and how they would divide their life into chapters. The researchers took a look at the attributions made in the stories.

Attributional styles evident in the narratives were related to depression. Individuals who explained negative events as stable and global were more likely to show symptoms of depression. Keep in mind that these were attributions that appeared spontaneously and were not solicited by the researchers through a questionnaire or direct questions about attributions.

Depression was also related to contamination sequences in stories. A contamination sequence occurs when a story begins well but is ruined or spoiled by negative events. For example, someone might tell a story about a fun day at the beach that was spoiled by a fight and ended in a car ride home in stony silence. The presence of these types of stories independently predicted depression, apart from attributional style.

Other evidence that stories can reveal the attributional style related to depression was found by Peterson and Ulrey (1994). They showed people pictures of ambiguous scenes and asked them to describe what was happening in the picture. The researchers analyzed the stories that were told. They found that individuals who told stories that explained events using a negative attributional style were at greater risk for depression. We may often think of depression as simply feeling bad about oneself and the world, but depression is related to the way we view and describe the world around us.

---

on your toes to cause you pain? Or was that person jostled by the crowd and stepped on your toes while trying to stay upright? Did the person in the supermarket cut in front of you because she wants to make you late? Or did she not see you or thought you were headed for another line? In making judgments about the actions of others, we can decide that others engaged in those actions to deliberately harm us. People who chronically make these kinds of judgments have a **hostile attribution of intent**, sometimes called hostile attribution bias (de Castro, Veerman, Koops, Bosch, & Monshouwer, 2002). If you believe someone has deliberately stepped on your toes or cut in front of you in line, your reaction is likely to be different than if you believe these actions were unintentional. Hostile attribution of intent does tend to lead to more aggressive behavior (at least in children, where this has been studied the most) (de Castro et al., 2002).

Conclusion

Our lives are full of things we need to explain, usually without complete information. How we do that follows specific patterns within our culture (fundamental attribution error) or within our own experiences (explanatory style and hostile attribution of intent). The fundamental attribution error leads us to make dispositional attributions for the behavior of others when situational attributions would be valid. The attributions we make about ourselves and our style of explanation can influence how we feel and how we act within the world. Chronically attributing hostility to the actions of others can change our own actions toward those we encounter.

Summary

Internal and External Attributions

When we make internal attributions we attribute an action to something internal to the person, such as personality. External attributions, on the other hand, involve attributions of actions to something outside the person, such as current circumstances. When we make internal attributions despite plausible external causes we are making the fundamental attribution error.

Other Attributions

Our habitual patterns of making attributions can vary in terms of whether we make an internal versus external, a stable versus unstable, and a global versus specific attribution. When we make internal, stable, and global attributions for positive things and external, unstable, and specific attributions for negative things, we are showing an optimistic explanatory style. Pessimistic explanatory styles are directly opposite optimistic styles. Patterns of attributions can also involve how much hostility one expects from others and therefore sees in actions, known as hostile attribution of intent.

Critical Thinking Questions

1. Consider a recent experience you have had where you were trying to explain another person's behavior. What explanations can you identify as internal attributions? What explanations can you identify as external attributions?
2. How might making the fundamental attribution error affect your relationships?
3. Within your own cultural tradition, is the fundamental attribution error common?
4. An optimistic explanatory style was represented as positive for well-being and persistence. When might an optimistic explanatory style be detrimental to a person?
5. Where might a hostile attribution of intent originate?

Key Terms

Attribution

Explanatory style

External attribution

Fundamental attribution error

Hostile attribution of intent

Internal attribution

Optimistic explanatory style

Pessimistic explanatory style

Expanding Your Knowledge: Links to Additional Material

What Are They Doing?

Describe what you see at the animation at this link: http://cogweb.ucla.edu/Discourse/Narrative/heider-simmel-demo.swf.

Most people tell stories about the shapes. One shape might be described as chasing the other shape or following along. If we quickly and naturally make attributions for shapes, how likely are we to use such language and thinking to describe people? Consider why causal attributions for behaviors of people and objects might be adaptive. In other words, why might saying "Joe did this because of X" be something that would help humans live successfully in the world? For more explanation of the animations, see http://cogweb.ucla.edu/Discourse/Narrative/Heider_45.html.

Martin Seligman

Martin Seligman, a prominent researcher in the area of explanatory style, has a website dedicated to his research. The site is primarily focused on his work on positive psychology, but some references to work on explanatory style and learned helplessness are provided.

Seligman's site: http://www.ppc.sas.upenn.edu/index.html.

Research Participation

Opportunities to participate in Seligman's ongoing research are available. Seligman is known for his work on explanatory style, so there may be some related to the material within the text. Seligman also does research in the area of positive psychology, studying human flourishing.

Research opportunities can be found at http://www.ppresearch.sas.upenn.edu/.

Attributional Style Questionnaires

If you are interested in assessing your own attributional style, information on how to access this questionnaire can be found at http://www.ppc.sas.upenn.edu/asq.htm. Note that this link does not provide you with the questionnaire but information on how to obtain it.

An article on the questionnaire (Peterson, Semmel, von Baeyer, Abramson, & Metalsky, 1982) can be found at http://www.metalsky.com/var/ax/46494/558758-1982_Attributional%2BStyle%2BQuestionnaire%2B(ASQ).pdf.

Another attributional style questionnaire was developed by Dykema, Bergbower, Doctora, and Peterson (1996). A copy of their article can be found at http://deepblue.lib.umich.edu/bitstream/2027.42/68618/2/10.1177_073428299601400201.pdf.

Optimism Questionnaire

The Authentic Happiness website provides a variety of questionnaires. The optimism scale link is in the Engagement Questionnaires. In order to take scales from this site you are required to register, but the site does not send spam or sell names and e-mail addresses.

The optimism scale can be found at http://www.authentichappiness.sas.upenn.edu/Default.aspx.

4 | Evaluating Others and Our World

Learning Objectives

By the end of the chapter you should be able to:

- Define attitude
- Differentiate between implicit and explicit attitudes
- Describe when behaviors and attitudes are likely to match
- Explain the theory of planned behavior
- Describe cognitive dissonance theory and insufficient justification
- Describe self-perception theory

Chapter Outline

4.1 Definition of Attitudes

Attitudes have long been considered important to social psychology (Allport, 1935). Throughout the years social psychologists have found the subject of attitudes a fruitful area of research (Crano & Prislin, 2006). **Attitudes** are evaluations. These evaluations are based on our reactions, both in terms of how we feel and what we think, to some attitude object. Attitude objects can be physical objects, other people or groups of people, abstract or concrete ideas, animals, behaviors, or even some aspect of ourselves (Eagly & Chaiken, 1993). The evaluations we have involve two aspects, strength and valence. We may have attitudes that are very strong or very weak. In terms of valence we may have attitudes that are on the positive side of the spectrum (you like cats) or the negative side of the spectrum (you hate elephants). Putting together strength and valence, you might have a fairly weak positive attitude toward cats and a very strong negative attitude toward elephants. (There is also a body of work on ambivalent attitudes, attitudes that are simultaneously positive and negative, see Armitage & Conner, 2000, or van Harreveld, van der Plight, de Vries, Wenneker, & Verhue, 2004.)

4.2 Implicit and Explicit Attitudes

When most of us think of attitudes we probably think of how we feel about objects, people, or groups. As noted earlier, you may have attitudes toward elephants and cats. Researchers have found that such consciously known and reported attitudes are only part of the attitude picture (Nosek & Smyth, 2007; Payne, Burkley, & Stokes, 2008). The attitudes we report, those that rely on our knowledge and beliefs about an attitude object, are called **explicit attitudes**. But there are other attitudes that we are often unaware that we hold. These attitudes are based in the automatic, unconscious reactions we have toward an attitude object and are called **implicit attitudes**.

If we are consciously aware of our attitudes we can, if we are willing to tell the truth, simply report on those attitudes (e.g., Yoo, Steger, & Lee, 2010). To assess implicit attitudes, researchers need to get a measure of our automatic reactions, reactions we

The attitudes and feelings we report and recognize are labeled "explicit." Some attitudes, however, are based on automatic, unconscious reactions, and are known as "implicit."

are not even aware of. Psychologists developed a test to look at implicit attitudes called the Implicit Association Test (IAT; Greenwald, McGhee, & Schwartz, 1998; Schnabel, Asendorpf, & Greenwald, 2008). The IAT measures implicit attitudes by evaluating reaction times. Test-takers match characteristics that are flashed in the center of a computer screen to category words in the upper corners of the screen. For example, if "good" is in the left corner and "bad" in the right, a word like "joy" should be matched to the left corner and "evil" to the right. The tricky part is that attitude objects are placed in the same corners as those words and respondents need to quickly match to the correct corner both words for the good and bad categories *and* words or faces associated with

Implicit attitudes are sometimes shaped by society and environment. For instance, your assumptions about other social groups might be influenced by how or where you grew up.

that attitude object. For a test looking at implicit attitudes toward older adults, "old" might be assigned to the left corner and "young" to the right. The respondent would need to quickly switch from a word (joy) to a face (older adult) and match each with the correct corner (left). A person who has a negative implicit attitude toward older adults should take longer to match the picture of an older person with the left "good" corner than to the right "bad" corner. This delay in matching an older person with a corner that also contains the category "good" provides evidence of a negative implicit attitude toward older adults.

We learn implicit and explicit attitudes through different systems. Explicit attitudes are based in language or, sometimes, logic or some other symbolic representation. Because of this we can learn them relatively quickly. For example, if someone were to tell you about a particular group you had not known about before (e.g., pygmies) and shared with you how much he or she liked this group, you might form a positive explicit attitude toward the group. Implicit attitudes are learned over time as we encounter the attitude object. For example, if you always encountered representations of a particular group (pictures of pygmies) that were positive, you might develop a positive implicit attitude toward them (Rydell & McConnell, 2006; Strack & Deutsch, 2004; Wilson, Lindsey, & Schooler, 2000).

Because of the way we learn implicit attitudes, people usually hold implicit attitudes that are held and communicated by society. The particular social environment and culture we are exposed to has a large impact on our implicit attitude (Shepherd, 2011). No one might say bad things about a particular racial or ethnic group, but if representations of these in the media are always paired with violence or poverty or negative things, individuals within the society tend to hold negative implicit attitudes. This also allows for people to hold opposite explicit and implicit attitudes. If people logically believe that a social group is good and report a positive explicit attitude, but the society has a negative view of that group and that has been communicated with individuals, they might hold a negative implicit attitude.

Implicit and explicit attitudes can both predict behavior, but generally do so for behavior in different realms. Researchers find that nonverbal behaviors are best predicted by implicit attitudes. For example, those with a negative implicit attitude toward people of a racial group tend to show nonverbal behaviors that indicate dislike for a member of the group they are interacting with, even when their verbal behavior is friendly and welcoming (Dovidio, Kawakami, & Gaertner, 2002). Consciously controlled, deliberate behaviors, like what we say, will go along with explicit attitudes (Jellison, McConnell, & Gabriel, 2004; McConnell & Leibold, 2001; Rydell & McConnell, 2006).

4.3 Behavior and Attitudes

Our attitudes involve evaluations of other people, behaviors, and objects. Logically, these evaluations should affect how we behave toward these attitude objects. For example, if you have a favorable attitude toward online dating, you should be more likely to engage in online dating than if you had a negative attitude. Early researchers believed this to be true (Allport, 1935; Droba, 1933). But even early on other researchers had difficulty finding this connection (LaPiere, 1934; Wicker, 1969).

LaPiere (1934) was one of the first to investigate the relation of attitudes to behaviors. LaPiere traveled around the United States with some friends of his. These friends were Chinese. In the 1930s many Americans held quite negative attitudes toward the Chinese, and LaPiere and his friends were concerned about the service they might get as they traveled. They had no reason to be worried. In all but one location, they were treated well, sometimes better than average. LaPiere was curious about this reaction, so several months later he sent questionnaires to the places he and his friends had visited as well as a number of hotels and restaurants they had not visited. Almost universally these businesses reported they would not serve someone who was Chinese. The negative attitudes were present, but LaPiere and his friends found that behavior did not match these attitudes.

Since the 1930s a great deal of work has been done to sort out this problem. Researchers have identified factors that can strengthen and weaken the ability of attitudes to predict behaviors. Attitudes that are particularly accessible are more likely to determine our behavior (Fazio, 2000). Generally if people respond quickly in reporting their attitudes, these attitudes are highly accessible. If you respond quickly that you hate blind dates, we are unlikely to find you on one. However, if it takes you some time to figure out that you are not fond of online dating, your behavior might not bear that out. The more closely the attitude assessment matches the behavioral assessment in specificity, the more likely the attitude is to predict the behavior (Weigel & Newman, 1976). For example, if you were asked about your attitude toward sports, your answer may not match well with your attendance at the local high school football game. If we asked about your attitude toward the local high school football team, we may have better luck predicting if we will see you at a game. Another factor is whether the behavior is easy or difficult to perform (Wallace, Paulson, Lord, & Bond, 2005). One might have a negative attitude toward smoking but continue to smoke because quitting is difficult. The social pressure one has to do

Logically, your attitude toward an activity—like skydiving—should be predictive of whether you'll engage in it. Researchers found there are other factors at play.

© Atlaspix, 2013. Used under license from Shutterstock, Inc.

or not do a behavior is also important. If a person feels a strong social pressure to engage in a behavior (wearing a seat belt) that person may engage in the behavior despite a negative attitude (Wallace, Paulson, Lord, & Bond, 2005).

A physiotherapist accompanies a patient with a prosthetic leg. The theory of planned behavior encompasses the individual's attitude and perceived behavioral control as well as the attitude of others.

Theory of Planned Behavior

One theory that puts a number of these factors together is the **theory of planned behavior**. According to this theory if we want to predict a behavior (or an intention to do a behavior) we need to know three things: (1) attitude toward that behavior, (2) subjective norms related to that behavior, and (3) perceived behavioral control (Ajzen, 1991). **Subjective norms** involve one's belief of how people in that person's environment view the behavior. For example, you might find that people in your social circle (friends, relatives) think healthy eating is a good idea but think online dating is silly. **Perceived behavior control** is your belief that you can engage in the behavior. For example, you might think that eating a healthy diet is a lot of trouble but joining an online dating site and posting a profile is easily accomplished. If someone has a positive attitude, positive subjective norms, and high perceived behavioral control, we can predict with some accuracy that they will engage in that behavior. You might become an online dater if you have a positive attitude toward online dating, if people in your environment think it is a good idea, and if you foresee no problems in creating an online profile on a dating site. The theory of planned behavior has been used to help explain an extremely wide variety of behaviors, everything from smoking cessation (Norman, Conner, & Bell, 1999) to using dental floss (Rise, Astrom, & Sutton, 1998) to composting (Kaiser, Wolfing, & Fuhrer, 1999). Looking across this wide variety with a technique called a meta-analysis, Armitage and Connor (2001) found that this model can accurately predict behavior and that each component is important to accurate prediction. The theory of planned behavior is also fairly helpful to prediction of behavior across cultures (Hagger et al., 2007; Van Hooft, Born, Taris, & Van der Flier, 2006).

Cognitive Dissonance Theory

Imagine you have agreed to be part of a research study. You come to the study and are asked to do two boring, repetitive tasks for an hour. As you finish the researcher looks distressed. He hesitates but finally tells you his dilemma. There is another student who is supposed to be coming and this student was going to introduce the tasks you just did to the next participant. The researcher tells you that they are interested in how expectations influence performance. This next participant is supposed to be told that these tedious tasks you just completed are fun and interesting. Haltingly, the researcher asks if you might be willing to help him out and tell the next participant that what you just did was fun. He is willing to pay you $1 for your effort. You agree. You tell the next participant that the task was interesting and exciting and off that person goes. A separate researcher asks you how interesting the tasks you just did were and whether you'd be willing to participate in similar types of studies in the future. How do you answer? Would your answer be different if the researcher had given you $20?

A group of male college students faced exactly this situation in a study by Festinger and Carlsmith (1959). In their study one third of participants received $1 to tell the next participant that the study they were about to participate in was fun and interesting, another third received $20, and the final third, the control group, was not asked to say anything to a future participant and was not given any money. Unbeknownst to the participants, the hesitant request was part of the experiment and the other participant was working for the experimenter. What the researchers were really interested in was whether the different amounts of pay would affect how participants felt about the study. Examine Table 4.1. Which group thought the research was most interesting, when later asked? Who was most interested in participating in similar studies in the future?

Table 4.1 Results from Festinger and Carlsmith's (1959) Study of Cognitive Dissonance

Interview Question	Experimental Condition		
	$1 Group	$20 Group	Control Group
Were the tasks interesting and enjoyable? (rated from −5, extremely dull and boring, to +5, extremely interesting and enjoyable)	+1.35	−0.05	−0.45
Would you have any desire to participate in another similar experiment? (rated from −5, definitely dislike to participate, to +5, definitely like to participate)	+1.20	−0.25	−0.62

Reprinted from the *Journal of Abnormal and Social Psychology*, Vol. 58, Festinger & Carlsmith, Cognitive Consequences of Forced Compliance, p. 207 (1959), with permission from Elsevier.

As you noticed in Table 4.1, the participants who received $1 seemed to like the study best. Any ideas on why? Festinger and Carlsmith proposed that those participants who received $1 for telling another person what amounted to a lie felt they had misled someone else and had **insufficient justification** for doing so. In other words, these participants lied for a very small amount of money and could not explain (justify) what they did as based in the monetary reward. So these participants were faced with two things: knowledge that the research was boring (the researchers had deliberately made it mind-numbingly tedious) and a behavior that involved telling someone else it was interesting. The gap between what they believed and what they did created a type of tension known as **cognitive dissonance**. They could not go back in time and change what they had done, so their only option was to change how they felt about the study. In the $20 condition there was also a gap between what they did and how they truly felt, but these people did not experience any tension. They had a reason, sufficient justification, for what they did: $20. The people in the $20 condition later reported that the study was boring because they had no need to justify what they did.

Cognitive dissonance can be reduced without changing one's attitude. For example, if you decided you needed to be on a diet but then went to a dinner and had chocolate mousse, you could change your attitude toward the diet (maybe you do not really need to diet), but

Cognitive dissonance can be reduced in a number of ways.

you could also reduce that tension by doing other things. One option would be to minimize the importance of one of the elements (Festinger, 1957). You could say that dieting is not that important to you or that chocolate mousse is not a big deal. Another option would be to reduce your perceived choice (Beauvois & Joule, 1999; Wicklund & Brehm, 1976). You might tell yourself it would have been rude if you had not eaten your host's dessert. You might also add consonant cognitions. For example, you could tell yourself that chocolate mousse is healthy; after all, chocolate contains flavonoids that are good for your health.

Cognitive dissonance theory can be helpful in understanding or promoting behavior change. Researchers have found that differences between attitudes about dating aggression and behaviors resulted in a decrease in dating aggression over time (Schumacher, 2004). In a study involving high school students at risk for eating disorders like anorexia or bulimia, researchers induced behavior change by creating dissonance (Stice, Rohde, Gau, & Shaw, 2009). The students were part of a program where they were asked to engage in behaviors that went against their unhealthy attitudes toward their bodies and food. For example, they were asked to write a letter to a young girl about the dangers of the thinness ideal, to share what they like about themselves, and to practice what they would say to others to challenge the thinness ideal. This intervention decreased risk factors in the participants for an eating disorder.

Cognitive dissonance does act differently across cultures (Hoshino-Browne et al., 2005). Individuals in independent cultures like that found in the United States are more concerned about their own individual identity and attributes. Internal consistency is therefore the primary goal for someone in an independent culture. Individuals in interdependent cultures, like that found in Japan, are more concerned about how they fit with the expectations of others, in particular others that are part of their own group. The approval of others is, therefore, of great importance. Since internal consistency is not as important, consistency between attitudes or behaviors may be important in interdependent cultures only when others are going to be appraised of one's behavior. Researchers find that when Japanese college students are aware of potential public scrutiny of their choices, they show greater dissonance. When others are not potentially aware of their choices, dissonance does not seem to come into play. For American college students, public scrutiny does not matter. Because the American students are attempting to be internally consistent, they show dissonance in both situations (Kitayama, Snibbe, Markus, & Suzuki, 2004). For more on cognitive dissonance, see the *Social Psychology in Depth* box.

Self-Perception Theory

There are other ways for attitudes and behaviors to connect. If you were wondering about your attitude toward online dating, one place you could look to determine your attitude is your behavior. If you have spent a lot of time and money on online dating, then you are

Social Psychology in Depth: Cognitive Dissonance, Children, and Monkeys

Where does cognitive dissonance come from? In investigating the origins of cognitive dissonance we would want to know whether children feel cognitive dissonance or whether it develops later in life. We may also want to know if cognitive dissonance occurs in nonhuman primates. Knowing whether cognitive dissonance is unique to humans may help us understand the potential evolutionary origin of the phenomenon.

Egan, Sanatos, & Bloom (2007) investigated cognitive dissonance in children and in monkeys. For both populations they created cognitive dissonance by having the child or monkey make a choice between two alternatives. When we make a choice between two equally attractive alternatives, we may experience cognitive dissonance. If both options were good, why did we choose the one we chose? To reduce the dissonance we will likely increase our liking of our chosen option and decrease our liking of the option we did not choose. In this study the participants made an initial choice and were then asked to make a second choice. The second choice included the option not chosen on the first trial and a new option. Presumably, if cognitive dissonance were at play, the participants would have decreased their liking of their unchosen option and be less likely to choose that option in the second trial. For example, if children originally rated stickers with a flower, a bird, and a rainbow equally, they might initially be asked if they wanted the flower or the bird sticker more. Having chosen the flower, they would then be asked to choose between the bird (the option not chosen in the previous trial) and the rainbow. If cognitive dissonance is in play, they should choose the rainbow. The initial choice would have created cognitive dissonance, leading the children to discount their liking of the bird sticker to reduce that dissonance. Children in this study were given choices of stickers; the monkeys, the choice of M&M candy colors.

Even though the participants initially liked all three options equally, after making a choice, they were less likely to choose the option they had not chosen on the first trial. The authors propose that because this effect is found among young children (4-year-olds) and monkeys, cognitive dissonance may operate before we have much experience in making choices. It may not need language or socialization for it to occur.

© Andrea Slatter, 2013. Used under license from Shutterstock, Inc.

A woman executes a "trust fall," believing her colleague will catch her. Researchers found that behavior does affect attitude.

likely to conclude that you have a positive attitude. If you have spent a lot of time making fun of people who meet dates online, then you might conclude, looking at these actions, that your attitude toward online dating is negative. This sense that we can figure out our attitudes by looking at our behaviors is the basis of **self-perception theory** (Bem, 1967).

To look into whether our actions could influence our attitudes Zak, Gold, Ryckman, & Lenney (1998) asked 64 dating couples to come to their lab. Each member of the couple was asked to provide information on how much they trusted their partner. The couples were separated and told one of three things. The first third of participants were told that their partner would be dancing with a research assistant to a Debbie Gibson or Madonna song. These participants were asked if that was OK with them, if they trusted their partner to dance with someone else. The next third of participants were told they would be dancing with a research assistant to a Debbie Gibson or Madonna song. The researchers told them that their partner had been asked if that was all right and their partner had said yes, they trusted their significant other. The final third of participants, the control group, were told that their partner would be listening to music. What the researchers wanted to know was whether acting in a trusting manner, that is, telling the researcher that they trusted their partner to dance with someone else, would increase trust. When the researchers assessed trust at the end of the study, they found that both the participants who acted in a trusting way and those who were trusted showed an increase in trust when compared to the control group. The bigger change, however, was with the participants who acted in a trusting matter. The act of trusting, it seems, increases trust.

Conclusion

Humans evaluate their environment and the things in that environment, forming attitudes. Although we may not always be aware of the attitudes we hold, they may still affect our behavior. Our attitudes can change because of our behavior (as in cognitive dissonance theory) or be formed because of our behavior (as in self-perception theory).

Summary

Definition of Attitudes

Attitudes involve an evaluation of an entity or behavior. Attitudes can be placed on a continuum from weak to strong and on a continuum of valence, from positive to negative.

Implicit and Explicit Attitudes

When people report on an attitude they are describing an attitude that they are consciously aware of, called an explicit attitude. Attitudes that emerge from automatic processes are implicit attitudes. Implicit attitudes can be assessed with the Implicit Association Test (IAT).

Behavior and Attitudes

Attitudes and behaviors are often misaligned. We are more likely to see attitude and behavior agreement when the attitude is accessible and it matches the behavior in level of specificity, the behavior is easy to perform, and social pressures support an alignment.

The theory of planned behavior allows for the prediction of behaviors from attitudes, subjective norms, and perceived behavioral control. Cognitive dissonance theory proposes that when our attitudes and behaviors do not match up and we have insufficient justification, we are likely to change our attitude. Self-perception theory involves figuring out our attitudes from observing our own behavior.

Critical Thinking Questions

1. If implicit attitudes are something we are not even aware of, do they matter?
2. How might we change our implicit and explicit attitudes?
3. What other influences on attitudes and behaviors might researchers study?
4. If you worked in a health care setting and wanted to promote positive health behaviors, how might you use the theory of planned behavior to implement an intervention?
5. Have you ever had an experience where your attitudes and actions did not match? Did you do any of the things suggested to reduce cognitive dissonance?
6. How could self-perception theory be used to promote positive attitudes?

Key Terms

Attitude

Cognitive dissonance

Explicit attitudes

Implicit attitudes

Insufficient justification

Perceived behavioral control

Self-perception theory

Subjective norms

Theory of planned behavior

Expanding Your Knowledge: Links to Additional Material

Defining Attitudes

A number of definitions of attitudes exist, some historic, some current. Several definitions from different sources and time periods in the history of attitudes research are available at http://www.psych.umn.edu/courses/spring06/borgidae/psy5202/images/attitude%20 definitions.pdf.

Pew Global Attitudes Project

If you would like to investigate a wide variety of attitudes from around the world, take a look at the Pew Global Attitudes Project website at http://pewglobal.org/. Reports on a variety of surveys are also available.

Research

Opportunities to participate in research can be found at http://www.yourmorals.org/explore.php. The site runs a variety of studies you can participate in and receive feedback concerning your results. The site is primarily focused on assessing morals and values of those who visit.

Intentional Action

To expand on the discussion of behavior provided by the text, visit the website below. The site is based on research on intentional actions. Visitors take part in demonstrations of research studies and read about the findings.

To take part in research: http://www.unc.edu/~knobe/experiments.html.

Joshua Knobe, the author of this demonstration and creator of the research paradigm, has a website at http://pantheon.yale.edu/~jk762/.

Knobe provides a number of links to some reports on his research. One link is to an amusing video that goes through a part of the demonstration: http://www.youtube.com/watch?v=sHoyMfHudaE.

Implicit Association Test

Information about implicit attitudes and the opportunity to take a variety of implicit association tests can be found at the Project Implicit website, http://www.projectimplicit.net/. On the initial page you can read about the project in general (under the For the Public tab). This page also offers more information about the project for researchers, and research papers.

At https://implicit.harvard.edu/implicit/, you can take an Implicit Association Test and participate in ongoing research. Most of the research studies take about 10 to 15 minutes, and participants must register before taking part in research. Participants are provided with a summary of their own results at the end of their participation. If you want to see what your scores might be but do not want to be part of a research study or register, you can take a demo test.

Attitude and Behavior Mismatch

Do your attitudes and behaviors always match? If you are similar to most people, you see distracted driving as dangerous, but also engage in the behavior.

A post on this issue can be found at http://theinvisiblegorilla.com/blog/2010/12/22/driving-and-distraction-california-survey/. The authors describe a study in California in which almost 60% of participants listed talking on the phone as a serious distraction for drivers while almost 46% admitted to making a driving mistake while talking on the phone.

ATTITUDES

Chapter Outline

Do our attitudes determine our behavior?

Does our behavior determine our attitudes?

Why do our actions affect our attitudes?

WHAT IS AN ATTITUDE?

ATTITUDES

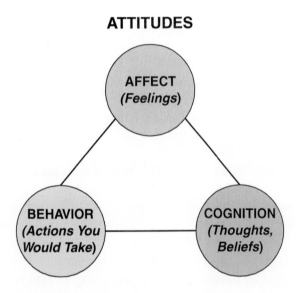

Do our attitudes determine our behavior?
- What is the relationship between what we are on the inside and what we do on the outside?
- Prevailing assumption is that our beliefs and feelings determine our public behavior.

Are we all hypocrites?

Prior to 1964
- Accepted the premise that attitudes predict behavior.
- Festinger (1964): Behavior is actually the horse pulling our attitudes.
- Wicker (1969): Expressed attitudes predict very little of the variation in their behaviors.
    —E.g., Attitudes regarding church are not likely to predict the behavior of going to church.
- Abelson (1972): "We're very good at finding reasons for what we do, but not very good at doing what we find reasons for."

When do attitudes predict behavior?

External influences--> Behavior<-->Attitude-->Expressed Attitude<--External Influences

- Our behavior and our expressed attitudes are both subject to social influences.
- Therefore, minimize the influences.

How to minimize social influences to measure attitudes?

- Bogus pipeline (Jones & Segall, 1971)
- Implicit Attitude Test

How to minimize other influences on behavior

- If people's expressions of attitudes are affected by outside influences, then other behaviors can be as well.
- Attitudes are like baseball averages in predicting behaviors.

Measuring attitudes specific to the behavior

When our attitude measurement is general, and our behavior is specific, we should not expect a close relationship (Fishbein & Ajzen, 1977, 1982)

- Health fitness attitude and jogging or dieting

Measuring attitudes specific to the behavior

- A third predictor is to make the attitude potent/relevant:
  - In a novel situation we think before we act;
  - Snyder & Swann (1976): For only those jurors allowed to reflect on their attitudes before deliberation did their attitudes predict their verdict.
  - Diener & Wallbom (1976): Cheating students and self-consciousness
  - Fazio & Zanna (1981): Cornell housing shortage

  → Attitudes guide our behavior only if they come to mind.

Summary thus far: Three conditions under which attitudes predict behaviors

1. When other influences upon our attitude statements and our behavior are minimized
2. When the measured attitude is specifically relevant to the behavior
3. When people are induced to focus on their attitudes by making them self-conscious

II. Does our behavior determine our attitudes?

- Sarah is hypnotized and told to take off her shoes when a book drops on the floor. Fifteen minutes later a book drops and Sarah quietly slips out of her loafers. "Hey, Sarah," asks the hypnotherapist, "why did you take off your shoes?" "Well . . . my feet are hot and tired. It has been a long day."
- George has electrodes temporarily implanted in the region of his brain that controls his head movements. When the electrode is stimulated by remote control, George always turns his head. Unaware of the remote stimulation, he thinks this activity is spontaneous. When questioned, he always offers a reasonable explanation: "I'm looking for my slipper." "I heard a noise." "I was looking for the bed."

II. Does our behavior determine our attitudes?

- Carol's severe seizures were relieved by surgically separating her two brain hemi-spheres. Now, in an experiment, a picture of a nude woman is flashed to the left half of Carol's field of vision and thus to the nonverbal right side of her brain. A sheepish smile spreads over her face and she begins chuckling. Asked why, she invents—and apparently believes—a plausible explanation: "Oh—that funny machine."
- Frank, another split-brain patient, has the word "smile" flashed to his nonverbal right hemisphere. He obliges and forces a smile. Asked why, he explains that "This experiment is very funny."

→ These all reflect the effect of what we do on what we "know."

II. Does our behavior determine our attitudes?

A. Role Playing

- Trost (1968): Role play a simulated conflict with Russia. Students' attitudes when assigned to be U.S. advisors became more hostile
- Liberman (1956) observed that those workers promoted to foreman developed more sympathetic attitudes toward management; stewards with unions.

II. Does our behavior determine our attitudes?

- College students: What is different about yourself now and how did this transfor-mation take place?

→ Attitude change as a result of different behaviors

II. Does our behavior determine our attitudes?

B. Sometimes saying becomes believing

- Tetlock (1981): Policy statements of U.S. presidents tend to be quite simplis-tic during the campaign. Immediately following, they become much more complex.
  → Lies? Shading views depending on who we're addressing

II. Does our behavior determine our attitudes?

- Jefferson (1785): "He who permits himself to tell a lie once finds it much easier to do it a second and third time, till at length it becomes habitual; he tells lies without attending to it, and truths without the world's believing him. This falsehood of the tongue leads to that of the heart, and in time depraves all its good dispositions."

II. Does our behavior determine our attitudes?

- Have students read a personality description of someone and then summarize it for someone else who was known to either like or dislike this person.

Results:

- Students gave more positive summaries of what they read to those who liked the person.
- Students came to like the description more themselves.

- Students remembered more positive descriptions than what was actually read.
  - → Once we have uttered our modified message, we tend to believe it.

II. Does our behavior determine our attitudes?
C. Foot-in-the-Door
- Ask to give to Cancer Society = 46% agreement
  Those contacted a day after agreeing to wear a pin for the cause = 92% agreement
- Ask for collection for the disabled = 53%
  Two weeks prior they signed a petition to build a rec. center for the disabled = 93%

II. Does our behavior determine our attitudes?
D. Low-Balling
- Volunteer for an experiment but the time is at 7 am = 24% attendance
- But if they first agreed to participate without knowing the time = 53% attendance

Consumer protection laws
- What can companies do to keep people from backing out of their commitments?
- Have them fill out the sales agreement. Leads to greater commitment.

II. Does our behavior determine our attitudes?
- → La Rouchefoucauld's Maxims (1665):
"It is not as difficult to find one who has never succumbed to a given temptation as
to find one who has succumbed only once."

II. Does our behavior determine our attitudes?
E. Actions and Morality?
- Action attitude sequence occurs not with just shading the truth but with more
  immoral acts as well.
- Cruel acts corrode the conscience (Abu Ghraib).
- Cruel acts lead to victim denigration, helping justify the hurtful behavior.
- We tend not only hurt those we dislike, but dislike those we have hurt.

II. Does our behavior determine our attitudes?
E. Actions and Morality?

NAZI cog plea during Nuremburg trials:

Q: "Did you kill people in the camp?"
A: "Yes."
Q: "Did you poison them with gas?"
A: "Yes."
Q: "Did you bury them alive?"
A: "It sometimes happened."
Q: "Did you personally help kill people?"
A: "Absolutely not. I was only the paymaster in the camp."
Q: "What did you think of what was going on?"
A: "It was bad at first but we got used to it."
Q: "Do you know the Russians will hang you?
A: (Bursting into tears) "Why should they?! What have I done?!"

II. Does our behavior determine our attitudes?

    E. Actions and Morality?

        Fortunately, the principle works in the other direction as well:

- Introduce children to a really neat battery-operated toy and instruct them not to play with it while I'm out of the room.
- Use severe threat with half of them and mild threat with the other half.
- Both conditions were sufficient to deter playing.
- Several weeks later, a different researcher leaves the child in the room with the toy.

Results:

14/18 (77%) under the severe threat, tore into the toy.

12/18 (66%) under the mild threat resisted playing with it.

    → Having made the conscious choice not to play with the toy, they internalized their decision and this newly acquired attitude controlled their behavior.

II. Does our behavior determine our attitudes?

    E. Actions and Morality?

- Chinese and POWs in the Korean War
- Little by little had them write and publicly speak anti-American trivia.
- Little by little greater demands were made of them: e.g., public confessions, self-criticisms in writing, etc.

Results:

- 100s cooperated
- 21 chose to remain upon being released
- Those who returned said that although Communism won't work for the United States, it's good for Asia.

    → Want to change your attitude? Start behaving!

Outline

Being Consistent

Balance Theory
Cognitive Dissonance Theory
What affects the desire for consistency?
Arousal and Preference for Consistency
Consequences and Salience
Consistent with What?

Being Consistent

Consistency Principle: The principle that people will change their attitudes, beliefs, perceptions, and actions to make them consistent with each other.

Balance Theory

We want to:

- agree with people we like.
- disagree with people we dislike.

- associate good things with good people.
- associate bad things with bad people.

Being Consistent

Balance Theory

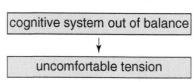

To remove this tension, we will have to change something in the system.

Balance Theory

Rhoda considers Mary her best friend.
Rhoda is strongly pro-choice.
Mary is strongly pro-life.

Balance Theory

Rhoda could restore balance by changing her feeling about abortion.

Balance Theory

Or she could restore balance by changing her feelings about her friend.

Being Consistent

Balance Theory

Or she could restore balance by changing Mary's feelings about abortion.

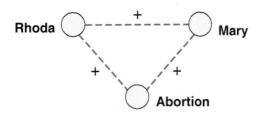

Being Consistent

Cognitive Dissonance Theory

Dissonance: The unpleasant state of psychological arousal resulting from an inconsistency within one's important attitudes, beliefs, or behaviors.

Being Consistent

Cognitive Dissonance Theory

Counterattitudinal action: A behavior that is inconsistent with an existing attitude.

Festinger and Carlsmith (1959):

  Students first performed a boring task (turning pegs in holes)

  Then were asked to tell another student it was interesting—and for this, they were paid either $1 or $20

  When later asked their attitudes toward the boring task:

  Those receiving $1 payment had come to see it as more enjoyable.

  Those receiving $20 hadn't changed their attitudes at all.

  Why? Dissonance theory explains:

  $20 provided adequate justification for misleading another student.

  $1 was insufficient justification, thus arousing dissonance.

  Changing beliefs about the task reduced the cognitive discomfort.

  Postdecisional dissonance is the **conflict** one feels between the knowledge that he or she has made a decision and the possibility that the decision may be wrong.

  Knox & Inkster (1968): Just seconds after placing a bet, gamblers are more confident their horse will win.

Being Consistent

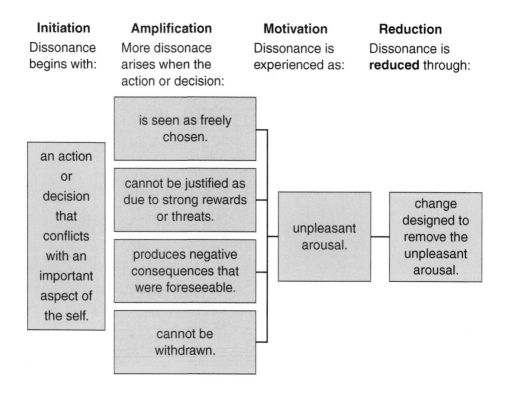

Initiation	**Amplification**	**Motivation**	**Reduction**
Dissonance begins with:	More dissonace arises when the action or decision:	Dissonance is experienced as:	Dissonance is **reduced** through:

an action or decision that conflicts with an important aspect of the self.

is seen as freely chosen.

cannot be justified as due to strong rewards or threats.

produces negative consequences that were foreseeable.

cannot be withdrawn.

unpleasant arousal.

change designed to remove the unpleasant arousal.

Arousal

No arousal = No dissonance = No need to change

- Cooper, Zanna, & Taves: Participants in an experiment who were given a **tranquilizer** (eliminating any dissonant arousal) did not change their opinions, even after writing a counter-attitudinal essay.

Being Consistent

Preference for Consistency

SAMPLE SCALE ITEMS:

1. I PREFER TO BE AROUND PEOPLE WHOSE REACTIONS I CAN ANTICIPATE.
   Strongly Disagree = 1…..   *Strongly Agree = 9*

2. IT IS IMPORTANT TO ME THAT MY ACTIONS ARE CONSISTENT WITH MY BELIEFS.
   Strongly Disagree = 1…..   *Strongly Agree = 9*

3. EVEN IF MY ATTITUDES AND ACTIONS SEEMED CONSISTENT TO ME, IT WOULD BOTHER ME IF THEY DID NOT SEEM CONSISTENT TO OTHERS.
   Strongly Disagree = 1……   *Strongly Agree = 9*

4. IT IS IMPORTANT TO ME THAT THOSE WHO KNOW ME CAN PREDICT WHAT I WILL DO.
   Strongly Disagree = 1......   *Strongly Agree = 9*

5. I WANT TO BE DESCRIBED BY OTHERS AS A STABLE, PREDICTABLE PERSON.
   Strongly Disagree = 1......   *Strongly Agree = 9*

6. THE APPEARANCE OF CONSISTENCY IS AN IMPORTANT PART OF THE IMAGE I PRESENT TO THE WORLD.
   Strongly Disagree = 1......   *Strongly Agree = 9*

7. AN IMPORTANT REQUIREMENT FOR A FRIEND OF MINE IS PERSONAL CONSISTENCY.
   Strongly Disagree = 1......   *Strongly Agree = 9*

8. I TYPICALLY PREFER TO DO THINGS THE SAME WAY.
   Strongly Disagree = 1......   *Strongly Agree = 9*

9. I WANT MY CLOSE FRIENDS TO BE PREDICTABLE.
   Strongly Disagree = 1......   *Strongly Agree = 9*

10. I MAKE AN EFFORT TO APPEAR CONSISTENT TO OTHERS.
    Strongly Disagree = 1......   *Strongly Agree = 9*

Being Consistent

Preference for Consistency

People low in preference for consistency:
- don't show typical consistency effects.
- tend to be equally positive toward an idea regardless of whether they had high or low choice in advocating it.

Being Consistent

Consequences

The more impact your behavior has had on the world, the more you will feel motivated to change your attitudes to fit the behavior.

Example: If you are on a committee that recommends a harsh penalty for a fellow student accused of cheating on a math test:

You will maintain your negative opinion of that student more to the extent that the consequence is expulsion from school as opposed to a lowered grade in the math class.

Being Consistent

Consequences and Salience

Negative consequences will spur more change only when they are foreseeable.

Factors that make inconsistency more salient will enhance dissonance.

Being Consistent

Consistent with What?

Different ads appeal to different self-related motives in different cultures.
Han & Shavitt (1994)
Asked Americans and Koreans to rate advertisements that suggested either:
- Personal benefits ("treat yourself")
- Group benefits ("share an experience")

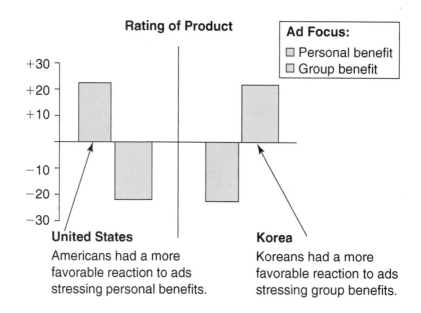

United States
Americans had a more favorable reaction to ads stressing personal benefits.

Korea
Koreans had a more favorable reaction to ads stressing group benefits.

Gaining Social Approval

The motivation to achieve approval is called impression motivation, because the goal is to create a good impression on others.
This motivation to create a good impression can sometimes conflict with the pursuit of the accuracy and consistency goals.

Gaining Social Approval

What affects the desire for social approval?
Self-monitoring and gender
The nature of the audience and the expectation of discussion
Expected discussions and social approval
Gaining Social Approval

Self-Monitoring

Snyder & DeBono
High self-monitors were more persuaded by ads promoting **socially appealing images** associated with particular brands of coffee, whiskey, and cigarettes than by ads touting the quality of the same brands.

Gaining Social Approval

Gender

Like high self-monitors, women tend to be sensitively attuned to relationships and inter-personal issues.
This sensitivity affects the way they respond to persuasive appeals.
Gaining Social Approval

The Nature of the Audience

Persuaders assign high intelligence to other people who quickly see the "wisdom" of their persuasive arguments.
However, outside observers assign low intelligence to people who are easily persuaded.

Gaining Social Approval

The Nature of the Audience

Most people are aware of this and use this information to gain others' respect.
If reporting an opinion to the persuader, people report a lot of change.
If reporting to an observer, more likely to say they were unmoved.

Gaining Social Approval

The Expectation of Discussion

People who expect to discuss a topic tend to hold more moderate opinions.
By seizing the middle, one not only gets to appear broadminded, but also gets to hold an especially flexible and defensible position.

Gaining Social Approval

Expected Discussion and Social Approval

When expecting a discussion:
High self-monitors (who pay more attention to social rewards) shift their attitudes and beliefs more that do low self-monitors.
People who have been reminded of the importance of social approval shift their attitudes more.

Stanford Prison Study

1. What parallels do you see between Abu Ghraib and this study?
2. What percentage of the population can you expect to commit such crimes?
3. How can normal people be brought to commit such crimes?
4. In times of war, are these things inevitable?
5. Is there anything inherent in the captor that brings about this behavior?
6. What are the most prevalent forces that can bring about abuse?
7. How do we prevent this from happening in the future?

Stanford Prison Study

1. What parallels do you see between Abu Ghraib and this Study?
   - Power differential: "It's not that we put bad apples in a good barrel. We put good apples in a bad barrel. The barrel corrupts anything that it touches."
   - Unless there is strict leadership and transparent oversight that prevent the abuse of power, that power will foster abuse. According to Zimbardo, in the case of Abu Ghraib, where everyone—guards and prisoners alike—was trapped in an alien setting and had neither a common language nor culture, the situation was likely to produce a classic case of abuse
   - There is given an acceptable justification for the behavior, akin to an ideology.
   - The guards (or teachers or participants) develop a distorted sense of the victims (or participants) as not comparable to themselves. Dehumanizing them as animals would be an extreme example.
   - Euphemisms, such as "learners" (instead of victims) are used.
   - There is a gradual escalation of violence that starts with a small step. Foot-in-the-door technique and dissonance theory.

Stanford Prison Study

2. What percentage of the population can you expect to commit such crimes?
   - It's not that two-thirds of the Milgram Pp went all the way, but that 100% went to the 300 volt level—a very powerful shock.
   - Why?
   - A powerful situation can bring anybody to commit acts outside of his or her normal range of possibilities simply as a function of conforming to the new situation—rules, norms, authority, symbols, language use, etc.

Stanford Prison Study

3. How can normal people be brought to commit such crimes? Everyone has the potential for sadism.
   - Everyone has the potential for sadism.
   - Confusing situation rife with frustration, fear, and hostility produces a group process of atrocity beyond any individual aberration.
   - Couple that situation with a universal human tendency to fear and distrust natural outsiders, makes the potential for abuse all the more likely.
   - Outgroup = "Enemy"

Stanford Prison Study

4. In times of war, are these things inevitable?
   - No. You must have personal accountability
   - A clear chain of command
   - Transparency
   - Respect for the enemy as a human combatant—not animal or anything less

Stanford Prison Study

5. Is there anything inherent in the captor that brings about this behavior?

    *   Power differential in this situation leads to dehumanization. Small step in that direction leads to further justification of such thinking.
    *   No external checks on the use of power, and social labeling play a part—i.e., "enemy," "foreigners," etc. Had they resembled more the ingroup, you could count on less abuse.

Stanford Prison Study

6. What are the most prevalent forces that can bring about abuse?

    *   Diffusion of responsibility
    *   Dehumanization of the enemy
    *   Secrecy of the operation
    *   Lack of personal accountability
    *   Conditions facilitating moral disengagement
    *   Relabeling evil as "necessary" and developing justifications for evil
    *   Social modeling
    *   Group pressures to conform in order to fit a macho cultural identity

Stanford Prison Study

7. How do we prevent this from happening in the future?

    *   Training
    *   Staffing: Prisoner-guard ratio
    *   Direction—watch prisoners, not "soften them up for interrogation" coming from covert CIA agents
    *   Supervision: Random site checks
    *   Accountability: If the prison is veiled in secrecy, abuse is much more likely. There needs to be very clear, transparent accountability.

Stanford Prison Study

1. What parallels do you see between Abu Ghraib and this study?
2. What percentage of the population can you expect to commit such crimes?
3. How can normal people be brought to commit such crimes?
4. In times of war, are these things inevitable?
5. Is there anything inherent in the captor that brings about this behavior?
6. What are the most prevalent forces that can bring about abuse?
7. How do we prevent this from happening in the future?

5 Making Judgments

Learning Objectives

By the end of the chapter you should be able to:

- Contrast conscious and automatic processes
- Define schemas and discuss their importance
- Define scripts and discuss their importance
- Describe the value of heuristics
- Identify and explain the availability heuristic
- Identify and explain the representativeness heuristic
- Describe how the conjunction fallacy and the base rate fallacy contribute to errors in judgment
- Identify and explain the affect heuristic
- Describe how the self-fulfilling prophecy can affect behavior

Chapter Outline

5.1 Conscious and Automatic Processes

When you make a decision do you weigh your options, carefully sorting out pros from cons? Have you ever made a decision because you had a gut feeling? Psychologists believe that our cognitive (thinking) processes operate at two levels, conscious and automatic. The conscious level includes the thought processes we are aware of and tend to direct. We might use this when we make a decision by carefully weighing our options. The automatic level involves processes that are done without our intention or awareness, such as when we make a decision based on our gut feeling. Researchers have called these a variety of names (Epstein, 1994; Kahneman, 2003; Peters, Hess, Vastfjall, & Auman, 2007; Reyna, 2004), but at their heart they all focus on some kind of rational, conscious process and another more emotional or experientially based unconscious process.

Table 5.1 summarizes the basic differences between these systems. As you can see from the table, the processing of the **automatic system** is something that we are generally not aware of. It processes things that come from the environment and when it has completed processing or gets stuck, something researchers call experiencing disfluency, it alerts the conscious system (Alter, Oppenheimer, Epley, & Eyre, 2007). The capacity of the **conscious system** is limited but it is a system we can direct. The unconscious system may be processing something you are not interested in working on; it is only the conscious system that allows you to deliberately focus on a particular idea, situation, or problem.

Table 5.1 Characteristics of the Automatic and Conscious Systems

Automatic System	Conscious System
Fast	Slow
Outside of conscious awareness	Within conscious awareness
Effortless	Effortful
Large capacity	Limited capacity
May do many tasks at once	Limited to very few tasks at once
Imprecise, general responses	Nuanced responses

5.2 Schemas and Scripts

In Chapter 2 on the self we met the idea of **schemas** as knowledge structures that organize what we know and that can affect how we process information. Self-schemas are knowledge structures about the self, but we can have schemas about many other things in our world, such as animals, objects, and places. When we are making judgments, schemas may affect those judgments.

Schemas can help us remember things, but may also create false memories for us (Lampinen, Copeland, & Neuschatz, 2001). If you were to sit in a professor's office for several minutes and then, outside of the office, after some time, were asked what you saw in that office, your schema could help you answer. You expect to see bookshelves with books, a desk, a computer, a stapler, and some pens in a professor's office. As you remembered, your existing schema might help you remember that you saw a bookshelf. But the schema may lead you to remember something that was not there. If you expected to see a stapler, you might report that a stapler was there, even if it was not.

Schemas can help us remember when we see something that violated our schema. If you were to see a stuffed teddy bear in a professor's office, you might remember and recall it because it was outside of your normal professor's office schema. This type of effect may have serious consequences when we examine the role of schemas in eyewitness memory. Researchers have found that schemas for crimes can influence the details people remember about crimes they witness (Tuckey & Brewer, 2003). People tend to be accurate about schema-relevant and schema-inconsistent information. Information that is irrelevant to the schema is most likely to be forgotten.

Schemas can be fairly broad or relatively narrow. Broader schemas take us longer to learn, as we encounter different ways to think about and view a particular entity or problem. But these broader schemas may allow us to be more flexible (Chen & Mo, 2004). For example, if you learned one situation in which calculus was helpful, in the future you might use calculus to solve problems when you encounter situations that were similar to the one you learned about. But if you were provided with examples of a variety of ways calculus could be helpful, you would be able to recognize those situations when you encountered them and use what you know to help solve all of those problems.

How do you know what to do when you go into a restaurant? How do you know what is expected on a first date? In our lives it is helpful to know what we should do when we are part of events. We know that on a first date it is likely the man will pick the woman up at her home, they will go to a restaurant, talk about their lives, and hope to impress one another, and perhaps then attend a movie. The man will likely pay for both the dinner and the movie. Not all first dates follow this pattern, but many do, and it is likely few of us were surprised by what was on the list (Laner & Ventrone, 2000). Psychologists call these expected series of events **scripts**, like the scripts in a movie or play that tell the actors what is going to occur next. Like schemas, scripts

© Rommel Canlas, 2013. Used under license from Shutterstock, Inc.

Just like in a play, a common script can help us know what to do or what is expected of us in a given situation.

are things we use to make sense of and organize our experience. Schemas involve our expectations for things, while scripts involve events or sequences of events.

Dating scripts can be quite detailed and can include behaviors that are different for men and women. Undergraduate students listed 19 different actions that women would engage in and 27 different actions for men. Most of these students agreed on what belonged in the script, indicating that scripts are shared within a culture (Rose & Frieze, 1989). College students noted that certain foods were date foods and others were not. Foods that could be eaten neatly, foods that were not too smelly, and foods that were likely to not cause bad breath were suggested (Amiraian & Sobal, 2009). Dating scripts go beyond the first date. Scripts may involve how a relationship should develop over time. When partners share a script for how their relationship should develop, they show greater relationship satisfaction (Holmberg & MacKenzie, 2002).

Scripts can be very helpful to us. When dates follow a script, both people know what to do and what is expected of them without having to discuss the process. If you have ever lived or traveled in a different country or if you are part of a subculture you know that others do things differently. You may have found yourself confused and unsure. In those kinds of situations you may feel like everyone knows what is going on but you. You do not know the script.

5.3 Heuristics

Our automatic system allows us to make short cuts and come to conclusions without taxing the conscious system (Shah & Oppenheimer, 2008). In fact, when our resources are depleted we are more likely to use the shortcuts offered by the automatic system (Masicampo & Baumeister, 2008). Schemas help us keep information organized and can help in memory. Scripts help us know what to do without expending a lot of energy trying to figure out what is appropriate in a given situation. Quick processing is a theme of our cognitive systems. When making judgments we also attempt to get quick answers. The shortcuts we use in making judgments are **heuristics**. Just as schemas and scripts can be helpful to us, heuristics can also be helpful. With heuristics we are likely to come up with a pretty good answer quickly. But they can sometimes get us into trouble. With schemas we sometimes remember that something was there when it was not. With heuristics we sometimes make an incorrect judgment. When researchers look at heuristics they most often focus on what happens when heuristics fail us and we make incorrect judgments. Such research helps us understand how heuristics work. Keep in mind, however, that despite the problems they sometimes create, heuristics quickly provide us with a good-enough answer most of the time.

Availability Heuristic

Consider the following question from Tversky and Kahneman (1973): "the frequency of appearance in the English language was studied. . . . Consider the letter R" (p. 211–212). Are we more likely to find R as the first letter of a word or the third letter of a word?

In answer to this question most people respond that there are more words with R as the first letter, estimating there are about twice as many with R as the first letter than with R as the third letter. Researchers are interested in how people make this judgment. Think about your own thinking. If you solved this like most people do, you thought briefly about how many words you knew that had R as the first letter (relatives, rainbow, rich, run). Then you thought about how many words you knew that had R as the third letter (park, more, marshmallow). As you made those calculations, you realized that you were able to come up with many more words with R as the first letter than R as the third letter. Words starting with R were more available to you in your memory.

Think of the availability heuristic in terms of a filing cabinet of memories and experiences. Your judgments will be based on what memories and experiences are most readily available.

Making a judgment this way, you and the research participants were using the availability heuristic. The **availability heuristic** involves the tendency to make judgments about the frequency of something or the likelihood of an event occurring by considering how available it was in memory. Instances that come more easily to mind, and thus are more available, are judged to be more likely. As noted earlier, these strategies often get us the right answer, but in the case of the position of the R our judgment is wrong. There are actually more words in the English language with R as the third letter than R as the first letter. Often this type of judgment will provide you with the right answer, but, as in this instance, there is room for error.

We can apply this to other realms and other experiences. How successful is online dating? Many people will tell you about a cousin or coworker who found someone on an online site and they are now happily married. You may have such a story yourself. But how often do you hear the stories about unsuccessful searchers who gave up on online dating in frustration? Occasionally, perhaps, but these are not widespread stories. Because we hear more of the happily-ever-after stories and few of the stories of frustration, many of us assume online dating is successful for the majority of those who engage in it.

Representativeness Heuristic

"Linda is 31 years old, single, outspoken, and very bright. She majored in philosophy. As a student, she was deeply concerned with issues of discrimination and social justice, and also participated in antinuclear demonstrations" (Tversky & Kahneman, 1983, p. 297). Which is more likely?

a. Linda is a bank teller.
b. Linda is a bank teller and active in the feminist movement.

If you are like most people you chose answer b. Why? Most people say they chose b because Linda sounds to them like someone who would be active in the feminist movement who happens to be a bank teller rather than just a stereotypical bank teller. If you answered this way, for this reason, you were using something called the representativeness heuristic. The **representativeness heuristic** involves making decisions based on how similar someone or something is to the typical, or representative, person or situation. Because Linda seems like your typical vision of someone in the feminist movement, you choose b.

The representativeness heuristic will often get you to the right answer when you are making quick decisions, but not in the case of Linda. It is logically impossible for someone to be more likely to be two things than to be one of those things. Linda is more likely to be just a bank teller than to be both a bank teller and active in the feminist movement. There are more bank tellers than there are bank tellers who are active in the feminist movement. When we rate two things occurring together as more likely than one of those things occurring alone, we have engaged in the **conjunction fallacy**.

Another piece of faulty reasoning that may be behind these heuristics is the **base rate fallacy** (Kahneman & Tversky, 1973). Consider the following: Walter is a 47-year-old man who reads poetry, watches PBS, and plays golf in his spare time. Which is more likely: that Walter is an Ivy League professor or that Walter is a truck driver? For most of us, Walter sounds like an Ivy League professor. Using the representativeness heuristic, we solve this problem by thinking about whether Walter is more like a typical Ivy League professor than a typical truck driver. But Walter is more likely to be a truck driver. Why? There are about 3.5 million truck drivers in the United States (TruckInfo.net, 2011), to say nothing of elsewhere in the world. Consider how many Ivy League professors there are. With only eight Ivy League schools, with between a little under 1,000 faculty (Dartmouth and Brown) to just over 4,000 (Pennsylvania and Columbia) per school, there are about 19,500 Ivy League professors. Given the very large number of truck drivers and relatively small number of Ivy League professors, it is much more likely that Walter is among the large group than the small group. When we make a decision about the likelihood of something and ignore the number of instances of that in the population (of people, actions, diagnoses, etc.) we are victims of the base rate fallacy.

Affect Heuristic

Imagine you are on a parole board deciding whether to parole an inmate. You are told that 20 in every 100 people released who are like this inmate go on to commit a violent crime. Would you parole the person or deny parole? What if you were told that 20% of people released who are like this inmate go on to commit a violent crime? Research participants have been asked similar questions. Those given information using relative frequency, the first form of question, believed there was greater danger than those with information in statistical form (Slovic, Monahan, & MacGregor, 2000). Rationally, we know that 20 out of every 100 people is equivalent to 20%, but we process these bits of information differently.

When this information is presented in relative frequency form, people imagine 20 perpetrators of violent crimes, a disturbing image. These images lead to a gut-level negative emotional reaction. The statistical form seems to separate us from that image, and

Social Psychology in Depth: Heuristics and Politics

When you vote, do you spend all the time and energy required to consider all the issues for all the candidates? Voters often use heuristics to make judgments about political candidates. The time required to find, sort through, and evaluate information on all the candidates is more than many people can afford. How, then, does that affect the decisions themselves?

R. R. Lau and D. P. Redlawsk (2001) note that voters often use party affiliation or candidate ideology to make quick decisions in voting. Most of the time such decision-making strategies get the voters what they want, but there are times when party affiliation or ideology can lead a voter astray. A candidate might be categorized incorrectly. For example, the media may say that a candidate for governor is a conservative when she is actually more of a moderate. Candidates may also differ from the party line. A voter may assume that because the candidate is Republican she is pro-life, but she may actually be pro-choice.

Beyond party affiliation and ideology, a voter might also use endorsements to make decisions. If a favorite celebrity shows support for a particular candidate, that voter might choose to vote for that candidate. Endorsements may come from individuals one trusts, like a close friend or a celebrity, or from organizations one believes in, like the National Rifle Association or the National Organization for Women.

Polling data also provides a simple cue to a voter. When a particular candidate is ahead in the polls, voters might vote for that candidate because he is popular or because they perceive he will win. Candidate appearance can also influence voters.

The researchers found that less sophisticated voters made poorer decisions when they relied on these heuristics. These voters would have been better served if they had examined the issues the candidates stood for and made a logical, rational choice rather than relying on heuristics. Using a short cut was detrimental to decision making. More sophisticated voters, those with greater interest and knowledge of the political system, made good decisions while using heuristics. This finding is somewhat ironic given that sophisticated voters are least likely to need heuristics, but they were the ones whose decision making did not suffer from using them (Lau, 2001).

therefore reduce the negative affect (emotional reaction). We use our gut-level reactions to help us make decisions (Slovic, Peters, Finucane, & MacGregor, 2005). This tendency to use affective (gut-level emotional reactions) as information to make judgments is called the **affect heuristic**.

If you have ever investigated online dating sites, you have likely found a significant number of stories touting their success. Television commercials and online ads for these sites show happy couples who found each other. The affect heuristic helps us understand why this might be. The site could explain that 20% of their members find a partner, or they could show a few happy couples. Our gut-level reaction to the percentage is not large. But a couple in love? We react viscerally, use that gut-level reaction to gauge our own likelihood of success, and sign on.

These heuristics are not just a novelty of research studies. They can affect our lives. In a study of women who were being tested for genetic vulnerability for breast and ovarian cancer, researchers found extensive use of the availability heuristic and the representativeness heuristic (Kenen, Ardern-Jones & Eeles, 2003). The women described vivid stories of others they knew who had been treated for or died of cancer. This affected how vulnerable these women felt in terms of their cancer risk. The representativeness heuristic came into play as the women judged their own risk for cancer by how similar they felt they were to others who had died of cancer.

Data might tell you that a certain percentage of children in the world are malnourished, but troubling images often evoke a more visceral reaction. This is the affect heuristic in action.

5.4 Self-Fulfilling Prophecy

Can our judgments about another person affect that person's behavior? In other words, can one person's expectations affect another person's behavior? This was a question investigated by Robert Rosenthal (with Jacobson, 1966). Rosenthal conducted his research with teachers and students. After giving students what appeared to be a test of intelligence, he told teachers that certain students were predicted to "bloom" over the school year, that is, these students were expected to make great intellectual gains. In reality these students' names were randomly chosen from each classroom. The students were not told anything about the tests or what their teachers expected of them. When the researchers returned at the end of the school year, they found that these randomly chosen students did indeed make gains. The researchers concluded that since the students were no different from their classmates at the beginning of the study, it must have been the teachers' expectations that affected their students.

This tendency for our expectations to affect the behaviors of others is called the **self-fulfilling prophecy**. We prophesy someone else's behavior, that is, we believe something will happen, and then, through our actions, we make that come true. Left alone, the prophesied behavior would likely not have happened, but because of the prophecy and our subsequent behavior, we managed to create a situation where the prophecy would come true.

Researchers have found that the self-fulfilling prophecy can have an effect outside of the classroom. Parent's beliefs about their child's underage drinking can create a self-fulfilling prophecy, leading to greater or lesser drinking later on, depending on the prophecy (Madon, Guyll, Spoth, Cross, & Hibert, 2003; Madon, Willard, Guyll, Trudeau, & Spoth, 2006). Within relationships, individuals with high rejection sensitivity—in other words, those who expect that the other person will reject them—act in ways that lead to rejecting responses, though the researchers found this only in women. These women prophesied rejection and by their actions created rejection in their romantic partners (Downey, Freitas, Michaelis, & Khouri,

1998). Self-fulfilling prophecy has even been proposed as partially responsible for the extreme violence found in the Pelican Bay State Prison (King, Steiner, & Breach, 2008). The prison is a supermax prison for extremely violent and dangerous prisoners. Expecting prisoners to be very violent in the prison environment, the researchers argue, creates behavior that leads to a fulfillment of that prophecy.

Conclusion

Our cognitive systems are designed to work as efficiently as possible, with the automatic system taking over as much as it can, while the conscious system deals with the nuanced and difficult problems that the automatic system cannot handle. The use of schemas and heuristics helps make this possible. These mental shortcuts can be helpful to us, but, at times, do lead to errors.

Summary

Conscious and Automatic Processes

The human cognitive system operates on two levels, a conscious level and an automatic level. The conscious system is directed by the individual and works slowly and deliberately on problems to provide nuanced answers. The automatic system works outside of conscious awareness and without intention. The automatic system works quickly, is largely effortless, and provides general answers.

Schemas and Scripts

Schemas are knowledge structures that allow for organization of information. Schemas can be helpful in memory but can also provide misleading cues when something we expect because of our schema is not present. Scripts are knowledge structures about events. Scripts can be helpful by allowing individuals to predict what will happen and to, therefore, engage in expected behavior.

Heuristics

The automatic system allows us to make quick judgments through the use of mental shortcuts called heuristics. When we use the availability heuristic, we judge the likelihood of an event based on how available that event is in memory. The representativeness heuristic involves judging the likelihood of an event based on how closely it resembles the typical case. When we make errors when making judgments using these heuristics it may be due, in part, to the conjunction fallacy or the base rate fallacy. With the conjunction fallacy, we judge the likelihood of two things occurring together as more likely than one of those occurring alone. When we ignore the rate of events and make judgments that suggest the unlikely event is more likely, we have engaged in the base rate fallacy. The affect heuristic is when we make judgments based on gut-level reactions to events.

Self-Fulfilling Prophecy

Others' expectations of us can influence our behavior. Researchers have found that prophecies for behavior—in other words, what people think others will do—can become self-fulfilling when individuals act in ways that elicit that behavior from the other.

Critical Thinking Questions

1. How might schemas be helpful and harmful in one's life?
2. What might your life be like if there were no scripts?
3. Consider a time when you might have used the availability, representativeness, or affect heuristic in making a judgment. How did that affect the accuracy of your judgment?
4. Although the examples in the chapter concern times when heuristics lead us to incorrect answers, why are heuristics helpful and used regularly by us?
5. Have self-fulfilling prophecies ever affected your life?

Key Terms

Affect heuristic	**Conscious system**	**Scripts**
Automatic system	**Heuristics**	**Self-fulfilling prophecy**
Availability heuristic	**Representativeness heuristic**	
Base rate fallacy	**Schema**	
Conjunction fallacy		

Expanding Your Knowledge: Links to Additional Material

Schema

An explanation of schemas and an activity are described by John Median, author of *Brain Rules*, and his friend Dr. Whitehead in the video found at http://www.youtube.com/watch?v=mzbRpMlEHzM&feature. Listen carefully to the directions and attempt to remember as much of the procedure as possible.

Heuristic Simulation

Want to think more about heuristics? You can participate in simulations of heuristics at http://cat.xula.edu/thinker/decisions/heuristics/. Two of the heuristics described in the text, the representativeness heuristic and the availability heuristic, are available on the site, and other heuristics are described as well. After making your own judgments, you can read about usual answers and explanations for these answers.

Affect Heuristic

Research on how people understand numbers shows that while frequencies and percentages are easily understood, absolute frequencies are given greater weight. Absolute frequencies are perceived to be larger than equivalent frequencies or percentages. Although there may be other things going on, the text explains this as at least partly due to the affect heuristic. We connect emotionally to absolute frequencies (30 people with cancer) in a way we do not with percentages (30% of the group has cancer).

A research study on how we understand numbers presented in different ways can be found at http://www.joe.org/joe/2007august/a1.php.

Or check out this link for an article explaining the research: http://www.sciencedaily.com/releases/2008/04/080422150652.htm.

Decision-Making Studies

If you would like to participate in research on decision making, check out http://www.decisionsciencenews.com/fun-experiments-to-try/. The studies change from time to time, but there are usually two or three you can participate in to learn about how research on decision making can be done. It is also possible to sign up to be a research participant for pay. Daniel Goldstein, author of the site, also provides links to articles on decision making at http://faculty.london.edu/dgoldstein/.

Self-Fulfilling Prophecy

An interesting blog post at http://www.psychologytoday.com/blog/science-small-talk/201003/just-i-expected summarizes the findings of Rosenthal's original study of the self-fulfilling prophecy and provides a description of subsequent research on the topic.

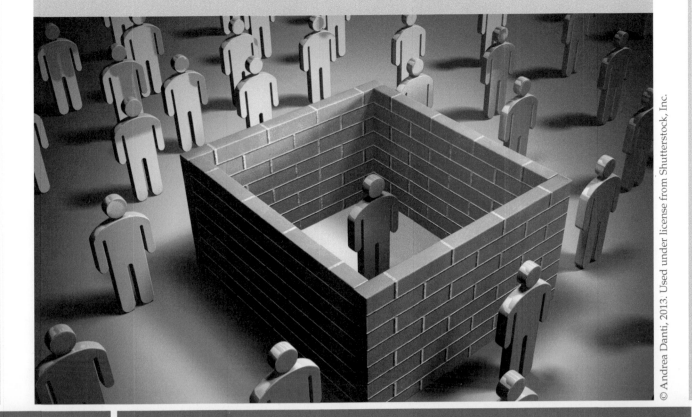

6 | Prejudice

Learning Objectives

By the end of the chapter you should be able to:

- Differentiate prejudice, stereotypes, and discrimination
- Describe how and why categorization occurs
- Define ingroup favoritism
- Define the outgroup homogeneity effect
- Describe how stereotypes and prejudice originate in social norms
- Explain why competition can lead to prejudice
- Identify how social inequalities are related to prejudice
- Describe how stereotype threat affects performance

Chapter Outline

6.1 Prejudice, Stereotypes, and Discrimination

Most people know about and have experienced prejudice, stereotyping, and discrimination. Social psychologists differentiate among these by focusing on whether they involve feelings (affect), cognition, or behaviors. Prejudice is the affect, or feeling, aspect of this trio. **Prejudice** involves a negative attitude toward individuals based on their membership in a particular group. The cognitive aspect is stereotypes. **Stereotypes** are beliefs about the characteristics of particular groups or members of those groups. Discrimination involves behaviors. **Discrimination** is negative behavior toward individuals or groups based on beliefs and feelings about those groups. One other bit of terminology surrounds our membership in different groups. A group you are a part of is called your **ingroup**. Ingroups might include gender, race, or city or state of residence, as well as groups you might intentionally join, like Kiwanis or a bowling league. A group you are not a part of is called your **outgroup**.

6.2 Social Cognitive Origins of Prejudice and Stereotypes

A variety of factors are responsible for our prejudice, stereotypes, and discrimination. One group of factors we can point to is those related to how we cognitively process information. Overall, these processes lead to generalizations about other people, generalizations that do not take into account the uniqueness of the individual.

Categorization

Making judgments about individuals based on their membership in a group relies, first of all, on perceiving that there are groups. Sorting people into categories has long been related to stereotyping and prejudice (Allport, 1954). Categories are helpful to human beings; they allow us to deal with large amounts of information. The cognitive energy-saving nature of categories was demonstrated in a study by Macrae, Milne, and

© Tumar, 2013. Used under license from Shutterstock, Inc.

Categorizing people can cause us to jump to conclusions about who they are—and perhaps what they can do.

Bodenhausen (1994). In their work they asked participants to remember a list of characteristics of people that were flashed on a computer screen. The participants were simultaneously asked to remember information on an unrelated topic from a recorded message. If both seeing words and listening to information seems like a lot to do at the same time, that was by design. The researchers were attempting to tax the participants' ability to process all the information they were seeing and hearing. When our systems are overloaded, anything that helps us will show clear effects.

The researchers wondered if having category labels would be helpful. Half of the participants saw a category label that might help them remember some of the characteristics on the list of names and characteristics they were supposed to remember. For example, Julian was labeled as an artist and then characteristics like creative, temperamental, and sensitive were flashed on the screen, to go along with our general stereotype of artist. Participants also saw characteristics that were not necessarily related to the category label, like cordial and generous. The other half of the participants saw the same names and characteristics, but they were not shown a category label such as "artist." When all the participants had seen all the different names and characteristics, the researchers quizzed them on how many of the characteristics they remembered for each name. They also quizzed the participants on how much they remembered about the unrelated recorded message.

Did having a category label help participants remember more of the category-related words? Participants who saw a category label remembered 4.42 category-consistent words, on average, while those who did not see the label remembered only 2.08. This shows that the label helped people remember things related to the label. In addition, the participants who saw a label also did better on the quiz about the unrelated message they heard. This suggests that being able to categorize freed up energy to listen to and process the unrelated message.

Categories help us by saving us cognitive energy and allowing us to process more information. Therefore we use categories liberally. That might not be a problem if all we did was categorize people, but it turns out that along with quickly and easily developing categories, we use them to make later decisions (Tajfel, 1970).

Ingroup Favoritism

In 1970 Tajfel published some surprising research results. For his study he brought boys age 14 and 15 into a psychological research laboratory. The boys were shown slides that had dots on them and were asked to estimate the number of dots. The boys were then told that they were either overestimators of dots or underestimators. In reality, the boys were assigned these two labels randomly. Later, when asked to assign money to other participants, the boys assigned more money to those who shared their group membership. This tendency to show preferential treatment toward members of one's own group is called **ingroup favoritism**. In later work Tajfel (Billig & Tajfel, 1973) found that even when participants were told that assignment to groups was random, they would still show preferential treatment toward members of their own group. Ingroup favoritism appears to work even when the reason for group categorization is relatively arbitrary (being an overestimator or underestimator of dots) or simply random.

Outgroup Homogeneity Effect

Beyond viewing one's own group as deserving more positive things than another group, individuals within a group tend to view their own group as more varied than someone outside the group views that group. This is called the **outgroup homogeneity effect**. Someone describing an outgroup will describe the members in that group as being more homogeneous, or similar. One reason why this might be is that when we are asked to describe an outgroup we are likely to access information at the group level, what we know about the primary tendencies of that group. However, when we are asked to describe our own groups, we access information about people within the group (Park & Rothbart, 1982). It is also possible that we simply know more people in our ingroup; it is our own group, after all. Because we know more people, we know more potentially different people, and therefore we judge the ingroup as being more diverse than the outgroup (Linville, Fischer, & Salovey, 1989).

Although categorization saves us cognitive energy and both ingroup favoritism and the outgroup homogeneity effect are understandable, there are dangers in these tendencies. Categorization denies the unique characteristics of individuals. For example, Germans as a whole may value timeliness and be prompt, but Hans may defy the stereotype and arrive late. Our judgments about people may be skewed because of these tendencies. We may perceive and make judgments based on similarities that do not actually exist or place individuals in categories in which they do not actually fit (Dotsch, Wigboldus, & van Knippenberg, 2011; Kosic & Phalet, 2006). We tend to go along with the judgments those in our ingroup make, without critically evaluating the content of those judgments (Binning & Sherman, 2011). For example, a woman might automatically agree with another woman regarding an issue, but would have carefully scrutinized the same statement coming from a man.

6.3 Societal Origins of Prejudice, Stereotypes, and Discrimination

Our prejudice and stereotypes come not only from the way our systems process information but also from the world around us. Societal origins of prejudice involve the norms in the world around us, the competition that exists between groups, and the social inequalities that exist in the world. Because categorizing happens naturally and is a helpful tool in many ways, all human cultures are likely to have stereotypes. Ingroup favoritism leads to unequal treatment of those we have categorized as in the outgroup. And outgroup homogeneity bias blinds us to the differences within the outgroup. But our beliefs about the characteristics of those outgroups and how stable our prejudice is relies on the particular culture in which we reside.

Norms

Prejudice and stereotypes have origins in the norms of our social groups. People learn negative attitudes toward groups by learning the norms of their social context (Sherif, 1936). We learn from our peers what stereotypes are appropriate. When participants in one study were led to believe that their stereotypes were different from those of their peers, those stereotypes were changed to be more in line with peer stereotypes (Stangor, Sechrist, & Jost, 2001).

We pick up prejudice and stereotypes from the norms in our social groups.

If our social norms tell us something about how prejudiced we should be toward certain groups, then social norms about groups should correlate with prejudice toward those groups. Crandall, Eshleman, and O'Brien (2002) found an almost perfect correlation. Social norms dictate that we dislike child abusers, terrorists, and members of the Ku Klux Klan. And these groups are groups we have strong prejudices toward. On the other hand, our norms tell us that farmers, family men, and those with physical challenges are people we should not have negative prejudice toward, and people report less negative prejudice toward these groups. Level of expressed prejudice toward different racial groups in the United States has been parallel to the perceived acceptability of prejudice (Dowden & Robinson, 1993). As society views prejudice as less acceptable, individuals are less likely to express prejudice.

We may see this in dating as well. People are most likely to form long-term commitments with those from a similar racial group (Blackwell & Lichter, 2004; Harris & Kalbfleisch, 2000). In the past we might have attributed this to lack of access to potential partners of other races because of geographic boundaries. But the Internet breaks down these boundaries and makes individuals of diverse backgrounds accessible. Even without the pressures of geography, people tend to prefer dating someone of their own race (Sweeney & Borden, 2009).

Competition for Resources

When groups exist together in a society they may be at odds with one another in competition for resources. Competition can create prejudice (Jackson, 1993; Sherif, 1966; Sherif & Sherif, 1953). Competition may be in the realm of economic interests, political or military advantage, or even threats to the safety or status of the group. A strong factor in creating prejudice is anger. When in competition we may feel angry that a rival group is taking away resources or prestige from our group. Individuals who feel angry are more likely to feel prejudice than those who feel sadness or more neutral emotions (DeSteno, Dasgupta, Bartlett, & Cajdric, 2004). Competition can certainly enhance prejudice, but is not necessary for prejudice to occur. Humans tend to show the social cognitive factors for prejudice, such as ingroup favoritism and outgroup homogeneity effect, even when competition is not in play (Luhtanen & Crocker, 1991).

This competition between groups can lead to problems for groups like immigrants. When immigrants do well in their new country, their success may be seen as coming at the expense of those already in the country. This competition for resources, real or perceived,

Social Psychology in Depth: Blue-Eyed and Brown-Eyed

How can a teacher teach about prejudice in a classroom with little diversity? Jane Elliott, a third grade teacher in a small Iowa town in the late 1960s, faced this problem and solved it. Shortly after the assassination of Dr. Martin Luther King Jr., Elliott decided to teach her students about the dangers of prejudice and discrimination by having them experience it. Elliot said "We've all been told those things. We know them, at least in the sense that we mouth them at appropriate times. Yet we continue to discriminate, or to tolerate it in others, or to do nothing to stop it. What I had racked my brain to think of the night before was a way of letting my children find out for themselves, personally, deeply, what discrimination was really like, how it felt, what it could do to you. Now the time had come to try it." (Peters, 1987).

She divided the class by the color of their eyes, blue-eyed versus brown-eyed students. On the first day the blue-eyed students were told they were smarter and better. Discriminatory policies were instituted for the brown-eyed children. Children with brown eyes got less recess time, were forbidden to use the drinking fountain, and could not play with the blue-eyed children. The next day roles were switched. The children quickly and easily joined in the game, and it swiftly became reality for them. A normally friendly, cooperative group of children were mean to one another and fought. The lower-status children became sad and withdrawn and angry. By the end of the second day the children had a taste of prejudice and a sense of what discrimination really feels like.

Since her lesson, Elliott has traveled around the world giving lectures and doing the same exercise with adults. The adults' reactions are similar to the children's. Both the children in Elliott's class and the adults in her seminars reported a profound long-term change in their understanding of prejudice and discrimination. Elliott received multiple awards for her work and has been the subject of a number of documentaries.

Her story is documented in a *Frontline* program titled "A Class Divided." You can watch the documentary at http://www.pbs.org/wgbh/pages/frontline/shows/divided/.

Elliott's website contains additional information and materials: http://www.janeelliott.com/index.htm.

may create tension, prejudice, and hostility. For the immigrant, lack of success could be just as problematic. An immigrant who requires social services or is not fully contributing to society may also be a target of prejudice and hostility (Esses, Dovidio, Jackson, & Armstrong 2001).

Social Inequalities

One way to justify one's prejudice is to justify the system in which it occurs. With this line of logic, people might argue that the low socioeconomic status of a person from a particular racial group is the result of negative qualities found in that group (for example, lack of intelligence or initiative). Such views justify stereotypes and prejudice (Fiske, 2001). Researchers have found that those with greater negative stereotypes also justified the system more than those with fewer stereotypes (De Oliveira & Damburn, 2007). Individuals who prefer more hierarchical power structures, what researchers call social dominance orientation, also tend to also support prejudice and racism (Pratto, Sidanius, Stallworth, & Malle, 1994). We find this across cultures (Pratto et al., 2000).

Social inequalities are maintained, to some extent, by legitimizing myths, beliefs, and attitudes that keep low-status groups in their place. They justify the place of those of higher status by emphasizing some aspect of the lower-status group that, according to the stereotype, indicates a flaw or weakness. Such beliefs allow individuals to feel justified in their privileged position, allow groups to maintain the positive image they have of themselves, and allow the status quo in the social system to be maintained (Jost, Banaji, & Nosek, 2004). Language helps maintain these legitimizing myths. Beliefs in social dominance relate to how funny people find the jokes that we tell that rely on stereotypes. These jokes allow the dominant group to maintain and legitimize their position of power (Hodson, Rush, & MacInnis, 2010).

6.4 Influences on Those Stereotyped

Do stereotypes influence our performance on tasks related to those stereotypes? Imagine you had to take a test to assess your performance that, based on the stereotype about your group, suggests you, as a member of that group, may not do well. If you were thinking about the stereotype while you took the test, would that affect your performance? Research suggests it would.

A student driver. Stereotype threat suggests that the fear of confirming or flouting a given stereotype can cause performance anxiety.

In a classic study by Steele and Aronson (1995), the researchers varied how much participants were thinking about a racial stereotype. The researchers told one group of African American and White participants that the test they would take would be diagnostic of intellectual ability, tapping into the stereotype for the African Americans that they are not as intelligent as those from other racial groups. For a second group of participants, the researchers emphasized that this test was *not* diagnostic of ability. The researchers found that African American participants in the first group did worse than their White counterparts, but in the second group, African Americans and Whites did equally well. Obviously, the African American participants were capable of doing just as well on the test as the White participants, so why the difference? Steele and Aronson suggest that the possibility that one is going to be evaluated on an ability about which others show a stereotype creates anxiety. This anxiety distracts people from doing as well as they might truly be capable of doing.

The researchers named this phenomenon stereotype threat. **Stereotype threat** refers to the risk of confirming a negative stereotype about one's group. The stereotype predicts poor performance, so the person has to deal with the possibility of confirming that stereotype. Awareness that one is being evaluated based on membership in a stereotyped group can, therefore, interfere with performance.

Stereotype threat is not just present for African Americans on intelligence tests. Researchers have found that women college students perform worse on tests of mathematics when in the presence of men (Inzlicht & Ben-Zeev, 2003). Huguet and Regner (2007) found similar results in sixth- and seventh-grade girls (girls 11 to 13 years old). Athletic performance of Caucasians showed stereotype threat effects (Stone, Lynch, Sjomeling, & Darley, 1999). Latinos showed poorer intellectual performance under situations of stereotype threat (Gonzales, Blanton, & Williams, 2002). All of us are part of social groups, which means all of us have the potential for our performance to be disturbed by stereotype threat.

Stereotype threat seems particularly strong when people care about the domain that is studied; for example, women who describe math as being important to them will show more stereotype threat (Aronson et al., 1999; Inzlicht & Ben-Zeev, 2003). Stereotype threat is also more of a problem when the test is difficult (Nguyen & Ryan, 2008; Walton & Cohen, 2003). Overall, then, when there is a stereotype about your group that you are thinking about, you care about what you are being tested on, and when a test is difficult, you are most likely to do badly.

6.5 Reducing Prejudice

How do we reduce prejudice and discrimination? During the civil rights movement in the United States in the 1950s and 1960s, the federal government instituted policies of desegregation in schools and the military. One hope of such policies was that putting people of different groups together would reduce prejudice, an idea named the **contact hypothesis**. But desegregation doesn't always work for this purpose, because simple contact is not always helpful in reducing prejudice. In fact, contact might increase prejudice in some situations (Allport, 1954).

Under certain conditions, though, contact is more likely to reduce prejudice (Dixon, Durrheim, & Tredoux, 2005). Here are some of the conditions found by researchers:

- Contact should be between people or groups at equal status.
- Contact should occur between people with common goals.
- Contact should include intergroup cooperation.
- Contact should be supported by the larger social context (e.g., authorities).

Working together, toward a common goal, can go a long way toward reducing prejudice and discrimination.

Contact has the most positive effect when these conditions are met, but even when they are not, contact can still reduce prejudice (Pettigrew & Tropp, 2006). One factor that may be necessary for contact to reduce prejudice is a reduction in anxiety. When we feel anxious and uncertain about how we should act, it is difficult for an interaction to go well (Brown & Hewstone, 2003; Stephan et al., 2002).

One interesting extension of the work on contact has been on indirect intergroup contact. Even if people have no real contact with people from another group, if they have a friend who does, their own prejudice can be reduced (Wright, Aron, McLaughlin-Volpe, & Ropp, 1997). It seems that this connection does not even need to exist. Researchers have found that imagined contact is sufficient to reduce prejudice (Turner & Crisp, 2010).

Common goals have long been viewed as important for the reduction of prejudice and conflict between groups. In the 1950s Muzafer Sherif and his colleagues studied the effectiveness of these shared goals, what he called superordinate goals, on the reduction of intergroup conflict (Sherif, 1958; Sherif, Harvey, White, Hood, & Sherif, 1961). **Superordinate goals** are goals held by both groups in a conflict that transcend the conflict and provide a common aim. Sherif's study brought two groups of boys to a summer camp setting. For a week each group did not know the other group existed. As you might imagine from the previous discussions of categorization and ingroup favoritism, each group of boys quickly and easily bonded as a group. When the groups discovered that another group was at the camp, conflict quickly escalated. The researchers then provided the boys with problems they could solve only if all of them worked together. In one such instance, the water supply to camp developed a problem (with the help of the researchers). The two groups of boys had to work together to fix the problem and restore water to the camp. After several such events, conflict between the groups reduced significantly and boys became friends without respect to the original grouping.

Conclusion

We all live with prejudice, stereotypes, and discrimination every day. Although we naturally form the categories that lead us to stereotypes, show discriminatory behavior toward those outside of our groups, and are part of societies that, intentionally or not, support prejudice and discrimination, we can still work hard to reduce prejudice, stereotypes, and discrimination through our interactions with others.

Summary

Prejudice, Stereotypes, and Discrimination

Prejudice includes the attitudes we have about individuals of a particular group based on their group membership. Stereotypes are the beliefs about individuals based on their group membership. Discrimination involves actions toward individuals or groups based on group membership. Those groups we belong to are our ingroup. Those outside our circle are our outgroup.

Social Cognitive Origins of Prejudice and Stereotypes

Our cognitive systems naturally categorize others. This categorization saves us cognitive energy. When we categorize others as members of our ingroup, we show ingroup favoritism. We see members of the outgroup as all similar, while we acknowledge that members of our ingroup are quite different from one another.

Societal Origins of Prejudice, Stereotypes, and Discrimination

Societies support stereotypes and prejudice, and therefore discrimination, through norms. All members of a group generally learn those norms. Groups in power maintain the social inequalities through legitimizing beliefs that justify their superior position.

Influences on Those Stereotyped

Stereotypes can interfere with performance. When people perform a behavior knowing their group is stereotypically not very good at that behavior, their performance may be less than their best. This phenomenon is called stereotype threat.

Reducing Prejudice

The contact hypothesis proposes that contact between members of groups that hold prejudice against one another may reduce prejudice. Contact can reduce prejudice when a number of conditions are satisfied. Common goals, called superordinate goals, are particularly helpful in bringing groups in conflict together.

Critical Thinking Questions

1. Humans naturally categorize; it is good for memory and saving cognitive energy. But categorization also leads to stereotyping. If we could somehow reverse our tendency to categorize, should we? What are the tradeoffs?
2. Have you seen ingroup favoritism or the outgroup homogeneity effect in your own experiences?
3. What effect would changing societal norms have on stereotypes and prejudice?
4. In your environment, in what ways do you see a justification of a social system to maintain status for the privileged and keep those with lower status in their place?
5. Everyone is part of a social group with a stereotype about how well people in that group perform at particular tasks. What stereotypes exist for your social groups? How might that affect your performance?

Key Terms

Contact hypothesis	Outgroup	Stereotype threat
Discrimination	Outgroup homogeneity effect	Stereotypes
Ingroup		Superordinate goals
Ingroup favoritism	Prejudice	

Expanding Your Knowledge: Links to Additional Material

Beyond Prejudice

The website Beyond Prejudice (http://www.beyondprejudice.com/) provides a great deal of interesting and accurate information on prejudice. The introduction provides a description of the concept of prejudice. The author differentiates between automatic prejudice and the unintentional prejudicial responses that may come with automatic prejudice, and more conscious and intentional prejudicial responses. Within the introduction suggestions are provided for reducing prejudice.

United Nations Declaration on Race and Racial Prejudice

To learn more about the international response to prejudice, read the United Nations Declaration on Race and Racial Prejudice, approved in 1978.

The statement can be found at http://portal.unesco.org/en/ev.php-URL_ID=13161&URL_DO=DO_TOPIC&URL_SECTION=201.html.

Test Yourself for Hidden Bias

The Southern Poverty Law Center provides a nice explanation of prejudice, focusing most thoroughly on implicit prejudice, or what they term hidden bias. Their Hidden Bias web page, at http://www.tolerance.org/activity/test-yourself-hidden-bias, defines prejudice and discrimination, explaining and providing a link to the Implicit Association Test. The connection between hidden bias and behavior is described, as well as how prejudice and stereotypes affect people. Some suggestions of what one can do about hidden biases are provided.

Interventions with Disadvantaged Groups

Interventions to reduce prejudice can affect individuals from disadvantaged groups differently from those in a more advantaged group. The authors of a study on prejudice-reduction strategies suggest that when advantaged groups undergo interventions or have more contact with people in a disadvantaged group, they show more support for programs that implement social change. Members of a disadvantaged group that have more contact with those of the advantaged group show more tolerant attitudes but also report less support for programs to implement social change and a lower likelihood to engage in activities to improve the social standing of their group.

The study can be found at http://www.psych.lancs.ac.uk/people/uploads/johndixon2010 0401T085019.pdf.

Reducing Stereotype Threat

The website ReducingStereotypeThreat.org (http://www.reducingstereotypethreat.org/) was developed by two social psychologists to describe and provide resources on the topic of stereotype threat. The site provides a very good introduction to stereotype threat and describes situations where stereotype threat occurs, the individuals who are vulnerable, the consequences of stereotype threat, and the mechanisms contributing to stereotype threat. Some suggestions for reducing stereotype threat and some unresolved issues on the topic of stereotype threat are also provided.

Research Participation

If you would like to participate in research on prejudice, visit the Yale School of Management eLab at https://elab.som.yale.edu/newlogin.php. The labs on this site include prejudice and intergroup relations as well as consumer decisions and behavior, organizational behavior, and food policy.

JUSTICE, POLITICS, and PREJUDICE REGARDING IMMIGRATION ATTITUDES

Robert R. Short
Arizona State

ABSTRACT

A number of theorists and researchers suggest attitudes resisting public policies and political initiatives intended to benefit nondominant, minority populations can actually be sophisticated disguises of racial prejudice (c.f., Gaertner & Dovidio, 1986; Sears, 1988). More recent research suggests that these attitudes may also function as a result of perceptions of justice (c.f., Bobocel, Hing, Davey, Stanely, & Zanna, 1998). The current investigation examines U.S. citizen attitudes toward immigration as a function of justice and prejudice. Based on political candidates' social stereotypes of Mexican immigrants, semantic differential scales were administered to participants (N = 247) in one of four scenarios in which is described an illegal or legal alien of Mexican or English-Canadian descent [1]. Consistent with notions of justice, participants indicated the greatest agreement with the pejorative nature of the themes when the immigrant described is of illegal status irrespective of national-ethnic background. Consistent with contemporary theories of prejudice, the legal Mexican immigrant was evaluated more harshly than the legal English-Canadian immigrant. The social, psychological and public policy implications of immigration as a political phenomenon are discussed.

Over the past decade in the United States, a societal debate regarding public policies and social phenomena including immigration, bilingual education, and affirmative action has become increasingly polarized. It is not surprising that immigration, particularly along the southern U.S. border, would be a focal point for such heated debate. Immigration as a social phenomenon is both revered and hated across ideological and political lines. For instance, one can find pro-business, political conservatives in favor of immigration as a means for cheap labor, while other conservatives are against it as a threat to national sovereignty. Political liberals can be found as pro-immigration as a means of social justice, whereas other traditionally liberal groups (e.g., Sierra Club) voice opposition for environmental reasons. The agency responsible for administering immigration issues, the Immigration and Naturalization Service (INS), has competing and often conflicting missions where at once they are responsible for providing a litany of services to immigrants— including, but not limited to, processing illegal aliens—while also enforcing immigration law. As a result, accusations of prejudice charged against those opposed to loosening immigration quotas and, in response, justifications of anti-immigration attitudes based on appeals for justice are common. Such inherent contradictions and competing views make it a ripe issue within which to investigate how justice-based appeals and prejudice mix together to create attitudes toward social policy.

Social psychology's foray into justice literature has been primarily confined to conceptualizations of procedural and distributive justice (c.f., Taylor & Moghaddam, 1994). Whereas procedural justice refers to perceptions of fairness regarding the manner by which a distributive allocation norm is implemented, distributive justice refers to the perceived fairness of resource allocation—i.e., how the resources are distributed (e.g., Adams, 1965; Homans, 1961; Thibaut & Walker, 1975). This body of research has produced interesting results leading to predictable attitudes toward, say, affirmative action policies depending on what combination of justice is violated. Typically, the more preferential the treatment implied by the program being evaluated, the more likely respondents perceive the program as unfair. For instance, when a beneficiary of the program is described as reaping a benefit over an equally qualified other because of a certain social identity (e.g., race), respondents voice opposition to the program, presumably because the description violates an egalitarian principle of justice. If, however, the respondents are primed with information highlighting sociological inequities that the program is designed to redress, preference of one candidate over an equally qualified other, irrespective of social identity, is perceived as fair (e.g., Bobocel, et al., 1998; Crosby & Clayton, 1990; Kravitz, 1995).

A number of scholars have raised the question of whether opposition to public policies is a result of genuine opposition motivated by violations of perceived justice or simply a matter of rationalized prejudice (e.g., Bobocel et al., 1998). Those arguing for the role of prejudice suggest that when racial and ethnic categories become intertwined with political initiatives and public policies, favor for or against the political initiatives can become opportunities to discriminate against particular populations without being socially reprimanded and accused of bigotry (cf., Dovidio & Gaertner, 1996; Sears, 1988). One can hide ones true attitudes about racial groups by championing political initiatives that appeal to universal abstract principles such as justice, egalitarianism, and equity.

These contemporary perspectives of psychological racism (cf., Dovidio & Gaertner, 1996; McConahay, 1986; Sears, 1988) apply seamlessly to immigration phenomena. For example, if a Latino of Mexican nationality has come to the United States illegally, by definition, that person has engaged in criminal behavior. Such a label psychologically makes it easier to discriminate against members of this ethnic group as one can do so under the guiding principle of being anti-crime, as opposed to anti-Mexican or anti-Latino. Consider the following story published in the *Arizona Republic*:

Joshua Ramirez . . . [is] a fourth-generation American of Mexican descent. His family did not immigrate, illegally or otherwise. Yet people assume that's how he got here. I get the wetback comments, . . .I'm asked to produce proof of citizenship when I apply for a job—and I don't even speak Spanish. . . . Ramirez remembers the night he was kicked and punched by a gang of boys who swore at him and told him they don't like illegal aliens. . . . I was leaving a restaurant . . .It was closing time and I was walking to my car at the far end of the parking lot. They jumped me. I never called police. I just thought it would be too much of a hassle (Amparo, 1999).

Recent immigration research supports the role of prejudice, regarding immigration attitudes (c.f., Short & Magana, 2002). From an aversive racism perspective this research found that respondents voiced the harshest immigration attitudes when provided with a non-race-based opportunity to express such attitudes. As such, respondents indicated that they were more likely to deport the immigrant, perceive the person as criminal, as a threat to national sovereignty and as an economic drain when the immigrant described was of Mexican descent and had accumulated several parking tickets. There was no difference in respondent attitudes when the immigrant described was of Mexican or English-Canadian descent and had not accumulated parking tickets, or was English-Canadian and had accumulated parking tickets. Had prejudice not been a factor, respondent attitudes should have been equivalent between the illegal English-Canadian and Mexican immigrant scenarios with accumulated parking infractions. Theoretically, the parking tickets served as a non-race-based rationale with which to express prejudiced attitudes without threatening one's nondiscriminatory self-concept.

It is important to note that one cannot determine racial attitudes simply by one's vote for or against certain political initiatives or political affiliation. Also, the attitudes uncovered within the aversive framework might also be fueled by perceptions of justice; that is, the illegal status of the immigrants described may have fueled the attitudes expressed. Indeed, those arguing for justice point out that justice-based opposition may be a rationale in its own right. Kleinpenning and Hagendoorn (1993), for instance, found that Dutch students' scores on racism were correlated more highly with their opposition to a question about equal opportunity in society than to a question about preferential treatment in job hiring. In another study investigating racial affect, self- and group-interest and perceptions of program fairness, Nosworthy, Lea, and Lindsey (1995) found that racism contributed most strongly and accounted for more variance over and above perceptions of fairness in the program that least likely violated perceptions of fairness. These works taken together indicate that justice can be a genuine cause of opposition toward social policy (Bobocel et al. 1998).

Research investigating procedural and distributive notions of justice have been confined to specific public policies, such as Affirmative Action. There is relatively scant literature investigating justice and prejudice as relates to immigration attitudes. Intuitively, however, as with affirmative action programs, immigration phenomena can be conceptualized in terms of procedural and distributive justice. For instance, much of the political rhetoric regarding Mexican immigration in mainstream U.S. media raises issues of justice in terms of legal and illegal immigration, adroitly differentiating between the two extolling the virtues of legal, hard-working immigrants and bemoaning the influence and presence of illegal immigrants (Magaña & Short, 2002). These findings fit conceptually with the justice literatures. That is, legal aliens did not violate a principle of justice—they conformed to the proper procedural norm as determined by the dominant majority; they did not violate national law to immigrate. As a result, they deserve equitable distribution of resources— legal status and access to federally protected social services. In contrast, however, the illegal alien has violated the proper procedural norm of how one should immigrate. By default, this labels the person as a criminal and justifies denying access to the distribution of resources. From a strict justice perspective, there is a right way, and a wrong way to immigrate; legal immigration is good, illegal immigration is bad, and, as a result, one would expect predictable immigration attitudes based on such justice principles.

Consistent with previous research, however, it is naïve to think justice would be the only factor in determining immigration attitudes. As noted, prejudice can also play a significant role. To date, however, measures of psychological justice have not been accounted for in understanding immigration attitudes. It may be true that aversive prejudice is less of a factor in predicting immigration attitudes than psychological perceptions of justice, especially in a southern U.S. border state. The current investigation is designed to address these two constructs as relates to immigration attitudes.

To the extent that there are meaningful psychological differences among various immigration scenarios that violate justice principles, i.e., legality, then individual differences in justice beliefs should predict harsher immigration attitudes when the immigration scenario violates justice principles and not when the scenario upholds those principles, irrespective of ethnic/national background. As a consequence, prejudice should predict harsh immigration attitudes less strongly for an illegal alien scenario relative to a legal alien scenario, irrespective of ethnic/national background. If, in contrast, the concern for justice is not a true determinant of immigration attitudes but instead a rationalization of prejudice, then respondents' scores on prejudice should predict harsher attitudes regardless of whether the alien scenario violates or upholds justice principles. Moreover, consistent with the nature of aversive prejudice, participants should exhibit ingroup bias more than outgroup derogation by equally voicing prejudiced attitudes regarding illegal immigrants, but voicing harsher attitudes for the legal outgroup immigrant than the legal ingroup immigrant. In this way, the participant's self-concept of being non-prejudiced and non-bigoted remains in tact.

Specifically, the hypotheses are as follows:

- Justice Hypothesis: Participants will voice stronger immigration attitudes toward an illegal immigrant than a legal immigrant irrespective of national/ethnic background.
- Aversive Prejudice Hypothesis: Participants will voice stronger anti-immigration attitudes toward a legal outgroup immigrant than a legal ingroup immigrant especially when the immigrant is representative of an ethnic outgroup.

For this study, intergroup boundaries were defined in a manner consistent with the ethnic composition of the research participants and that of the society at large; that is, the dominant, ingroup alien ethnicity as Anglo (national origin: English-Canadian) and the minority, outgroup alien ethnicity as Latino (national origin: Mexican). Justice violations were manipulated by describing an alien who has come to the United States either legally (non-justice-violating) or illegally (justice-violating). Consistent with the logic presented above, immigration attitudes were assessed in a randomized, between-subjects, 3 (ethnicity) x 2 (legality) factorial survey design and in regression analyses using a measure of individual prejudice and psychological perceptions of justice.

METHOD

Participants

Participants from a large, southwestern university were recruited from introductory psychology courses as part of their research requirement. Per university admissions policy, all participants are either American citizens or possess legal immigration status. A total of 242 people participated, including 155 females and 86 males with one not indicating sex. Of these there were 185 Whites, 2 Blacks, 11 Asians, 28 Latinos, and 15 indicating other and one not indicating ethnicity. This ethnic breakdown mirrors the institutional ethnic composition of the university as a whole. The median age of the participants was 20 years with a range from 18 to 50. The median estimated annual family income was reported as $70–80K. A median estimate of political conservatism was 5.00 on a scale of 1 to 10, where 1 is Very Liberal and 10 is Very Conservative.

Measures

In order to generate response items and an appropriate dependent variable relevant to immigration attitudes, a systematic analysis of mainstream newspaper accounts of political candidates characterizations of Mexican immigration between January 1, 1993 and

June 30, 1998 were analyzed (see Appendix A for a listing of newspapers). The criterion of using political candidate characterizations of immigration phenomena as opposed to non-politicians was set under the assumption that they have a pulse on constituent concerns regarding immigration issues. The source of data came from Lexis-Nexis, an archived database of full-text newspaper articles. The purpose for this qualitative approach was to find a source of themes concerning immigration phenomena generated by politicians that could then be turned into semantic differential response items for research participants.

The final sample of articles containing political candidate comments and statements regarding Mexican immigration numbered 553. As a means to generate thematic content, an independent researcher unfamiliar with the hypotheses was instructed to select every tenth article from the sample, read the article, and note the predominant topics the political candidate was addressing with respect to Mexican immigration. Consistent with related research, this approach yielded three topics of interest: (1) Issues of legality; (2) Economic implications; and (3) Issues of nativism (e.g., Esses, Dovidio, Jackson, & Armstrong, 2001). The entire sample of articles was then searched for references to those three themes using the key words legal/illegal, economic influence and national sovereignty (see Table 6.1).

While this approach generated typical political portrayals of immigration phenomena, such a procedure is not without limitations. Most importantly, there were no inter-rater reliability strategies employed to verify that the identified themes are those most prevalent. As such, any replication of this work requires efforts to control for possible researcher bias in theme generation. Without such inter-rater estimates, one cannot assume that these three broadly framed themes are the only possible, relevant immigration topics voiced by political candidates. In addition, in using this data base, the researcher approaches it with key terms in mind for a specific period in history, thereby further increasing the probability of researcher bias influencing the data. A second concern regards the electronic database used. There are no known reliability estimates regarding the use of Lexis-Nexis for research purposes. While I believe that the use of the same terms input for the same period of history explored would generate the same sample of articles, I have no estimates to verify this belief. Finally, an improvement on this method would be to subject the entire sample to analysis, not a random sample of it. Using a random sample may have unwittingly limited the source with which to generate the relevant themes potentially leaving out other, perhaps more important areas of investigation.

These themes were used to develop a six-item, 10-point semantic differential scale measuring immigration attitudes as the dependent variable (see Appendix A). In addition to scale internal reliability estimates using Cronbach's alpha (alpha = .87), a principal components

Table 6.1 Political candidate portrayals of Mexican immigrants by theme

Themes raised by candidates	Frequency of newspaper articles	
	N	Percent
Legality	349	63%
Economics	179	32%
Nativism	166	30%

Note: N = 553; Sum of themes is greater than 553 as one article may contain more than one theme.

factor analysis using Varimax rotation confirm that the scale represented one factor with an eigenvalue of 3.72 accounting for 62.01% of the variance. As discussed theoretically, it is possible that one's attitudes toward immigration may function as a result of individual prejudice and/or individual attitudes regarding justice. For this reason, respondents also responded respectively to McConahay's (1986) Modern Racism Scale modified to refer to the immigrant populations (alpha = .76), and Lipkus' (1991) Personal Justice Scale (alpha = .63).

The independent variables embedded in the developed scenarios described an immigrant of either Mexican or English-Canadian national origin/ethnicity (race) who either immigrated legally or illegally. Finally, included were various demographic questions of Age, Sex, Year in School, Race, self-perceptions of political conservatism (1 = Very Liberal to 10 = Very Conservative), and how typical the scenario was perceived to be (1 = This scenario is NOT typical at all; to 10 = This scenario is VERY typical).

Procedure

Vignettes were randomly distributed to participants on an individual basis. Upon entering the office for research participation, participants were handed a survey packet, told that all data collected were anonymous, and to fill out the packet alone outside the office. After completing the packet, the respondent was then debriefed regarding the theoretical and social implications of the study.

RESULTS

Data Screening and Evaluation of Measures

To ensure that participants did not respond equally to the legal and illegal scenarios, an independent samples t-test on criminality by condition was run as a manipulation check. Participants interpreted the illegal scenarios as possessing greater criminality than the legal scenarios (M = 3.66 and M = 1.81, respectively, $t(240) = 6.40$, $p < .001$).

A one-way ANOVA on typicality by condition revealed that each scenario was not perceived equally typical ($F(3, 241) = 6.25$, $p < .01$). The mean values are presented in Table 6.2.

Table 6.2 Mean values of participant estimates of scenario typicality by condition

Condition	Mean of Typicality	sd
Illegal Mexican	8.65	1.41
Legal Mexican	7.53	2.40
Illegal English-Canadian	7.84	1.81
Legal English-Canadian	7.03	2.12

Note. The higher the value, the more typical on a scale of 1 to 10. N = 240.

Post-hoc Least Significant Differences tests comparing the mean difference between conditions revealed that the Illegal Mexican scenario was perceived to be more typical than the Legal Mexican, Illegal Canadian, and Legal Canadian scenarios (Mean difference = 1.12, .81, and 1.62 respectively, N = 240; all values were significant at alpha = .05). In addition, the more typical the scenario is perceived, the harsher the attitudes expressed but only for the Legal Mexican and the Illegal Canadian scenarios (r = .25, and r = .30, p < .05, respectively). It should be noted that while there is a statistical difference in perceived typicality, be mindful that such a difference may not be meaningful considering that all of the typicality ratings are quite high with relatively small standard deviations. These statistical relationships suggest that in a post-9/11 society, there is much better understanding of immigration policies and the myriad ways by which immigrants enter the country—both legally and illegally—than had existed prior to that date. Stated differently, these data suggest that all scenarios are possible and indeed probable but statistically, the vignette that better reflects popular understandings of U.S. immigration phenomena, albeit slight, is the illegal Mexican vignette. While these differences are small, nonetheless they warrant control for perceived typicality throughout the analyses as a covariate.

A one-way ANOVA on age, sex, and political conservatism by scenario revealed no significant differences (F (3, 239)= .80, F (3, 240)= 1.08, F (3, 239)= 1.28, p >.05, respectively). Age did not correlate significantly with immigration attitudes (r = -.02 p > .05, respectively, N = 238). Sex, however, did correlate with immigration attitudes such that women expressed less harsh attitudes than men (r = .11, p < .05, N = 239). In addition, political conservatism significantly correlated with immigration attitudes suggesting that the more conservative ones political views, the more harsh are the attitudes toward immigration expressed (r = .18, p < .01, N = 238). This finding is consistent with previous research investigating party affiliation and attitudes toward immigrant populations (cf., Magaña & Short, 2002). To control for this effect, political conservatism is included as a covariate in the analyses.

Finally, participant race is included as a factor in the analyses as a means to investigate its role in influencing immigration attitudes. The rationale for doing so is theoretical. Depending on one's generation, attitudes toward a shared ethnicity with immigrant populations may influence their response and most likely in a more favorable direction than the population at large. This may be particularly so in using a sample from a region in the United States where immigration issues are most salient. In addition, it is important to note that ethnicity is controlled for while being cognizant that the identity of being an American university student participating in a university sponsored research project may be a more salient identity issue than that represented by the singular demographic box checked on the back of the form (c.f., Espenshade & Belanger, 1998).

Test of the Justice Hypothesis Using All Participants

The number of cases for this test is 236 with 2 missing cases each for political conservatism, typicality, and immigration attitudes. The harshest immigration attitudes were reserved for the immigrants of illegal status (See Tables 6.3 and 6.4).

Table 6.3 Descriptive Statistics for Each Factor by Immigration Attitudes

Source	Legality	Race	Mean	Standard Deviation	N
Mexican Immigrant					
	Legal	White	20.91	10.68	46
		Latino	8.14	2.54	7
		Other	24.63	8.99	8
		Total	19.93	10.75	61
	Illegal	White	31.51	12.41	43
		Latino	21.00	12.00	5
		Other	26.60	11.03	10
		Total	29.76	12.39	58
Canadian Immigrant					
	Legal	White	15.60	7.50	45
		Latino	14.50	6.52	8
		Other	16.57	7.28	7
		Total	15.57	7.25	60
	Illegal	White	31.62	10.37	47
		Latino	16.14	14.23	7
		Other	31.33	22.28	3
		Total	29.70	12.41	57
Total					
	Legal	White	18.28	9.57	91
		Latino	11.53	5.90	15
		Other	20.87	8.97	15
		Total	17.76	9.41	121
	Illegal	White	31.57	11.33	90
		Latino	18.17	13.00	12
		Other	27.69	13.35	13
		Total	29.73	12.35	115
Overall Total	Total	White	24.89	12.40	181
		Latino	14.48	10.07	27
		Other	24.04	11.53	28
		Total	23.60	12.45	236

Table 6.4 Mean Differences of Nationality and Legality on Immigration Attitudes

Scenario	Mean	Mean Difference (I-J)	Standard Error
Mexican (I)	21.64	.48	1.32
Canadian (J)	21.16	−.48	1.49
Legal (I)	17.01	−8.61*	1.28
Illegal (J)	25.70	8.61*	1.53

Note. The higher the value, the harsher immigration attitudes expressed.

*A priori pairwise comparisons using ANOVA indicate the mean values for the legal scenarios are significantly different from the legal scenarios at p < .05.

Table 6.5 illustrates the confirmation of mean differences using a 3 X 2 ANOVA revealing a significant between-subjects main effect for Legality (F (1, 236) = 18.56, p. < .001) and Race (F (2, 236) = 11.37, p. < .001) (see Appendix B for correlation matrix). The main effect for Race reflects the unequal distribution of Races across conditions. As expected, the strongest attitudes were reserved for the Illegal immigrants however, statistically there were no meaningful interactions for Nationality by Legality (F (1, 236) = .88, n.s.), Nationality by Race (F (2, 236) = .64, n.s.) or Nationality by Legality by Race (F (2, 236) = 2.66, n.s.). Again, given the unequal distribution of Race across conditions, statistical power is limited in detecting meaningful interactions with this factor. These analyses support the hypothesis that justice (immigrating legally or illegally) is important in shaping immigration attitudes. In addition, it is important to note that the magnitude of these scores hover around the midpoint of the scale and below (the scale ranges from 6.00 to 60.00). These findings are consistent with previous research suggesting that among traditional university populations, attitudes regarding important, potentially divisive public policies such as affirmative action (e.g., Crosby & Clayton, 1990), politics and authoritarianism (e.g., Altemeyer, 1988), race (e.g., McConahay, 1986, Sears, 1988), and now, immigration are likely to fall in the center to center-left of the political continuum. In short, the responses comport to their self-reported estimates of political conservatism (5.00 on a scale of 1 to 10) and statistically reflect attitudes forged through perceptions of justice over that of ethnic nationality.

Table 6.5 Analysis of Variance for All Participants Testing Legality by Nationality with Political Conservatism and Perceived Typicality as Covariates

Source	Type III Sum of Squares	df	F	Sig.
Corrected Model	14073.81	13	10.75	.000**
Intercept	1119.81	1	11.12	.001**
Typicality	798.24	1	7.93	.005**
Political Conservatism	788.39	1	7.83	.006**
Nationality	5.88	1	.06	.809
Legality	1869.54	1	18.56	.000**
Race	2289.53	2	11.37	.000**
Nationality x Legality	88.73	1	.88	.35
Nationality x Race	129.01	2	.64	.53

(Continued)

Source	Type III Sum of Squares	df	F	Sig.
Legality x Race	275.14	2	1.37	.26
Nationality x Legality x Race	535.94	2	2.66	.07
Error	22356.97	222		
Total	167845.00	236		
Corrected Total	36430.76	235		

Note: R-Squared = .386 (Adjusted R Squared = .350). N = 236, missing cases = 2 for Typicality, 2 for Political Conservatism and 2 for Immigration Attitudes. ** significant at p. < .01

Test of the Aversive Prejudice Hypothesis Using Only White participants

Table 6.6 Descriptive Statistics for Each Condition by Immigration Attitudes (Whites only, N = 181)			
Source	Mean	Standard Deviation	N
Mexican			
Legal	20.91	10.68	46
Illegal	31.51	12.41	43
Canadian			
Legal	15.60	7.50	45
Illegal	31.62	10.37	47
Total			
Legal	18.29	9.57	91
Illegal	31.57	11.33	90
Overall Total	24.89	12.39	181

Table 6.7 Mean Differences of Nationality and Legality on Immigration Attitudes (Whites only, N =181)			
Scenario	Mean	Mean Difference (I-J)	Standard Error
Mexican (I)	25.74	1.69	1.50
Canadian (J)	24.05	−1.69	1.50
Legal (I)	19.04	−11.71*	1.53
Illegal (J)	30.75	11.71*	1.53

Note: * significant at p.< .05

Table 6.8 illustrates the confirmation of mean differences using a 2 X 2 ANOVA revealing a significant between-subjects main effect for legality (F (1, 181) = 58.65, p. < .001) and a statistically significant interaction for Nationality X Legality (F (1, 181) = 4.26, p. < .05). Again, perceptions of justice are the strongest effect using only White participants, however, prejudice against an immigrant outgroup is also evident. That is, issues of legality did not affect participant attitudes equally across all conditions. Indeed, the simple effect is most pronounced between Mexican and Canadian legal immigrants (M = 20.91 vs. M = 15.60, respectively). These findings are consistent with an aversive prejudice interpretation; that is, participants are less likely to voice outgroup prejudice that threatens their egalitarian self-concept as much as they are likely to voice ingroup bias (e.g., Dovidio & Gaertner, 1996).

Table 6.8 Analysis of Variance for White Participants Testing Legality by Nationality with Political Conservatism and Perceived Typicality as Covariates

Source	Type III Sum of Squares	df	F	Sig.
Corrected Model	10520.75	5	21.50	.000**
Intercept	1208.95	1	12.35	.001**
Typicality	1190.07	1	12.15	.001**
Political Conservatism	546.93	1	5.59	.019*
Nationality	123.14	1	1.26	.264
Legality	5740.62	1	58.65	.000**
Nationality X Legality	416.47	1	4.26	.04*
Error	17129.05	175		
Total	139777.00	181		
Corrected Total	27649.79	180		

Note: White participants only (N = 181).
* significant at p< .05, ** significant at p<.01.

Linear regression analysis was run using all participants to investigate the role individual difference variables on prejudice and perceptions of justice play in predicting immigration attitudes (see Table 6.9).

Table 6.9 Summary of Simultaneous Regression Analysis for Variables Predicting

Immigration Attitudes (N = 225 valid cases, missing values = 11 personal justice, 3 modern racism, 1 sex, and 2 age).

Variable	B	SE B	β
Modern Racism	1.19	.46	.46**
Sex	−2.33	1.53	.12
Age	−.036	.208	.86
Ethnicity	−.64	.56	.25
Personal Justice	.05	.07	.04

Note. R^2 = .25
**p < .001.

Prejudiced attitudes are the strongest predictor of immigration attitudes in this analysis. Participant perceptions of personal justice did not play a significant role in determining immigration attitudes. These findings are further bolstered by the finding that participants' racial attitudes correlate positively with immigration attitudes ($r = .49$, $N = 242$, $p < .01$) whereas individual perceptions of personal justice did not ($r = .06$, $N = 229$, $p =$ n.s.).

DISCUSSION

This study empirically explored the roles racial prejudice and perceptions of justice play in shaping immigration attitudes, thereby addressing an important gap in this literature as identified by previous researchers (e.g., Bobocel, Hing, Davey, Stanley, & Zanna, 1998). Consistent with previous research, evidence was presented showing that both issues of justice and prejudice influence attitudes toward immigration. However, the specific roles each of these constructs play is not so clear. Clearly, procedural justice defined in terms of having immigrated legally or illegally indicate that individuals are more likely to voice anti-immigration sentiments when that principle is violated (e.g., illegal immigration). Recall, however, that contemporary theories of prejudice espouse that people are reluctant to voice prejudicial attitudes unless they can do so in ways that cannot be attributed to race, thereby maintaining their self-concept in tact as being fair, egalitarian, non-prejudiced, etc. (cf., Dovidio & Gaertner, 1996; McConahay, 1986; Sears, 1988). In using the entire sample including all ethnicities, it appears that the legal-illegal procedural distinction in these data does not serve as a non-race based opportunity to voice such sentiments as the participants did so irrespective of ethnic/national background. However, when analyzing the data using only self-reported White participants, the differences suggest that legality may be used as a rationale for voicing stronger immigration attitudes. In addition, these data indicate that the more prejudiced the individual, the more harsh are the immigration attitudes expressed. So, how are these competing constructs to be reconciled theoretically in shaping immigration attitudes?

In previous research, the roles of procedural justice were clearly defined in terms of a specific, concrete public policy context—i.e., Affirmative Action (cf., Bobocel et al., 1998; Crosby & Clayton, 1990). In contrast, I propose that the use of procedural justice in terms of an illegal-legal distinction is relatively more abstract, or with more universal appeal. That is, another way of conceptualizing how justice and prejudice may be intertwined in this work is to suggest that abstract forms of justice do not lend themselves to convenient social categorizations that can clearly lead to ingroup biasing and outgroup derogation (cf., Tajfel, 1981). Appeals to abstract (or universal) principles of justice are assumed to be equally relevant to all social groups; there is no work or sense-making necessary to understand the phenomenon with which to selectively voice prejudiced attitudes. In contrast, concrete justice appeals such as those presented in the context of a specific public policy proposal, or of having engaged in socially undesirable behavior, are borne of immediacy, a relevance to the social context and, therefore, are subject to our universal tendencies to stereotype and categorize as a means to make sense of the social world (cf., Short & Magaña, 2002). Perceptions of abstract principles of justice are more likely to be attributionally ambiguous, whereas concrete principles of justice are more likely to be attributionally defined (cf., Semin & Fiedler [1991] for a psycholinguistic interpretation of abstract versus concrete social sense-making). In short, one may harbor prejudiced

114

attitudes toward certain immigrant populations, but such attitudes do not override the weight of perceived procedural justice violations when referring to a general, abstract social phenomenon such as immigration.

Limitations and Future Research

While the psychometric properties of the dependent measure of immigration attitudes comport to conventional statistical scaling criteria, there remain important areas of further development regarding its validity. As previously mentioned, the themes generated with which to create the scale were not subject to important inter-rater reliability assessments. As a result, I cannot rule out the potential threat of researcher bias in its construction. Future research must control for this threat to internal validity while also examining the scales' behavior with respect to related theoretical constructs to establish sound content validity. In short, the findings presented above and their interpretation should be cautioned given the remaining work needed to be done regarding the dependent measures' validity.

Given that these data are based on a convenience sample, namely, university undergraduates, it is possible that the findings do not generalize to the population. In addition, immigration phenomena are complex and multifaceted and do not lend themselves to easy, convenient interpretations. For instance, attitudes toward immigration are not necessarily specific to any particular social group, status, political affiliation, race, or gender (Espenshade & Belanger, 1998). Therefore, to assume our sample—albeit from a large public university—is a sufficient snapshot into the general population should be interpreted with caution. As a means to address this limitation, we suggest future investigations be replicated with more nontraditional populations. Such a direction would have important applied and theoretical interests.

One avenue of future research that would benefit from using nontraditional populations would be to assess immigration attitudes among first-generation immigrants: How do they see legality as relates to immigration phenomena? According to Social Identity Theory (c.f., Tajfel, 1981), might newly arrived immigrants express harsher immigration attitudes than members of the dominant majority as a means to differentiate oneself from a stigmatized media group—i.e., illegal aliens? Or does a shared component of social identity as being an immigrant predict more favorable attitudes toward immigration? These empirical questions among others are raised by the data in the current study and would benefit from investigation using more nontraditional populations.

Finally, these results have applied research implications, especially with respect to racial profiling. Do individuals differentiate between those of the stigmatized group (illegals) and those who are not? Psychologically, it is not likely that we process social information in such a convenient fashion. That is, our perception of individuals is colored by numerous factors including, but not limited to, social stereotypes, attributes, and the like. The danger of negative social constructions in the mainstream press by the politically powerful may influence a tendency to associate immigrant populations with socially undesirable characteristics. As a result, arguably, immigrant groups are more susceptible to prejudiced attitudes and discriminatory behaviors that can impede their successful transition to a new society. Clearly we rely on convenient heuristics to guide our behavior, even if that behavior has important civil rights implications including, but not limited to, rounding up potential illegal immigrants, justifying internment camps, soliciting identification, and racial profiling in traffic stops.

REFERENCES

Altemeyer, B. (1988). *Enemies of freedom: Understanding right-wing authoritarianism.* San Francisco: Jossey-Bass.

Amparo, J. (1999, August 2). Lets rid our state of hatred. *The Arizona Republic*, p. D1.

Bobocel, D. R., Hing, L. S., Davey, L. M., Stanley, D. J., & Zanna, M. P. (1998). Justice-based opposition to social policies: Is it genuine? *Journal of Personality and Social Psychology, 75* (3), 653–669.

Crosby, F., & Clayton, S. (1990). Affirmative action and the issue of expectancies. *Journal of Social Issues, 46* (2), 61–79.

Dovidio, J. F., & Gaertner, S. L. (1983).The effects of sex, status, and ability on helping behavior. *Journal of Applied Social Psychology, 13*, 191–205.

Dovidio, J. F., & Gaertner, S. L. (1986). Prejudice, discrimination, and racism: Historical trends and contemporary approaches. In J. F. Dovidio & S. L. Gaertner (Eds.), *Prejudice, discrimination, and racism* (pp. 1–34). Orlando, FL: Academic Press.

Dovidio, J. F., & Gaertner, S. L. (1996). Affirmative action, unintentional racial biases, and intergroup relations. *Journal of Social Issues, 52* (4), 51–76.

Dovidio, J. F., Gaertner, S. L., Anastasio, P. A., & Sanitioso, R. (1992). Cognitive and motivational bases of bias: The implications of aversive racism for attitudes toward Hispanics. In S. Knouse, P. Rosenfeld, & A. Culbertson (Eds.), *Hispanics in the workplace* (pp. 75–106). Newbury Park, CA: Sage.

Espenshade, T. J., & Belanger, M. (1998). Immigration and public opinion. In M. M. Suarez-Orozco (Ed.), *Crossings* (pp. 365–403). Cambridge, MA: Harvard.

Esses, V., Dovidio, J., Jackson, L., & Armstrong, T. (2001). The immigration dilemma: The role of perceived group competition, ethnic prejudice, and national identity. *Journal of Social Issues, 57* (3), 389–412.

Gaertner, S. L., & Dovidio, J. F. (1977). The subtlety of white racism, arousal, and helping behavior. *Journal of Personality and Social Psychology, 35*, 691–707.

Gaertner, S. L., & Dovidio, J. F. (1986). The aversive form of racism. In J. F. Dovidio & S. L. Gaertner (Eds.), *Prejudice, discrimination, and racism: Theory and research* (pp. 61–89). Orlando: Academic Press.

Lipkus, I. (1991). The construction and preliminary validation of a global belief in a just world scale and the exploratory analysis of the multidimensional belief in a just world scale. *Personality and Individual Differences, 12* (11), 1171–1178.

Luhtanen, R., & Crocker, J. (1992). A collective self-esteem scale: Self-evaluation of ones social identity. *Personality and Social Psychology Bulletin, 18*, 302–318.

Magaña, L., & Short, R (2002). The social construction of Mexican and Cuban immigrants by politicians. *The Review of Policy Research, 19* (4).

McConahay, J. B. (1986). Modern racism, ambivalence, and the modern racism scale. In J. F. Dovidio & S. L. Gaertner (Eds.), *Prejudice, discrimination, and racism* (pp. 91–125). Orlando, FL: Academic Press.

Sears, D. O. (1988). Symbolic racism. In P. A. Katz & D. A. Taylor (Eds.), *Eliminating racism: Profiles in controversy* (pp. 53–84). New York: Plenum Press.

Short, R., & Magaña, L. (2002). Political rhetoric, immigration attitudes and contemporary prejudice: A Mexican American dilemma. *Journal of Social Psychology* (6), 142.

Stephan, W. G. (1986). Intergroup relations. In G. Lindzey & E. Aronson (Eds), *The handbook of social psychology* (3rd ed., pp. 600–658); New York: Random House.

Tajfel, H. (1981). *Human groups and social categories: Studies in social psychology.* Cambridge, UK: Cambridge University Press.

Taylor, D., & Moghaddam, F. (1994). *Theories of intergroup relations: International social psychological perspectives.* Westport, CT: Praeger.

AUTHOR BIOGRAPHY

Dr. Robert Short is an Academic Associate in the Department of Psychology at Arizona State University. Correspondence concerning this article may be addressed electronically to Robert.Short@ASU.edu.

ENDNOTES

[1] While some readers may have preferences for the use of terms such as undocumented or documented in place of illegal and legal, or person in place of alien, for ease of readability and consistency, I will use the terminology used by the Federal Immigration and Naturalization Service throughout this document.

APPENDIX A

Scale questions generated from political candidate portrayals regarding Mexican immigration

Theme	Question
Legality	To what degree do you feel the person described should be deported? 1 (No, definitely should NOT be deported) to 10 (Yes, definitely should be deported); To what degree do you feel this person is a criminal? 1 (No, this person definitely is NOT a criminal) to 10 (Yes, this person definitely IS a criminal);
Economics	To what degree do you feel this person is a drain on the American economy? 1 (No, this person definitely is NOT a drain on the economy) to 10 (Yes, this person definitely IS a drain on the economy);
Nativism	To what degree does this scenario represent a cultural invasion? 1 (No, this scenario definitely is NOT representative of a cultural invasion) to 10 (Yes, this scenario definitely IS representative of a cultural invasion) To what degree does this scenario represent a threat to national sovereignty? 1 (No, this scenario does NOT represent a threat to national sovereignty) to 10 (Yes, this scenario represents a threat to national sovereignty) To what degree does this scenario represent an inability for the U.S. to control its borders? 1 (No, this scenario does NOT represent an inability on the part of the U.S. to control its borders) to 10 (Yes, this scenario DOES represent an inability on the part of the U.S. to control its borders).

Note. Cronbach's reliability analysis for the six-item scale: alpha = .84

Sample items from McConahay's (1986) modern racism scale (Mexican immigrant version). Scale items range from +2 Strongly Agree to -2 Strongly Disagree.

Item
1. I favor strong open housing laws that permit Mexican immigrants to rent or purchase housing even when the owner does not wish to rent or sell.
2. It is easy to understand the anger of Mexican immigrants in America.
3. Discrimination against Mexican immigrants is not a problem in the United States.
4. Mexican immigrants have more influence on what is taught in school than they ought to have.
5. It is a bad idea for Mexican immigrants and existing citizens to marry one another.
6. Mexican immigrants should not push themselves where they are not wanted.
7. If a Mexican immigrant family with about the same income and education as I have moved next door, I would mind it a great deal.

Note: Cronbach's alpha = .76.

Sample items from Lipkuss (1991) Personal Justice Scale

	Strong Disagreement Strong Agreement
1. I think that I deserve the reputation I have among the people who know me.	1------2------3------4------5------6
2. When I get lucky breaks, it is usually because I have earned them	1------2------3------4------5------6
3. When I take examinations, I rarely seem to get the grade I deserve	1------2------3------4------5------6
4. As a child, I was often punished for things that I had not done	1------2------3------4------5------6
5. I am less likely to get hurt in traffic accidents if I drive with caution	1------2------3------4------5------6
6. I have found that people who work the hardest at their jobs are not always the ones who get promoted	1------2------3------4------5------6
7. If I watch what I eat, I will live longer	1------2------3------4------5------6

Note: Alpha = .63

APPENDIX B

Descriptive statistics for all variables and all participants used in ANOVA and regression analyses

Variable	Mean	Standard Deviation	Minimum	Maximum	N	Missing Cases
Political conservatism	5.09	2.29	1.00	10.00	240	2
Racial attitudes	−3.09	4.80	−14.00	14.00	239	3
Immigration attitudes	3.74	2.08	1.00	10.00	240	2
Age	20.78	3.43	18.00	50.00	240	2
Personal justice	113.88	11.00	45.00	139.00	231	11

Note: The higher the number, the stronger the attitudes in the direction of political conservatism, racist attitudes, anti-immigration attitudes, and sense of personal justice.

Correlation matrix for all variables used in ANOVA and regression analyses

		Political conservatism	Age	Racial attitudes	Immigration attitudes	Personal justice
Political conservatism	Pearson correlation	1.00	.007	.287**	.200**	−.022
	Significance	.	.455	.000	.001	.371
	N	240	239	237	238	229
Age	Pearson correlation	.007	1.00	−.015	−.014	−.070
	Significance	.455	.	.409	.414	.145
	N	239	240	237	238	229
Racial attitudes	Pearson correlation	.287**	−.015	1.00	.488**	.018
	Significance	.000	.409	.	.000	.392
	N	237	237	239	237	229
Immigration attitudes	Pearson correlation	.200**	−.014	.488**	1.00	.059
	Significance	.001	.414	.000	.	.187
	N	238	238	237	240	229
Personal justice	Pearson correlation	−.022	−.070	.018	.059	1.00
	Significance	.371	.145	.392	.187	.
	N	229	229	229	229	231

Note: ** $p < .001$.

PART III | Influencing Others

> "*Character may almost be called the most effective means of persuasion.*"
>
> —*Aristotle*

7 | Persuasion: Who, What, to Whom

Learning Objectives

By the end of the chapter you should be able to:

- Describe the characteristics of communicators that make them more persuasive
- Describe the characteristics of a message that make it more persuasive
- Describe how culture, sex differences, and self-esteem affect persuasion
- Differentiate the central route from the peripheral route to persuasion within the elaboration likelihood model
- Describe the difference in the strength of attitudes changed by the central or peripheral route to persuasion

Chapter Outline

7.1 Introduction: Infomercials and Advertisements

Every day we face other people trying to persuade us to buy or do something. Advertisements on television, the Internet, or the radio attempt to persuade us to buy a product. Family members, friends, and employers ask us to do things for them. Some of these messages we quickly dismiss, but others convince us and we buy that brand of paper towels or bake cupcakes for that fundraiser.

We see ads every day trying to persuade us to buy something.

© Morgan Lane Photography, 2013. Used under license from Shutterstock, Inc.

Imagine watching an infomercial for an exercise machine. The product is described by an attractive and trim fitness expert to a mildly skeptical person in front of an enthusiastic studio audience. The machine is demonstrated, the positive benefits and ease of use of the machine are touted, and viewers are offered the product at a low, low price. By the end of the infomercial the skeptic is convinced of its miraculous powers and you find yourself picking up the phone to order one for yourself. What makes such communications persuasive? Why do we do what others ask sometimes but not other times? Social psychology can help us find the answers to these questions and, perhaps, better resist being persuaded in the future.

As we explore persuasion we can divide the persuasive communication into three parts: the communicator, the message, and the audience. First we will deal with what characteristics of persuaders make people more likely to be persuaded. Next, we will think about characteristics of the message that lead people to change. Finally, we will explore what characteristics of the audience can lead them to be persuaded.

7.2 Who—Characteristics of the Persuader

Credibility: Expertise and Trustworthiness

As you watch an infomercial, a central communicator is likely to offer arguments for the product. Whether or not you listen to this person likely depends on how credible you view that person to be. **Credibility** has two aspects: expertise and trustworthiness (Hovland, Janis, & Kelley, 1953). A communicator with **expertise** is one who appears to have knowledge and is able to communicate it. A **trustworthy** communicator is one we believe is giving us accurate information.

We are more likely to believe someone who we see as a credible expert. That's why many medicine commercials use pharmacists or doctors as spokespeople.

Messages from expert sources are persuasive when the message includes strong arguments from within that expert's field of knowledge (DeBono & Harnish, 1988; Petty, Cacioppo, & Goldman, 1981). Messages that come from an expert source but are weak are less persuasive than messages coming from someone who is less of an expert, but who has strong arguments (Bohner, Ruder, & Erb, 2002; Tormala, Brinol, & Petty, 2006). Expert opinion is generally only persuasive within that expert's domain of expertise. For example, you might believe what fitness experts say about exercise but not what they say about cake decorating. Children, who are generally not experts, can be persuasive when a message focuses on their social role. For example, using children to demonstrate the safety features in a new vehicle may resonate with an adult's perceived role as protector and nurturer (Pratkanis & Gliner, 2004).

At times we may receive a message and not have the time or energy to think carefully through the arguments. In those instances trustworthiness of the communicator can serve as a cue as to whether we should trust the message. If we perceive that the communicator is providing us with accurate information, we may not feel it necessary to carefully examine the message itself. When we perceive the communicator to be less trustworthy, we may carefully examine the message to determine if we can trust it. A message can, in this instance, still be persuasive if it contains strong arguments. A nonexpert who cites a study by the American Heart Association showing that the exercise equipment improves heart health in 90% of users has a strong argument, despite lack of expertise. An expert who points out that the stainless steel frame of the equipment will match any decor has a weak argument. Strong messages from nonexpert sources can be persuasive because people carefully examine the arguments (Priester & Petty, 2003). Such careful examination creates stronger and more long lasting attitude change.

Physical Attractiveness and Likeability

The attractiveness of the communicator is another factor in the persuasiveness of the message. In general, more physically attractive communicators are more persuasive and less attractive communicators are less persuasive (Chaiken, 1979; Debevec, Madden, & Kernan, 1986; DeBono & Telesca, 1990). Individuals we like are also more persuasive to us. You might buy Girl Scout cookies from the neighbor who you know and like, but the Girl Scout from across town will likely sell you fewer cookies. Physically attractive communicators are relatively easy to find, but advertisers have found tricky ways to make it appear that an appeal is coming from someone we know and like. An envelope that appears to be addressed by hand and have a note inside is more likely to be opened and read than one that is clearly mass produced. In one study of this idea, a number of car owners in Dallas were sent an ad for car wax that appeared to have been ripped from a magazine, with a handwritten sticky note attached; if the recipient was named Mary, for example, the note would read "Mary—Try this. It works!—J," with "J" being the supposed sender. The ad contained a mail-in card for a free sample of the car wax. The ad was sent in an unmarked white envelope, hand-addressed, with a first-class stamp. Other participants were mailed the same ad, but in a typed envelope sent through metered mail, and the ad inside was simply printed on a sheet of paper with no note attached. When the message in the ad was strong and it appeared to come from someone they knew, more participants requested a free sample (Howard & Kerin, 2004).

Should the communicators make their desires to persuade explicit? To maintain credibility and avoid reactance, advertisers generally avoid stating that they are trying to persuade; however, in some contexts such information can be helpful. You would likely attribute selfish motives to the fitness expert who is trying to sell exercise equipment he designed. But your doctor presumably has your best interests in mind, so his or her obviously persuasive message about exercise may be received well (Campbell & Kirmani, 2000; Eagly, Wood, & Chaiken, 1978). Researchers have found that physically attractive communicators do well if they make their desire to persuade explicit. Unattractive communicators are not very successful in this instance. For the less attractive, keeping persuasive intent hidden is a better strategy. Similarly, disliked sources should keep persuasive intent under wraps, while liked sources are more persuasive when they are open about persuasive intent (Reinhard, Messner, & Sporer, 2006).

7.3 What—Characteristics of the Message

Emotion

Within a persuasive appeal, a communicator might attempt to elicit an emotion. Emotions contain both physiological and cognitive elements. Our bodies are involved in our emotions. For example, when you are frightened your blood pressure and your heart rate increase. Cognition is also important. The same bodily state may be interpreted differently depending on the context. You might feel fear if you are in a dark alley and a stranger approaches. In the context of a thrilling video game, that same racing heart could be interpreted as excitement (Schacter & Singer, 1962).

We learn to appropriately display our emotions from our culture and social context. For example, in some cultures it is not considered acceptable to display anger in front of others, while in others public displays are customary (Averill, 1980). We may also learn from those around us what emotions are appropriate to feel. This is one way persuaders may use emotion to convince us to do something. Convinced that you should feel guilty if your home does not smell like flowers, you buy a candle. Having learned from an advertiser that a new car will make you happy, you purchase a new vehicle.

A graphic warning label such as this—required by the Food and Drug Administration starting in fall 2011—might scare people into rethinking their smoking habits.

Persuaders can also elicit specific emotions to motivate people to act. If an infomercial salesperson is trying to convince you to buy the exercise equipment, would it be best to scare you with the potential consequences of not exercising? Researchers have long been interested in how fear influences persuasion (Hovland et al., 1953, is an early example). The relationship was hypothesized to follow the pattern of an inverted U. At low fear levels, persuasion would be low because there was not enough motivation to change. At a moderate rate of fear persuasion should be highest; here people would be motivated to make a change but not so scared that they become paralyzed. At high levels of fear, according to this hypothesis, persuasion once again becomes less likely, as people become too frightened to process the information and respond to it. At this level, individuals may become defensive and ignore the content of the message.

The problem with this hypothesis is that research support is spotty (Eagly & Chaiken, 1993; Janis & Leventhal, 1968). The most important predictor of behavior when faced with a fear appeal seems to be not the level of fear aroused, but the belief of individuals in their ability to engage in actions that will allow them to avoid the feared consequence (Ruiter, Abraham, & Kok, 2001). Smokers might be exposed to a message that evokes a great deal of or very little fear about lung cancer, but if they do not believe they can quit, thereby avoiding cancer, the level of fear in the appeal does not seem to matter much (Hoeken & Geurts, 2005; Timmers & van der Wijst, 2007; Witte, 1998). The fitness expert should, then, scare you enough to motivate you to start exercising and convince you that the advertised product will make exercise easy.

Some persuasive appeals may use guilt to attempt attitude change. Charities, for example, might describe people who are hungry or sick or homeless in an attempt to persuade someone to give money or time. Guilt appeals can be successful. The more guilty people feel, the greater their intention to donate. However, if recipients are generally skeptical of emotional appeals and believe the communicator is manipulative, they will not feel as much guilt and therefore not be as likely to donate (Hibbert, Smith, Davies, & Ireland, 2007).

Advertisers can tap into other emotions in making their message persuasive. Happy holiday shoppers are likely to be persuaded by a happy message. The sweet and sappy commercials for engagement rings will do well with those who are in love and feeling sweet and sappy toward their significant other. Overall, a match between the emotional state of the person and the emotional overtones of the persuasive message creates the most persuasion (DeSteno, Petty, Rucker, Wegener, & Braverman, 2004).

Framing

Should the infomercial you are watching emphasize what you would gain by buying the equipment or what you might lose by not buying the equipment? Would a message that tells you about health improvement with exercising using this equipment be more persuasive than one that emphasizes your vulnerability to chronic health problems without the purchase of this machine? Messages can vary in whether they emphasize gains or losses. A message that focuses on benefits is described as being **gain framed**. If you were buying a vehicle, for example, the message that buying this car, with all of its safety features, will keep you safe in a crash emphasizes the things you would gain. A message that focuses on losses is **loss framed**. For example, a salesperson might suggest that if you do not buy this car with all of its safety features, your likelihood of experiencing major injury in a crash is increased. By emphasizing what you would lose, the message becomes loss framed. Framing can influence responses to persuasive messages.

When people are in a good mood they are more responsive to loss-framed messages. Happy people would respond well to a message that indicates that not exercising can increase your risk of dying of heart disease. When people are in a bad mood, gain-framed messages are more persuasive. Those who are upset or sad would respond better to a message that emphasizes your lowered risk of dying of heart disease with regular use of the exercise equipment (Keller, Lipkus, & Rimer, 2003).

One-Sided and Two-Sided Messages

When sharing a persuasive message the question arises whether presenting both sides of the argument is advantageous or whether presenting both sides would weaken the message. For example, if a car salesperson wanted to convince someone to buy an electric car, would presenting the positive features of the car alone be best or should the salesperson point out both the positives and negatives of owning an electric car? A communicator must also decide whether to simply describe the alternate position or also refute it. Should the electric-car salesperson simply mention the drawbacks of owning such a vehicle (the fully charged vehicle goes only 100 miles fully charged), or also explain why those are not of great concern (most trips people take are well under this distance)?

Overall, two-sided messages are more persuasive when they provide a refutation of the option the communicator is arguing against. If both sides are simply offered, with no refutation, one-sided messages are more per-suasive (Allen, 1991; Buehl, Alexander, Murphy, & Sperl, 2001). In our infomercial example this means that the drawbacks of owning one's own equipment should be discussed by the communicator, but those drawbacks should be refuted. Owning one's own equipment, for example, means taking care of it and storing it, but, the fitness expert might argue, this equipment takes almost no care and can easily be stored in the corner of a room.

Narratives and Rational Appeals

In the exercise equipment infomercial, the story of one customer is shared. She describes her struggle with poor health and the decision to purchase the equipment. After regular use, she explains, she lost weight, felt great, and was able to go off medication for a chronic health problem. Is this sort of personal story more persuasive than statistics on the health of users? In other words, are people more persuaded when they hear a story or when they hear statistics? What is persuasive may depend on the strength of the arguments. Individuals are persuaded by stories if the stories

Testimonials about substantial weight loss can convince us to try a new weight-loss program or exercise machine.

are good even when arguments are weak. On the other hand, when a message is shared not in a story but as a rational appeal, arguments that are weak are not persuasive. In a rational appeal, only strong arguments lead to attitude change (Escalas, 2007). People presented with personal narrative of a health risk viewed themselves as being more at risk and said they were more likely to get tested than those presented with statistical information (deWit, Das, & Vet, 2008).

Stories can be persuasive, but those stories need to be well done. The key element in persuasive stories is something called **transportation**. In the context of story, transportation is the joining of feelings, attention, and thoughts (Green & Brock, 2000). Transportation involves getting lost in a story. Overall, if you have a good story, no matter the strength of your arguments, you should persuade with a story. Use rational appeals only when you have strong arguments.

Sleeper Effect

Generally messages are most persuasive when they are first encountered. Over time the effect of the message gradually declines. For instance, you might be quite motivated to exercise after your doctor tells you about the importance of exercise. A few months later, however, you find your gym clothes collecting dust in the corner. In some instances messages become more persuasive with time, a phenomenon called the **sleeper effect**

(Peterson & Thurstone, 1933/1970). For the sleeper effect to occur, individuals need to spend enough time thinking about the message that the message sticks around (Priester, Wegner, Petty, & Fabrigar, 1999). People may discount a message when they first encounter it but over time forget their reasons for doing so, leading to greater persuasion after some time has elapsed (Kumkale & Albarracin, 2004). Some of the power of narratives may lie in the sleeper effect. The things individuals learn through a narrative are retained and any reasons for discounting it (it was just a fictional story) may be lost with time (Appel & Richter, 2007).

7.4 To Whom—Characteristics of the Audience

Culture

A large-scale difference in audiences for a persuasive messages is the cultural background of the audience. In Chapter 2 different ways of viewing the self were discussed. People from Western cultures, like the United States, most often view themselves as independent and unique individuals; they are part of an independent culture. People from many Asian cultures, such as Korea, have a more interdependent view of themselves; they are part of an interdependent culture. In interdependent cultures, people see themselves as enmeshed within a social context, with the sense of self arising out of social roles and relationships.

Persuasive messages follow this pattern. Persuasive messages in the United States focus more on uniqueness and individual preferences. In Korea, advertisements and other persuasive messages are more likely to focus on harmony with others, particularly family or other ingroups (Han & Shavitt, 1994). Recent research has shown that this difference can vary depending on the particular group within a culture. Affluent Generation X consumers in China were more persuaded than older Chinese consumers by an advertisement for a car that emphasized uniqueness, an independent culture value (Zhang, 2010). With greater exposure to Western values, these young people in China were more persuaded by advertisers emphasizing those values.

Western values usually emphasize independence and uniqueness, while Asian values often focus more on social roles and ingroups.

Sex Differences

Are men or women easier to persuade? Although the difference is quite small, overall, researchers have found that women are slightly easier to persuade than men (Becker, 1986; Eagly & Carli, 1981). This difference is not true in all circumstances. In situations where women traditionally know more than men, men are easier to persuade. For example, men may be more persuaded by an advertisement for a cleaning product, since house cleaning is the traditional purview of women. Women are easier to persuade in situations where their gender has traditionally been less well-informed (Eagly & Carli, 1981).

Self-Esteem

Individuals' level of self-esteem can influence how easy it is to persuade them. When it comes to differences among people, William McGuire (1968), an early researcher of persuasion, proposed that persuasion depended on both receptivity and yielding. Receptivity means that one has the ability and is willing to pay attention to and understand a message. Yielding means that the individual changes his or her mind as a result of the message. In order for a message to be considered persuasive, the individual must both be receptive to the message and yield to it.

When evaluating the effect of self-esteem on persuasion, both receptivity and yielding are important (Rhodes & Wood, 1992). Individuals with low self-esteem are likely to be yielding. As people who do not trust their own opinion, they are likely to yield to what others say. But those with low self-esteem lack receptivity: they are less likely to pay attention and remember a message. On the other end of the spectrum, receptivity is high among those with high self-esteem. Individuals with high self-esteem are likely to pay attention to and remember a message. But those with high self-esteem are less yielding. Confident in their own judgments, they are not persuaded by what others say. It is those in the middle, with moderate self-esteem, that are likely to have the combination of receptivity and yielding that makes persuasion likely. Overall, research findings support this claim, although many variables interact with self-esteem, meaning that given the right circumstances individuals with high or low self-esteem are more persuadable (Sanaktekin & Sunar, 2008).

Elaboration Likelihood Model

One model that brings together persuader, message, and audience variables is the **elaboration likelihood model** (Petty & Cacioppo, 1986). According to this model, people differ in their motivation and ability to process a persuasive message. When people are motivated and able to process a message, they will take more time to think about and evaluate the message. Elaboration refers to this engagement with the message. Those high on the spectrum of being willing and able to process a message will use what researchers have named the **central route to persuasion**. When using the central route, individuals process the message deeply, evaluating the strength of the persuasive arguments. If messages are strong, people are likely to respond with positive attitude change. But when arguments in a message are weak, those taking this route to persuasion may reject the message.

Being distracted prevents us from evaluating the message properly.

We tend to elaborate when a message is relevant to us and we have the time and energy to process it. For example, if a commercial for exercise equipment were shown during a television show you were watching, you might listen closely if you were thinking about buying such equipment and you had the time to listen. If you had a gym membership and were happy with your exercise routine, you might largely ignore the message. Distraction can stand in the way of taking this route to persuasion. When we are distracted we do not have the focus needed to evaluate a message (Petty & Brock, 1981; Petty, Wells, & Brock, 1976).

Our elaboration of a message can also depend on how much we feel the need to evaluate aspects of our lives in general. **Need for cognition** is a term researchers use to describe an individual difference in how much people enjoy thinking (Cacioppo & Petty, 1982). In a scale to assess need for cognition research participants are asked about their agreement with statements such as "I really enjoy a task that involves coming up with new solutions to problems" or "I would prefer a task that is intellectual, difficult, and important over one that is somewhat important but does not require much thought." (Cacioppo & Petty, 1982, p. 120). Whether or not something is personally relevant, people who are high in need for cognition tend to take the central route to persuasion (Cacioppo, Petty, & Morris, 1983).

Prior knowledge of a subject can influence people in a similar way. If you knew a great deal about exercise equipment, you would have an easier time processing a message. In this instance you would likely perceive a message with strong arguments as more convincing and quickly dismiss one with weak arguments or with only an attractive communicator to recommend it (Wood & Kallgren, 1988). As with need for cognition, even when a topic is not personally relevant someone with prior knowledge is still more likely to use the central route to persuasion (Chebat, Charlebois, & Gelinas-Chebat, 2001). Even if you are not presently in the market for exercise equipment, if you stumble across an advertisement for such equipment and have knowledge about equipment, you are likely to pay attention.

When people are less motivated or do not have the time or energy to process a message, they use the **peripheral route to persuasion.** With this route individuals use other cues to evaluate the persuasive arguments. These other cues include the number of arguments presented, the supposed credibility of the source, how many other people seem to be persuaded, and many other factors (Maheswaran & Chaiken, 1991; O'keefe, 2002; Petty, Caciopppo, & Schumann, 1983). For example, an online shopper using the peripheral route might be persuaded by the number of reviews for a product rather than the quality of those reviews (Sher & Lee, 2009).

When our self-control has been tested, we are more likely to take the peripheral route to persuasion. If you studied hard for a test, using all of your self-control to keep working through class material, an advertisement with an attractive communicator would be more persuasive to you, regardless of the strength of that communicator's arguments. Recall from the chapter on the self that ego depletion creates a problem for later volitional acts.

Social Psychology in Depth: Word of Mouth and Persuasion

When making decisions about products to buy, restaurants to visit, or movies to see, we often ask our friends and relatives. A friend who raves about a new movie is probably more likely to get you to the theater than an advertisement on television. This passing of information about products or services through informal social networks is known as word of mouth. Traditionally, word of mouth has its strongest impact when a relationship is close (Brown & Reingen, 1987) and the message is rich or vivid (Kisielius & Sternthal, 1986; Sweeney, Soutar, & Mazzarol, 2008).

A new frontier for persuasion through word of mouth is the Internet. Many websites offer customer reviews of their products or services. These reviews, known as electronic word of mouth or e-word of mouth, can significantly affect popularity and sales (Ye, Law, Gu, & Chen, 2011; Zhang, Ye, Law, & Li, 2010). E-word of mouth is different from traditional word of mouth because many of the comments or reviews one might read about a product or service are from strangers, not friends or relatives.

Online shoppers tend to use certain clues to evaluate e-word of mouth. While considering the e-word of mouth for a product, shoppers look at the agreement among evaluations. If all reviewers are in agreement (all positive or all negative), that may sway a shopper (Chiou & Cheng, 2003). If the reviews for a camera you were considering purchasing were uniformly negative, would you buy the camera? One bad review among many, however, will not necessarily scare off a shopper. A set of perfect reviews may be seen as suspicious, too good to be true (Doh & Hwang, 2009). Overall, the greater the ratio of positive to negative reviews, the more positive the attitude of the shopper and the greater the intention to buy the product (Doh & Hwang, 2009).

Online reviews of products may be evaluated differently depending on the shopper. Online shoppers high in need for cognition were more persuaded by high-quality reviews than by low-quality reviews. The quality of the review had no impact on persuasion for those with low in need for cognition (Lin, Lee, & Horng, 2011). A large number of reviews was more convincing to those low in need for cognition, but did not affect persuasibility for those high in need for cognition (Lin et al., 2011). Individuals who were largely unfamiliar with a product were also more swayed by the number of reviews for a product. Expertise of reviewers, not number of reviews, was more important to those who knew more (SanJose-Cabezudo, Gutierrez-Arranz, & Gutierrez-Cillan, 2009).

The way individuals engage in e-word of mouth may be different in different countries. In a study of discussion boards in the United States and China, researchers found greater information seeking but less information provision by the Chinese than the U.S. participants. Chinese participants were also more concerned about the country of origin, as opposed to the quality, of the products they were investigating (Fong & Burton, 2008).

The peripheral route is used when we do not have the time or energy to consider a persuasive message carefully, so when the ego is depleted we use this route. When individuals engage in self-control earlier they are more likely to give in to persuasive messages that come through the peripheral route (Fennis, Janssen, & Vohs, 2009).

The persuasive message itself can influence what route we would take. Personalization in websites is one way online retailers have sought to influence the buying public (Tam & Ho, 2005). Many companies that sell products online now keep track of where consumers look on their sites, what they click on, and what they eventually buy. With all of that information, the retailer is able to make suggestions for an individual site visitor or for the general shopper who visits and shows interest in a product. You may have visited a website that, after you purchase or even just click on a few products, offers suggestions of other products you might be interested in; that site is using personalization strategies. Because personalization makes messages relevant to individuals, according to the elaboration likelihood model it should lead to greater central route processing, and, when a product is good, potentially more purchasing of that product.

When we are persuaded using the central route, our attitudes are stronger. Stronger attitudes tend to last longer and are less likely to be changed when attacked (Haugtvedt & Petty, 1992; Wu & Shaffer, 1987). Attitudes changed by the central route are more likely to lead to behavior in line with that attitude (Wu & Shaffer, 1987). All of this

Sometimes defending our attitudes can make them stronger. An elementary example is a child who is adamant that she doesn't like a certain food.

means that when you are trying to persuade someone, if you want the attitude to stick around for the long term you should use the central route. The problem is that it is generally easier to change someone's attitude using the peripheral route.

When someone tries to persuade us and we need to defend our beliefs and attitudes, that defense can make those attitudes stronger (Tormala & Petty, 2002). For example, imagine someone told you that you should no longer buy and eat your favorite brand of cereal. You would likely defend your cereal, describing its great taste, healthy ingredients, or low price. Having successfully defended your breakfast food, you would likely feel even more strongly about your cereal.

However, if our attitudes are attacked and we believe we did a poor job of defending those attitudes, we may hold the same attitudes as we did before, but with less certainty (Tormala, Clarkson, & Petty, 2006). Imagine someone attacked your breakfast cereal and you found yourself saying the box it came in has a nice design. Even if you still eat the cereal, you might think of the reason you gave for eating it an unsubstantial reason. When we hold our attitudes with less certainty, those attitudes are less predictive of our behavior. If your cereal were attacked again, researchers have found, you would be more likely to change your attitude and your breakfast choice.

When presenting a persuasive message, it is important for the communicator to avoid making the audience defensive. Affirming what others believe and validating their concerns can increase message scrutiny and lead to a change in behavior (Correll, Spencer,

& Zanna, 2004). When students' concerns about availability of recycling containers were validated (we know it's a long walk but . . .) and they were encouraged to use the containers that were available, even if it was inconvenient, their recycling behavior increased and lasted longer (Werner, Stoll, Birch, & White, 2002). Reactance, the tendency to reassert one's freedom in the face of demands from others, can be reduced by affirming what that person believes. Acknowledging concerns works by reducing criticism of a persuasive message, opening the individual up to consideration of the message (Werner, White, Byerly, & Stoll, 2009).

Conclusion

In evaluating persuasion we need to take into account where the message comes from, what the message contains, and the intended audience. Each of these factors interact with one another, so a particular communicator may be quite persuasive using a certain type of message with a certain audience but less persuasive when conditions change.

Summary

Who—Characteristics of the Persuader

Those who have the most credibility are persuasive. Credible sources convince their audience they are expert and trustworthy. Attractive sources tend to be more persuasive. Persuasion is also higher with sources we like.

What—Characteristics of the Message

Some amount of fear and guilt can make a message more persuasive. Whether a persuader wants to use a gain-framed message or a loss-framed message depends on whether the audience is in a good mood or a bad mood. Two-sided messages are more persuasive than one-sided messages, but only if refutations of the opposing arguments are offered. People find narratives persuasive, but only when those narratives are well-written and transport the reader into the story. Rational appeals can also be persuasive, but arguments need to be strong. When a message is not a strong one it can become more persuasive with time through the sleeper effect.

To Whom—Characteristics of the Audience

Culture, self-esteem, and gender all affect persuasion. The elaboration likelihood model helps us sort out when persuasive messages might be persuasive. When people are attentive and have the time and energy to think about a message, the central route can be more persuasive. When people are distracted or uninterested, messages that take the peripheral route are more persuasive.

Critical Thinking Questions

1. What other communicator characteristics do you think might make the communicator more persuasive?
2. Consider the last infomercial you saw. How did characteristics of the communicator, the message, and your own interest in the product affect the degree to which you were persuaded?
3. If you are currently trying to persuade another person or group of people, how might you use the content from this section to help you?
4. In what circumstances might taking the peripheral route to persuasion be more appropriate? When might the central route be more appropriate?

Key Terms

Central route to persuasion	Gain framed	Sleeper effect
Credibility	Loss framed	Transportation
Elaboration likelihood model	Need for cognition	Trustworthy
Expertise	Peripheral route to persuasion	

Expanding Your Knowledge: Links to Additional Material

Propaganda

Governments, political parties, organizations, and individuals have all used persuasive communications in an effort to sway the public. The website Propaganda Critic (http://www.propagandacritic.com/), from the Institute for Propaganda Analysis, offers a look at propaganda, including a page on why investigating propaganda matters and analysis of a number of propaganda techniques.

Scams

If you are curious about scams and why people fall for them, check out the blog post at http://mindhacks.com/2009/05/17/the-psychology-of-being-scammed/. The author summarizes a report on scams from the Office of Fair Trading in the U.K.; the full report is available at http://www.oft.gov.uk/shared_oft/reports/consumer_protection/oft1070.pdf.

Crimes of Persuasion

The Crimes of Persuasion site (http://www.crimes-of-persuasion.com/) provides information on a variety of scams and frauds involving persuasion. The material is quite broad, including information about sweepstakes scams, investment fraud, and business opportunity or money laundering scams. There are sections on the criminals as well as laws and victims.

The Persuaders

An interesting program on persuasion is PBS's *Frontline* episode "The Persuaders," which can be viewed at http://www.pbs.org/wgbh/pages/frontline/shows/persuaders/. The program discusses in depth the current issues persuaders face—such as the fact that we all encounter advertising all the time. To cut through the clutter, advertisers have developed new ways to find out what we want and capture our attention.

Framing

For a demonstration of framing research, visit http://www.philosophyexperiments.com/framing/. The demonstration uses the scenarios created by two researchers in the field, Kahneman and Tversky. After you read the scenarios and make two decisions, the site describes why you might have made those choices and how they are related to loss and gain.

8 Persuasion Techniques

Learning Objectives

By the end of the chapter you should be able to:

- Describe the persuasion techniques involving initial small requests
- Describe the use of reciprocity as a persuasion technique
- Explain how techniques that begin with a large request work
- Explain how persuasion techniques using scarcity work

8.1 Introduction

Watching a series of infomercials or a shopping channel, you may have noticed that some phrases keep coming up. Most offers are for a limited time only. The shopping channel may show you how many of the products are left and count them down until they are all gone. Some infomercials ask you to send no money now or offer you a full refund if you are not completely satisfied. Others offer the product and then let you know that if you order now you could get a free gift. All of these are based on persuasion techniques researched by social psychologists and others.

Three persuasion techniques are based on small requests or what appear to be small requests. The foot-in-the-door technique begins with a small request and moves to a larger request. With the low-ball technique, a request is made and accepted before the full cost is revealed. The legitimization-of-paltry-favors technique validates small contributions. We investigate these three techniques first. Later in this chapter we will look at persuasion techniques involving reciprocity, large initial requests, and scarcity.

8.2 Foot-in-the-Door

If you have ever bought a car, you may have found yourself visiting a lot of dealerships or used car lots. At a dealership you might be asked to sit in a new car or offered a test drive. In doing all of this the salesperson might say that there are no strings, but is that really true? A persuasive technique that is behind the behaviors is called foot-in-the-door. With the **foot-in-the-door technique** a small request is made and agreed to, followed by a larger request. The salesperson might first ask if you would like to take a test drive and only after that test drive ask if you would like to buy the car. Because people have said yes to the first request (test drive) they are more likely to say yes to the second request (buying the car). The second

The foot-in-the-door technique suggests that if you're able to get your foot in with a smaller request, the rest of your body (or a larger request) is more likely to follow.

request is really the target for the salesperson. Depending on the situation, this technique can bring 15% to 25% compliance with the second request (Dillard, 1991).

In early studies on this technique, researchers called one group of housewives and asked some of them about the types of soaps they used. Another group of women were asked if they would be willing to be asked such questions, though the questions were not actually asked. A third group of women were told about the organization doing the survey. These last two groups were, therefore, familiar with the organization. A fourth group was not called initially. Later on the researchers called the women in all the groups and asked if a team of five people could come over and catalog all products in their kitchens and storage places. The women were told the task would take 2 hours and the five guests would need to have access to all areas of the house. Women who had answered questions about the soaps they used, agreeing to a small initial request, were much more likely to agree to have the 2-hour visit, the large, target request, than any of the other groups. About 53% of this first group agreed, while agreement in the other groups ranged from 22% to 33%. Having their foot in the door with the first group, the researchers were able to elicit higher agreement. In a similar study, the researchers asked participants to put a small sign in their front window or car that read "Be a safe driver." When those who had agreed were later contacted, many more were willing to place a large, somewhat ugly "Drive Carefully" sign in their front lawn (55% agreed) than those who had not been asked to comply with the first request (20% agreed) (Freedman & Fraser, 1966).

One explanation for the foot-in-the-door technique's success is related to self-perception theory. Self-perception theory involves attitude formation. When we want to know what our attitudes are, we look at our behavior. With foot-in-the-door the same process might be happening as people look to their initial behavior (agreeing to a small request) to determine what they should do for another behavior (agreeing to the larger, target request) (Burger, 1999; Burger & Caldwell, 2003). Use of the technique requires a delicate balancing act. The first request needs to be small enough to be accepted, but the larger the first request the more likely individuals are to say yes to the second request (Seligman, Bush, & Kirsch, 1976).

Foot-in-the-door technique might be used outside of commercial purposes. When individuals visit a website for a charitable organization, those who agree to sign a petition are more likely to donate money than those who are not asked to sign (Gueguen & Jacob, 2001). Teen smokers intercepted at the mall were asked to answer a few questions about smoking. When called later with a request to be part of a smoking cessation program, the ones who answered questions were more likely to agree (Bloom, McBride, Pollak, Schwartz-Bloom, & Lipkus, 2006). In another study, researchers found that young women were more likely to agree to have coffee with a young man if they were first asked to give him directions or light his cigarette (Gueguen, Marchand, Pascual, & Lourel, 2008).

8.3 Low-Ball

Seeing a commercial on a website for a computer at a low price, you click on the ad. You are in the market for a new laptop computer so you are very interested, and you know this price is a good one. You quickly decide on this computer and, excited about your potential purchase, begin the order process. Partway through providing your name, address, credit card information, and desired color for your new computer, you are asked whether you'd like to buy a power cord for only $19.99, antivirus software for only $39.00, a carrying case for only $34.99, and four other products you had thought were included in the initial price. At the end of the purchase you find you spent $200 more on the laptop and all its accessories than comparable products elsewhere. By the time all of the small additions are made, you realize your good deal is quite a bit more expensive than you thought.

This is the **low-ball technique**. A request is made that is reasonable, but after the person agrees, additional things are added that make the overall request less reasonable. Because individuals have already made a commitment to the item (e.g., the computer) they are reluctant to walk away. If they had known about all of the costs initially, however, it is unlikely they would have agreed (Cialdini, Cacioppo, Bassett, & Miller, 1978; Gueguen, Pascual, & Dagot, 2002). The initial request seems small, but when all is revealed it is not. This can be used beyond the salesroom. Someone might ask you as a favor to hang up posters for an upcoming event. If you agreed and then later found out you also needed to pick up the bulky, heavy posters from a location 10 minutes away and transport them to where you are to hang them up, you might still do it, even though you would not have had you known all the details in the first place (Burger & Petty, 1981).

Unlike foot-in-the-door, with low-ball the initial request is the target request. The initial request is small, or at least reasonable, and it is only when the full cost is revealed that individuals realize the large commitment they have made. The initial request is one that people must agree to for this technique to work. With this technique the persuader needs to be careful to offer the initial product at a price people will be interested in and then make the additional requests reasonable enough so that the agreement continues as the deal becomes less of a deal.

8.4 Legitimization-of-Paltry-Favors

A neighbor child comes to your door, collecting money for a well-known charity. Your budget is tight and you give elsewhere so you are about to respond with a polite no, but the child says, "Even a penny will help." You have a penny, right in your pocket, so you can't really say no to the request. But you don't feel right about contributing just a penny. Reaching into your wallet, you pull out a couple of dollars and hand them over. Congratulations, you have just been persuaded by the technique called legitimization-of-paltry-favors.

As the name implies, the **legitimization-of-paltry-favors technique** catches us by making a very small contribution acceptable. It is difficult to refuse when even a very small amount is described as legitimate. But few would give a paltry amount even if it is acceptable, so we give more than just that penny. Notice that a penny was not suggested, but legitimized. With this technique it should be clear that while a very small amount is okay,

Social Psychology in Depth: Resistance to Persuasion

Persuasive messages are designed to change our minds but we are not without defense. In the battle for our wallets and our minds, resistance to persuasion plays a part. One way in which we resist persuasive messages is through arguing our own point of view, or counterarguing. Hearing a message you do not agree with, you come up with a number of arguments why your position is right and the alternate position is wrong. Such an activity will have an effect on your initial attitude. When people counterargue successfully, they become more certain of their initial attitude, particularly when the other message comes from an expert source (Tormala & Petty, 2004a; Tormala & Petty, 2004b). However, when people believe they have done a poor job at counterarguing, they may actually become less certain of their attitudes. The attitudes themselves may not change, but they are now more vulnerable to future attacks and are less likely to predict behavior (Tormala, Clarkson, & Petty, 2006).

At times we resist persuasion not because of well-thought-out arguments but simply because we are reacting to manipulation. Reactance is our response to threatened freedom; we do the opposite of what someone wants us to do because we want to reassert our right to make our own decisions. If a high-pressure salesperson is advocating a particular product, we may choose another because we want to assert our freedom to make our own choices. We generally think of reactance as a simple knee-jerk reaction to a threat to freedom, but reactance can also lead us to the kind of counterarguing described in the first paragraph (Silvia, 2006).

While we can and do resist persuasive messages, our view of our vulnerability to persuasion is distorted. We believe we are less vulnerable to persuasion than others (Douglas & Sutton, 2004). While we tend to judge the vulnerability of others accurately, we judge ourselves as being less vulnerable to persuasion than we really are. When our attitudes do change, we underestimate the degree of change (Bem & McConnell, 1970; Markus, 1986). For example, if a salesperson convinced us to buy a product, we might say we were leaning toward that choice already even if we were not.

When it comes to resistance to persuasion, our vulnerability is higher when we have exerted self-control. Previous experiences that have resulted in ego depletion, such as controlling our emotions, making decisions, or engaging in an undesired task, make us more vulnerable to persuasive messages. With depleted resources we are less able to counterargue (Burkley, 2008; Wheeler, Brinol, & Hermann, 2007). The reverse also appears to be true: Engaging in resistance to persuasion makes us less able to engage in tasks requiring our self-control (Burkley, 2008).

it is certainly not desired. Such a technique tends to increase the number of people who give while not affecting the amount each individual gives (Cialdini & Schroeder, 1976). There is some evidence that this technique works best in face-to-face interactions and is less effective in direct mail situations (DeJong & Oopik, 1992).

8.5 Reciprocity

Wandering through the supermarket, you come upon a small table with the offer of free samples. You are hungry and the samples look good so you take one. Smiling your thanks to the person offering the samples, you reach for a package of the product. Considering that the product was not on your shopping list and you may not have known it even existed before your encounter with the sample, why would you buy this product? Even if you do not buy the product, why would the company send someone out to your local grocery store to offer samples? Do they actually sell more of the product that way?

Reciprocity is about exchange: We may feel obligated to give someone a gift if he or she has given us one first.

© StockLite, 2013. Used under license from Shutterstock, Inc.

The technique being used here is the **reciprocity technique**. Reciprocity is considered a rule of social behavior, a rule that appears to be present in most cultures, if not all. When others do something for us, we feel obligated to do something for them (Gouldner, 1960; Wright, 1994). Communicators use our natural tendency toward reciprocity to get us to do what we otherwise might not. When provided with something we did not ask for, we tend to reciprocate, at times giving more in return than was invested in the original gift. In one study, for example, some research participants were given a 10-cent soda by a confederate. Later in the study, when the participants were asked by the confederate to buy 25-cent raffle tickets, the ones who had been given the soda were more likely to buy the raffle tickets than those who had not been given a soda (Regan, 1971). In another example of reciprocity, researchers have found that food servers who provide their customers with mints or candy get increased tips (Lynn & McCall, 2000). Although reciprocity will be slightly higher in a public context, we still tend to reciprocate even when our behavior is private (Whatley, Webster, Smith, & Rhodes, 1999).

When we are providers of a favor to others, it seems reciprocity is still desired. In a field study in France, researchers asked smokers on the street for a cigarette. When the researchers offered a small amount of money in exchange the money was usually refused, but the smokers were more likely to give up a cigarette (Gueguen & Pascual, 2003).

8.6 Door-in-the-Face

Two techniques begin with a large request and move on from there. In the door-in-the-face technique, a large request is made, which is refused. After receiving the refusal the communicator makes the real request, which, in contrast, seems more reasonable. The that's-not-all technique also begins with a large request, but the communicator does not allow time for refusal before adding additional incentives.

As you watch an infomercial for exercise equipment, the advertiser shows four different machines and the price for each. As you contemplate the expense of such equipment, you quickly reject the idea of ever owning exercise equipment. A request to buy four different machines is too much. But wait, the advertiser says, you *can* afford exercise equipment. The advertiser then displays a machine that will do everything the first four machines can and is small and relatively inexpensive. Relieved that there is a product you can afford, you pick up the phone to order one of your own.

The infomercial used a technique called door-in-the-face. Unlike foot-in-the-door, where a small request is followed by a larger request, the target request, the **door-in-the-face technique** begins with a large request. When the message recipient says no to the first request, the persuader follows with a second, more reasonable request, the actual target of the communication. In the original study on the technique, college students were asked if they would be willing to counsel juvenile delinquents for 2 hours a week for 2 years. The students declined. Then, those students and others were asked if they would be willing to take the juveniles to the zoo for a day. Of the students who had not been previously asked to make a 2-year commitment, about 17% agreed to chaperone the kids. Of the students who had been asked, and refused, 50% agreed to the chaperoning (Cialdini et al., 1975).

One explanation for why this technique works has to do with the discomfort we feel when we refuse someone's request. In their second request the persuader makes a concession, so we feel as though we should make a reciprocal concession. Wanting the students' help with juveniles for two years, the persuader appears to be making a concession with just a day at the zoo. Wanting to do nothing, the students make a concession from nothing to a day at the zoo. When researchers emphasized to participants that the second request would reduce feelings of guilt, they found greater compliance with that request (Millar, 2002). Further research has found that emphasizing the concession made by the person making the request increases persuasion (Ebster & Neumayr, 2008) or feelings of obligation (Abrahams & Bell, 1994). Perhaps because of this, compliance is highest when requests are close to one another in time (within the same interaction, ideally) rather than separated (Cann, Sherman, & Elkes, 1975). It seems the person needs to see a clear connection between the first request and the second request in order to feel a need for reciprocal concession.

As with the foot-in-the-door technique, a balance needs to be struck with size of the requests. In the initial study on the technique, the first request was a very large request that everyone was expected to refuse (counseling juveniles 2 hours per week for 2 years). When moderate initial requests are used, compliance actually declines in some studies (Even-Chen, Yinon, & Bizman, 1978). With moderate requests that are refused, self-perception theory would suggest that participants can look to their behavior to determine that perhaps they do not support that cause or desire that product. When the request is one any reasonable person would refuse, self-perception does not kick in.

8.7 That's-Not-All

On late-night television you might find an infomercial that explains an exercise machine and the wonderful things it does. After offering the product and telling you the price, the announcer says "And that's not all" and offers a lower price or some exercise towels that you will get with your purchase. When sellers offer a product and before the customer can respond offer something else with the sale or offer to lower the price, they are using the **that's-not-all technique**.

This technique might work because of reciprocity. The seller is seen as willing to negotiate the sale of his or her product, so the buyer should reciprocate that flexibility by buying. Another factor may be a concept known as anchoring. The initial price for the individual piece is seen as the anchor. When the price is lowered or additional things are added, the consumer sees this as a good deal. If originally offered the entire package at the lower price, consumers take that as the anchor and do not view it as a good deal (Burger, 1986).

The that's-not-all technique seems to work best when the initial request is a reasonable request (Burger, Reed, DeCesare, Rauner, & Rozolis, 1999). This means that when using the technique, sellers need to be careful in setting the initial price. A high initial price can shock people into considering whether they really need the product or really need to spend that much money. High initial prices tend to lead to greater refusal when the that's-not-all technique is used. Adding additional items to the initial offering may not alleviate that initial shock (Pollock, Smith, Knowles, & Bruce, 1998).

8.8 Scarcity

Often advertisements for products will emphasize the fact that the item is only available for a limited time. Deals available on the day after Thanksgiving are sometimes only available for a few hours after the store has opened. Why do advertisers limit the time frame for such bargains?

Overall, people do not like it when their freedom to act is restricted. When products may not be available for long, we tend to buy those products so we can access them if we want. This type of behavior is called reactance. **Reactance** is acting in a way that protects one's freedom. Although we may have never intended to buy a certain product in the first place, if we think it will no longer be available we may purchase it. Researchers have found evidence of reactance in a wide variety of circumstances. When we feel like others are restricting our freedom in a parking lot by waiting for our parking space, we may actually stay in the space longer than if no one was waiting (Ruback & Juieng, 1997).

The idea of scarcity prompted Black Friday shoppers to line up in front of this Best Buy in Idaho starting at 9:15 p.m. Thursday.

© K2 Images, 2013. Used under license from Shutterstock, Inc.

Limited-time offers are not the only type of offers where we have this reaction. We may also buy when we believe there are few of the product in existence, in other words, when the number of items is restricted. Any advertisement that refers to the product as being a limited edition or in short supply leads us to a similar reaction. This reaction may rely in part on our need for uniqueness (Lynn, 1991). We do not want to look like or have the same things as everyone else, so we buy rare products to express our individuality. When commercials offer a product for a limited time or describe the limited number available, the advertisers are using the **scarcity technique**.

When products are seen as available for only a limited time, it is possible that respondents actually increase their scrutiny of the persuasive message. Knowing the product may only be available briefly provides motivation to think about the merits of the message (Brannon & Brock, 2001). Scarcity works particularly well in romantic contexts (such as when watching a romantic movie) but can backfire when in the context of fearful events (such as when watching a scary movie). Romantic situations remind us how scarce opportunities can be; after all, how often does Mr./Ms. Right come along? In these situations you want to stand out from the crowd so you can be noticed by that potential significant other or impress the partner you have. When we are thinking of romance, therefore, a commercial that tells us to get one of the few products available is more likely to be persuasive. In the context of fear, however, we may not want to stand out or have the only one of something. When an attack is possible it is better to be among many others and not stand out in any way, lest we be the one harmed. We do not, therefore, want a unique product when we are scared; we want to be just like everyone else (Griskevicius et al., 2009).

Table 8.1 Persuasion Techniques: Definitions and Examples

Technique	Definition	Example
Foot-in-the-door	An initial small request is made and accepted. A large request, the target request, is then made.	You are asked to sign a petition to support blood donation. After you sign, you are asked to donate blood.
Low-ball	An initial request, the target request, is made, but only later are the full costs revealed.	You are asked to volunteer 20 minutes of your time. Only later is it revealed that the time will involve blood donation, with accompanying needles and slight pain.
Legitimization-of-paltry-favors	Small favors are described as acceptable, although not desired.	A small donation to support blood donation, just $0.25, is acceptable, although a larger donation would be appreciated.
Reciprocity	A request is made after a gift has been given.	After receiving a cookie you are asked if you would be willing to donate blood.
Door-in-the-face	A large request is made and refused. Then the target request is made.	You are asked if you could volunteer 2 hours a week for the next year. When you refuse, you are asked if you could spend just a half hour now donating blood.
That's-not-all	A large request is made, but before the individual can refuse additional incentives are added.	You are asked to donate blood, but before you say no you are told you will get a cookie and a sticker and your name will be published in the paper.
Scarcity	A potential customer is told that an item will be at a certain price for a limited time, or that there is a limited supply.	On "Black Friday" a big box store offers TVs at half price but only until 10 a.m.

Conclusion

Persuaders have a large and varied bag of tricks. Each persuasion technique can affect behavior or attitude when used carefully and correctly.

Summary

Foot-in-the-Door

With the foot-in-the-door technique persuaders make small requests and then a larger, target request. Compliance with the larger request is higher when an initial request is accepted than if no initial request is made.

Low-Ball

Seemingly low-cost requests grow with the low-ball technique. For the low-ball technique the target request is made and accepted because it seems reasonable. Only later are additional costs revealed.

Legitimization-of-Paltry-Favors

When small favors are legitimized, larger favors may follow with the legitimization-of-paltry-favors technique. The small favors, like a penny, while legitimized, are not the true target. Persuaders hope for larger favors, such as several dollars.

Reciprocity

Small gifts may provide large returns with reciprocity. When given a gift we feel compelled to give something in return. Persuaders use this natural tendency by providing us with a small gift, in the hope of a large return on their investment.

Door-in-the-Face

Large requests followed by persuasion are hallmarks of the door-in-the-face technique and the that's-not-all technique. When large requests are refused and then a smaller target request is offered, compliance with the second request is higher; this is the door-in-the-face technique.

That's-Not-All

With the that's-not-all technique, a large request that might be refused may be accepted if additional things are added to it before the target of the request can refuse.

Scarcity

Techniques involving scarcity stress that products or options may be available in limited quantities or for a limited time so that the products will receive special consideration. Feeling our freedom threatened, we respond by buying the product or taking the option provided by the persuader.

Critical Thinking Questions

1. Look through a magazine or your junk mail. What persuasion techniques seem to be made in those communications?
2. In watching commercials or visiting a store, have you noticed use of these techniques?
3. How might you use techniques involving large requests, the door-in-the-face technique, or the that's-not-all technique, in an situation where you are attempting to persuade another person?
4. How might you arm yourself against falling victim to these techniques?

Key Terms

Door-in-the-face technique	Low-ball technique	Scarcity technique
Foot-in-the-door technique	Reactance	That's-not-all technique
Legitimization-of-paltry-favors technique	Reciprocity technique	

Expanding Your Knowledge: Links to Additional Material

Influence by Cialdini

Persuasion researcher Robert Cialdini has spent decades studying influence. His books are very accessible and may be particularly interesting if you are planning to work in business or sales. His books are titled *Influence: Science and Practice*, *Influence: The Psychology of Persuasion*, and *Yes!: 50 Scientifically Proven Ways to Be Persuasive*.

Cialdini's website: http://www.influenceatwork.com/.

An interview with Cialdini that appeared in the American Psychological Association's magazine the *Monitor*: http://www.apa.org/monitor/2011/02/persuasion.aspx.

Persuasion Techniques

For broad information on persuasion, see the Changing Minds.org website at http://changingminds.org/techniques/techniques.htm. The techniques described include everything from body language to hypnotism. To read about specific techniques, click on General Persuasion Techniques and then Sequential Requests. The Sequential Requests page provides descriptions and examples for several of the techniques discussed in the text, as well as some that may be new to you.

Door-in-the-Face Video

A short video involving speech-to-text technology describes door-in-the-face in an amusing way. The two cartoon characters, and a laugh track, demonstrate and then discuss the technique, differentiating it from foot-in-the-door. View the video at http://www.youtube.com/watch?v=79cYfK1KTi0.

Jonestown

The People's Temple, led by Jim Jones, was a cult that became famous for the mass suicide of its members in Jonestown, a settlement the group made in Guyana. Over 900 members died. A PBS documentary called *Jonestown: Life and Death of Peoples Temple* describes the cult from its beginnings, with interviews from former members, others who encountered the cult, and archival recordings and images. Jones used a variety of persuasive techniques to encourage members to join his group and to stay. Watch the documentary about Jonestown and consider how persuasion techniques were used.

PBS site: http://www.pbs.org/wgbh/americanexperience/films/jonestown/.

Watch the documentary (not great image quality) at http://topdocumentaryfilms.com/jonestown-the-life-and-death-of-peoples-temple/.

To learn more about Jonestown, check out the article at http://www.trutv.com/library/crime/notorious_murders/mass/jonestown/index_1.html, and explore the Department of Religious Studies at San Diego State University's Jonestown collection at http://jonestown.sdsu.edu/.

9 | Persuasion by a Group: Conformity

Learning Objectives

By the end of the chapter you should be able to:

- Explain Solomon Asch's study of conformity
- Differentiate injunctive norms from descriptive norms
- Differentiate normative influence from informational influence
- Describe how conformity may result in either acceptance or compliance
- Explain the power of minorities

Chapter Outline

9.1 Conformity

You have been invited to be a participant in a research study. When you show up you find that seven other participants have already arrived. All of you are seated around a table and are asked to be part of a study that, at least by appearances, is investigating visual perception. You are shown a line, called the stimulus line, and are asked which of three other lines the stimulus line matches. This looks to be a simple task; you expect to be a little bored. For the first couple of rounds the study goes as expected, each person around the table choosing the line that obviously matches the stimulus line. Then something odd happens. The first person chooses the wrong line. You are surprised; the line he chose is obviously not the right one. You wait for the second person to choose the right line. But she agrees with the first person. The third and fourth also agree. The fifth person chooses the same wrong line and then the sixth. Finally, it is your turn. You need to decide whether to go along with the group, a group that is unanimous, or trust your eyes and choose what you perceive is the right line. What do you do?

This scenario was faced by participants in Solomon Asch's (1958) study of conformity. **Conformity** means going along with a group in actions or beliefs. The study was designed to pit individuals against a unanimous group, to see whether people would go along with the group or stick with what their eyes were telling them was right. In this study, one third of judgments made by participants went along with the majority opinion. Looking at how likely individual participants were to conform, Asch found that one quarter of all participants never went along with the majority. On the other side, one third of participants conformed 50% of the time or more. The rest of the participants showed at least occasional conformity. Altogether, three quarters of participants conformed to the group judgment at least once. See Figures 9.1 and 9.2 for more on the specific test Asch used and the results.

Participants who did not go along with the group were not unaffected by the fact that their judgments were going against the group. Some seemed confused or hesitant in their answers, but persevered anyway. Even those who were more certain of their judgments were chagrined at their own deviance. Of those who went along with the group, some thought that the answers that they and the group were giving were wrong, but nevertheless went along with the group. Others came to believe that the group was right.

What would you do if you were part of the described experiment? Would you point out that everyone else is wrong?

Asch followed up his original study with variations. He varied the size of the group. He found that a unanimous group of one or two others was not as persuasive as three, but there were only minimal gains after adding the third person. He also

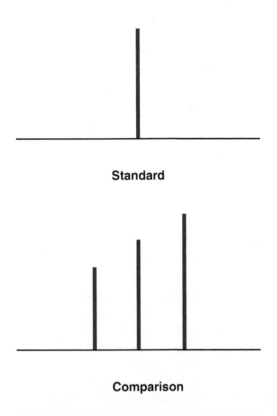

Standard

Comparison

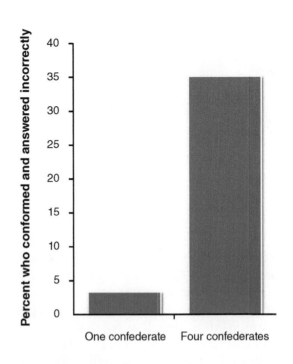

Figure 9.1

Asch used this visual perception test. Participants were asked which comparison line was the same length as the standard line. The participants were unknowingly mixed with confederates. The confederates purposefully agreed on the wrong answer. Asch measured how many participants agreed with the confederates (even though they were wrong) and how many did not.

Figure 9.2

When participants were grouped with a single confederate in Asch's study, they were generally as accurate as if they had been alone. When they were grouped with four confederates, they agreed with the incorrect confederates more than 30% of the time.

had a variation in which another person in the group gave an accurate judgment. The presence of another person who went against the group and gave the right answer decreased conformity. In other words, even when it goes against the majority opinion, having one other person around who agrees with us allows us to express what we believe is right.

Conformity occurs in all cultures, although rates may be slightly different. In independent cultures we generally find less conformity than in interdependent cultures (Bond & Smith, 1996). One caveat to this is the rates of conformity found by researchers in Japan. In one study, rates of conformity were lower in Japan than in the United States, a surprising finding given that Japanese culture is more interdependent than U.S. culture (Frager, 1970). Later researchers found that in Japan when the group was made up of friends, conformity was much higher (Williams & Sogon, 1984). Conformity has declined slightly since Asch did his study in the early 1950s; conformity is somewhat less likely now than it was in Asch's time (Bond & Smith, 1996).

If recycling is a norm in your neighborhood, you might be more likely to recycle, too.

© Sunsetman, 2013. Used under license from Shutterstock, Inc.

Most of the time in our lives we are not sitting in a room with seven other people deciding on the length of lines, so what the group is doing is not always clear. However, we develop ideas about what the collective is thinking or doing. For example, you might believe that the majority of people brush their teeth at least twice a day and that most people are against removing educational services for children with disabilities. These beliefs about what the group is thinking or doing are called **norms**.

Two types of norms may influence our behavior. Norms for what is approved or disapproved of are called **injunctive norms**. Norms describing what most people do are **descriptive norms** (Cialdini, Kallgren, & Reno, 1991). Sometimes these two types of norms are in conflict; for example, a high school student may believe that the majority of people are not in favor of underage drinking (injunctive norm) but also believe that the majority of teens engage in underage drinking (descriptive norm). Often the two are similar. For example, most people agree that we should not steal from one another (injunctive norm) and that most people do not steal (descriptive norm). We can also be wrong about one or both of these norms. The high school student may be right that most people disapprove of underage drinking but wrong that most students engage in it (Borsari & Carey, 2003).

One place we get information about norms is the environment itself. For example, if you are in a public place and see trash all around, the descriptive norm the environment is providing is that everyone litters. This may lead you to litter as well (Cialdini, Reno, & Kallgren, 1990). If the injunctive norm against littering were more prominent, for example if there were signs asking you not to litter and easily accessible trash cans were available, you may not litter (Cialdini et al., 1990; Reno, Cialdini, & Kallgren, 1993). Norms that come from the environment will differ from place to place and culture to culture.

Telling people about descriptive norms can be helpful in encouraging positive behaviors. In a study of energy consumption, households that used more than the average amount of energy reduced energy consumption when informed of the descriptive norm. However, households that were below the average for energy consumption actually increased consumption when told about the descriptive norm, creating a boomerang effect. This can be addressed by including the injunctive norm with the descriptive norm. Households that were told they were lower than average in energy consumption (told of the descriptive norm) and then praised for their conservation (indicating an injunctive norm) maintained their low rate of energy consumption (Schultz, Nolan, Cialdini, Goldstein, & Griskevicius, 2007).

General descriptive norms about positive behaviors are helpful for encouraging those behaviors, but more specific norms are even more helpful. If you have stayed in a hotel recently you have probably seen a sign about towel reuse. The hotel will replace your towel but, if you want to save water and electricity, you can choose to reuse your towel. Does it matter if you know what others do in this situation? When told that the majority of other guests in the hotel reuse their towels, guests are more likely to reuse their towels.

But this can be strengthened with greater specificity. When told that 75% of people that stayed in their specific room (e.g., Room 201) reused their towels, guests were more likely to reuse their towels than if they were told 75% of people staying in the hotel reused their towels (Goldstein, Cialdini, & Griskevicius, 2008). Greater specificity of a norm leads to greater conformity to that norm.

Social Psychology in Depth: Drinking Norms

Drinking on college campuses is a problem. Around 80% of college students report drinking. Despite a minimum legal drinking age in the United States of 21, almost 60% of students aged 18 to 20 report drinking. Much of this drinking is binge drinking, that is, consuming at least four drinks (for women) or five drinks (for men) in a 2-hour period. Over 40% of college students report binge drinking at least once in a 2-week period (National Institute on Alcohol Abuse and Alcoholism, 2011). Besides alcohol poisoning, such behavior contributes to injuries, assaults, unsafe sex and sexual assault, academic problems, and vandalism (Centers for Disease Control and Prevention, 2010; National Institute on Alcohol Abuse and Alcoholism, 2011).

Alcohol use for college students depends, in part, on perceived injunctive and descriptive norms (Park, Klein, Smith, & Martell, 2009). Approval of drinking is an injunctive norm; the perception of how much drinking is being done is a descriptive norm. Not all norms are created equal. Researchers have found that people closer to a student are more likely to influence that student's behavior. Perceived approval for drinking (injunctive norm) by close friends and parents is more important than the approval for drinking of typical students, even same-sex students (Lee, Geisner, Lewis, Neighbors, & Larimer, 2007; Neighbors et al., 2008). Similarly, students' beliefs about how much their friends drink has more of an impact than the perceived behaviors of others (Cho, 2006; Lee et al., 2007).

Norms involve what we believe others approve of or are doing, but beliefs are not always accurate. In the case of norms about drinking, U.S. and Canadian students overestimate the quantity and frequency of drinking by other students. Along with this, personal alcohol use is more influenced by the inaccurate norm than by the real norm for drinking on campus (Perkins, 2007; Perkins, Haines, & Rice, 2005).

Does correcting these misperceptions reduce drinking? Overall, yes. At schools where the perceived norm is more in line with the lower actual norm, there is less problematic drinking (Perkins et al., 2005). Campaigns to change social norms tend to change perceived norms and bring down problematic drinking behaviors (Perkins et al., 2010). For binge drinkers, the descriptive norms for friends influence behavior more than descriptive campus norms or injunctive norms. Non-binge drinkers were more influenced by campus descriptive norms (Cho, 2006). Unfortunately, interventions with those most at risk, high binge drinkers, can backfire if students perceive the messages as restricting their freedom to do as they like (Jung, Shim, & Mantaro, 2010).

Social norm information can be used to convince people to behave in a more prosocial way. An advertising campaign in Montana targeted at drinking and driving among 21-to-34-year-olds used information about social norms to encourage this age group to reduce drinking and driving and use designated drivers (Perkins, Linkenbach, Lewis, & Neighbors, 2010). In research on college campuses, researchers have found that the norms for friends are more influential on binge drinkers' behavior than campus norms are. Non-binge drinkers were more influenced by campus norms, that is, more influenced by the descriptive norms of the campus than by descriptive norms for friends or injunctive norms (Cho, 2006). Interestingly, in one study, although norms were actually the most influential, individuals rated norms as having the least amount of influence on their behavior (Nolan, Schultz, Cialdini, Goldstein, & Griskevicius, 2008).

9.2 Normative and Informational Influence

Why do we conform? Conformity may occur because we believe that a group has some knowledge we do not. Imagine yourself at the zoo. You walk up to the lion enclosure and notice that a lot of people are over on the right side and no one is on the left. If you want to see the lion, where do you go? Your best bet is to the right, where all the people are. It's likely that no one is on the left because the lion is not over there. The crowd knows something you do not—where the lion is—and so by following the crowd you are more likely to see the lion. When we conform because we believe the crowd knows something, we are experiencing **informational influence** (Castelli, Vanzetto, Sherman, & Luciano, 2001).

Conformity may also occur because we want to be liked and accepted by the group. In high school you might have worn a certain style of clothing or acted in a particular way not because you believed it was the right thing to do but because you wanted to be liked and accepted. When we conform because we want to be liked and accepted by the crowd, we are experiencing **normative influence** (Deutsch & Gerard, 1955).

Because of informational influence, you may want to look over the railing, too—These people may know something you don't.

© Planet5D LLC, 2013. Used under license from Shutterstock, Inc.

These different forms of influence can lead to different types of persuasion. If you believed the group knew information, you would likely act as the group does as well as come to believe as they do. If you were in a theater and suddenly everyone started running for the exits yelling "Fire!," you may follow the crowd, truly believing there is a fire somewhere, even if you have not seen any evidence of it. When we both behave and believe as the group does we have experienced **acceptance** of the social norm. We more often find acceptance in the case of informational influence. On the other hand, if you were in that theater following everyone as they rushed toward the exits but you did not believe there was a fire, you would be acting in a way that goes along with the group norms while privately disagreeing. Such action without belief is called **compliance**. We find more compliance in the case of normative influence.

Advertisers can use conformity to their advantage. By telling us how many people switched their car insurance, an insurance company is suggesting that these other people know something we do not. If everyone else discovered cheaper insurance, perhaps we should join them and switch too; informational influence is at work. Another advertiser might show us a lot of happy people wearing a particular brand of jeans, suggesting that if we want to fit in we should buy and wear these jeans. When we buy what others do to be liked or accepted, we are conforming due to normative influence. There are times when we are more susceptible to conformity pressures. Individuals are more likely to go along with the crowd when they are in a good mood (Tong, Tan, Latheef, Selamat, & Tan, 2008) and are more involved with the topic at hand (Huang & Min, 2007).

9.3 Minority Influence

So far it in this chapter it has appeared that norms have a great deal of influence and that the individual is likely to go along with what everyone else is doing. But individuals have power too. In the 1957 film *12 Angry Men*, one juror brings the other 11 jurors over to his side of thinking. Although at the beginning of the film he is the only one who believes in the innocence of the accused, at the end they all believe the young man accused of the crime is not guilty.

When an individual goes against the majority, that action can influence the majority. The majority is more likely to find a minority viewpoint persuasive if the minority viewpoint is distinct and the position is held consistently. When a minority holds one point of difference from the group but agrees with the majority on other points, this creates **distinctiveness**. If a friend believes as you and others do on all aspects of school reform except the use of student achievement for teacher evaluation, you might be more willing to hear out that friend and be convinced by his arguments (Bohner, Frank, & Erb, 1998). Consistently held positions are also more persuasive. If your friend waivered in his beliefs about teacher evaluations, you would be less willing to hear his arguments (Moscovici & Lage, 1976). Minorities can also become more persuasive when there are defections from the majority. If your friend were to convince someone who used to agree with you over to his line of thinking, you would be more likely to also change your opinion (Clark, 2001)

Whether or not minorities convince the majority of their beliefs, minorities do create greater creativity and complexity in the thinking of the majority (Legrenzi, Butera, Mugny, & Perez, 1991; Nemeth, Mayseless, Sherman, & Brown, 1990). When minorities do change the opinion of the majority, that change tends to be more stable and more resistant to change (Martin, Hewstone, & Martin, 2008). Minorities perform a service for the majority, even if they do not convince anyone in the majority over to their way of thinking.

Having a group move from agreeing with you on an issue to disagreeing with you is an unsettling experience. Individuals who began in the majority and maintain their opinion as the rest of the group goes over to the minority opinion tend to have hostile feelings toward the group and expect negative future interaction. On the other hand, those who began in the minority and have a group adopt their opinion tend to like the group more and expect positive interactions with the group in the future (Prislin, Limbert, & Bauer, 2000).

Conclusion

Conformity affects our everyday behavior. We might follow what everyone else is doing or what we think others would like us to do; we might follow because the crowd evidently knows something we do not know or because we want acceptance from the crowd. But minorities can also influence behavior, particularly when they maintain a consistent, distinctive position.

Summary

Conformity

When we do as others do we are conforming to the behavior of the group. At times our conformity is due to what we believe others want us to do. In this instance we are influenced by injunctive norms. Descriptive norms refer to what most people do, not necessarily what most people approve of.

Normative and Informational Influence

When we conform we may do so to be liked or accepted by the group. Normative influence produces this type of conformity. When we conform to be liked or accepted we may act as others do without believing that action is right; we show compliance to the social norm. Informational influence brings about conformity because we believe the group knows something we do not. At such times we may both act and believe as the group does, showing acceptance of the social norm.

Minority Influence

Majorities are powerful, but minorities can have an influence too. Minorities with distinctive positions, that are consistent in their position, and that gain defections from the majority are most persuasive.

Critical Thinking Questions

1. Have you ever been in a situation where you changed your behavior, or observed others changing their behavior, due to conformity? What was that situation like?
2. In your own life, where might you have seen injunctive norms and descriptive norms?
3. How might knowledge of the difference between normative and informational influence help you in your everyday life?
4. If you held a minority opinion in a group and wanted to convince the rest of the group to join you in that opinion, what might you do to convince them?

Key Terms

Acceptance	Descriptive norms	Injunctive norms
Compliance	Distinctiveness	Normative influence
Conformity	Informational influence	Norms

Expanding Your Knowledge: Links to Additional Material

Demonstration of Asch's Research

A number of videos show reenactments of Asch's conformity study. To get a sense of how the study was done, watch one or more of the videos accessed through the links below. The first is a reenactment of Asch's study by Pratkanis, to see if individuals today would conform. He found results similar to Asch. The second and third are older clips, but still clearly show Asch's paradigm. The third clip provides discussion on why participants make the decisions they made and some variations on Asch's original study.

Videos: http://www.youtube.com/watch?v=-qlJqR4GmKw; http://www.youtube.com/watch?v=iRh5qy09nNw; http://www.youtube.com/watch?v=TYIh4MkcfJA.

Music and Conformity

Why do people like particular songs or artists? Is it the song, or something else? Research suggests that conformity has a great deal of influence on our preferences. In an online study involving more than 14,000 mostly teen participants, researchers allowed participants to listen to songs from unknown artists and download them. While listening to the songs, participants were shown the name of the artist and the song title; some of the participants were also shown how many others had downloaded the song. Information about the preferences of peers affected the choices of the teens. Songs that others appeared to like were downloaded more frequently; songs that were apparently liked by few others were chosen more rarely. To see a *Scientific American* story on this research, visit http://www.scientificamerican.com/article.cfm?id=hit-songs-unpredictable-t.

Conformity and Cheating

Others do not have a uniform effect on our behavior. In a study of cheating behavior, researchers asked participants to engage in a task that, without cheating, was impossible to do well. When another participant who appeared to be like them and clearly cheated was in the room, participants were more likely to cheat than if that other participant appeared to be from a rival school. Participants were most likely to cheat when someone like them also cheated. With the presence of a rival, cheating was almost eliminated. Read more about the study at http://scienceblogs.com/cognitivedaily/2009/09/were_more_likely_to_behave_eth.php.

Changing Social Practices

Practices within a particular culture have their origin and support in a number of places, but one important place is clearly conformity. When a cultural practice harms individuals, how might that society change the practice? An article in the *New York Times*, http://www.nytimes.com/2010/10/24/magazine/24FOB-Footbinding-t.html?_r=1, describes how the Chinese practice of foot binding faded away, in some parts of the country within one generation.

Minority Influence

The post at http://www.simplypsychology.org/minority-influence.html offers a discussion of Moscovici's work on minority influence. The post describes how minorities can change what the majority believes and the factors related to minority influence.

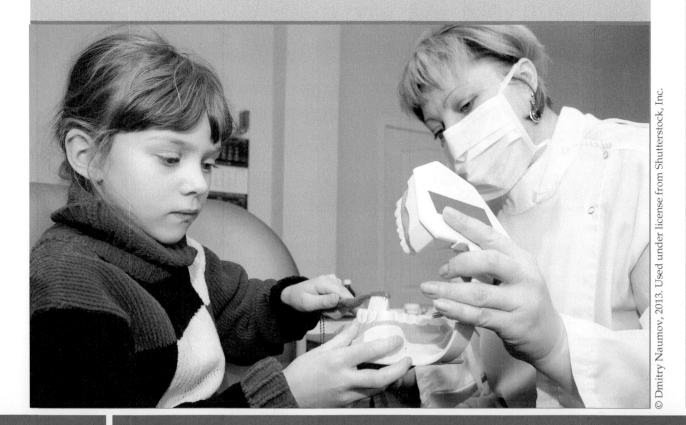

10 | Persuasion by an Individual: Obedience

Learning Objectives

By the end of the chapter you should be able to:

- Describe Milgram's study of obedience
- Explain factors that make obedience more or less likely to occur
- Describe the ethical issues with Milgram's study and Milgram's response
- Describe how obedience can be used to persuade
- Define leadership
- Differentiate the three main types of leadership

10.1 Obedience to Authority

It began like many other research studies. Having answered a newspaper advertisement asking for research participants, participants entered the research laboratory and were told they were going to be part of a study of performance and punishment. They met another participant and were told they would each be taking on a role, the role of teacher or the role of learner. They chose these roles randomly, from little slips of paper in a hat. The learner was brought to a separate room. In the initial study all the participants were male. Electrodes were connected to the learner's arm and he was strapped to a chair. He was told, in the hearing of the teacher, that the shocks would be painful but they would cause no permanent damage. The teacher returned with the experimenter to the other room and was told he would be teaching the learner a series of words, using electrical shocks to punish the learner for wrong answers.

As the teacher and learner worked through the word list, the teacher increased the shock level by 15 volts for every wrong answer, as instructed by the experimenter. At first the

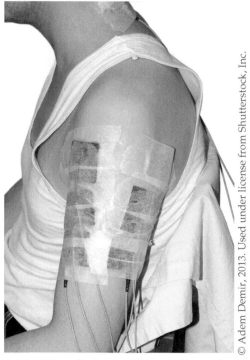

experiment was uneventful, but at 75 volts the learner uttered an "Ugh!" after the shock. After several more of these sorts of verbalizations from the learner at the 150-volt level the learner said "Ugh! Experimenter! That's all. Get me out of here. I told you I had heart trouble. My heart's starting to bother me now. Get me out of here please. My heart's starting to bother me. I refuse to go on. Let me out" (Milgram, 1974, p. 56). When the teacher asked the experimenter what to do, the experimenter replied that he should go on. After that, if the teacher continued the learner protested until the 330-volt level. (See Table 10.1 for a summary of protests.) After the 330-volt level the learner fell silent, not providing any further protests, but also not answering any questions. The highest shock level possible was 450, a level denoted with XXX, past the denotation of Danger: Severe Shock.

In the described experiment, electrodes attached to the learner's arm would supposedly shock the learner whenever he got the answer wrong.

© Adem Demir, 2013. Used under license from Shutterstock, Inc.

Before the study began, psychology undergraduates, adults, and psychiatrists were asked to predict how far on the shock generator the teachers would go. They predicted that only 1 in 1,000 would go all the way to the end of the shock

Social Psychology in Depth: Bad Apples or Vinegar Barrels?

If only there were evil people somewhere insidiously committing evil deeds, and it were necessary only to separate them from the rest of us and destroy them. But the line dividing good and evil cuts through the heart of every human being. And who is willing to destroy a piece of his own heart?

—Alexander Solzhenitsyn, *The Gulag Archipelago* (1973)

When we hear about some of the bad things that happen in our world, we often describe the individuals doing those things as bad people. Though that may be true for some, prominent psychologist Philip Zimbardo argues we apply such terms too liberally and fail to recognize the capacity for evil that we all hold, given the right set of circumstances (Zimbardo, 2004; 2008).

Take, for example, the Abu Ghraib prisoner-abuse scandal. In 2004 pictures began to emerge of U.S. prison guards (Army reservists) at the Abu Ghraib prison in Iraq abusing the Iraqi prisoners. The images were graphic. Prisoners were shown naked, in humiliating poses, on leashes, being threatened by dogs. Our initial instinct is to say the guards were bad people, bad apples who should never have been allowed into the Army (Shermer, 2007). In making such a conclusion we make a fundamental attribution error, ignoring situational factors and blaming dispositional factors for behavior.

Milgram's experiment shows us how powerful situational factors can be. Normal, ordinary Americans were willing to inflict great harm on another person simply because of the orders of a man in a white lab coat. If such behavior can be elicited in a relatively short period in a largely innocuous psychology laboratory situation, might even more brutal behavior be expected in over a longer period in a frightening and unfamiliar situation?

Despite focusing on the situation in explaining evil events, Zimbardo does not advocate excusing bad behavior. Understanding the situation that brought about the behavior does not condone it. Those who do bad things should be punished for what they have done. But without some attention to the situation, more people will engage in the behaviors, creating more pain and suffering in the world.

Zimbardo (2004) writes: "'While a few bad apples might spoil the barrel (filled with good fruit/people), a barrel filled with vinegar will *always* transform sweet cucumbers into sour pickles—regardless of the best intentions, resilience, and genetic nature of those cucumbers.' So, does it make more sense to spend our resources on attempts to identify, isolate, and destroy the few bad apples or to learn how vinegar works so that we can teach cucumbers how to avoid undesirable vinegar barrels?" (p. 47).

generator, with about 4% even making it to the 300-volt level (Milgram, 1974). In the study, 62.5% of the participants (25/40) went to the end. (See Table 10.1 for a breakdown of obedience.) Many teachers protested along the way, showing signs of extreme stress, but continued to the end. What the participants did not know was that the learner was not getting any electrical shocks; he was working with the experimenter, his "random" assignment as learner

Table 10.1 Obedience and Learner Protests in Milgram's Obedience Experiment		
Volts	**Percentage Obeying Orders to Continue (40 total participants)**	**Learner's Protest**
Slight Shock		
15, 30, 45, 60	100%	
Moderate Shock		
75, 90, 105	100%	Ugh!
120	100%	Ugh! Hey this really hurts.
Strong Shock		
135	97.5% 1 participant refuses to continue	Ugh!
150	85% 5 more refuse to continue	Ugh!!! Experimenter! That's all. Let me out of here. I told you I had heart trouble. My heart's starting to bother me now. Get me out of here, please. My heart's starting to bother me. I refuse to go on. Let me out.
165	82.5% 1 more refuses to continue	Ugh! Let me out!
180	80% 1 more refuses to continue	Ugh! I can't stand the pain. Let me out of here!
Very Strong Shock		
195	80%	Ugh. Let me out of here. Let me out of here. My heart's bothering me. Let me out of here! You have no right to keep me here! Let me out! Let me out of here! Let me out!! Let me out of here! My heart's bothering me. Let me out! Let me out!
210	80%	Ugh! Experimenter! Get me out of here. I've had enough. I won't be in the experiment any more.
Intense Shock		
225, 240	80%	Ugh!
255	80%	Ugh! Get me out of here.
270	80%	Ugh! (Scream) Let me out of here. Let me out of here. Let me out of here. Let me out. Do you hear? Let me out of here.
285	77.5% 1 more refuses to continue	Ugh! (Scream)
300	75% 1 more refuses to continue	Ugh! (Scream) I absolutely refuse to answer. Get me out of here. You can't hold me here. Get me out. Get me out of here.

Volts	Percentage Obeying Orders to Continue (40 total participants)	Learner's Protest
Extreme Intensity Shock		
315	67.5% 3 more refuse to continue	Ugh! (Scream) I absolutely refuse to answer. I'm no longer part of this experiment.
330	67.5%	Ugh! (Scream) Let me out of here. Let me out of here. My heart's bothering me. Let me out. I tell you. Let me out of here. Let me out of here. You have no right to hold me here. Let me out! Let me out! Let me out of here! Let me out!
345	67.5%	No more protests or answers from participant.
360	62.5% 1 more refuses to continue	
Danger: Severe Shock		
375, 390, 405, 420	62.5%	
XXX		
435, 450	62.5%	

Singular tabular adaptation of table (p. 35) and text (pp. 56–57) from *Obedience to Authority: An Experimental View* by Stanley Milgram. Copyright © 1974 by Stanley Milgram. Used by permission of HarperCollins Publishers.

was rigged, and his verbalizations throughout the study were recordings. The study was designed to investigate obedience, and the primary interest of the researcher was whether the participant (the teacher) would obey even when it meant harming another person.

Many found these findings surprising, even Stanley Milgram, the researcher (Milgram, 1963). Results of this study suggest that people are willing to harm another person if told to do so by an authority. They may protest, express disapproval, and ask the authority figure to let them stop, but when the authority figure says they should continue, they will. Milgram found greater obedience than anyone expected.

Milgram undertook his study in part to try to better understand the events that occurred in Nazi Germany (Milgram, 1963). Many ordinary people went against their own moral codes and their own ethics and participated in the degradation, imprisonment, and killing of Jewish civilians and other innocent people. Milgram argued that one reason for that behavior was obedience. But could obedience be so powerful? Milgram's study suggests it is. Even given amoral orders to continue to hurt another person, people tend to obey.

Obedience is a deeply engrained tendency, one we are taught from early on in life. And most of the time obedience is a positive behavior. Driving your car through an intersection at a green light, you hope that those stopped for the red light on the cross street will obey traffic laws and stop. Obedience to authority prevents many thefts, murders, and kidnappings. In fact, we may wish for more obedience in regards to violent and nonviolent crimes. But as Milgram showed and history has taught us, there is also a dark side to obedience.

10.2 Factors in Obedience

Milgram (1974) completed a variety of related experiments to get at the factors that contribute to obedience. In one set of studies Milgram varied how far away the learner was from the teacher (the participant). In one study the learner was in another room and had no communication with the teacher, except in providing answers and, at the 300- and 315-volt level, banging on the wall. For this obedience was raised only to 65% (26 out of 40 participants) from 62.5% in the first study. In another study the learner was in the same room as the teacher. In another the learner and teacher were next to one another. In this experiment the learner had to touch a shock plate every time he got an answer wrong. He eventually refused to touch the plate and the teacher had to physically move his hand and force it down on the shock plate. In these studies Milgram found that the closer the learner was to the teacher, the lower the obedience. When the learner was far removed, obedience was very high; well over half of the participants obeyed the experimenter. When the learner was in the same room obedience declined to 40%, and it further declined to 30% when physical contact was required.

In another set of studies the distance between the experimenter (the authority figure) and the teacher was varied. In one study the experimenter provided directions by telephone or through a prerecorded message. When the authority figure was distant, the participants were less likely to obey. The legitimacy of the authority was also varied. Milgram moved the study to an office building in Bridgeport, Connecticut, out of the Yale University laboratory he had been using. Participants believed they were participating in a study for the "Research Associates of Bridgeport" and saw no connection of the study to prestigious Yale University. In this study obedience declined some, from 65% to 48%. Other researchers found similar results with an authority figure without legitimate authority (Mantell, 1971; Rosenhan, 1969). With almost half of participants still obeying an authority figure with very little legitimacy giving an immoral order, the implications are frightening.

© Julie DeGuia, 2013. Used under license from Shutterstock, Inc.

If the authority figure is distant, obedience is less likely.

When others were part of the study, Milgram found that compliant others led to compliant participants and defiant others led to defiant participants. In these studies Milgram had confederates who appeared to be other participants do a variety of teaching tasks. In one study the participant watched as a confederate gave shocks. In this study 90% of participants were fully obedient. In another study two confederates and one participant were assigned to give shocks. At the 150-volt level, when the learner makes his first long protest (see Table 10.1), the confederate giving the shocks

166

refused to continue. The second confederate was then given the job of giving shocks. At the 210-volt level this second confederate joined in the protest, getting up from his chair by the shock generator and refusing to continue the study. At that point the actual participant was asked to continue the study on his own. When the two other teachers (the confederates) quit, obedience declined significantly, to 27.5% (Milgram, 1965).

Would we harm those we know well? In one of Milgram's studies, participants brought a friend along. The friend was enlisted as the experimenter's helper and fulfilled the role of learner, including giving all the protests the confederate learner had offered in the original study. The researchers found much lower obedience in this condition. Only 15% (3 out of 20) of participants were willing to go all the way to the end of the shock generator when their friend protested (Rochat & Modigliani, 1997).

Unlike many studies in social psychology, Milgram used community members for his research, not college undergraduates. His participants were from a variety of education levels, from not completing high school to having obtained doctoral degrees, and varied from age 20 to age 50. Milgram's original studies used only male participants, thus the use of male pronouns above. When Milgram expanded his study to include women, he found no appreciable differences between men and women, nor have later replications (Shanab & Yahya, 1977). Age does not seem to matter either. Children aged 6 to 16 years were about as obedient in a replication of Milgram's study, with no differences based on age (Shanab & Yahya, 1977).

Are we as obedient today as we were in the 1960s? Because of ethical issues the most recent research on obedience stopped after the 150-volt level, the level that seemed to be the decision point for most of Milgram's participants (Packer, 2008). When the learner provided his first longer protest, most of those who would drop out did. In a recent follow-up study, Burger (2009) found roughly the same rate of obedience as Milgram found. Seventy percent of participants were obedient to the 150-volt level. Similar findings to Milgram's were found when the study was done in an immersive video environment (Dambrun & Valentine, 2010). An immersive video environment is one in which the user is surrounded by the sights and sounds of a virtual environment, often with projections on walls within sight and the ability to manipulate objects within the virtual environment (Loomis, Blascovich, & Beall, 1999). Culture can also contribute to obedience. In the United States, independence is a dominant value and parents tend to pass on those values to children through childrearing. With social harmony a high value in interdependent cultures like that found in China, children are socialized to be obedient (Xiao, 1999). There are variations in the value of obedience within a culture. Researchers find that middle-class parents in the United States are more likely to be concerned with emphasizing independence with their children while working-class parents tend to focus more on obedience (Gecas & Nye, 1974; Xiao, 2000). In cultures where authority is highly valued, we are more likely to see the kind of destructive obedience that Milgram studied and that we find in genocide and other horrible human actions (Staub, 1999).

10.3 Ethics of Obedience Research

The participants in Milgram's studies underwent an experience that was very stressful. According to an observer of the study:

I observed a mature and initially poised businessman enter the laboratory smiling and confident. Within 20 minutes he was reduced to a twitching, stuttering wreck, who was rapidly approaching a point of nervous collapse. He constantly pulled on his earlobe, and twisted his hands. At one point he pushed his fist into his forehead and muttered: "Oh God, let's stop it." And yet he continued to respond to every word of the experimenter, and obeyed to the end (Milgram, 1963, p. 377).

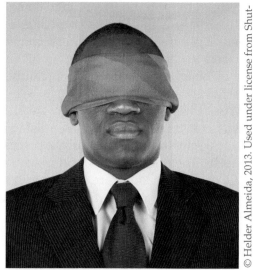

Is it ethical to put unsuspecting people into stressful situations for experiments?

Entering into an experimental situation, participants in research put themselves into the hands of the experimenter. After Milgram's study other researchers asked if placing unsuspecting people into these kinds of situations was ethical. The main problems identified were that participants had a very stressful experience and that they might learn something about themselves they would need to live with after the study ended, all within a situation based on trust (Baumrind, 1964).

Milgram (1964) responded to these criticisms by noting that the findings of his studies and the reaction of the participants was unexpected. When he asked psychologists and others what to expect, they did not believe participants would go all the way to the end of the shock generator and be as obedient as they were. At the end of the experimental session the experimenter reunited the confederate with the participant so the participant could see that he was unharmed in any way. The experimenter was supportive of whatever decision the participant made in terms of obedience.

The study involved a great deal of deception. The participants were lied to about the purpose of the study, about the complicity of the other participant, and about what was actually happening. Critics of the study argued that this type of deception may have an impact on the participants themselves, as they feel duped by the researcher. But deception could also have an impact on the general public's view of psychological research. When researchers use deception a great deal, the public may become suspicious of all research studies and wary of participating in research, even research that does not in fact involve deception. Milgram (1974) contacted participants after their participant to ask how they felt about the study. The vast majority said they were glad or very glad to have been part of the study (83.7%). Only 1.3% of the participants reported being sorry or very sorry to have participated. Almost three fourths of participants reported learning something of personal importance.

10.4 Obedience and Persuasion

Milgram's study shows us that authorities influence our behavior. Even when an action ordered by an authority will cause another person pain or harm, we often still obey. An example of this sort of behavior outside of the laboratory setting comes from a study of nurses in a hospital. An unfamiliar physician called nurses on duty at the hospital and asked them to administer what they would have known to be an unsafe level of a drug to a patient. Before being intercepted on their way to give the drug, 95% of the nurses

We are often more likely to take directions from someone in uniform.

obeyed (Hofling, Brotzman, Dalrymple, Graves, & Pierce, 1966). The trappings of authority can lead us to be obedient. If a security guard asked you to stand on the other side of a bus stop sign, would you do it? Even though the request was really not part of the security guard's domain, most people asked by a uniformed person to do a simple act did so (Bickman, 1974).

Advertisers know of these tendencies and put a person in a white lab coat on television touting a drug or toothpaste. On an infomercial you are likely to see someone claiming to be a fitness expert selling exercise equipment. Scammers know about the tendency to obey and arrive at one's door or in one's e-mail inbox claiming some authority. We should listen to our doctors, the police, and the people at our bank about health, safety, and money, so the cons we are likely to fall for rely on the tendencies that overall make us healthier, safer, and wealthier.

We can be taught to resist such appeals. Students who were taught to check on whether the authority in an advertisement was a legitimate authority were less likely to be persuaded by illegitimate authorities (Sagarin, Cialdini, Rice, & Serna, 2002). Unfortunately we do not do as good of a job at rejecting illegitimate authority as we could. People generally believe they are less vulnerable than others to be persuaded by an illegitimate authority and therefore are less likely to notice and reject such messages (Perloff, 1999).

10.5 Leadership

Leadership is an important topic when thinking about obedience. **Leadership** involves influencing a group and its members to contribute to the goals of the group and coordinating and guiding those efforts (Kaiser, Hogan, & Craig, 2008). If leaders are good leaders who make good decisions, then obedience is appropriate. What makes a good leader? When are leaders most effective?

A number of models for describing types of leadership exist. One model offers two main categories of leadership. Leaders can lead by offering an exchange of rewards for effort from followers. This type of leadership is called **transactional leadership**. By contrast, some leaders offer their followers a common purpose and ask that individual interest be put aside so the group can work together toward that goal. This leadership style is called

Leadership is an important factor in obedience.

transformational leadership (Bass, 1985). **Laissez-faire leadership** can also be included in this list. Such leadership is characterized by a hands-off approach, with the leader simply allowing the followers to do what they would like without substantial input from the leader (Yammarino, Spangler, & Bass, 1993).

Transactional leaders focus on contingent rewards and active management. Transactional leaders work out with followers agreements that will satisfy both parties. These contingent rewards are provided once the followers have held up their end of the bargain. This type of leadership may also involve active management, where the leader monitors what the follower is doing to redirect, if needed, and enforce the rules that have been agreed upon. Transactional leaders do not always actively manage their followers. At times they take a passive management approach, intervening when problems are brought to their attention (Bass, 1997).

Transformational leaders are characterized by charisma, inspirational motivation, intellectual stimulation, and individualized consideration. Charisma, in this context, means influence toward an ideal that can be accomplished through the leader displaying conviction about the goal, presenting and taking stands on important issues, and emphasizing trust. When leaders clearly articulate a vision, provide encouragement, and show optimism, they display inspirational motivation. Intellectual stimulation within transformational leadership is modeled by leaders in their welcoming of new ideas and perspectives. Finally, transformational leaders tend to focus on individual gifts, abilities, and needs, offering individual consideration for followers (Bass, 1997). Along with these qualities, transformational leaders are generally self-confident and are able to handle pressure and uncertainty well. Optimistic and self-determined, such leaders are able to cast a vision for their followers (van Eeden, Cilliers, & van Deventer, 2008).

Do leaders matter? Success of a leader can be defined in a variety of ways. Successful leaders might be the ones who have helped their followers reach a goal (Kaiser & Hogan, 2007). Even without reaching or moving toward obtaining a goal, leaders might be defined as successful if their group is satisfied or motivated or, simply, if followers rate the leader as successful (e.g., Tsui, 1984). Looking from a strict monetary perspective, 14% of the variance in the financial results of a business are due to the leadership provided by the CEO (Joyce, Nohria, & Robertson, 2003). Although we often think of transformational leaders as better leaders, leading, as they do, by inspiring followers, generally there are no overall differences in effectiveness of transformational versus transactional leaders (Judge & Piccolo, 2004).

Conclusion

Overall people tend to be obedient, a positive tendency that allows for a well-ordered and safe society. But obedience is often still high even when it involves harming others, as found in Stanley Milgram's famous study of obedience. Obedience is higher when the authority figure is close, the victim is distant, and others are also obeying. Milgram's studies were attacked for being unethical, as his participants were put under extreme stress within a context where trust is important.

Summary

Obedience to Authority

Stanley Milgram completed a study of obedience where participants were asked to follow the orders of an experimenter despite the protests of a victim. In his study 62.5% of participants were fully obedient.

Factors in Obedience

When Milgram varied the distance of the authority figure from the participant, obedience declined as the authority figure's presence was less prominent. The victim's presence led to a decrease in obedience. When the legitimacy of the authority figure was lessened, obedience was lower, though still quite high. Individuals were found to be less willing to follow an authority to harm a friend, although obedience in this circumstance was still 15%. More recent research has shown that obedience has not declined significantly.

Ethics of Obedience Research

Milgram's study of obedience placed participants in a situation of great stress in an environment of trust. Milgram's follow-ups with his participants indicated that most were happy to have participated and had no long-term ill effects from the study.

Obedience and Persuasion

Advertisers and others use authority, and the trappings of authority, to persuade us to buy or do what they would like us to buy or do.

Leadership

Leadership styles may involve a transaction of rewards for effort, known as transactional leadership, or inspiration toward a common goal and purpose, known as transformational leadership. Laissez-faire leadership involves leadership without substantial input from the leader.

Critical Thinking Questions

1. Milgram investigated the closeness and legitimacy of the authority figure, the closeness to and identity of the victim, and the actions of others in relation to degree of obedience. What other factors might influence obedience?
2. If you had been part of Milgram's study of obedience, what do you think you would have done?
3. What do you think about the ethics of Milgram's studies of obedience? Do you think they should have been done, or are the ethical issues too great?
4. Think of a time when you have been a follower. How would you characterize the leader of your group?
5. What effect have different styles of leadership had on your behavior as a member of a group?

Key Terms

Laissez-faire leadership   **Transactional leadership**   **Transformational leadership**

Leadership

Expanding Your Knowledge: Links to Additional Material

Milgram's Journey

Where did Milgram's ideas for studying obedience come from? How did he come up with his research paradigm? A short and interesting article by Nestar Russell investigates Milgram's work and traces its development. To read the article complete with figures and sketches from Milgram's original study, click on "View the complete article as a PDF document" at http://www.thepsychologist.org.uk/archive/archive_home.cfm?volumeI=23&editionID=192&ArticleID=1729.

On the same topic, Blass published an article on the major influences on Milgram. His full-text article can be found at http://www.sfu.ca/cmns/courses/marontate/2009/801/Readings/MilgrimReplication/Blass_FromNewHaventoSantaClara.pdf.

Game Show

In a surprising replication of Milgram's study of obedience, a French television station recruited 80 people to be part of what they believed was a new television game show. The victim appeared to be another contestant, although he was an actor. Contestants were asked to give him electrical shocks when he gots a wrong answer. The contestant was encouraged by the presenter and chants from the audience of "Punishment!" The audience, in this case, was also naïve to the deception. The actor appeared to be in great pain, begged to be let go, and appeared to die, yet over 80% of the contestants gave the maximum shock of 460 volts. With the added element of television cameras and a cheering audience, greater compliance with immoral orders was found than in Milgram's original study. Links to stories on the game show are provided below.

http://www.france24.com/en/20100317-fake-torture-tv-game-show-reveals-willingness-obey# (clip with connections to Milgram's study)

http://news.bbc.co.uk/2/hi/europe/8571929.stm (with brief clip)

http://www.theage.com.au/world/gameshow-electricity-reels-in-the-torturers-20100317-qfkg.html

http://www.time.com/time/arts/article/0,8599,1972981,00.html

Zimbardo on Evil

Phillip Zimbardo described the social psychological factors in destructive behaviors in his book *The Lucifer Effect*. Although obedience is only a part of the explanation, if you are interested in learning more about why people act in ways that hurt others, check out this book.

Zimbardo also wrote two shorter pieces on this topic: a chapter in an edited book titled *The Social Psychology of Good and Evil: Understanding Our Capacity for Kindness and Cruelty* and a short article for the magazine *Eye on Psi Chi*. The book chapter explores what Zimbardo calls a situationist perspective on evil. A full-text copy of the chapter can be found at the second link below. The reading from *Eye on Psi Chi* is very short, only four pages, and includes a short reflection on how we can combat the forces that seem to lead us to evil. The third and fourth link provide access to this reading.

Zimbardo, P. G. (2008). *The Lucifer effect: Understanding how good people turn evil.* New York: Random House. Information on the Lucifer Effect is available at http://www.lucifereffect.org/. Zimbardo, P. G. (2004). A situationist perspective on the psychology of evil: Understanding how good people are transformed into perpetrators. In A. Miller (Ed.) *The social psychology of good and evil: Understanding our capacity for kindness and cruelty* (pp. 21–50). New York: Guilford. Read this book chapter at http://www.zimbardo.com/downloads/2003%20Evil%20Chapter.pdf.

Zimbardo, P. G. (2000). The psychology of evil. *Eye on Psi Chi, 5 (1)*, 16–19. Read this article at http://www.psichi.org/Pubs/Articles/Article_72.aspx or http://www.zimbardo.com/downloads/2000%20Psych.%20of%20Evil,%20Eye%20on%20Psi%20Chi.pdf.

Did Milgram Study Obedience?

In partially replicating Milgram's study, Burger and colleagues (Burger, Girgis, & Manning, 2011) came to question whether the classic study of obedience was really assessing obedience. As described in this chapter, the participants in Burger's study showed about the same rate of obedience as those in Milgram's study. But when Burger and his colleagues examined the participants' responses to the experimenter's prompts, they found that as the prompts became more forceful (moved from "please continue" to "You have no other choice, you must go on"), they became less effective. If, as Burger argues, this was truly obedience then stronger encouragement from the authority figure should result in greater obedience, not less. Read a blog posting on this topic at http://bps-research-digest .blogspot.com/2011/02/milgrams-obedience-studies-not-about.html.

What Was It Like?

Wondering what being a participant in Milgram's study might have been like? Joseph Dimow describes his experience as a Milgram study participant (story available at http:// www.jewishcurrents.org/2004-jan-dimow.htm). Dimow was one of the participants who refused to continue and he describes that experience as well as the debriefing afterward. He reflects on why he might have been in the smaller group of participants who refused to obey the orders of experimenter. A unique and interesting perspective.

Interactionist Perspective on Milgram

Were Milgram's results due to the situation or due to something about the individuals in the study? Blass (1991) questions whether Milgram's article shows as strong a situational impact on behavior as is often attributed to Milgram's work. Blass makes the point that personality does have an important effect on obedience. He suggests that the best understanding of the results of Milgram's study can be gained from an interactionist perspective that takes into account both the situation and the person and how they interact with one another.

Blass, T. (1991). Understanding behavior in the Milgram obedience experiment: The role of personality, situations, and their interactions. *Journal of Personality and Social Psychology, 60*, 398–413. The article can be read at http://www.stanleymilgram.com/pdf/understanding% 20behavoir.pdf.

PART IV | Interacting with Others

© Lorraine Swanson, 2013. Used under license from Shutterstock, Inc.

"I get by with a little help from my friends."

—The Beatles

11 | Aggression

Learning Objectives

By the end of the chapter you should be able to:

- Define aggression and differentiate instrumental aggression, hostile aggression, and violence
- Describe the possible origins of aggression
- Explain whether men or women are more aggressive, what age group shows the most aggression, and how age and gender interact with types of aggression, including relational aggression
- Explain catharsis and whether it works to reduce aggression
- Describe displaced aggression and triggered displaced aggression
- Explain the factors that influence our aggression: frustration, media, weapons, alcohol, and environmental factors

Chapter Outline

11.1 Introduction: At the Train Station

© Stuart Monk, 2013. Used under license from Shutterstock, Inc.

What sort of interactions would you anticipate seeing or hearing in a train station?

Sitting in a train or bus station, airport, or other transportation hub, you have probably had time to observe the people around you. Over in the next waiting area you may notice two children wrestling with one another. In front of you someone hurrying by drops her ticket; a fellow traveler picks it up and runs after her to return it. You eavesdrop on the cell phone conversation the woman sitting near you is having with her husband. In these next modules we will explore some of the interactions you might see and experience while waiting.

11.2 Aggression

As you wait for the train you observe two children wrestling with one another. The man and woman in the corner are yelling at one another and the woman begins to cry. Are these behaviors aggression? **Aggression** is intentionally harming someone who is motivated to avoid that harm. In order to be labeled as aggression the behavior does need to be intentional. The result does not matter as much as the intent. Whether or not the punch connects, the behavior is aggression. If you were swinging your arm around with no intention of hitting someone and accidentally did, your behavior may be careless but it is not aggression. Both the children and the couple appear to satisfy this requirement: Their actions have intention. To be labeled as aggression the behavior must also have the intent of harm. Harm may be relational, such as an insult, or physical, such as a punch. Harm can also differ in whether it is direct, like an insult or a punch, or covert, like gossip or adding poison to someone's drink. The wrestling children might qualify as expressing aggression, if their actions are intended to harm one another and not to relieve the boredom of waiting. The fighting couple is likely showing aggression, as their words seem to be designed to harm each other. For a behavior to be labeled as aggression, the person toward whom the behavior is aimed must be motivated to avoid the harm. A visit to the oral surgeon, for example, may result in pain. But the oral surgeon was not acting aggressively when she took out your wisdom teeth, as you willingly submitted to the surgery.

We might engage in deliberate actions that harm someone else without the action being aggressive. When competing for a job, our getting the job does harm the other candidates, but we were not being aggressive in our actions. The intent of the action was not harm; the intent of this action was employment (Felson, 2002). At times we engage in aggressive acts as a means to an end, not as an end in itself. A bomber pilot who drops a bomb on a terrorist training camp intends to harm individuals there, but the pilot's final goal is to stop terrorist attacks, not cause harm to those particular individuals. Boxers throw punches

Intentionally spreading a hurtful rumor can also be considered aggression.

to win a boxing match, not because of a desire to cause lasting harm on their opponents. When aggression is a means to an end we call it **instrumental aggression**. If one member of the couple in the train station was saying hurtful things in order to bring about a breakup, that would be instrumental aggression. In contrast, at times the harm an aggressive behavior is intended to cause is our goal. A fifth grader who spreads a rumor about an enemy may have hurting that enemy as his or her final goal. This type of aggression is called **hostile aggression** (Baron & Richardson, 1994). Physical aggression that has the potential of severely harming someone is **violence** (Felson, 2002; Krug, Dahlberg, Mercy, Zwi, & Lozano, 2002). A gunshot to the chest is violence, while a slap on the cheek is better described as aggressive behavior.

Origins of Aggression

Where does aggression originate? We find aggressive behavior in a variety of human cultures and find evidence of aggression in the remains of early humans, suggesting that aggression is something that is innate to the person (Buss & Shackelford, 1997). Sigmund Freud, for example, believed that all people were endowed with aggressive energy, called thanatos. Human cultures, he argued, were needed to control this aggressive drive. Today, evolutionary psychologists suggest that humans evolved a tendency toward aggression because aggression provides an evolutionary benefit (Buss & Shackelford, 1997). Inflicting harm on a rival is one way of gaining territory or mates, thus making it advantageous to use some degree of aggression in human relationships.

Although most cultures exhibit some degree of aggression, wide variations exist between cultures and over human history, suggesting that aggression is to some extent affected by the social environment (Bond, 2004; Munroe, Hulefeld, Rodgers, Tomeo, & Yamazaki, 2000). For example, rates of aggression against partners tend to differ depending on the level of gender equality and individualism in a culture. In cultures with greater gender equality and more individualism, violence toward women is lower, although victimization of men tends to be higher in these cultures (Archer, 2006). Overall aggression is an inborn tendency that appears in most cultures and is either increased or decreased by the norms of that culture.

Just as aggression rates among cultures vary, so do rates among individuals. Differences in rates of aggression between individuals are due to a combination of inborn or innate qualities (nature) and the environment (nurture). Some degree of the difference between people in rates of aggression can be traced to genetic differences. Identical twins, who share the same genes, are more similar to one another in rates of aggression than fraternal twins, who share only half of their genes (Hines & Saudino, 2009). But differences between twins with the same genes still exist, suggesting that, in the end, it is neither just genes nor just environment that influence aggression. Individuals whose genes predispose them toward aggression may become more aggressive in an environment that encourages aggression or not show this predisposition in an environment that does not encourage aggression. For example, in one study of adoptees, only 10.5% of the adoptees whose biological and adoptive fathers did not commit a crime committed a crime. These individuals had neither the genetic predisposition toward crime nor the environment to support criminal actions. Those whose environment but not biology included criminality, in other words those whose adoptive father but not biological father committed a crime, did not show much more criminal behavior than the previous group. Only 11.5% committed a crime. When the biological father, but not the adoptive father, committed a crime, 22% of the adoptees committed a crime themselves. Finally, of those individuals whose biological father and adoptive father committed a crime, 36.2% committed a crime (Hutchings & Mednick, 1977). In the end, then, biology is an important factor in aggression. Individuals with inborn tendencies toward aggression are likely to be more aggressive than those who do not have such inborn tendencies. But the environment also contributes to expression of aggression, building on those genetic predispositions.

Gender and Age Differences in Aggression

As you sit at the train station, you hear some kind of aggressive behavior happening behind you. When you turn around, who do you think would be most likely to be the perpetrator? A man or woman? A boy or girl? How old would you expect that person to be? When we look into differences in aggression we find that men show more physical aggression than women. This does not mean that women are never physically aggressive; they simply show less of this type of aggression than men. Women are generally more verbally aggressive than men (Bettencourt & Miller, 1996; Card, Stucky, Sawalani, & Little, 2008; Eagly & Steffen, 1986; Ostrov, 2006). Some of this difference may come from gender roles. Women are expected to be less aggressive than men, and women may therefore show less physical aggression in order to be in line with the expectations for their gender. Such an idea is supported with the finding that when individuals are angered or aggression is instigated, essentially no differences in aggression are found between men and women (Bettencourt & Kernahan, 1997). Given the right situation women can be as aggressive as men.

The most physically aggressive age group is, surprisingly, toddlers. Children begin to use physical aggression in their second year and this aggression decreases as they learn that hitting, kicking, and biting are not socially acceptable behaviors. Because the hit of a 2 year-old is generally not going to do much damage, we

© Cheryl Casey, 2013. Used under license from Shutterstock, Inc.

Toddlers are the most physically aggressive group.

Social Psychology in Depth: Mean Girls

The 2004 film *Mean Girls* follows one teenage girl as she is plunged into an American high school and mentored into meanness by a group of girls called the Plastics (Michaels, Shimkin, & Waters, 2004). When conflict erupts because of a romantic entanglement, the girls engage in a variety of activities to discredit and harm one another. Do high school girls use the tactics shown in this movie to make friends or manipulate situations?

Research on aggression focused for a long time on the types of physical aggression that leave physical traces. Relational aggression, aggression that is focused on the destruction of relationships or social status, has become a more important topic in the last couple of decades (Crick & Grotpeter, 1995). Girls and women tend to show more relational aggression than boys and men, although this gender gap is larger in high school than in elementary school (Crick & Werner, 1998; Kistner et al., 2010; Smith, Rose, & Schwartz-Mette, 2010). Researchers find that girls report being both victims and perpetrators of relational aggression at least once within a year (Reynolds & Repetti, 2010). Around 20% of girls are described as aggressive (Crick & Grotpeter, 1995), although all girls, not just this 20%, may use relational aggression at some point.

The most commonly used and experienced types of relational aggression are talking about people behind their back and intentionally ignoring someone, known as giving that person the silent treatment. The silent treatment is most often motivated by revenge. Spreading rumors about or excluding someone may also be used as a tactic for revenge, although these tactics are also described as ways to become closer to one's friends or have some fun (Reynolds & Repetti, 2010).

Both victims and aggressors report feeling sad, confused, and hurt at the time of the aggression. Aggressors also feel guilty, while victims feel angry and betrayed. Guilt is felt by victims when they perceive the aggression as revenge. Victims feel guiltier when they are receiving the silent treatment than when they are the victim of rumors or exclusion (Reynolds & Repetti, 2010). Those most hurt by the aggression are most likely to cope by becoming passive and using avoidant strategies (Remillard & Lamb, 2005).

Over the long term, relational aggression is related to peer rejection and mental health problems (Crick, 1996; Tomada & Schneider, 1997; Werner & Crick, 1999). Relational aggression has been related to depression (Ellis, Crooks, & Wolfe, 2009), borderline personality, and bulimia (Werner & Crick, 1999).

Relational aggression is used as a weapon. The most common reason for engaging in relational aggression is getting back at the victim of aggression. The next most common is to get closer to one's friends by aggressing against someone one's friends do not like. Victims correctly perceive these reasons. Victims believe they are being punished for something they did to the perpetrator (Reynolds & Repetti, 2010). Fictional though *Mean Girls* may be, research shows that the tactics used in the movie are not at all fiction.

usually do not think about the frequency of physically aggressive behaviors in this age group (Tremblay, 2000). Overall, physical aggression tends to decrease through adolescence, though there is a great deal of variability amongst individuals (Underwood, Beron, & Rosen, 2009). For at least a subset of individuals, aggression increases in adolescence and young adulthood (Loeber & Farrington, 1998; Loeber & Stouthamer-Loeber, 1998).

Relational aggression shows a different developmental trajectory. **Relational aggression is aggression focused on the destruction of relationships or social status through direct actions, reputation attacks, or exclusion** (Crick & Grotpeter, 1995). When a person spreads a rumor designed to damage someone's reputation, excludes someone from a social group, or tells someone they cannot join one's group unless they do a favor, that individual is engaging in relational aggression. Original research on the concept included direct, rather than covert, acts, but much of the subsequent researchers have focused primarily on the nondirect types of aggression, such as spreading rumors or exclusion (Crick & Grotpeter, 1995; Geiger, Zimmer-Gembeck, & Crick, 2004; Tomada & Schneider, 1997). Relational aggression largely begins in the preschool years and rises through childhood. Children learn how to use techniques like ostracism and gossip to harm others and get their way. Girls and women tend to use more relational aggression than men (Crick & Grotpeter, 1995). Relational aggression is common between cultures (Tomada & Schneider, 1997).

High aggression in childhood and adolescence can have negative long-term effects, including increased risk of alcohol and drug abuse, divorce, unemployment, and mental illness (Farrington, 1991; Loeber, Farrington, Stouthamer-Loeber, Moffitt, & Caspi, 1998; McCord, 1983; McCord & McCord, 1960; West & Farrington, 1977). Both physical aggression and relational aggression have negative effects (Crick, 1996).

11.3 Catharsis: The Myth Lives On

Have you ever been told to vent your anger? Do you believe that expressing aggression toward the object of your aggression or some other object will reduce your aggressive urge? If so, you believe in catharsis. **Catharsis** refers to the idea that engaging in aggressive actions reduces aggression. Sigmund Freud believed that verbally venting one's aggressive urges would reduce aggression. He proposed that without the release of emotions, the energy for these emotions would build up inside and cause physical or psychological problems (Breuer & Freud, 1893–1895/1955). People engage in cathartic activities because they believe these will improve their mood or to reduce the likelihood they will express aggression in the future (Bushman, Baumeister, & Phillips, 2001).

The problem with catharsis is that it does not work. In study after study, researchers found that engaging in aggression did not reduce feelings of aggression or the likelihood of acting aggressively in the future (Berkowitz, 1964; Bushman, 2002; Geen & Quanty, 1977; Mallick & McCandless, 1966). In some cases, acting out increased rather than decreased aggression. Believing catharsis works does not make it work. Research participants who read a message convincing them that catharsis was helpful in reducing aggression were not less aggressive after punching a punching bag; in fact, they showed more aggression (Bushman, Baumeister, & Stack, 1999). Acting out aggression, particularly if you are ruminating on the object of that aggression while you are acting out, seems to serve as practice for more aggression.

In acting out aggression, people may direct anger to a punching bag, some other inanimate object, or a person other than the real target. This targeting of aggression toward some other person or entity is **displaced aggression**. If you threw a pencil at the wall rather than hitting your boss when the boss made you angry, you would be displacing your aggression. We displace aggression for a variety of reasons. We might displace aggression if the object of our anger is unavailable. When the bus drives away without you, the garbage can is the only thing left for you to yell at and kick. Other times we displace aggression because it would not be acceptable or advantageous to act aggressively toward the true focus. If your boss made you angry, you may not express it toward him or her for fear of losing your job.

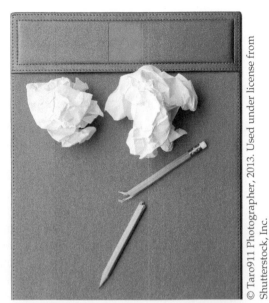

Sometimes the recipient of aggression, like this pencil, is not the true object of anger. Do you think catharsis works?

If you have ever been unreasonably aggressive toward a person who did something minor to annoy you, you may have experienced a type of displaced aggression called **triggered displaced aggression**. With triggered displaced aggression the person you are upset with has done something to bother you, but your reaction to this minor event is really due to the larger event that happened earlier. Here your aggression is triggered by some minor incident and displaced upon the cause of that minor event. In line with research on catharsis theory, when we ruminate on the cause of our aggression, we tend to show more displaced aggression when we are triggered (Bushman, Bonacci, Pedersen, Vasquez, & Miller, 2005).

What should you do if you are feeling aggressive? If you want to lower your aggression, doing nothing is a better idea than venting your anger. Doing something opposite your aggressive urges may be even more helpful. Write a thank-you note to someone, pet the cat, or look at a picture of your family (presuming that it's not your family you're mad at).

11.4 Aggression Cues

A variety of factors may lead to aggression or make aggression in a particular circumstance more likely.

Frustration-Aggression Hypothesis

If you have been delayed in a train or bus station or airport you know what frustration feels like. Early on in the study of aggression, a link was made between frustration and aggression. Originally the authors made the statement that "the occurrence of aggression always presupposes the existence of frustration and, contrariwise, that the existence of frustration always leads to some form of aggression" (Dollard, Miller, Doob, Mowrer, & Sears, 1939, p. 1). **Frustration**, in this context, refers to the blocking of behavior that

© Edward Fielding, 2013. Used under license from Shutterstock, Inc.

Frustration does not always lead to aggression, particularly if it is not because of another person.

would have moved the person toward a particular goal. For example, if you want to get to Atlanta but the plane is having mechanical problems, you are blocked from your goal. Reread the statement about the connection between frustration and aggression and notice the use of the word *always*. The authors quickly realized that the use of terms like *always* would get them into trouble (Miller, Sears, Mowrer, Doob, & Dollard, 1941). While people might respond to frustration with aggressive behavior, a frustrated person does not always do so. That person might respond with a variety of other behaviors. A frustrated 3-year-old might hit his mother in response to his frustration but could also cry, go into another room, or start to whine.

At times frustration does not lead to aggression at all (Buss, 1966). Frustration that comes about because of another person is more likely to lead to aggression than frustration from an outside cause. Attack, rather than frustration, is more likely to lead to aggression (Tedeschi & Felson, 1994). If the bus you were waiting for passed you by, you would be frustrated. If this seemed a deliberate attack from a bus driver that did not like you, you might respond with aggression. If, however, the bus had a sign on it that said it was headed to the garage for a repair you would be less likely to respond with aggression (Pastore, 1952).

Media

Another possible source of aggression is the media. Children's television often shows violence. On average there are 14 acts of violence per hour in children's programming (Wilson et al., 2002). Does this affect the amount of aggression children engage in? Children copy what the adults in their lives do. If adults act aggressively children are likely to as well. But will children copy what they see adults doing on TV or other forms of media? One of the earliest studies to show this used children who were 3 to 5 years old. The children were divided into a number of groups and each group observed different things. Some children watched as an adult across the room beat up a 5-foot-tall inflatable doll with a weight in the bottom, called a Bobo doll. Other children watched as the same adult did the same actions on film. In one other condition the children saw a cartoon cat doing the same things the adult did. After frustrating the children by not allowing them to play with attractive toys, the researchers put the children in a room with a variety toys, including a 3-foot-tall Bobo doll. No matter how the children saw the aggression toward the Bobo doll—real life, film, or cartoon—they showed more aggressive behavior toward the doll and more total aggression than children who did not see any aggressive behavior (Bandura, Ross, & Ross, 1963).

Television viewing can increase both physical aggression and relational aggression (Ostrov, Gentile, & Crick, 2006). Violent video games also increase aggression. Aggressive behavior, thoughts, and feelings are increased over the short term and long term through the playing of violent video games (Anderson et al., 2010; Williams, 2009). Video game play may leave players with less empathy for others and a higher desensitization to violence and other disturbing materials (Staude-Muller, Bliesener, & Luthman, 2008), though this effect may be different for individuals who play often versus those who do not (Glock & Kneer, 2009). A bout of game play may provide a mood improvement for those who play often (Ferguson & Rueda, 2010).

Weapons

The presence of weapons is related to greater aggression. When research participants were in the presence of a revolver rather than a badminton racket, they acted more aggressively toward another (fictitious) participant (Berkowitz & LePage, 1967). This increase in aggression in the presence of weapons is called the **weapons priming effect**, or the weapons effect. Familiarity with weapons can affect how this effect works. Individuals with prior experience with guns, such as hunters, do not show an increase in aggressive thoughts when shown pictures of hunting guns, although those without prior experience with guns, nonhunters, do show an increase. This effect of familiarity is quite specific. When hunters are shown assault rifles, they do show an increase in aggressive thoughts (Bartholow, Anderson, Carnagey, & Benjamin, 2005).

Alcohol

Alcohol and aggression have been linked. When people are intoxicated they may find themselves less able to think about long-term consequences and less able to curb impulses. In the face of provocation, this can lead to greater aggression (Giancola, 2000). An insult that might have been ignored when someone is sober may result in a swinging fist when the insulted person has had a few drinks (Denson et al., 2008). Alcohol may also affect aggression simply because it is expected to affect aggression. When research participants were given a substance that tasted and looked like alcohol but did not have any intoxicating qualities, they showed just as much aggression as when they were given actual alcohol (Rohsenow & Bachorowski, 1984). Recent research has suggested that one does not even need to consume the alcohol to show increased aggression. As with the presence of weapons, simply being in the presence of alcohol or alcohol-related images (alcohol advertisements) is associated with increased aggression (Bartholow & Heinz, 2003; Subra, Muller, Begue, Bushman, & Delmas, 2010).

© Ejwhite, 2013. Used under license from Shutterstock, Inc.

Alcohol has been linked with aggression.

Environmental Factors

Environmental factors that make people uncomfortable are associated with aggression. If the waiting area at the train station were crowded, do you think you would feel more aggression? Research suggests that you would. In a study of nightclubs, researchers found more acts of aggression when nightclubs were more crowded than when they were less crowded (Macintyre & Homel, 1997). Bars that were unpleasant in other ways, such as smoky and unclean, also had more aggression (Graham, Bernards, & Osgood, 2006). Noise, particularly noise one cannot control, is connected to higher aggression as well (Donnerstein & Wilson, 1976)

Discomfort in the form of heat is related to aggression. Uprisings, as well as assaults, murders, and rapes, are more likely in hot summer months than in cooler times of the year (Anderson, 1989). Generally, greater heat is related to more aggression (Baron & Lawton, 1972). One surprising finding about this connection deals with baseball. Researchers counted the number of batters hit by a pitch per game for three years of major league baseball games as well as how hot it was while those games were being played. The number of batters hit when the temperature was 79° Fahrenheit or below was quite low. When the temperature was 80°–89° the number of batters hit rose some, with a dramatic rise in hits with temperatures 90° and higher (Reifman, Larrick, & Fein, 1991).

Conclusion

Aggression is a behavior with a variety of causes. Aggression comes from within the person and is affected by external forces. A single factor may not determine whether someone is aggressive, but several factors together may lead to harm.

Summary

Aggression

Aggression involves intentional harm, although we may harm because the harm itself is our goal, called hostile aggression, or we may harm as a way to reach another goal, called instrumental aggression. When aggression causes severe harm we call it violence. Aggression has origins within the person as well as the environment. Men and women show different rates of aggression, depending on the type, and aggression varies with age.

Catharsis

Catharsis is an idea with a long history. Although many believe that expressing aggression will reduce feelings and likelihood of engaging in future aggression, it does not. In catharsis we may direct our aggressive feelings toward other, often safer, targets, as in displaced aggression.

Aggression Cues

Aggression is more likely when someone is frustrated or attacked. Aggression can also be affected by media, the presence of weapons, the consumption or even the presence of alcohol, and environmental factors like crowding, noise, and heat.

Critical Thinking Questions

1. The chapter described a variety of factors that may increase aggression. What other factors might affect aggression?
2. What are your beliefs about catharsis? Now that you know catharsis does not decrease aggression, what might you do when you are feeling aggressive in the future?
3. If factors like media and alcohol increase aggression, is there something we as a society could do to lessen those effects?
4. Have you ever been in a situation where the heat, crowding, and noise made you feel more aggressive?

Key Terms

Aggression	Hostile aggression	Triggered displaced aggression
Catharsis	Instrumental aggression	
Displaced aggression	Relational aggression	Violence
Frustration		Weapons priming effect

Expanding Your Knowledge: Links to Additional Material

Psychology and Law

The justice system uses the terms *murder* and *manslaughter* to differentiate between a crime involving forethought and one that may have happened in the heat of the moment. Fontaine (2007) offers a discussion of the legal definitions of manslaughter and murder and how they relate to the psychological definitions of instrumental and hostile aggression at http://works.bepress.com/reid_fontaine/2/.

Culture of Honor

Are people from the southern and northern United States different? Although we often study differences between the cultures of different countries, differences also exist within a country's borders. In an interesting study by Cohen, Nisbett, Bowdle, & Schwarz (1996), the researchers looked at differences in aggression between college-age men from the northern and southern parts of the United States. In this series of studies the researchers found differences between the two groups of men when they were insulted by a confederate. The researchers attributed these differences to the existence of a culture of honor in the South but not the northern United States. Read the article to see what they found: http://faculty.som.yale.edu/keithchen/negot.%20papers/CohenNisbettEtAll2_SouthCultureHonor96.pdf.

Modeling: The Bobo Doll Study

In the study by Bandura, Ross, and Ross (1963) described in this chapter, the researchers found that children readily copied the aggressive behaviors toward a Bobo doll modeled by adults. Go to http://video.google.com/videoplay?docid=-4586465813762682933# to see video clips of both an adult and children beating up the Bobo doll. The children are shown copying the adult directly, being more attracted to guns, and engaging in what Bandura describes as "creative embellishments" on the aggression they saw the adult perpetrate.

Youth Violence Prevention

The U.S. Department of Justice provides a number of resources to encourage the prevention of youth violence. If you are interested in youth violence or are planning to be involved in youth work, follow the links at http://www.ojp.usdoj.gov/programs/youthviolenceprevention.htm.

Teaching Gentleness

If we desire to not just prevent violence in children but teach more positive behaviors, how do we do it? Two articles from the American Psychological Association Help Center suggest ways to promote gentleness in children and help them resist violence.

What Makes Kids Care? Teaching Gentleness in a Violent World: http://www.apa.org/helpcenter/kids-care.aspx.

Raising Children to Resist Violence: What You Can Do: http://www.apa.org/helpcenter/resist-violence.aspx.

12 | Prosocial Behavior

Learning Objectives

By the end of the chapter you should be able to:

- Define altruistic motives and egoistic motives
- Differentiate ultimate goals from instrumental goals and unintended consequences
- Explain the empathy-altruism hypothesis and debate whether true altruism exists
- Explain how the norm of reciprocity, social norms in general, kin selection, and personal differences determine helping
- Explain the steps to helping and the factors that may cause someone to not help
- Define and describe the underpinnings of the bystander effect

Chapter Outline

12.1 Altruism

In the train station waiting for your scheduled departure you notice a woman drop her ticket. The man behind her picks it up and returns it to her. She accepts it with a smile of relief and hurries off to catch her train. This may be an ordinary occurrence, but it leaves us with the question of why the man helped the woman by returning her ticket. Was he hoping to make a connection and get her phone number? Was he hoping for a reward? Did he want to look like a hero? Or, even though he was a stranger and not helping would not have affected him, was he just trying to make sure she made her train? When we help others, do we help because we truly care about the welfare of the other person, or are we helping with the hope of helping ourselves? This is the basic question in the debate about altruism. Altruism occurs when our motive for our behavior is entirely for the interest of others and is not motivated by self-interest. On the other hand, when we do something entirely for self-interest, we are being egoistic.

Imagine you bought the person sitting next to you in the train station coffee and a bagel. If you bought those treats for your neighbor entirely because you wanted to make that person happy, you would have acted altruistically. Your ultimate goal was the happiness of the other person. An **ultimate goal** is the true goal, the end toward which one is aiming. In these types of situations we can also talk about another type of goal called an instrumental goal. **Instrumental goals** are the things we do to obtain our ultimate goal. Your instrumental goal was to buy the coffee and bagel and give them to your neighbor. As stepping stones toward our ultimate goals, instrumental goals may change depending on our ability to do them. If coffee and a bagel were not available, you might have told your neighbor a funny story or given him or her $5 to reach your ultimate goal of making that person happy.

This person decided to be altruistic and help pick up the fallen papers, rather than rushing off to his own destination. Why do you think he did this?

When you engage in actions for **altruistic** motives, your ultimate goal is the welfare of the other person, not yourself. You might receive benefits for your action. The other person might show gratitude, your significant other might be impressed by your generosity and give you a kiss, or you might look good in front of your boss who is waiting in the train station with you. If you received benefits for

190

an action, was your action still altruistic? Yes: when self-benefits are an unintended consequence of an action, that action may be truly altruistic. With altruism, the ultimate goal is still the welfare of others, and the action would have been done whether or not the self-benefits were present (Batson, 2010).

Using this terminology, actions undertaken for **egoistic** motives involve an ultimate goal of self-benefit (that kiss from your significant other) with the happiness of the other person being only an instrumental goal. If there had been another way to reach the goal of impressing your significant other, you may have taken that option instead. If you have ever volunteered so that you would have something to put on your resume, you engaged in volunteering for an egoistic motive. The type of volunteering you might choose to do may depend on whether you are egoistically or altruistically motivated (van Emmerik & Stone, 2002). Table 12.1 shows how our ultimate and instrumental goals are related to egoistic and altruistic motivations.

Table 12.1 Ultimate and Instrumental Goals of Altruistic and Egoistic Actions		
Motive	**Welfare of the Other**	**Self-Benefits**
Altruistic	Ultimate goal	Unintended consequence
Egoistic	Instrumental goal	Ultimate goal

Based on Batson, 1990.

We engage in altruism, according to researchers, when we feel empathy for another person. By adopting that other person's perspective we are able to act in an altruistic way. This is called the **empathy-altruism hypothesis** (Batson, 1990; Batson, Duncan, Ackerman, Buckley, & Birch, 1981). You might know what it is like to be hurrying through a train station, hoping to make your train, so when you see someone else hurrying you may help because you have been in that person's shoes. If we see that someone else is in trouble and needs help but do not adopt that person's point of view, we feel not empathy but personal distress. For example, if someone slipped and fell in front of you and you did not feel empathy, you might instead be upset that you had to see blood or be inconvenienced by someone else's clumsiness. In this case you might help so you do not need to see the injury or so you can be on your way quickly, not because you truly care about that person's well-being. Egoistic (self-focused) motives might involve personal distress, a concern about how one might be viewed by others, or a desire to feel better about oneself.

The problem researchers face in examining whether we engage in activities for truly altruistic motives is that the action itself does not clearly show the motive behind the action. That coffee you bought for your neighbor in the train station may have earned you a kiss from your significant other, but was your action egoistically motivated by that potential kiss or altruistically motivated by a desire to make your neighbor happy? On the surface the action and reaction are identical.

To look into altruism, researchers set up situations in which participants who were feeling empathy for someone else could either help that person or get out of the situation without looking or feeling bad. For example, in one study the participants could help by taking the place of another participant (actually a confederate) and receive electrical shocks in her place. For some participants, escape from the situation, and therefore their own distress, was easy. For other participants, escape was difficult. The idea was to see whether people were motivated by true altruism (they would help whether escape was difficult or easy) or egoism (they would help only if escape was difficult). In this, and other studies like it, researchers found that when empathy was high people seemed to act in truly altruistic ways. Even when they could escape the situation or leave feeling happy or looking good without helping, they still helped (Batson et al., 1989; Batson et al., 1991; Batson et al., 1988). Altruism can even occur when it violates the principle of justice. When we feel strong empathy for someone, we may act to increase that person's welfare even when that act will be unfair to others. An individual might cover for a co-worker whose mother has died even when that is unfair to another co-worker or the department in general (Batson, Batson, Todd, & Brummett, 1995; Batson, Klein, Highberger, & Shaw, 1995).

Altruism does vary from culture to culture (Cohen, 1972; Fehr & Fischbacher, 2003; Gurven, Zanolini, & Schniter, 2008). For example, altruism is higher in Thailand than in the United States. The reasons for such differences are likely quite varied, but in interviews Thais remarked that their Buddhist religion was an important factor in their desire to help others (Yablo & Field, 2007). Even when given the same resources, older individuals tend to donate more than younger people, suggesting that altruism is something one, in part, learns from culture (Rai & Gupta, 1996). This is not to say altruism is entirely based in culture. Evolutionary psychologists propose that altruism is at least partially genetically based and it is an interaction of genetic influences and cultural influences that determine altruism (Gintis, Bowles, Boyd, & Fehr, 2008; Knafo & Israel, 2010).

12.2 Reasons Behind Helping

Besides altruism there are a variety of reasons we might help. One reason we might help is because we want others to help us. Recall the discussion in Chapter 8 of reciprocity as a persuasion technique. We generally want to get as much as we give and give as much as we get (Gouldner, 1960). You might give a friend a ride to the airport with the implicit understanding that your friend will give you a ride when you need one. Helping, then, is really a form of social exchange.

People often have different reasons for helping others. Perhaps this young woman is just naturally helpful. Or perhaps she is related to this man and feels inclined to help him.

© Arek_Malang, 2013. Used under license from Shutterstock, Inc.

Helping may also be part of a general social norm (Staub, 1972). Recall from Chapter 9 that we often engage in behavior because we believe others do (descriptive norms) or because others think we should (injunctive norms). We may help, therefore, because we believe it is what others do and what others think we should do (Schwartz, 1975). For example, in a study of potential bone marrow donors, women who had a norm toward donating bone marrow and ascribed that responsibility to themselves were more likely to volunteer to donate than those did not have the norm or the feeling of responsibility (Schwartz, 1973). Norms for who we help may be different in different cultures. Indians were more likely than Americans to judge as immoral a failure

Social Psychology in Depth: Helping After Natural Disasters

In 2005 Hurricane Katrina slammed into the U.S. Gulf Coast and brought death and devastation. More than one million residents of the Gulf Coast were displaced and over 1,800 lost their lives (Katrina Facts Online, 2010). Private donations for hurricane relief in the Gulf Coast was over 3.5 billion dollars (Center on Philanthropy, 2006) with Red Cross workers coming to help from all 50 U.S. states and the U.S. territories (Kelson, 2005). When asked, 77% of Americans say they want to help in the face of such disasters (Marchetti & Bunte, 2006). What determines helping in such disasters?

Our emotional reactions to disasters are important to our response. According to the empathy-altruism hypothesis we should help altruistically when we feel empathy for others. Feelings of empathy and sympathy are related to a desire to help and eventual helping (Amato, 1986; Amato, Ho, & Partridge, 1984; Marjanovic, Greenglass, Struthers, & Faye, 2009; Avdeyeva, Burgetova, & Welch, 2006). Personal distress also affects helping. Individuals who reported shock, horror, or sickness in response to major bush fires in Australia donated more money than those who did not report feeling these emotions (Amato, 1986).

As would be expected from kin selection theory, individuals with friends or relatives affected by a disaster are more likely to provide assistance (Amato, Ho, & Partridge, 1984) and those individuals in need of assistance tend to receive more help in networks that are more kin dominated (Beggs, Haines, & Hurlbert, 1996).

Women are more likely to provide assistance (Amato, Ho, & Partridge, 1984) and to both seek and receive it when they are the victims of a disaster (Beggs, Haines, & Hurlbert, 1996). Those with higher self-efficacy, more education, and greater religious attendance feel more positive responsibility for helping (Michel, 2007). Individuals with higher income are more likely to provide monetary help, perhaps because they have the resources to give (Amato, Ho, & Partridge, 1984).

Integration in one's community and social network is important. Those who are involved in their community are more likely to help community members in need (Penner, Dovidio, Piliavin, & Schroeder, 2005). Studies of a couple of disasters, including Katrina, show that people with large social networks and networks that are dense, that is, have a lot of ties between members, are more likely to gain assistance when they need it (Beggs, Haines, & Hurlbert, 1996; Hurlbert, Beggs, & Haines, 2006).

To read more about how social scientists understand and explain the Hurricane Katrina disaster, see http://understandingkatrina.ssrc.org/.

to help strangers or others in only moderate or minor need (Miller, Bersoff, & Harwood, 1990), suggesting a stronger norm for helping in India than in the United States

Evolutionary theorists have suggested people help to gain benefits through promoting the genes of those related to them (Hoffman, 1981). Individuals are more likely to help their own child than a stranger's child. We are more likely to help a sibling than a cousin, and more likely to help a cousin than a stranger. Generally, the closer the genetic similarity, the greater the likelihood of helping. This tendency allows our own genes to be passed on to future generations. This tendency is called **kin selection** (Essock-Vitale & McGuire, 1980).

Are there some people who are simply more helpful than the rest of us? Some similarities exist in those who are particularly helpful. Individuals who helped Jews in Nazi Europe had greater empathy and beliefs in the equality of people than those who did not help, though they were similar to others in most other personality characteristics (Oliner & Oliner, 1988). Helpful people tend to be high in self-esteem and self-efficacy (feelings of competence). Helpful people also tend to have a strong belief that their own actions will affect what is happening in the world (something called an internal locus of control) and attribute responsibility for making those changes to themselves (Schwartz, 1974). Moral development is also more advanced in those who are helpful (Piliavin, Dovido, Gaertner, & Clark, 1981; Rushton, Chrisjohn, & Fekken, 1981; Staub, 1978).

Altruistic types of helping increase with age. Preschool children show few instances of altruistic helping, while older children show these types of actions much more (Bar-Tal, Raviv, & Goldberg, 1982; Eisenberg, 1986). Children learn to help altruistically from adult models, particularly parents (London, 1970; Piliavin & Callero, 1990; Rosenhan, 1970).

12.3 Bystander Helping in Emergencies

In 1964 a woman named Kitty Genovese was murdered in New York City. According to the *New York Times*, 38 people watched for a half hour as she was stalked and stabbed. By the time anyone called the police, she was dead (Martin, 1989). Although later reports suggested some changes to the basic facts (neighbors may have heard but not seen her attack), the city and the country were horrified that people could be so apathetic in the face of an unfolding tragedy. Why, everyone wanted to know, didn't someone help?

Examples of such incidents are not hard to find. In 2008, in Connecticut, Angel Arce Torres was hit by a car while crossing the street. He lay paralyzed on the sidewalk as cars and pedestrians passed by (Goren, 2008, June 11). In 2009 a 15-year-old girl at Richmond High School, in California, was gang-raped and beaten during a homecoming dance, while at least 10 observers watched and took pictures (Martinez, 2009, October 27). When we encounter such events, when do we help and what factors might lead us to turn away? Social psychologists decided to answer that question. There are five major steps to helping. At each step one can continue to the next step or fail to continue.

Step 1: Noticing an Event Is Occurring

Before people can help, they need to first notice that there is a situation present where help is needed. While you are sitting in the train station someone screams. If you are listening to an iPod or are in a place where there is a lot of noise, you might not hear the scream (Page, 1977). If you do not know the event is occurring you will not help.

Other than not physically hearing or seeing something, we might also be less likely to notice an event if we are in a hurry. In a study by Darley and Batson (1973) the researchers recruited seminary students to be part of a study supposedly focusing on vocational careers for seminary students. The students participated in the first part of the study and were asked to go to another building to complete the second part of the study. One third of the participants were told that they were late and needed to hurry over to the next building. Another third were told to go right over, they would be right on time. The final third were told they were early but could go over to the other building to wait. While walking from one building to the next, the participants encountered a man—actually a confederate of the researchers—sitting in a doorway who coughed twice and slumped down as they went by. Of the participants who were not in a hurry, 63% stopped to help the man. Of those who were told they would be right on time, 43% helped. Being in a hurry had a dramatic effect on helping. Of those in the high hurry group, only 10%

We might be too distracted or rushed to notice when someone needs help.

helped. This study suggests that being distracted from one's surroundings due to hurry decreases helping.

Step 2: Interpreting an Event as an Emergency

If a person has noticed an event has occurred, the next step is interpreting that event as an emergency. Is the person slumped in a seat at the train station asleep or ill? Is the person pulling to the side of the road having car trouble or stopping to discipline a whiny child? When an event is ambiguous, we are less likely to take the next step in helping. The man who clutches his chest and groans "heart attack" is fairly clearly having a heart attack. The man slumped in a seat at the train station is less clearly in need of help.

One way we try to figure out if someone needs help is to look to other bystanders. If others look alarmed at the sound of the scream in the train station, you might interpret the event as an emergency. If others look unconcerned you might interpret the same scream as nothing to worry about. When research participants were placed in a room and smoke was piped in through the heating vent, those who were alone reported the smoke fairly quickly, normally within 2 minutes of noticing it, with 75% reporting it within 6 minutes. Participants who were with confederates who showed no reaction to the smoke rarely reported the smoke. Out of the 10 people in this condition, only 1 (10%) reported the smoke after 6 minutes. (See Figure 12.1.) When three actual participants sat in the room filling with smoke, only 38% reported the potential emergency (Latane & Darley, 1968). Our tendency to collectively misinterpret situations in this way is called **pluralistic ignorance**. Pluralistic ignorance can be reduced if we know the other people we are with, perhaps because friends are more likely to discuss what is going on rather than rely on the nonverbal signals strangers are likely to send. In a study involving a potential emergency two friends responded more quickly than two strangers, though individuals waiting alone still responded most quickly (Latane & Rodin, 1969).

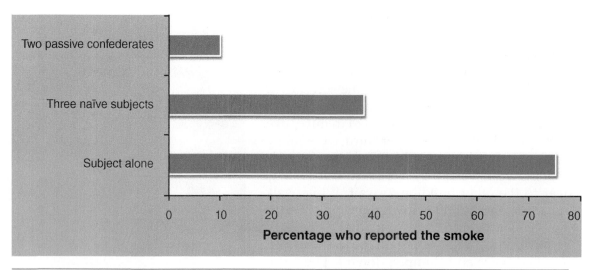

Figure 12.1 Effect of Group Membership in Emergency Situations

In the Latane and Darley (1968) study, only 1 out of 10 subjects reported the smoke when paired with two unalarmed confederates. Seventy-five percent reported it when left alone.

We interpret situations differently depending on what we believe is the relationship of those involved in the situation. In an emergency involving a victim and an attacker, we are less likely to intervene when we believe there is a relationship between the individuals. A tragic example of this phenomenon occurred in the U.K. in 1993 when 2-year-old James Bulger was killed by two 10-year-old boys. James was kidnapped by the boys from a shopping mall and dragged 2½ miles to railroad tracks where he was killed. Many people saw the boys together and noticed little James's distress but assumed it was two older brothers taking home a reluctant little brother. This type of interpretation and reaction was supported in research. When researchers staged an attack of a woman, three times as many people intervened when she said "I don't know you" (65% intervened) to her attacker than when she said "I don't know why I ever married you" (19% intervened) (Shotland & Straw, 1976).

Step 3: Taking Responsibility for Helping

Once we have interpreted an event as an emergency, we may still not help if we fail to take responsibility for helping. In a study investigating this step to helping, research participants heard another participant apparently having an epileptic seizure in another room (Darley & Latane, 1968). One group of participants believed they were the only one hearing the seizure, another group that there was one other person besides them, and a third group believed that four others were also hearing the seizure. After 6 minutes, 85% of those who believed they were alone, 62% of those who thought there was one other person, and 31% of those who thought there were four other people went to find help. The individuals who did not seek help were still concerned. When the researchers went to get them at the end of the study they showed signs of nervousness and asked about the condition of the person apparently having the seizure.

Having a larger group observing an emergency seems to inhibit helping. The responsibility for helping gets diffused, or parceled out, in large groups. In a group of four you might figure that someone else can take responsibility for helping, because you are not the only one hearing about the emergency. The result of this **diffusion of responsibility** is that less helping occurs with a larger population of bystanders. This phenomenon can be affected by whether or not the other bystanders are friends and by the gender composition of the group. In some situations, such as when a female group is confronted with an emergency involving a female victim, having a larger group can actually increase helping (Levine & Crowther, 2008).

Step 4: Deciding How to Help

Once we take responsibility for helping, we may still not help if we cannot decide how to help. If you see someone along the road with a car trouble, you have several options for helping. You could stop and see if you can fix the car yourself. You could call a repair shop or the police yourself or stop and offer your cell phone to the stranded motorist so they could call for help. Of course, you would only stop and fix the problem yourself if you knew how. Competence or training makes helping in this way of helping more likely. For example, individuals with Red Cross training in first aid were more likely than those who did not have such training to offer direct help to someone who appeared to be bleeding (Shotland & Heinold, 1985).

Step 5: Helping

Even if someone notices an event, interprets it as an emergency, takes responsibility, and decides how to help, that person may still fail to help in the end. One reason for lack of actual help is feeling embarrassed or self-conscious in the presence of other people. This reaction is called **audience inhibition** (Latane & Darley, 1970). (See Figure 12.2 for data on the effect of group size according to Latane and Darley's research.) This type of inhibition applies to more than emergency situations involving helping. When a coupon for a free cheeseburger was available to riders in an elevator, these individuals were less likely to take a coupon when others were present (Petty, Williams, Harkins, & Latane, 1977). The presence of an audience makes us generally less willing to act.

Individuals may also fail to help if they determine that the costs outweigh the benefits of helping. For example, if you see a hitchhiker on the side of the highway, you may decide you are the only one who could help (the highway is deserted) and know how to help (give the person a ride), but decide that the potential costs to you are too great. If an individual decides the potential costs are too high and the potential benefits too low, they may decide not to help (Avdeyeva, Burgetova, & Welch, 2006; Morgan, 1978). The cost-benefit calculation may be, in part, responsible for the finding that in some dangerous situations, where the victim's life may be in danger, greater helping has been found with larger groups (Fischer, Greitemeyer, Pollozek, & Frey, 2006). In these types of situations, the benefit of potentially saving the life of the victim may outweigh the potential costs to the helper, and the group may actually protect the individual helper from harm from, for example, a large, potentially dangerous attacker. Within this cost-benefit calculation is also the costs of not helping. If people could help but do not, they may feel guilty or lose social status. Helping might bring praise

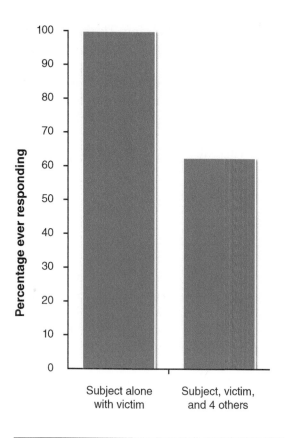

Figure 12.2 Effect of Group Size on the Likelihood of Responding in an Emergency

Based on Latane and Darley (1970).

Would you pick up this hitchhiker? Would your answer change if it were a woman? If it were at night? If you were alone?

© Kiselev Andrey Valerevich, 2013. Used under license from Shutterstock, Inc.

or other rewards (Fritzsche, Finkelstein, & Penner, 2000; Piliavin, Dovidio, Gaertner, & Clark, 1981). If the benefits for helping were high, the costs of not helping were high, and the costs of helping were low, the logical thing would be to help. Looking at the five steps together, we see that a person in need of help is less likely to get that help in a crowd than with one other person present. Kitty Genovese, who was murdered while 38 of her neighbors watched or listened, would have been more likely to get help if a neighbor knew, or believed, he or she was the only one to hear Kitty's struggles. This combination of factors that makes helping less likely with more people present is called the **bystander effect**.

Reducing the Bystander Effect

If you are the one in need of help, what should you do? Take a few minutes to consider before looking at the suggestions below.

Step 1: Make the emergency situation noticeable. The first step to helping is noticing something is happening, so if you are part of an emergency situation make that situation noticeable to others. Depending on the situation, yell, put up signs, light a flare, or wave your arms.

Step 2: Make it obvious that the event is an emergency. While bystanders might notice something is happening, they may not offer you help if they do not realize the event is actually an emergency. Individuals yelling "Help!" are more likely to get help than those who are silent (Shotland & Heinold, 1985). If others are present, remember the danger of pluralistic ignorance and do not rely on the nonverbal signals of others. Make friends with others and discuss whether you think an emergency situation is occurring. Remember that friends respond more quickly than strangers (Latane & Rodin, 1969). If you are the victim of an attack, remember that you are more likely to get help if bystanders believe your attacker is a stranger (Shotland & Straw, 1976).

Step 3: If you have an emergency situation, you want to be sure someone takes responsibility for providing help, so single someone out to help you. Point to someone, say his or her name if you know it, and ask that person specifically to provide help (Markey, 2000). If you have ever been through CPR training you know that one of the first things you are asked to do is point to some-

To reduce the bystander effect, make it clear that you need help and what kind of help you need.

one specific and ask them to call 911 while you do CPR. The Red Cross knows about bystander research and has implemented the research findings in their training.

Steps 4 & 5: Make the type of help you need evident and do what you can to reduce costs and increase benefits. Individuals who know what help to provide will be more likely to actually provide the help. If you need someone to call 911, say so. If you need help changing a tire, make that clear as well. A clear task or instructions on what to do may help reduce audience inhibition. As we learned from Milgram's studies of obedience, individuals who are acting on specific orders feel less responsible for their actions and, therefore, may feel less inhibition to help even when observed by others.

Conclusion

People may help for a variety of reasons. Whether one of those reasons is altruism, truly caring about another without any self-focus, is a matter of debate within social psychology. Helping may occur because of reciprocity, social norms, or evolutionary benefits. Some individuals may be more helpful than others. Bystander helping in emergencies takes place when the steps to helping have been taken, with people generally less likely to help when other people are present.

Summary

Altruism

Helping that occurs for altruistic motives occurs when the ultimate goal is to increase the welfare of the other and any self-benefits are an unintended consequence. According to the empathy-altruism hypothesis, when we feel empathy for another person we may help for altruistic reasons.

Reasons Behind Helping

Helping may occur because others have helped us in the past or we hope they will help us in the future. A general social norm also promotes helping those in need. Evolutionary theory suggests we help to promote our own genes, so we help those who are genetically similar. Individuals with particular qualities or personality traits may be more likely to help.

Bystander Helping in Emergencies

There are five steps to helping. One must first notice an event and then must interpret that event as an emergency. When individuals are busy or distracted they may not notice an event. The presence of others who do not react to an event may cause one not to react either, leading to pluralistic ignorance. Once the event is seen as an emergency, one must take responsibility for helping. When others are present we may not take responsibility because of diffusion of responsibility. The final steps are deciding how to help and helping. When others are present individuals may not help because of audience inhibition. The overall tendency to not help when others are present is the bystander effect.

Critical Thinking Questions

1. Do you believe true altruism exists? Why or why not?
2. Does it matter whether we do things for altruistic or egoistic motives if another person is helped in the end?
3. A variety of things are suggested in this chapter to increase likelihood of helping in emergency situations. What other things do you think might be helpful?
4. Think about a time when you were deciding if a situation was an emergency and whether you should help. How do the steps to helping apply in that situation?

Key Terms

Altruistic

Audience inhibition

Bystander effect

Diffusion of responsibility

Egoistic

Empathy-altruism hypothesis

Instrumental goal

Kin selection

Pluralistic ignorance

Ultimate goal

Expanding Your Knowledge: Links to Additional Material

Volunteering

If this chapter on prosocial behavior inspires you to volunteer, here are some links to find helping opportunities.

Feeding America: http://feedingamerica.org/

Volunteer Match: http://www.volunteermatch.org/

United We Serve: http://www.serve.gov/

Volunteer in U.S. National Parks: http://www.volunteer.gov/gov/

Global volunteering: http://www.globalvolunteernetwork.org/

Be Inspired

The Carnegie Hero Fund Commission recognizes individuals who perform acts of heroism. At http://www.carnegiehero.org/, click on Carnegie Medal Awardees to read the stories of some past winners of the Carnegie Medal. To watch a video about the award, click on Resources and a Century of Heroes.

Kitty Genovese

If you want to learn more about Kitty Genovese, check out the links below. The *New York Times* has published a number of stories about Kitty Genovese's murder. The website TruTV also has a substantial piece on Genovese.

New York Times articles: http://www.nytimes.com/keyword/kitty-genovese

TruTV page: http://www.trutv.com/library/crime/serial_killers/predators/kitty_genovese/1.html

Some contend that the *New York Times* was inaccurate in its reporting on the case. A blog post on this can be found at the link below. The blogger also describes Darley and Latane's work.

Blog post: http://riverdaughter.wordpress.com/2009/08/02/a-fascinating-intersection-of-true-crime-psychology-and-media-misinformation/

10 Notorious Bystander Stories

For additional stories about the bystander effect, take a look at Listverse's list of 10 notorious bystander stories at http://listverse.com/2009/11/02/10-notorious-cases-of-the-bystander-effect/. Some you may know about, some may be new to you. The list includes Kitty Genovese's story as well as stories about big events like the Holocaust and smaller-scale tragic events like the torture and murder of Ilan Halimi.

Bystander to Genocide

At times we are bystanders of not just small scale emergencies but large ones. This article from the *Atlantic* magazine describes what at least some individuals within the U.S. government knew about the genocide in Rwanda and their response to that knowledge: http://www.theatlantic.com/magazine/archive/2001/09/bystanders-to-genocide/4571/.

To expand on this subject take a look at the *Frontline* episode "Ghosts of Rwanda," at http://www.pbs.org/wgbh/pages/frontline/shows/ghosts/. The site contains a timeline of the genocide, interviews with those outside the tragedy who might have helped, and video clips.

13 | Attraction

Learning Objectives

By the end of the chapter you should be able to:

- Describe how proximity, attractiveness, matching, similarity, and equitability influence attraction
- Describe what is attractive in being hard to get
- Explain the two factors of the need to belong
- Describe how human tendencies toward social bonds and our emotions show the need to belong
- Describe the effects of being deprived of belonging

Chapter Outline

13.1 Factors in Attraction

Many of us meet a variety of people each day. Sitting in the train station you would likely meet a variety of people. Some we become friends with, others remain strangers. We may begin a romantic relationship with one person but refuse to even date another. What attracts us to some people and not others? Throughout this chapter we investigate a variety of factors related to attraction.

We Like Those Who Are Close to Us

Surprisingly, simple proximity has a lot to do with who we meet and become friends with. First-year students were more likely to develop a friendship with someone they sat next to during an introductory session than those they were not sitting near (Back, Schmukle, & Egloff, 2008). In a student apartment building, individuals were more likely to make friends with those living in apartments next to theirs, as opposed to those down the hall or up the stairs. The one exception to this was for those living near the mailboxes. The people in the apartments by the mailboxes saw individuals from all areas of the building frequently and thus became friends with those on different floors or farther down the hall (Festinger, Schacter, & Back, 1950; also Cadiz Menne & Sinnett, 1971). The most important factor in our liking of those who are close to us is repeated exposure. Exposure does not need to be in a face-to-face context. When we frequently interact with someone online, such as in a chat room or online classroom, we show greater liking for that person (Levine, 2000).

We tend to become friends with people near us, including co-workers and neighbors.

Repeated exposure to objects and people is related to greater liking for that person or object (Monahan, Murphy, & Zajonc, 2000; Zajonc, 1968). A piece of modern art, for example, that you thought was merely interesting the first time you saw it may, with repeated exposure, become well loved. This tendency to have greater liking for things we see often is the **mere-exposure effect**. In one study of mere exposure women who attended more class sessions were better liked by their classmates, even when they did not interact with those classmates (Moreland & Beach, 1992).

One interesting byproduct of the mere-exposure effect is our tendency to prefer mirror images of ourselves, while our friends prefer our true image. Because most people see themselves in a mirror more than they see their true image, they come to like their mirror image more than their true image. Friends and family rarely see our image in the mirror, so they prefer the true image (Mita, Dermer, & Knight, 1977).

We Like Those Who Are Attractive

Imagine you are beginning school at a large university and have signed up to be part of a welcome week dance. For the dance you are paired with another student of the opposite sex by a computer based on your answers to some questionnaires. You meet your date and the two of you try to get to know each other over the course of the evening. As part of this dance you are asked to evaluate your partner and are asked whether you would like to date him or her again. What might influence your answer? Would how intelligent your date is matter? His or her sincerity? Other personality factors? When researchers did this study they found none of these predicted evaluations of the date. The only predictor of the evaluation students gave of their partner was how physically attractive the date was. The partners of more-attractive dates liked them more and showed a greater desire to go out with them again (Walster, Aronson, Abrahams, & Rottman, 1966). All other things being equal, we prefer highly attractive individuals as dates, as friends, and to interact with in a general situation (Black, 1974; Byrne, London, & Reeves, 1967). For example, in a study of speed daters the strongest predictor of attraction for both men and women was attractiveness of the partner (Luo & Zhang, 2009). In another study involving third and eighth graders, physical attractiveness was an important factor in a desire for friendship with a peer (Zakin, 1983).

Attractiveness appears to be most important for initial phases of a relationship. In a study of newlyweds, attractive individuals were not any more satisfied with their marriage than those who were less attractive. In fact, more attractive husbands were less satisfied. Partners behaved best when the wife was more attractive than her husband and worst when the husband was more attractive than his wife (McNulty, Neff, & Karney, 2008). Physical attractiveness has been found to have no effect on established friendships (Johnson, 1989).

We Like Those Who Match Us

While individuals might desire a relationship with an attractive other, the attractive person might not desire a relationship with the not-so-attractive individual. Most people, therefore, expect to and tend to end up with someone who is close to them in physical attractiveness (Berscheid, Dion, Walster, & Walster, 1971; Montoya, 2008). This tendency to have relationships with those who match us is called the **matching hypothesis**. The next time you have a chance to observe couples, perhaps at a party, look around and notice whether the couples are about the same in attractiveness.

We Like Those Who Are Similar to Us

Do the values or interests of a potential relationship partner make a difference in our liking of that person? In general, we like and want to interact with those who are similar to us in values and interests (Byrne, London, & Reeves, 1967; Johnson, 1989). Among those who are already our friends, researchers find, the intensity of friendship is greater among those who perceived similarity (Selfhout, Denissen, Branje, & Meeus, 2009).

We are usually friends with people who are like us or share similar interests.

Similarity may be a more long-term relationship factor than a short-term factor. Speed daters showed no greater attraction to those who were similar (Luo & Zhang, 2009). As we discovered above, it was attractiveness that was more important. Even when we desire similarity in our friendships, we may not actually be friends with similar people if our options are limited. Friends in the United States tend to show greater similarity than friends in Japan. Researchers found that this was because of a difference in the ability of individuals within those cultures to form new relationships. With fewer opportunities for new friendships to form, we tend to stick with friends who are not necessarily similar to ourselves but are close in geographic proximity (Schug, Yuki, Horikawa, & Takemura, 2009).

We Like Those We Have Equitable Relationships With

Have you ever had a relationship where you felt you were giving more than you were getting from the other person? If so, you were part of an inequitable relationship. **Equity** involves receiving benefits proportional to what one provides (Hatfield, 1983). According to equity theory, it is not the overall amount one receives from a relationship that is important, it is whether or not what one gives and what one gets are equal. A partner who gives more than he or she receives in a relationship is **underbenefited** in the relationship. A partner who receives more than she or he gives in a relationship is **overbenefited**. As you might imagine, underbenefiting is more distressing to individuals. If you have ever invested in a relationship and have not gotten rewards proportional to your input, you were likely unhappy with that relationship. This theory also predicts that overbenefiting is problematic. When one relationship partner overbenefits, that person gains rewards he or she knows are undeserved, causing distress (Sprecher, 1986; 1992; Stafford & Canary, 2006).

Although there is some support for this theory, some have suggested the overall amount of benefits in a relationship is more important than equity (Cate, Lloyd, Henton, & Larson, 1982; Cate, Lloyd, & Long, 1988). If one is in an equitable relationship, but is neither giving nor receiving much from that relationship, it is unlikely to be a relationship for very long. Some people may expect fairness and pay attention to equity; others may be satisfied with an unbalanced relationship (Donaghue & Fallon, 2003). There may also be certain domains where equity is more important. Housework and childcare often fall inequitably to married women, creating problems within the relationship (Davis, Grenstein, & Marks, 2007). Equitability in these areas may, therefore, be more important to relationship success for married couples than equity in other domains (Gottman & Carrere, 1994).

We Like Those Who Are Hard to Get

The idea of playing hard to get is part of our culture. A variety of websites give advice on how to play hard to get (wikiHow.com; Dahlstrom, 2011). But does it work? Are individuals who play hard to get liked better? Individuals who play **hard to get** are selective in their social choices. Much of the advice about playing hard to get, and therefore the research on the idea, focuses on women playing hard to get in their potential romantic relationships.

In an impressive series of studies, Elaine Walster and colleagues (Walster, Walster, Piliavin, & Schmidt, 1973) investigated whether those who were more selective in their romantic interactions were liked more than those who were less selective. They found no greater liking for someone who was selective when they asked students to read a story about a woman who was not all that interested in a potential romantic partner (Studies 1 and 2) nor when male college students called up a woman who was hesitant about accepting his invitation to go out (Studies 3 and 4). Using a unique confederate, a prostitute, the researchers found that her clients seemed to like her less and were less likely to call her in the future when she played hard to get (Study 5). Finally, they discovered that targeted selectivity is what is most attractive (Study 6). Women who appeared to like and wanted to date the man in question, but not other men, were more attractive than women who were uniformly hard to get or who were willing to date anyone. The men were most likely to report wanting to date the women who liked them but no one else, liked her most, and expected fewer problems in dating. Interacting with someone who likes you but not other people may provide a boost in self-esteem (Matthews, Rosenfield, & Stephan, 1979). Others have expanded this finding of selectively hard-to-get individuals being most liked to include both men and women and within actual dating situations (Wright & Contrada, 1986).

13.2 Need to Belong

There are a variety of reasons why we might pursue relationships with some people but not others, but the question remains of why we would pursue relationships at all. Our desire for relationships is, arguably, a fundamental human need (Baumeister & Leary, 1995). Within the **need to belong** are two parts (1) the need for frequent positive contact with others and (2) the need for enduring connections marked by mutual concern for the welfare of the other.

Social Bonds

This need to belong can be seen in the ease with which we form social bonds and the trouble we have breaking those bonds. Waiting at the train station you might find yourself chatting with the person sitting next to you, easily forming a friendship. After a short stay at summer camp as a child you may have promised your bunk mate or the other kids in your cabin that you would be friends forever. Humans quickly, and relatively easily, form social bonds. Research evidence of this can be found in the ease to which the boys in Sherif's study of conflict and superordinate goals made friends with the boys in their own group

(Sherif, Harvey, White, Hood, & Sherif, 1961). Recall from Chapter 6 on prejudice that within a week these boys were a close-knit group. Ingroup favoritism quickly developed when participants were placed into groups, even when these groups were based on something as unimportant as the number of dots they estimated was on a slide (Billig & Tajfel, 1973; Tajfel, 1970).

Friends and family are generally a source of positive emotion.

Emotion

We generally view social connections as a source of positive emotions. In other words, our friends and family generally make us happy. When children say they made a friend at school, parents usually rejoice. New relationships are greeted with joy. We celebrate births and marriages (Baumeister & Leary, 1995). One predictor of happiness and satisfaction with life is social relationships (Myers, 1992).

Threats to relationships are associated with negative emotions. The loss of a loved one is very stressful (Holmes & Rahe, 1967). Even the possibility that an important relationship might end is met with sadness (Leary, 1990; Leary & Downs, 1995; Leary, Tambor, Terdal, & Downs, 1995) or jealousy (Pines & Aronson, 1983). Our reactions to discrimination may, in part, be rooted in our need to belong (Carvallo & Pelham, 2006). When ostracized from a social group, we feel pain, anger, and sadness (van Beest & Williams, 2006; Williams, 2001) though initially we may feel numbness (DeWall & Baumeister, 2006). The status of our relationships and our emotions are closely linked.

Deprivation

What happens if we are deprived of belonging? Consider this startling statistic: For all causes of death in the United States, rates are higher for individuals who are divorced, widowed, or single than those who are married (Berkman & Syme, 1979; Sorlie, Backlund, & Keller, 1995). A variety of factors may be behind that statistic, but one is likely the long-term affective bond, normally accompanied by frequent contact, that marriage provides. In other words, married people are more likely than those in the other groups to fulfill the need to belong. It is not necessarily marriage that is key here, but fulfillment of the need to belong. Individuals with limited social ties, including family and friendships, had poorer physical health (Berkman, 1995; House, Robins, & Metzner, 1982). Individuals who do not fulfill the need to belong are also more vulnerable to mental illness (Broadhead et al., 1983; Thoits, 1995).

Loneliness is the feeling of being without desired social connections. It is possible to fulfill one piece of the need to belong, frequent contacts, without fulfilling the second, ongoing relationships involving mutual caring. Loneliness involves a problem with the second part of the need to belong. Someone can be lonely, therefore, even when that person has frequent contacts with others. Loneliness may be understood and experienced differently in different cultures. Cultures have different ways of understanding the nature of

Social Psychology in Depth: Ostracism and Aggression

On April 20, 1999, Erick Harris and Dylan Klebold killed 12 fellow students and one teacher and wounded 23 other people at Columbine High School in Littleton, Colorado. Since then there have been over 45 other school shootings around the world (Information Please Database, 2010). Many of the perpetrators of these school shootings had been ostracized by their classmates (Gibbs & Rocher, 1999; Leary, Kowalski, Smith, & Phillips, 2003).

Ostracism is something most people experience and use to control others. Ostracism can be used for a variety of purposes. Individuals with high self-esteem ostracize to end relationships while those with low self-esteem use ostracism as a defense against the expected rejection or criticism by others (Sommer, Williams, Ciarocco, & Baumeister, 2001). Ostracism has positive effects for the group as it increases group cohesion (Gruter & Masters, 1986).

Ostracism interferes with our need to belong, particularly when we are unsure of the cause of our ostracism (Sommer, Williams, Ciarocco, & Baumeister, 2001). Ostracism might also affect our self-esteem. Recall from Chapter 2 the sociometer theory, the idea that acceptance and rejection are important for self-esteem. Ostracism tells us that others do not value us as much as we value them (van Beest & Williams, 2006). To get back in the good graces of those around us, we often act in compliant or prosocial ways when we have been ostracized (Cater-Sowell, Chen, & Williams, 2008; Williams, 2007). For example, an ostracized teen might buy gifts for the friends who ostracized her in an attempt to secure entry back into the group and demonstrate that she is a valuable member of the group.

When we are ostracized, life seems to lose meaning (Stillman et al., 2009) and we feel out of control (Williams, 1997). Ostracism that affects our sense of purpose or control is more likely to result in antisocial behavior (Williams, 2007). The interaction of ostracism and control may be particularly important for aggression. Warburton, Williams, and Cairns (2006) used a game of toss to ostracize research participants and then exposed them to an unpleasant blast of noise. Some of the participants were able to control the noise and others were not. Participants were then asked to decide how much hot sauce to put in the food of a stranger, knowing that the individual did not like spicy foods but would be required to eat all of the food. Participants who had no control over the noise wanted to put four times more hot sauce in the stranger's food than those who had control over the noise. Placing hot sauce in the food of someone who does not like it is an aggressive act, an act made more likely when people felt they were ostracized and had no control over their circumstances.

The fact that school shooters have often been ostracized by their classmates does not excuse their behavior. Knowing about the effects of ostracism can, however, help us understand the behavior and provide us with a potential area for intervention.

relationships, so, while loneliness appears to be common across cultures, it is understood differently depending on the culture (Rokach, 2007; van Staden & Coetzee, 2010). Lonely people have the physical and mental health issues discussed above. One major issue with loneliness is that it can lead to depression (Cacioppo, Huges, Waite, Hawlkey, & Thisted, 2006).

Bullying may, in part, be due to a deprivation and desire for acceptance from other children. Boys involved in bullying desired acceptance from other boys involved in the types of antisocial activities they were involved in (other bullies) and from other boys in general (Olthof & Goossens, 2008). Nearly all student perpetrators of school shootings felt they had been rejected and excluded by their classmates (Leary, Kowalski, Smith, & Phillips, 2003). Not fulfilling the need to belong is dangerous for our own physical and mental health and may potentially be harmful to those around us.

Conclusion

We like those we interact with often, those who are attractive, those who match us, those who are similar to us, and those we have equitable relationships with. We also like those who like us exclusively. We form relationships quickly and easily and are happier and healthier because of these relationships. Our need for interaction and close bonds is a need, not just a want, in our lives.

Summary

Factors in Attraction

A variety of factors exist that help determine our liking of others. We like those we see or interact with often, as the mere-exposure effect predicts. We also like those who are attractive. Although we would prefer to interact with those who are attractive, we usually end up with those who are similar to us in attractiveness, as proposed by the matching hypothesis. We tend to like those who are similar to us in values and interests rather than those who are different. We prefer to not overbenefit or underbenefit in a relationship but have a relationship characterized by equity. We also tend to like those who like us and only us.

Need to Belong

The need to belong has two factors, frequent contact and enduring connections. Evidence of this need is seen in our ease of forming and reluctance in ending relationships. The need is also evident in our happiness when we have social bonds and the negative emotions (anger, sadness) associated with lack of connection. Deprivation is associated with mental and physical health detriments. In loneliness we may interact with others, but do not feel that we have a close connection to anyone.

Critical Thinking Questions

1. Have you had an experience with any of the factors related to attraction? For example, do you find yourself friends with your neighbors? Is your significant other, if you have one, similar to you in attractiveness?
2. If you were a scientist looking into liking, what other factors might you want to investigate?
3. What kinds of situations could you imagine in which someone would fulfill one aspect of need to belong, but not the other? How would that affect the person?
4. How could you assist others whose need to belong is not fulfilled ? For example, if older adults in nursing homes lack frequent contacts with others, how might that be alleviated?

Key Terms

Equity	Matching hypothesis	Overbenefited
Hard to get	Mere-exposure effect	Underbenefited
Loneliness	Need to belong	

Expanding Your Knowledge: Links to Additional Material

Mere Exposure and Art

For in-depth coverage of the mere-exposure effect and art, take a look at the chapter found at http://people.psych.cornell.edu/~jec7/pubs/103.pdf. Cutting (2006) describes the mere-exposure effect and how it relates to the frequency of publication of particular works of art. An interesting twist on the research here is the comparison of adult preferences to the preference of children. Children tended to prefer pieces of art at a relatively random rate (basically 50/50 for commonly seen versus less commonly seen pieces of art). Adults, on the other hand, tended to prefer works of art that were more often published, despite the fact that they showed no recognition of these works. In other words, adults showed a decided preference for art they had been exposed to, even when they did not recognize that exposure.

Does Beauty Matter? It Depends

As suggested in the chapter, we like those who are attractive, but this matters more in some contexts than in others. Plaut, Adams, and Anderson (2009) found that attractiveness (assessed by waist-to-hip ratio) was more important for social connections for those in urban, as opposed to rural, environments. They suggest that the increased choices in an urban environment allows people to choose attractive over unattractive relationship partners to a greater extent than in rural environments. For a short article reporting on this finding, see http://www.sciencedaily.com/releases/2009/12/091215112043.htm.

Pickup Lines

What do those pickup lines really mean? In an article on PsyBlog (http://www.spring.org.uk/2007/08/hidden-purpose-of-chat-up-lines.php), the authors describe different types of pickup lines (what they call "chat-up" lines), different kinds of men, women with different personalities, and how these all fit together. When a man uses a pickup line he may actually be testing to see what kind of women he is talking to. For example, if the pickup line contains a joke he might be seeking an extroverted woman, as this is the type of line she responds to.

Ostracism

For more information on social ostracism beyond what is covered in the *Social Psychology in Depth* box check out Kip Williams's website at http://www1.psych.purdue.edu/~willia55/Announce/Compass%20Supplements.htm.

Loneliness Scale

If you are interested in taking a loneliness scale, try one of these options.

The Differential Loneliness Scale can be accessed here (about half way down the list): http://www.yorku.ca/rokada/psyctest/.

A six-item loneliness scale can be found within this article: http://home.planet.nl/~gierv005/ResonAging.pdf.

This article provides the 20-item Revised UCLA Loneliness Scale and a three-item scale (see page 660): http://psychology.uchicago.edu/people/faculty/cacioppo/jtcreprints/hwhc04.pdf.

14 | Relationships

Learning Objectives

By the end of the chapter you should be able to:

- Describe the differences in the way people talk about love and being in love
- Explain the difference between companionate love, passionate love, and compassionate love
- Explain the difference between a communal relationship and an exchange relationship
- Explain Sternberg's triangular theory of love
- Describe how interdependence theory works
- Explain the components of the investment model
- Describe John Gottman's findings about relationship maintenance
- Explain the process and results of relationship dissolution

14.1 Love

Sitting in the train station, you hear the woman next to you say "I love you" to her husband before hanging up the phone. Someone sitting across from you exclaims "I love donuts" when her friend brings her one to eat. A mother tells her child she loves him. "Love" is a word with a multitude of meanings. To say you love your mother is different from saying you love your shoes or you love your romantic partner or you love chocolate donuts. When Fehr and Russell (1991) asked college students to list all the kinds of love they could up with, the students were able to list 216 different kinds of love. Puppy love, brotherly love, romantic love, and maternal love are all different types.

To further investigate our conception of love, Meyers and Berscheid (1997) asked people to write down the initials of everyone they loved, everyone they were in love with, and everyone they felt a sexual attraction or desire for. After sorting out where the lists overlapped, the researchers found that the *love* list was long. We love a lot of people. Most people who were on the *in love* list were also on the *love* list (93% of the *in love* list were on the *love* list). The *love* list contained a number of people that were not on the *in love* list (23% of the *love* list were on the *in love* list). This suggests that when we talk about being *in love* we are talking about something similar to *love* but more selective in some way. It was the last list that helps us sort out how *in love* differs from *love*. Many of the people on the *in love* lists were also on the sexual attraction or desire for list (87% of the *in love* list were also on the sexual attraction list). This suggests that when we say we are *in love*, we are describing a type of love that includes a sexual or desire component.

Three Types of Love

One way we might break down love is to put it into a few categories, two of these roughly analogous to the *love* versus *in love* dimensions above. One type of love is the affection we hold for friends and family, what some researchers have deemed companionate love. **Companionate love** is characterized by deep caring for another person, comfort and trust, and enjoyment of shared experiences (Berscheid, 2010). Marriages characterized by companionate love tend to be lasting and satisfying (Gottman, 1999). The importance of companionate love may be surprising to some, as a more passionate type of love is often expected and striven for in marriage, but researchers find that a more romantic view of love does not do as good of a job of predicting well-being within a marriage (Orbuch, Veroff, & Holmberg, 1993; Grote & Frieze, 1994) or general well-being (Kim & Hatfield, 2004). Companionate love does a better job of predicting well-being in these situations.

There are many different kinds of love. How many types can you think of?

© Robert Kneschke, 2013. Used under license from Shutterstock, Inc.

Social Psychology in Depth: Love Online

Finding love online has become popular. Estimates vary but it seems that somewhere around 40% of single Internet users have visited a dating site and/or posted a profile (Madden & Lenhart, 2006; Valkenburg & Peter, 2007). Seventy-four percent of Internet users who are single and looking for relationships have used the Internet in their quest for love: flirting with someone online, being introduced to someone online, joining a chat group in hopes of finding a date, and even searching for information on a potential date (Madden & Lenhart, 2006). Online daters appear to come from all age groups and income brackets, although individuals who are divorced are more likely than those who are never-married or widowed to use online dating services (Valkenburg & Peter, 2007).

Most daters anticipate meeting and potentially forming intimate relationships with the individuals they find online. Individuals who expect to meet in the real world and establish long-term relationships tend to be more honest in their online communication. They also disclose more information consciously and intentionally (Gibbs, Ellison, & Heino, 2006).

That is not to say that online daters never misrepresent themselves, provide idealized portrayals, or are mistaken about their own attributes. Online daters attempt to counter this misrepresentation while looking at online profiles by assuming the image they get from a profile is a bit rosier than reality. Men, for example, might be a little shorter than they claim, women a little heavier (Ellison, Heino, & Gibbs, 2006).

People go through a decision process while engaging in online dating. The first is when looking at profiles. Some profiles are rejected because they do not fit what one is looking for in terms of age, location, or some other factor. Some online daters describe this as shopping for a date. The dater scans what is available and makes a decision based on the presence of desired qualities. Ironically, having more choices has been found to lead to poorer choices as well as objectification of future partners (Heino, Ellison, & Gibbs, 2010; Wu & Chiou, 2008). Another point in the decision process comes with online communication. A budding relationship may be ended at this point because of rejected overtures for communication or communication that is slow, uncomfortable, or reveals inaccuracies. When communication moves from online to phone or face-to-face, online daters face another decision point. At this point daters need to decide whether the online profile matches reality and whether any chemistry found online is present in the real world (Heino, Ellison, & Gibbs, 2010).

When individuals who met online meet face-to-face, a significant minority experience disappointment. In fact, the longer the couple spends engaging in computer-mediated communication the more likely they are to be disappointed when they meet face-to-face (Ramirez & Wang, 2004; Ramirez & Zhang, 2003). The limited information an online dater receives about his or her match can lead to idealized or inaccurate ideas of the qualities the potential partner possesses (Hancock & Dunham, 2001).

Accurate data on the success of online dating is hard to come by. Of the people who have visited online dating sites, about half say they have had positive experiences, with a third describing negative experiences. The vast majority (97%) of currently married or committed people did not meet online. That number is skewed, however, by the fact that many met before online dating was an option. Many online daters know someone who found a long-term romantic partner online (43%). Of the Americans who have looked for love using Internet dating sites, about a quarter are in committed relationships. Those numbers sound hopeful until you consider that almost half of those who have visited online dating sites have not found a relationship partner (Madden & Lenhart, 2006). The Internet may be a good tool, but it seems finding Mr./Ms. Right is just as hard as it has ever been.

Passionate love would describe the in love type of love from above. Passionate love involves intense emotional arousal and physical attraction. (Fehr, 1994; Regan, 1998). This strong desire for another person may be the draw into a relationship, which could then transition into a relationship characterized by companionate love (Berscheid, 2010). Unlike companionate love, which seems to increase over time given the right conditions, passionate love tends to decline over time (Hatfield et al., 2008; Tucker & Aron, 1993).

Another category of love is the self-giving, caregiving type of love called **compassionate love**. Compassionate love might describe a parent child relationship or a long-term friendship. The caring and concern for the welfare of the other present in compassionate love has been described by Margaret Clark and colleagues as part of communal relationships (Clark & Mills, 1979; Clark & Monin, 2006). In **communal relationships**, partners respond to the needs of the other person, not worrying about when or how their contributions will be repaid. **Exchange relationships**, by contrast, are those where contributions and rewards are counted and immediate repayment is expected. We tend to act in a more communal manner, showing compassionate love, in close friendships or dating or marriage relationships (Sprecher & Fehr, 2005). Exchange relationships are more common in our interactions with acquaintances, strangers, or co-workers.

Sternberg's Triangular Theory of Love

Robert Sternberg (1986) divides love into even more distinct categories. In his **triangular theory of love** he describes three aspects of love. Each can be thought of as a point on a triangle. **Intimacy** is one component, described as feelings of closeness or bonds to another person. Intimacy may include sharing of oneself and one's possessions with another, counting on that person in times of need, and receiving emotional support from and providing emotional support to the other person. We tend to grow in intimacy within a relationship. Intimacy is moderately stable over time. Typically, intimacy is quite important in long-term relationships. We have some control over how much intimacy we have in a relationship though we may not be consciously aware of how much we have.

The second component of love in the triangular theory is passion. **Passion** involves physical attraction to another person and/or expression of desires and needs. Passion is not necessarily stable in our relationships. Generally we do not have a great deal of control over passion, though we are often aware of how much passion we are feeling for someone else.

The final component is **decision/commitment**. According to Sternberg, this can be a short-term commitment, the decision to love a particular other person, or a long-term commitment, the decision to stay with someone over the long term. We control the amount of commitment we have in a relationship, and it is important for long-term relationships.

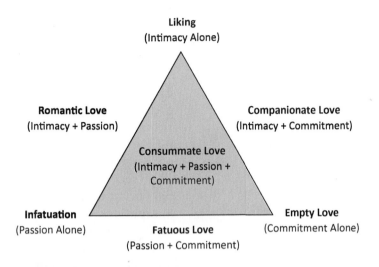

Figure 14.1 Robert Sternberg's Theory of Love

Within the triangular theory of love these three components are combined to describe different kinds of love. For example, infatuated love is a type of love that includes passion but no intimacy or commitment. Companionate love, on the other hand, includes intimacy and commitment but no passion. The types of love are shown in Figure 14.1.

14.2 Relationship Maintenance

What keeps partners in relationships? One way to look at our relationships over the long term is to use the **interdependence theory** (Kelley & Thibaut, 1978; Thibaut & Kelley, 1959). With this theory we can determine satisfaction and dependency within relationships. The way we determine satisfaction is to look at the rewards and costs in a relationship and the comparison level. Imagine you were in a relationship and found there were a lot of costs. Your partner left messes around the house, often borrowed money without paying it back, and had several annoying habits. The relationship also held some rewards. Your partner was sweet and affectionate and when you went out heads turned because your partner was very good looking. When you put it all together, though, the costs outweighed the benefits. You might be dissatisfied with a relationship where the outcome was not good, but there is some variation here. Some individuals do not expect a lot of rewards in their relationships, so having a relationship with a lot of costs and only a few rewards might still be satisfying for these people. Others might be dissatisfied even with large rewards because

We often determine satisfaction based on rewards and costs. Perhaps your partner brings you breakfast in bed, but is also extremely messy.

they expect highly rewarding relationships. This expectation for the outcomes in a relationship is the **comparison level**.

This theory also involves a calculation of dependence. In this context, dependence is the degree to which we believe our current relationship is the best we can do, in other words, how dependent we are on this particular relationship. Our calculation of dependence involves a comparison level of alternatives. The **comparison level of alternatives** is the outcomes we would expect to receive if we were in an alternate relationship. Imagine you were in a city where a number of neat and solvent relationship partners were available, all of whom were also likely to be affectionate and good looking. Given the alternatives, you would be unlikely to stay with your present messy, annoying partner. If, however, you looked around and found that alternative partners were no better than or were worse than your present partner, you might stay, even though you are unsatisfied. Within this theory you might be satisfied in a relationship (your rewards outweigh the costs) but still leave that relationship because there are other attractive alternatives.

An expansion of this idea is the **investment model**. According to this model, the level of commitment one has for a particular relationship is a function of satisfaction with the relationship, quality of alternatives, and investment (Rusbult, 1983). As you might imagine, individuals who are more satisfied with a relationship are more likely to be committed to a relationship. But satisfaction alone is not enough to predict commitment. As in the interdependence theory, alternatives are also important. If one has good alternatives to a current relationship, that person might move to another relationship even if satisfaction is not low. This model also includes one's investment in the relationship. **Investment** may take the form of intrinsic investments like time and emotional energy. Investments may also be extrinsic investments like shared possessions or even mutual friends that might be lost if one were to leave the relationship. Even when satisfaction is low and alternatives are good, people might stay in a relationship because of their enormous investment in the relationship, an investment they would lose by leaving. Putting this all together, a member of a couple who is very satisfied, has few alternatives, and has high investments will likely be quite committed to a relationship and make the decision to remain in the relationship. An individual who is not satisfied, has a number of alternatives, and has a small investment is likely to show low commitment to the relationship (Rusbult, Drigotas, & Verette, 1994; Rusbult, Martz, & Agnew, 1998).

Though this may all seem more like economics than relationships, other researchers have also played a numbers game with relationships and have been quite successful in predicting relationship outcomes. John Gottman and his colleagues are able to predict with over 90% accuracy the likelihood of divorce for a couple with their mathematical model (Gottman, Swanson, & Swanson, 2002). Couples may follow a variety of patterns, but overall, the researchers found that a ratio of five positive to every one negative behaviors must be maintained for relationships to last. A couple that fights often might have a long relationship if that fighting is balanced with expressions of fondness toward one another (Gottman, 1993). Couples that largely avoid both conflict and positive interactions may last for a while, but eventually divorce (Gottman & Levinson, 2002).

A particularly destructive interaction pattern is called the demand-withdraw pattern. One member of the couple brings up an issue he or she needs to talk about and the other member attempts to avoid the discussion. The person bringing up the issue is critical and contemptuous; the member responding comes back with defensiveness, eventually withdrawing (Gottman, 1998). Note that anger is not among these emotions. Properly expressed anger is not necessarily a problem for a relationship, provided it is expressed within the context of positive interactions. Four behaviors—criticism, contempt, defensiveness, and stonewalling (withdrawal)—are so important to the success, or lack of success, in a relationship that Gottman calls them the four horsemen of the Apocalypse (Gottman, 1994).

14.3 When Relationships End

About half of all first marriages end in divorce (Bramlett & Mosher, 2002; Rogers, 2004), with subsequent marriages ending at even higher rates (Cherlin, 1992; Glick, 1984). A vast number of nonmarital relationships end each year as well (Sprecher & Fehr, 1998). Many of the same factors that attract us to others may also affect our likelihood of ending a relationship. When relationships do not feel equitable or there are differences in educational aspirations, the relationships of college students are more likely to end. Mismatched couples, in terms of attractiveness, are also more likely to break up (Hill, Rubin, & Peplau, 1976). Divorce is often preceded by problems like infidelity, incompatibility (general disagreement about a variety of issues), money issues, substance abuse, jealousy, and growing apart and by personal factors like moodiness and irritating habits (Amato & Previti, 2003; Amato & Rogers, 1997).

A variety of factors may be behind breakups, but one we often do not think about is the calendar. The school year had an affect on when couples broke up in one study of college student relationships (Hill, Rubin, & Peplau, 1976). Valentine's Day is also a dangerous time for relationships that are not doing well. A cultural expectation exists for couples on Valentine's Day. For partners whose relationship is already in choppy waters, the time and energy needed to successfully navigate Valentine's Day activities may be more than the members can handle. A couple might not want to put the time and money into a Valentine's celebration for a relationship that appears troubled, and therefore they break up before getting to Valentine's Day. Couples may also find that the ideal

Relationships end for a number of reasons.

of love that Valentine's Day promotes was not present in their own celebration and break up post-Valentine's Day. In a study of college student couples, the number of breakups increased in the two-week time period around Valentine's Day (Morse & Neuberg, 2004).

The breakup process may begin with a personal realization of the need to end the relationship, followed by a negotiation with the partner for dissolution of the relationship. A couple is not done breaking up when they have agreed to break up; they must recover from the breakup, and others in their environment must be told of the breakup (Duck, 1982). Someone who wants to break up might use a variety of strategies. These can be grouped into four categories. A person might withdraw from the relationship and avoid contact with the partner, hoping the partner will get the message that the relationship is over. Another strategy involves using other people or other indirect ways to break up. For example, one might have a friend tell the significant other that the relationship is over. A partner might attempt to set a positive tone, describing the other person's positive qualities. Perhaps you have heard the phrase "you're a great person but. . . ." Finally, a more direct approach stating a desire to break up may be used to end the relationship (Baxter, 1982; Wilmot, Carbaugh, & Baxter, 1985). The particular strategy one uses may depend on the reason for the breakup as well as the degree of compassionate love one has for the partner (Sprecher, Zimmerman, & Abrahams, 2010).

A variety of emotions accompany a breakup. The primary emotions are love, anger, and sadness (Sbarra & Ferrer, 2006). If you have experienced a breakup you may remember the rollercoaster of emotions that accompanied it. Emotions tend to be very variable in the first few weeks after a breakup (Sbarra & Emery, 2005). Love and sadness tend to occur together. For example, one might listen to a song that provides a reminder of the love that was shared and this brings along with it feelings of sadness. Continued attachment (love) is not generally positive for people and may be associated with depression (Sbarra & Emery, 2005; Sbarra & Ferrer, 2006). Sadness does tend to get better with time. In one study of dating breakups in college students, at the end of a month most participants showed no more sadness than those in intact relationships (Sbarra & Emery, 2005). Anger may actually be somewhat of a positive emotion in breakups as it serves to more firmly sever the bond, provided one does not get stuck on anger. In line with the investment model, individuals who had greater investment (dated longer and felt closer) and who saw fewer positive alternatives showed more distress at the ending of a relationship (Simpson, 1987).

Breakups are sometimes mutual, but often not (Baxter, 1984; Hill, Rubin, & Peplau, 1976; Sprecher, 1994), so the initiator and the partner who is left may be dealing with different emotions. Sadness is a common emotion in those who have been broken up with (Boelen & Reijntjes, 2009). For the one who does the leaving, emotions may be different. Though guilt about hurting one's partner and regret may be present (Emery, 1994; Vaughn, 1986), there might also be a sense of relief or freedom (Sprecher, Felmlee, Metts, Fehr, & Vanni, 1998). Generally, the initiator of the breakup does better than the one who is broken up with (Thompson & Spanier, 1983).

Breakups can have a positive impact on someone's life. If a relationship was fraught with conflict or abuse, a breakup of that relationship can produce positive change (Nelson, 1989; 1994). When asked about positive changes that occurred because of a romantic relationship breakup, the most common had to do with things learned about the self. People mention being more self-confident and independent. Individuals also learn things from the relationship, such as what they want from a relationship or how to do better in future relationships. Other relationships can also grow because of a breakup. Friends and family may be seen as more important or these relationships might be closer than they were in the past (Tashiro & Frazier, 2003).

Conclusion

Love comes in a variety of guises, at times including passion or friendship or compassion. The staying power of relationships depends on factors inside the relationship, like costs and rewards; factors inside of the person, like comparison level; and factors outside the relationship, like available alternatives. When relationships end, the emotions experienced may depend on one's status as an initiator of the breakup and the quality of the relationship before it ended.

Summary

Love

Love is a concept with many facets. Companionate love involves a deep caring for another person, passionate love includes desire for another, and compassionate love is a self-giving type of love. Love can also be characterized according to the amount of intimacy, passion, and decision/commitment involved, according to Sternberg's triangular theory of love.

Relationship Maintenance

Interdependence theory predicts satisfaction with a relationship by bringing together costs, rewards, and the expectations one has for costs and rewards in a relationship. Dependence on a particular relationship, according to this theory, is determined by costs, rewards, and possible alternatives. The investment model predicts commitment to a relationship through a combination of satisfaction, quality of alternatives, and investments in the relationship. One relationship researcher with an impressive track record at predicting relationship success, John Gottman, notes that a ratio of at least five positive for every one negative behavior must be maintained for relationships to last. Those relationships characterized by criticism, contempt, defensiveness, and stonewalling are likely to fail.

When Relationships End

Breakups normally follow a pattern of individual realizations about the relationship, a breakup of the partnership, telling others about the breakup, and recovery. Love, sadness, and anger are all emotions felt in a breakup. One's status as initiator of a breakup and quality of the relationship before the breakup can affect the emotions one feels after a relationship dissolves.

Critical Thinking Questions

1. Some researchers describe three types of love (companionate, passionate, and compassionate), others three aspects of love (passion, intimacy, commitment). Are there other types or aspects of love not covered by these?
2. Consider some of your own relationships. Based on Sternberg's theory of love, how would you characterize these relationships?
3. How might you apply interdependence theory or the investment model to relationships you are part of or know about? What do the theories predict about the long-term success of these relationships?
4. If you have experienced a relationship breakup, does the research on this topic fit with your experience? Is there anything these researchers are missing?
5. Love, anger, and sadness are three of the primary emotions dealt with in a relationship breakup. What other emotions might be felt?

Key Terms

Communal relationships	Compassionate love	Investment
Companionate love	Decision/commitment	Investment model
Comparison level	Exchange relationships	Passion
Comparison level of alternatives	Interdependence theory	Passionate love
	Intimacy	Triangular theory of love

Expanding Your Knowledge: Links to Additional Material

Face-to-Face and Facebook

For an expansion on the *Social Psychology in Depth* box, read this blog post on liking face-to-face and liking online (http://bps-research-digest.blogspot.com/2009/05/people-judged-as-likable-in-flesh-also.html). It turns out the people we like in real-life conversations have Facebook pages we like as well.

Love from PBS and the BBC

Both PBS (http://www.pbs.org/kqed/springboard/segments/59/) and the BBC (http://www.bbc.co.uk/science/hottopics/love/index.shtml) have web pages on love. If you would like to explore websites on love these are good, reliable sources.

The Brain and Love

What does one's brain look like when in love? An article in the *New York Times* (http://www.nytimes.com/2005/05/31/health/psychology/31love.html) describes research involving brain scans of college students in love. As described in the article, in the initial phases of love our brains show activity similar that shown for drives like hunger, thirst, and drug cravings. The cycling from euphoria to depression found in this stage of love is what we would expect with this sort of brain activation. The brain scans also show that this intense feeling is likely to fade. Different parts of the brain were activated for those in one-year or longer relationships.

State of Marriage and Divorce

For an interesting report on marriage and divorce within different states check out the report from the Pew Research Center at http://pewresearch.org/pubs/1380/marriage-and-divorce-by-state. The report looks at age of marriage, rates of divorce, and some correlations to marriage and divorce patterns. Pew also offers an interactive map for rates of marriage and divorce at http://pewsocialtrends.org/2009/10/15/marriages-and-divorce-a-50-state-tour/.

John Gottman

Additional information on Gottman and his work, including workshops and DVDs, can be found at his website: http://www.gottman.com/.

PART V | Groups

© Ammit Jack, 2013. Used under license from Shutterstock, Inc.

"You think because you understand 'one', you must understand 'two', because one and one make two. But you must also understand 'and'."

—Ancient Sufi saying

15 | Group Actions, Cognition, and Dilemmas

Learning Objectives

By the end of the chapter you should be able to:

- Describe what a group is and the various types of groups
- Explain the positive and negative effects of social facilitation
- Differentiate social loafing from the Köhler effect
- Explain what deindividuation is and when it occurs
- Explain brainstorming techniques that increase or decrease the number of ideas developed
- Describe the effect of group polarization on group decisions
- Explain the antecedents, characteristics, and consequences of groupthink
- Explain other factors in group decision making, particularly those that occur in jury decision making
- Differentiate the following social dilemmas: tragedy of the commons, resource dilemma, prisoner's dilemma

Chapter Outline

15.1 Introduction: The Jury

The federal jury that convicted former Illinois Governor Rod Blagojevich on 17 of 20 counts in 2011, finding he abused the powers of his office.

About 154,000 jury trials take place every year in the United States (Graham, 2009). Almost 30% of Americans have served as a trial juror in their lifetime, with about 32 million Americans being summoned each year to serve on a jury (Burnett, 2009; Read, 2009). Jury trials are used in the United States, the United Kingdom, Canada, Australia, and many other countries around the world.

Jury trials were adopted by the United States in 1791, with the 14th Amendment in the Bill of Rights. Jury trials were seen as a way for citizens to make decisions for themselves and to prevent political leaders or others who might be in power from unfairly or unjustly prosecuting citizens. Juries involve a small group of people, normally between 6 and 12 jurors, making a decision together. Jury trials take, on average, four to five days. When juries make their decisions, they take about four hours for deliberation (Burnett, 2009).

Juries are one example of a small group working together to make a decision or accomplish a goal. Every day groups of people engage in actions, large and small, that affect their own lives and the lives of others. A family may jointly decide what restaurant they will eat at that night. A group of executives may decide to engage in a hostile takeover of a rival company. Citizens of a nation may rise up together to overthrow their leaders, as occurred in Tunisia and Egypt in January and February of 2011. Understanding how groups think and act together is important.

15.2 Group Actions

In life we act with groups or in the presence of groups in a variety of settings. A child jumping rope may do so with an audience of other children. A basketball player throwing a free throw may be affected by the presence of the crowd. A team on a factory floor may produce different amounts of product than would be expected based on each member's individual production. A mob of angry protesters may act in ways uncharacteristic of its individual members. Groups can affect individual behavior in positive ways and in negative ways. In this section we investigate these types of situations, focusing primarily on the way individuals act, think, and interact.

What Is a Group?

When a jury enters a jury room and begins debate, they are fairly clearly a group. Would a dozen people standing at the bus stop qualify as a group? What about three students studying at the same library table? We generally define **groups** as involving at least two people who are interacting and who form some kind of coherent unit (Cartwright & Zander, 1968; Dasgupta, Banaji, & Ableson, 1999). According to this definition, those bus riders or studying students might qualify as a group if they are doing something together. If the students are interacting and quizzing one another on class material, they would qualify as a group. If the bus riders are simply standing together they are unlikely to qualify.

We can also differentiate different types of groups. Relatives or friends—that is, groups of individuals who are related to one another or enjoy one another's company—are **intimacy groups**. Groups that engage in tasks together, like juries, are **task groups**. **Social categorization**, like being a woman or a Japanese American, can be the basis of a group. Groups might also be described by **loose associations**, like those who like hip-hop music or football (Lickel, Hamilton, & Sherman, 2001). When people think about each of these types of groups, they think about them differently. Intimacy groups are assumed to be small and long lived, involve a lot of interaction, and be relatively impermeable to outsiders. Social categories, on the other hand, are likely to be large and involve less interaction, but, like intimacy groups, be long lived and relatively closed to outsiders. Because task groups work together on tasks, we see them as having common goals and interacting to meet those goals, but they are less likely to be of long duration. Loose associations are likely to be short lived and open to outsiders, with little interaction (Lickel et al., 2000).

This group of golfers enjoying each other's company would likely be an intimacy group.

Social Facilitation

When people are together and interacting with one another, they may act differently than if they are alone. You will recall from Chapter 1 that in the 1890s Norman Triplett noticed that bicycle riders clocked different times depending on whether they were bicycling alone or with others. When bicyclists competed against the clock and

Some people tend to perform better when watched; others do not.

there were no other bicyclists cycling with them they went slower than when other bicyclists were there. Triplett's study is considered by many to be one of the first studies in social psychology.

Triplett began by looking at the records of cyclists, but discovered that a large number of other variables, extraneous variables, might affect the findings. For example, when bicyclists race together they draft one another, allowing the group to go at a faster pace than an individual might be able to achieve. To focus in on the impact of the group and to control extraneous variables, Triplett looked at the behavior of 40 children. He asked these children to wind up a modified fishing reel. Sometimes the children were alone and sometimes other children were present, winding up their own fishing reels. On average the children wound most quickly when other people were there.

Later researchers found results similar to Triplett's. Participants performed better when others were present. For example, when people engaged in tasks like doing easy multiplication problems or crossing out all the vowels in a written passage, they did better when others were there (Allport, 1920; 1924). But some researchers found that the presence of others caused problems. In one study participants did worse on a memory task when others were present than when they performed the task alone (Pessin, 1933). This left researchers with the question of whether the presence of others actually helped performance or hindered it.

An explanation for this difference was provided by Robert Zajonc ("Zajonc" rhymes with "science"). He proposed that the presence of others increases arousal. Increased arousal, he argued, increases the dominant response tendency. The dominant response tendency depends on the nature of the task. For simple, easy, or well-learned tasks, our most likely (dominant) action (response tendency) is to do the task well. For difficult, new, or complex tasks, our most likely action is to do the task poorly. If the presence of others increases our arousal and arousal increases our dominant response tendency, then we should do simple or easy tasks particularly well in the presence of others. On the other hand, if the presence of others increases our arousal and arousal increases our dominant response tendency, then we should do difficult or new tasks poorly. If you were a star basketball player in high school and shooting a free throw is a well-practiced response, you should be more likely to make the basket in a packed gym because your increased arousal due to the audience would drive your dominant response of the free-throw shooting behaviors. Alternatively, if you have played basketball rarely and making a basket is a relatively new and difficult task for you, an empty gym would provide you with the best chance to make that basket because your arousal would be lower.

When the presence of others affects task performance, **social facilitation** has occurred. Evidence of this can also be found in animal as well as human behavior. Zajonc and colleagues set up an experiment using cockroaches (Zajonc, Heingartner, & Herman, 1969). They created both complicated and simple mazes for the cockroaches and provided tiny Plexiglas audience boxes for observer cockroaches. When other cockroaches were in the audience boxes, the cockroach in the maze completed the simple maze faster, but completed the complicated maze more slowly. Similar effects have been found with rats and chickens (Tolman, 1967; Wheeler & Davis, 1967; Zentall & Levine, 1972). People show social facilitation just like these insects and animals. Good pool players play better when watched, but poor players tend to do worse with an audience (Michaels, Bloommel, Brocato, Linkous, & Rowe, 1982).

Zajonc (1980) argued that social facilitation could occur simply because others are there, what he called mere presence, not because of other factors. Other researchers suggested that the presence of others creates distraction or concern about being evaluated and it is this distraction or concern that is the true cause of the social facilitation effects (Cottrell, 1972). There is some support for these alternate explanations. In one study participants completed a task in a room where another person was present. The other person either quietly observed or was blindfolded, presumably because the person was waiting for a study of vision to begin soon and needed to have his or her eyes adapt to darkness. If social facilitation occurs simply because of the presence of others, there should be no difference in how well the participant completes the task because in both conditions the "mere presence" of another exists. This study, however, showed no social facilitation effects when the other person was blindfolded (Cottrell, Wack, Sekerak, & Rittle, 1968). Although this study suggests that social facilitation requires more than the mere presence of others, later studies (e.g., Platania & Moran, 2001) showed that mere presence is enough, and the effect of apprehension about evaluation remains a question.

Some researchers have questioned whether arousal is the mechanism behind social facilitation (Aiello & Douthitt, 2001). More recent ideas have proposed cognitive-neuropsychological mechanisms. The presence of others seems to put demands on the frontal lobes of the brain and the cognitive system that manages the other systems, diminishing the capacity of the system to deal with new or difficult tasks (Wagstaff, Wheatcroft, Brunas-Wagstaff, Blackmore, & Pilkington, 2008). The frontal lobes of the brain are particularly important for planning for the future, attention in the present, and initiation of actions, so such an explanation makes logical sense.

Social Loafing and the Köhler Effect

In studies involving social facilitation the individual performing the action was simply in the presence of others, with the others either doing an action at the same time or observing. What happens when the others are working with the individual doing the action? When a group performs actions together to accomplish a goal, do the members of the group act differently than if they were engaging in that action alone?

About the same time as Triplett, Max Ringelmann completed a set of early studies in social psychology that were designed to look into that question. Ringelmann, a French agricultural engineer, investigated the amount of work individuals versus groups put into tasks. He suggested that two or more individuals working together did not accomplish as much as one individual alone because of a difficulty in coordinating their efforts, termed **coordination loss**. Though he knew there might also be issues with motivation of the members of a group, he left it up to later researchers to investigate this possibility (Kravitz & Martin, 1986).

Individuals tend to socially loaf when they do not expect their contributions to lead to something they value.

The tendency for individuals to produce less or not work as hard when working with others is called **social loafing**. Social loafing occurs when individuals are working together toward a shared goal and their efforts are pooled. When our work is combined we tend to have less motivation or show less effort. In one study of this phenomenon, participants were asked to pull a rope as hard as they could in a simulated tug-of-war type setting (Ingham, Levinger, Graves, & Peckham, 1974). The researchers measured how hard participants pulled when they were pulling alone and knew it and when they thought they were pulling with others. (Participants completed the task blindfolded so they would not know they were the only one pulling.) When participants thought a number of other people were pulling, they pulled with less force than if they thought the task was theirs alone.

If your efforts toward a group goal, like a class project, were pooled, but you knew that each person's piece could be clearly identified, would you engage in social loafing? One key factor in social loafing is the identifiability of individual effort. When one's work is pooled with others but one's effort can be identified individually, social loafing declines or disappears. To figure out if identifiability was important, research participants were asked to yell as loud as they could under three conditions: when they were yelling alone and knew they were alone, when they thought they were yelling with one other person, and when they thought they were yelling with five other people (Williams, Harkins, & Latane, 1981). The participants had headphones and blindfolds on so they could not actually see or hear what others were doing. The researchers found that when people thought they were yelling with one other person, they produced 69% as much sound as when they were yelling alone. When participants thought they were part of a group of six, they produced 63% as much sound. The researchers were able to eliminate this reduction in sound production by putting individual microphones on participants and telling them that when they were yelling with others their individual efforts were identifiable.

When individuals do not expect their contributions to lead to things that they value, they are most likely to socially loaf. This could happen either because they perceive that their contributions are not going to be meaningful or because they do not value the outcome of the group. In a tug-of-war you might feel that your additional effort is not going to add much to the group, so you would pull less when the group is pulling with you. You might also feel that any praise you would get would be quite small in the tug-of-war, since it would be divided amongst your group members. It follows, then, why individual identifiability is important. When your contribution can be recognized it becomes meaningful and the outcome more valued.

We also find less social loafing when we know the other people in our group and have a cohesive group. Perhaps knowing your friends are relying on you is different from having strangers rely on your contributions. We also loaf less when the outcome depends on us in some way (e.g., the project will not be completed without our contribution), or the task is meaningful, important, or enjoyable to us in some way (Karau & Hart, 1998; Karau

& Williams, 1993; Smith, Kerr, Markus, & Stasson, 2001). If you know your group cannot finish the class project without you or you simply enjoy investigating the topic or putting together a report, you may not loaf.

Social loafing varies depending on both culture and gender. Men are more likely to socially loaf than women (Karau & Williams, 1993; Kugihara, 1999). Women tend to show more equal inputs whether working alone or with a group. Individuals from more interdependent cultures are also less likely to socially loaf than those from independent cultures (Gabrenya, Wang, & Latane, 1985; Klehe & Anderson, 2007). Within each culture, though, women are less likely to loaf than men (Kugihara, 1999).

In some instances groups can positively affect performance by eliciting motivation to work harder (rather than engage in social loafing). Imagine you were recruited to be part of a basketball team. Though you know the rules and have played before, your background in basketball is limited. When you are playing with a team of great players, will you try as hard as you can or not as hard as you can? Most likely you would be motivated to work hard and would put a lot of effort into your play, hoping you will not let your team down. The tendency for individuals who are less capable than their group to work harder has been called the **Köhler effect** (Hertel, Kerr, & Messe, 2000; Kerr, Seok, Poulsen, Harris, & Messe, 2008). That increased motivation may come from comparing oneself to other group members and realizing that one's performance is lacking. It could also come from a realization that the group's outcome will only be as good as one's behavior, as the weak link, allows (Kerr, Messe, Park, & Sambolec, 2005; Kerr et al., 2008; Stroebe, Diehl, & Abakoumkin, 1996).

Deindividuation

Have you ever attended a sporting event and found yourself yelling at the top of your lungs in a way you would not ever do if you were alone? If you have ever been in a crowd and found yourself acting in a way you would not act alone you may have experienced deindividuation. **Deindividuation** is the tendency to engage in behaviors with a group that one would not engage in alone. Yelling insults, throwing objects onto the field at a sporting event, or looting have all been part of deindividuated behavior.

Researchers have proposed a variety of factors that could lead to deindividuation. A reduced sense of individual responsibility for action, high physiological arousal, a lower awareness of personal values and beliefs, novel situations, and a sense of anonymity have all been proposed as factors that increase deindividuation (Prentice-Dunn & Rogers, 1982; Zimbardo, 1969). Imagine the types of situations where such things are true. When a mob is involved in looting, individuals know their own behavior is unlikely to be traced back to them. At a sporting event people are excited and may be distracted from awareness of their inner

Deindividuation causes people to do things they might not do if they were on their own, like rioting, looting, and trashing a neighborhood after a sports team loses.

thoughts by the action on the court/field/rink. At a rock concert, low lighting and wearing a band t-shirt like many others may allow one to feel anonymous. Researchers looked further into the factors that seem to lead to deindividuation using a technique called meta-analysis. Meta-analysis involves looking at as many studies as possible on a particular topic and using a statistical technique to summarize those findings. When researchers did this for factors that promote deindividuation, they found that feelings of individual responsibility were most important (Postmes & Spears, 1998). This means that, while a novel situation or high physiological arousal might have a small impact on tendency to engage in deindividuation, feeling like one is not accountable for actions is essential.

Deindividuation most often leads to negative behavior such as stealing and cheating (Postmes & Spears, 1998). For example, one Halloween trick-or-treating children were told that they were supposed to take only one piece of candy. When the adult who had given the children these instructions left, researchers watched from a hidden location to see how many pieces of candy the children actually took. Children who were more anonymous and were in a group were more likely to steal candy than those who were more identifiable or trick-or-treating alone (Diener, Fraser, Beaman, & Kelem, 1976). In another study, Halloween masks that hid children's identities led to greater stealing of candy (Miller & Rowold, 1979).

Most research and most examples you will find of deindividuation involve behaviors like yelling insults, stealing, or cheating, but this sort of behavior is not inevitable. In a study by Johnson and Downing (1979) participants were placed either in a situation to induce deindividuation or in a situation where their actions were clearly identified as their own. The participants were asked to put on one of two costumes. For half of the participants a nurse's uniform was provided, with the explanation that the costumes had been borrowed from the hospital for the study. The other half were asked to put on a robe that the researcher had supposedly made himself. He said "I'm not much of a seamstress so these ended up looking kind of Ku Klux Klannish" (p. 1534). The idea was that the costumes might provide participants with different cues toward behavior. The researchers thought the nurse's uniform would provide people with an environmental cue to be helpful, since we generally think of nurses as helpful. The robe could provide people with an environmental cue toward negative, aggressive behavior, since the KKK is and has been a violent organization.

Participants were asked to select an electrical shock level when another participant responded incorrectly. They had the option of either raising the shock level, up to a positive 3, or reducing it, down to minus 3. By raising the shock level participants were engaging in an action that inflicted additional harm on the other participant. By lowering the shock level they were helping the other participant by making the shock less painful. The other participant they were supposedly shocking did not really exist; no one received a shock in this study. The researchers were wondering if deindividuation could actually create helpful behavior, if the environmental cues were right, or if anonymity always lead to negative behavior. Table 15.1 shows the results of the study.

Table 15.1 Average Shock Level Increase or Decrease of Participants in Different Groups in Johnson and Downing's (1979) Study of Deindividuation		
	Individuated	Deindividuated
Cue for helpfulness	—0.35	—1.47
Cue for aggression	0.76	0.95

Based on Johnson and Downing (1979).

As you can see from the table, deindividuated individuals with the aggressive cue showed more aggressive behavior: They increased the shock level. Those who had something in their environment that suggested helpfulness tended to do what they could to reduce the pain someone else would experience, particularly when they were deindividuated. Deindividuation has the potential to create positive behavior if the environment supports it.

Overall, deindividuation increases the individual's responsiveness to the situation or the group norms (Postmes & Spears, 1998). The person will take on the norms of the group, the group identity, and engage in behavior that goes along with those norms, good or bad. You can think of the impact of individual identity and group identity on our behavior as working like a teeter-totter. When one side of a teeter-totter goes down, the other goes up. When our reliance on our individual identity goes down, the identity of the group becomes more important. On the other hand, when we are very aware of our own individual identity, the group is less of a determinant for our behavior. This is the idea behind the **social identity model** of deindividuation effects. As people lose their own identity, they take on the identity of the group around them.

15.3 Group Cognition

In the previous section we explored how groups affect the actions of individuals. When in groups, people also seem to think differently than they do individually. Individuals in groups may think together to generate ideas or make decisions. Group discussions may also affect individual attitudes.

Brainstorming

When groups think together, coming up with ideas as a group, it is called **brainstorming**. Brainstorming has been proposed as a way to develop a wide variety of solutions or new and creative ideas (Osborn, 1957). Common brainstorming rules include trying to generate as many ideas as possible, with encouragement to combine, improve, or expand on previous ideas.

Many people think brainstorming generates more ideas, but it might actually generate fewer ideas if individuals interrupt one another or become distracted.

Brainstorming seems, to many, to generate more ideas than individuals working alone (Paulus, Dzindolet, Poletes, & Camacho, 1993). In fact, overall, brainstorming actually provides fewer ideas per person than individuals would provide on their own. This may be because of issues related to production with a group. Individuals might interrupt one another or spend time in social conversations unrelated to the task at hand (Diehl & Strobe, 1987). As groups get bigger and there are more people to interrupt or get off topic, groups show a greater loss of productivity (Mullen, Johnson, & Salas, 1991).

Some people are anxious in social situations and may put a damper on group interactions while brainstorming. Researchers have found that those high in interaction anxiety were not as helpful in brainstorming sessions. They were unwilling to participate orally. When highly anxious people were in a group with those who were not anxious, the low anxiety individuals tended to show poorer performance as well (Camacho & Paulus, 1995). Interaction anxiety puts a damper on both those who suffer from it and those with whom they interact.

To maximize the potential of brainstorming, the standard technique of getting all members of the group into a room and speaking their minds may not be most effective. Combining individual idea generation and group brainstorming can be helpful. The greatest number of ideas are developed when the group brainstorms together and then each person brainstorms alone (Brown & Paulus, 2002). The group may prompt individuals to think in directions the individuals would not have thought about on their own. Following the group session with an individual session allows individuals to come up with a number of ideas without the loss of productivity due to interruptions by other members of the group and without the social anxiety of the group context. Talking over other group members can also be avoided by having members write down their ideas and read the ideas of others, rather than speaking ideas, or by using a computer to type up one's ideas and send them electronically to other group members (Brown & Paulus, 2002).

Group Polarization

Do group discussions change the way people think? When the opinions of individuals are surveyed before and after a group discussion of opinion-related topics, opinions tend to shift farther toward an extreme. If we think of opinions on a continuum, with strong agreement on one pole and strong disagreement on the other pole, people tend to polarize. **Polarization** involves a shift closer to whichever pole people were initially leaning toward.

There are a variety of possible reasons why this occurs. During a group discussion, individuals might hear arguments in favor of their own position that they had not heard or thought of before (Burnstein & Vinokur, 1977). People might also realize that their opinion is more common than they already thought (Myers & Lamm, 1976). Such a realization may lead us to make our own attitude more extreme as we strive to be distinctive from the group. Thus, group discussion may provide us with more arguments bolstering an already held opinion and the motivation to make that opinion stronger. People are more persuaded by their ingroups than by an outgroup (Mackie & Cooper, 1984) and more persuaded by unanimous groups than by groups with a dissenter (Williams & Taormina, 1993).

Polarization can occur not only with group discussion but also with repeated exposure to or stating of an attitude or with dedicated time spent thinking about the attitude (Brickman, Redfield, Harrison, & Crandall, 1972; Downing, Judd, & Brauer, 1992; Tesser, 1978). Part of the effect of polarization may, therefore, come not because of the group but because the interaction allows someone to state their own opinion and time to think about their attitude. Polarization also occurs with juries. In general, individuals who initially want to be lenient have a greater slant toward leniency after some jury deliberation. Those whose initial leaning is toward a severe punishment become more severe after discussion (Bray & Noble, 1978). When juries deliberate, the first vote most often predicts the outcome of the deliberation (Kalven & Zeisel, 1966; Sandys & Dillehay, 1995), particularly when the initial vote favors acquittal rather than conviction (MacCoun & Kerr, 1988).

Groupthink

In 1961 a group of 1,600 U.S.-funded and -trained Cuban exiles invaded Cuba at the Bay of Pigs. Their mission was to lead a popular movement to overthrow Fidel Castro and his communist regime. The mission failed entirely. The exiles were captured or killed, and the world was outraged that the United States invaded a sovereign country. Far from being overthrown, Castro remained in power for nearly 50 years, when ill health forced him to cede power to his brother in February 2008.

President Kennedy and a small group of advisors made the decision to move forward with the invasion plan, hatched during the Eisenhower administration. Kennedy was in favor of it and his advisors seemed to agree. They were confident the plan would succeed and were shocked when it turned into a disaster. Neither Kennedy nor his advisors seem to have seen how flawed the concept of an invasion with such a small force really was. The tactics, the numbers, the weapons, and even the intelligence from Cuba added up to a flawed plan doomed to failure (Sidey, 2001). Despite the characterization of Kennedy's group of advisors as "the best and brightest" (Halberstam, 1972), Kennedy later asked, "How could we have been so stupid?" (Sorenson, 1966).

Groups are often involved in decision making. With the adage "two heads are better than one," many of us believe that a decision made with others is better than a decision made by an individual. But the Bay of Pigs Invasion shows that groups can and do make bad decisions. Similarly disastrous decisions were made by groups in the failure of the United States to prepare for Pearl Harbor in 1941, the escalation of the Vietnam war, and even in the *Challenger* space shuttle disaster. Many of these group decisions share common characteristics. Researcher Irving Janis studied these types of group decisions and developed a model to describe how groups could make such bad choices (Janis, 1972; 1982).

Janis's model involves a process including the antecedents, characteristics, and consequences of this type of group decision making. He named it **groupthink**, a decision-making process that occurs when a desire for harmony and consensus within the group interferes with appropriate information seeking and leads to bad decision making. To begin, the antecedents are the conditions that must be in place for groupthink to occur. Here is a list of conditions that need to be present:

- The group is highly cohesive.
- The group is insulated from other viewpoints.
- The group has a directive leader.
- The group has poor procedures for searching out and evaluating alternatives.
- The group is under high stress or is threatened.

Notice that these conditions revolve around an insular, cohesive group that follows a leader with a certain plan. The group does not seek outside input but looks into itself for answers.

The antecedents lead to a group decision-making process with particular characteristics. These characteristics are the natural outgrowth of such an insular group. The characteristics are as follows:

- The group feels invulnerable.
- The group assumes the moral correctness of its viewpoint.
- The group stereotypes outsiders, particularly opponents.
- The group engages in self-censorship, not sharing concerns, doubts, or disagreements.
- Dissenters from the group are pressured to conform to group opinion.
- The group has an illusion of unanimity.
- The group members act as mindguards, protecting the leader from alternative viewpoints.

When a group is showing characteristics of groupthink, that group supports its own viewpoint and dismisses or ignores those of others. Even those within the group who disagree are silenced. Because of what are called **mindguards**, individuals who protect the leader from hearing a viewpoint contrary to their own, the leader never hears about dissenting opinions. For example, had Presidents Kennedy, Johnson, and Nixon appointed at least one person whose job it was to challenge proposed decisions, historical courses of action may have been different.

The consequences of such a process can be devastating, as the historic examples illustrate. The particular consequences of groupthink for the group are

- The group does not fully consider its true objectives.
- The group does not consider alternatives to the proposed course of action.
- The group does not fully examine risks of the proposed course of action.
- The group does a poor information search.
- The group does not develop appropriate contingency plans.

Because the group does not consider alternatives or risks or develop a contingency plan when things go wrong, the group is surprised and left scrambling for answers.

Social Psychology in Depth: The Wisdom of Crowds

Want to know what movie will do big at the box office this weekend?

Want to know the answer to that tough question on the game show *Who Wants to Be a Millionaire?*

Want to know how many jelly beans are in the jar?

All these questions are best answered by groups. Throughout this chapter groups have been described as doing stupid things or making poor judgments, but groups are not as dumb as we think. The average estimate for the group is usually closer to the real number of jelly beans in a jar than any individual estimate. The studio audience picks the right answer 91% of the time on *Who Wants to Be a Millionaire?* Friends give correct answers only 65% of the time (Surowiecki, 2004).

Prediction markets use the wisdom of the group to predict events. Within these markets individuals use real or fake money to bet on the likelihood of an event (though other types of predictions are used, see Wolfers & Zitzewitz, 2004) and their collective wager is normally quite accurate. The Iowa Electronics Market (http://tippie.uiowa.edu/iem/) correctly predicted Obama's presidential victory in 2008, with closer accuracy than any of the major polling companies (Rowe, 2010). This was not a fluke; such markets have been more accurate than polls for a variety of races (Berg, Forsythe, Nelson, & Reitz, 2001).

According to James Surowieci, author of *The Wisdom of Crowds*, groups are helpful with three types of problems: cognitive, coordination, and cooperation. Cognitive problems are those that require judgment. If you poll 100 people about the month and year humans first set foot on the moon, the group will get closer than almost all of the members of that group. This holds true for prediction as well as facts. Want to know who will be awarded an Oscar? Take a look at the Hollywood Stock Exchange (http://www.hsx.com/) to find out (Pennock, Lawrence, Giles, & Nielsen, 2003). Groups also show wisdom in the coordination they engage in. Walking down a sidewalk you might find yourself drifting to the right side while the foot traffic coming toward you inhabits the left. Because of this coordinated action, you rarely crash into another pedestrian. Finally, crowds show cooperation. At the beach the group may collectively watch over one another's possessions and the small children playing the waves, all without talking about or knowing one another.

Not all crowds are wise. The key to good collective decision making is independence (Postmes, Spears, & Cihangir, 2001; Surowiecki, 2004). Each member of a group needs to make an independent judgment for the collective response to be accurate. Solomon Asch, who performed his classic studies of conformity, would agree. In comments about Asch's work, Levine (1999) wrote, "[T]he bottom line is that, because people are involved in cooperative efforts to understand the world, they have a responsibility both to assert their own viewpoint, which involves independence, and to pay attention to others' viewpoints, which can lead to conformity" (p. 360).

Though we would expect to find groupthink when the antecedents for groupthink are present, this does not always happen. The antecedents set the stage, but a group might still avoid groupthink. Not all antecedents are necessary for groupthink to occur. Cohesive groups, insulated from other viewpoints, with directive leaders are most vulnerable (Ahlfinger & Esser, 2001; McCauley, 1989).

Although a decision-making process characterized by groupthink does not use the best decision-making strategies, decisions made this way are not always disastrous. It is possible for a groupthink decision to turn out well, if the group happens to stumble on a good solution or gets lucky in the outcome of its actions. Groups making decisions without groupthink do not always make the best decisions either (Tetlock, Peterson, McGuire, Chang, & Feld, 1992). However, a decision made when groupthink is in play is more likely to turn out badly than one made by a group not involved in groupthink.

Group Decision Making

Research on juries, as well as other groups, has revealed that a variety of factors can affect the process and the outcome of group decisions. Groups that make decisions together are affected by the information individuals bring to the table and whether they share that information, the size of the group, and if the group is required to make unanimous decisions.

Unique Knowledge

When a group comes together, each member comes with a unique perspective. For example, if your work group was making a decision and you were the only one that knew about a new product the rival company was developing, it would be useful to your group if you shared that information. For many group decisions, each member could help the group most by clearly and concisely sharing his or her unique knowledge. Despite what would be best for the group, often group members focus on what all of them know or hold in common, ignoring the unique, potentially useful, information they as individuals have (Stasser & Titus, 1985). For example, a jury might discuss most of the aspects of the case they all remember or best understand. Jurors who remember other aspects or have knowledge that could help everyone understand particular aspects of the case are less likely to bring those up, at least initially.

Unique information is more likely to come up later in a group discussion, suggesting that longer discussions are more likely to yield diverse information (Fraidin, 2004; Larson, Christensen, Franz, & Abbott, 1998). People also tend to bring up information when they know it is their task to do so. By giving different members of the group different tasks and asking them to report on those, groups can have broader information when they come together (Moreland, Argote, & Krishnan, 1996; Stasser, 2000). Groups that are persuaded of the value of diverse opinions are also more likely to share diverse information amongst themselves (Homan, van Knippenberg, Van Kleef, & De Dreu, 2007).

Unanimous Versus Nonunanimous Decision Rules

Groups that are required to come to a unanimous decision act differently than those who can quit deliberation when a majority agrees. With majority rule, group members who hold alternative opinions can be outvoted. Traditionally, unanimous decisions were required of juries. In research on juries a nonunanimous verdict is associated with taking less time to reach a verdict (Davis, Kerr, Atkin, Holt, & Meek, 1975; Foss, 1981; Hastie, Penrod, & Pennington, 1983). Given that longer group deliberation is more likely to include discussion of information unique to particular members, it is likely that these nonunanimous juries are making decisions having not fully explored the knowledge of all members. Nonunanimous juries are more likely to be able to come to a decision, that is, they hang less often (Nemeth, 1977; Padawer-Singer, Singer, & Singer, 1977). Nonunanimous juries are more likely to come to a decision because they do not need to convince those final few people to agree with the majority.

Group Size

Differently sized groups make decisions differently. Juries in the United States have traditionally been made up of 12 members, but may be made up of as few as six members. Smaller juries tend to deliberate for a shorter period of time. In smaller juries, more people participate and there is less variability among the members in the amount they participate. In general, smaller groups tend to share more information (Cruz, Boster, & Rodriguez, 1997). But larger juries are more likely to contain members of ethnic and racial minorities (Saks & Marti, 1997). Generally, larger groups bring more ideas to the table and offer more diverse ideas that may be applied to solve a problem than small groups. A payoff may be at work with group size. Both small groups and large groups have their advantages. Small groups are efficient and members may have more chance to participate, but larger groups offer more diversity of opinion and are more likely to contain people with a diversity of backgrounds or ideas (Cummings, Huber, & Arendt, 1974).

Group Diversity

Some groups are quite homogeneous, with members having similar backgrounds and racial or ethnic identities, while others are quite diverse. How does diversity affect decision making? Overall, diverse groups tend to have less group cohesiveness and lower morale (Jackson, 1991; O'Reilly, Cadwell, & Barnett, 1989). At times diverse groups do not perform as well as less diverse groups (Ancona & Cadwell, 1992; Mullen & Copper, 1994). However, diverse groups can do better than more homogeneous groups.

Diverse groups tend to do better with complex decisions or decisions that require creative thinking as opposed to decisions that require settling on one answer or doing a simple task (Levine & Moreland, 1998). One important factor in this distinction is differences in the ways individuals from different backgrounds share information and in their willingness to share. When diverse groups are encouraged to share diverse information, they can make good decisions (Kooij-de Bode, van Knippenberg, & van Ginkel, 2008). In a study of diversity in juries, juries with minority members spent more time deliberating, discussed a wider range of information, and made fewer

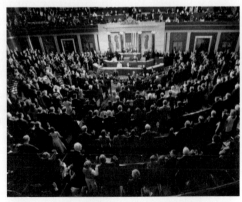

The U.S. Congress illustrates how group size and majority rules can affect decision making.

errors in their discussion of the case. This was not solely due to the contributions of the minority members of the groups. Majority members brought up more information and made fewer errors in the diverse groups than similar members in homogeneous groups (Sommers, 2006).

15.4 Social Dilemmas

After emptying a can of soup, what do you do with the can? Putting it in the trash might be easiest. The trash bin is right there and you are taking out the trash soon anyway. But if you throw it in the trash you know that the can will end up in a landfill. The recycling bin might be harder to get to and require a special trip. Recycling, however, is better for the environment, saving energy and landfill space and reducing pollution. Do you do what is best or easiest for you, at least in the short term, or do what is best for the larger group? You are facing a social dilemma.

When individuals face decisions whose outcomes create a tension between what is best for the individual and what is best for the collective (or group), they are facing a social dilemma. For these dilemmas, what is best for the individual is not what is best for the group. The individual would be best served by being selfish. But those individual behaviors are harmful to the collective and may, in the end, come back to harm the individual.

Tragedy of the Commons

Imagine you lived in a village with a common grazing field. Each person in your village could graze one cow on that common green space. As you consider the field you realize that adding one more cow would harm the field only a small amount. You need the milk to get you through the winter, so you add one or two more cows. Your neighbor comes to the same conclusion, as do a number of other villagers. With the addition of many animals the common field becomes a field of mud and no cows are able to graze. In other words, the individual can gain the best outcome by taking advantage of a collective resource, but if too many in the group take advantage of the resource it will not be sustainable and will no longer be available. This phenomenon is called **tragedy of the commons** or the commons dilemma (Hardin, 1968).

River pollution is one example of tragedy of the commons. What other examples can you think of?

Commons dilemmas are a part of a variety of social problems: overfishing, pollution, overpopulation, forest depletion, and overuse of energy.

For each of these what is best for the individual, at least on the short term, is to act in a self-interested way. A fisherman needs to make a living so making a large catch is important. If only a few individuals took advantage of a collective resource the outcomes might not be as good for the collective, but the resource does allow for some of that behavior. If only a few fishermen take large catches, there will still be fish to reproduce and provide future fishing opportunities. The tragedy occurs when large numbers act in a self-interested way. This depletes the resource. For a commons dilemma, what we view as fair is equal outcomes for all (van Dijk & Wilke, 1995). Even if a fishing resource could sustain some additional catches by some fisherman, what we view as fair is for each fisherman to take an equal amount of fish from that resource.

Resource Dilemma

With the tragedy of the commons, individuals have the option of gaining from a collectively owned resource that will naturally renew itself. A related social dilemma is called the resource dilemma. With the **resource dilemma**, individuals contribute to a resource from which all may benefit. Public television and public radio in the United States is funded to a large extent by those who watch or listen, but within a viewing or listening area everyone with a radio or television has access to PBS and public radio regardless of their contributions. The best individual strategy would be to not contribute and take advantage of the resource. Blood banks also encounter a resource dilemma. Individuals who become ill or have an accident may need blood, so we all hope that blood is available when we need it. But what is best for us as individuals is to avoid blood donation and the time and discomfort associated with donation. The dilemma is that if no one were to contribute, the resource would not exist.

In commons dilemmas, benefits are individual and costs are shared by the group. In resource dilemmas, benefits are shared by all and costs are borne by the individual. For the resource dilemma, we view fairness in terms of equity. Those who benefit most from a resource should contribute the most and those who benefit little can contribute little and be seen as being fair in their contributions (van Dijk & Wilke, 1995).

Prisoner's Dilemma

The commons dilemma and the resource dilemma involve groups of people. One dilemma that can involve only two people is called the **prisoner's dilemma**. To understand how this dilemma works, imagine you are a thief. The police caught you and your partner engaging in a minor crime. The police take the two of you into separate interrogation rooms and offer you this deal: If you confess to a major crime they suspect you of and implicate your partner, you will go free and your partner will spend 20 years in jail. The police tell you they are offering the same deal to your partner: If your partner confesses to the major crime, you will go to jail for 20 years and your partner will go free. If you both confess to the major crime, you will both spend 5 years in jail. If neither one of you confesses to the major crime, you will both be charged with the minor crime you were arrested for and spend a year in jail. (See Table 15.2.) What do you do?

Table 15.2 Prisoner's Dilemma Matrix		
	Partner	
	Confess *(do not cooperate with you)*	**Do not confess** *(cooperate with you)*
Confess *(do not cooperate with partner)*	Partner 5 years You 5 years	Partner 20 years You 0 years
Do not confess *(cooperate with partner)*	Partner 0 years You 20 years	Partner 1 year You 1 year

It would be best for you if you confessed and your partner did not. Collectively, it would be best if the two of you cooperated and spent only a year in jail each. If you both try to get the good deal, both of your sentences will be appreciably longer than if you had cooperated with one another.

When the prisoner's dilemma is played by two players several times in a row, called iterated prisoner's dilemma, players can use a number of different strategies. One strategy would be to always cooperate with one's partner, no matter what the partner did. If the partner always cooperates, this is a good strategy. By always cooperating, the two of you are able to, collectively, get the best outcome. The drawback comes if the partner realizes you always cooperate and is willing to take advantage of that. If so, you will get the worst outcome while your partner gets the best. Another strategy would be to always compete. Such a strategy would avoid the danger that you will be taken advantage of and may get you the best outcome (0 years) if your partner cooperates. If your partner is willing to cooperate consistently, competition prevents the best collective outcome.

Another strategy for the prisoner's dilemma game is the **tit-for-tat strategy**. With tit-for-tat you would use whichever strategy your partner did on the previous turn. If your partner cooperated on turn 2, you would cooperate on turn 3. If your partner competed on turn 3, you would compete on turn 4. If your partner cooperated on every turn you would also cooperate on every turn. If your partner consistently competed, you would also compete. A problem with the tit-for-tat-strategy is that if both members are using it and competition becomes the norm, each side reciprocating with competition, you have a negative outcome, individually and collectively. Because tit-for-tat can result in this negative cycle of responding, some have proposed a generous tit-for-tat strategy, where the individual cooperates more than would be strictly done in response to a partner's competition (Wedekind & Milinski, 1996).

Another strategy where you change depending on what your partner does is called the **win-stay, lose-shift strategy**. With this strategy you would continue with whatever strategy is providing you with the best outcome. If cooperating is getting you the best outcome, you would continue to use it until it starts to be a problem, then you shift to competition (Nowak & Sigmund, 1993). Other strategies exist, but overall the generous tit-for-tat and win-stay, lose-shift strategies have consistently had the best outcomes (Axlerod, 1984; Nowak & Sigmund, 1993; Wedekind & Milinski, 1996).

Dealing with Social Dilemmas

Pitting self-interest against collective interest, social dilemmas are difficult to solve. There are some factors, however, that make cooperation more likely. One factor that increases cooperation most of the time is communication (van de Kragt, Dawes, Orbell, Braver, & Wilson, 1986). Individuals playing the prisoner's dilemma game or engaging in a laboratory simulation of the tragedy of the commons are more likely to cooperate with one another if they can communicate with one another. This may be particularly important when unforeseen circumstances affect a behavior. For example, if someone playing the prisoner's dilemma game on a computer accidentally hit the wrong button they could apologize for taking advantage of their partner, if communication were possible, and promise to be cooperative in the future. If communication was not possible, the same action could send the players into a stint of competition (Tazelaar, Van Lange, & Ouwerker, 2004).

Cooperative behavior is more likely when payoffs make cooperation more attractive, either through punishment for selfish behavior or through rewards for cooperative behavior (Dawes, 1980; Shaw, 1976; van de Kragt et al., 1986). Changing payoffs to punish self-interested behavior or reward cooperation may involve oversight by a government or other organization. The problem with oversight is that it can cost resources to implement, police, and maintain. Societies need to be sure such oversight does not cost more resources than it saves.

Social dilemmas may continue because we do not see the effect our behavior is having on the collective. In a tragedy of the commons, if people see that the common resource is likely to soon be depleted they will normally cut down their use of that resource (Messick et al., 1983; Samuelson, Messick, Rutte, & Wilke, 1984). If fishermen were able to see how many fish were in the sea, they may reduce consumption of fish when supplies are low. When the effect of behavior cannot be seen or people are unable to engage in a behavior for reasons beyond their control, they may be unlikely to engage in cooperative behaviors. If one's recycling is only sporadically picked up or if the transportation system keeps changing the bus route, one may cease to recycle or take public transportation (Brucks & VanLange, 2008).

Social forces can be powerful in encouraging cooperative behavior. Individuals might recycle, despite the trouble, if it becomes a norm. Knowing one's friends and neighbors would be disappointed or disapproving may motivate the individual to do what is best for the collective and make a personal sacrifice (Dawes, 1980). Along with this, if we know well the people that may be affected by our self-interested behavior, we are less likely to compete. Therefore we tend to find more cooperation in social dilemmas that involve smaller groups (Seijts & Latham, 2000). We are more likely to cooperate with friends than with strangers (Majolo et al., 2006).

Is there any reason to do what is best for the collective despite the costs to oneself? Individuals who always cooperate might be viewed as suckers. These cooperative individuals will, in many situations, be taken advantage of and gain little self-benefit for their actions (Deutsch, Epstein, Canavan, & Gumpert, 1967; Solomon, 1960). But their actions as consistent contributors may influence their fellow group members toward better behavior. When their cooperative actions tell the rest of the group that cooperation is valued and expected, it may spark reciprocal cooperation and, in the end, lead the entire group to better behavior (Weber & Murnighan, 2008).

Conclusion

Although groups are made up of individual people, groups are qualitatively different from individuals. We cannot predict group behavior by simply combining individual behavior. Groups need to be studied as entities in and of themselves. Groups affect how the individual acts and thinks. In some instances, the person needs to sort out group interests from individual interests to determine behavior. Given the amount of time most of us spend in groups and how the decision of groups affect our lives, understanding groups is important.

Summary

Group Actions

A group is a collection of at least two individuals who are interacting in some way. A group can affect individual performance positively or negatively depending on the task. This is called social facilitation. Being in a group can also affect a person's production. When individual inputs cannot be identified, people tend to engage in social loafing, that is, not putting in full effort. The group can have positive effects on individual performance, as proposed by the Köhler effect, when an individual attempts to rise to the level of performance common in their group. Groups may also induce individuals to act in ways they normally would not. When individuals feel they cannot be identified they tend to take on the identity of the group and engage in actions with the group.

Group Cognition

Although some believe that brainstorming as a group can provide the largest number of ideas, in actuality a combination of both individual and group brainstorming is best for idea generation. When groups discuss attitudes, the attitudes of individual members tend to polarize. With polarization, individuals become more extreme in their attitudes after a discussion than they were before. When groups get together to make a decision, specific weaknesses in decision making can be identified amongst cohesive groups with strong directive leaders. Group decision making in general is affected by the willingness of individual members to share unique knowledge, by the decision rules imposed on the group, by the size of the group, and by the diversity within the group.

Social Dilemmas

Social dilemmas pit individual self-interest against the interest of the group. In the tragedy of the commons, a common resource can sustain a small amount of selfish behavior, but too much self-interest will destroy the resource. When individuals can contribute to a common resource that all, regardless of contribution, benefit from, a resource dilemma might develop. It is advantageous to the individual to take advantage of the resource without contributing, but the resource disappears without some individual contributions. The prisoner's dilemma involves a situation where cooperation yields the best collective outcome but competition can provide the individual with a better outcome, provided that cooperation is present on the other side. Mutual competition results in a poor outcome for both. Social dilemmas can be tamed by allowing for communication among the parties, by making cooperation more attractive and self-interested behavior more costly, by making individuals aware of their effect on a common resource, and by using norms that encourage cooperative behavior.

Critical Thinking Questions

1. If you were assigned to do a group project for a class, how might the research on social loafing help you encourage equal participation in your group?
2. Have you experienced deindividuation? What forces lead you to deindividuation? Were the effects positive or negative?
3. When might group polarization have a positive effect? When might group polarization have a negative effect?
4. If you were concerned a group was likely to engage in groupthink, what might you do to combat that?
5. Social dilemmas are common in a variety of venues, from friendships to international relations. Where have you seen social dilemmas at work? How might they be satisfactorily resolved?

Key Terms

Brainstorming	Loose association	Social identity model
Coordination loss	Mindguards	Social loafing
Deindividuation	Polarization	Task group
Group	Prisoner's dilemma	Tit-for-tat strategy
Groupthink	Resource dilemma	Tragedy of the commons
Intimacy group	Social categorization	Win-stay, lose-shift strategy
Köhler effect	Social facilitation	

Expanding Your Knowledge: Links to Additional Materials

Famous Trials

For information on a variety of famous trials check out this wonderful resource from Douglas O. Linder of the University of Missouri: http://law2.umkc.edu/faculty/projects/ftrials/ftrials.htm. For each of the trials you can access information on the case, forensic evidence (if applicable), and a wide variety of other resources.

Triplett

You can read Triplett's classic study of social facilitation at http://psychclassics.yorku.ca/Triplett/index.htm. Triplett offers a number of possible explanations for his observations, including theories like the suction theory, the brain worry theory, and the theory of hypnotic suggestions.

Cuban Missile Crisis

Irving Janis's work on groupthink began with an examination of the Bay of Pigs Invasion, which was a contributing factor to the Cuban missile crisis. To read more about this crisis, access *Washington Post* articles from the time of the event at http://www.washingtonpost.com/wp-srv/world/digitalarchive/index.html. These offer a fascinating glimpse into what was being reported at the time.

The National Security Archive provides another perspective on the Bay of Pigs Invasion and the missile crisis:

National Security Archive: Bay of Pigs Timeline: http://www.gwu.edu/~nsarchiv/bayofpigs/chron.html

National Security Archive: Bay of Pigs interview transcripts: http://www.gwu.edu/~nsarchiv/bayofpigs/press1.html#cia

National Security Archive: Missile Crisis: http://www2.gwu.edu/~nsarchiv/nsa/cuba_mis_cri/

Improving Group Decisions

A short reflection on how to help groups make better decisions is offered on the British Psychological Society site Research Digest, http://bps-research-digest.blogspot.com/2009/04/how-to-improve-group-decision-making.html. The authors review a few research studies that looked at group decision making and the factors that stood in the way of good decisions.

Prisoner's Dilemma Game

You can play the prisoner's dilemma game online at http://www.iterated-prisoners-dilemma.net/ or http://serendip.brynmawr.edu/playground/pd.html.

Intergroup Relations, Social Identity, and How the Individual Mind Can Morph into a Group Mind

Goal: Overview of the development of Social Psychology leading to the need for a Social Identity approach

<u>Theory</u>

Social Identity defined: "The individual's knowledge that he belongs to certain social groups together with some emotional and value significance to him or the group membership" (Tajfel, 1972).

- Identity is inextricably linked to group belongingness.
- Belongingness is psychological—it is phenomenologically real with important self-evaluative consequences.

<u>Social Psychology defined</u>

Early: The scientific study of social behavior.

- Humans are law-governed machines that react to stimuli much like any physical object
- Therefore, experimentation is the ideal (Wundt/Lewin with physics backgrounds; although Wundt thought introspection was critical to understanding Volkerpsychologie)

Revolt: Study the individual holistically.

- Focus on subjectivity, history—e.g., social constructivism, humanism, ethogenics, dramaturgy, post-structuralists
- Retain faith in experimentation but employ multiple methods

  ➜ Bricks in a brickyard; no cohesion; rat labs

- <u>Where's the "Social"?</u>
  Early: Social is limited to the presence of others (e.g., Triplett/social facilitation, etc.)
  - Focus on dyad (73% of all naturally formed groups are dyads)
    ➜ Leaves out values, opinions, attitudes, beliefs

Allport: "Attempt to understand, using scientific methods, how thought, feeling, and behavior are influenced by the actual, imagined or implied presence of others."

- Attitudes are social because they orient us toward other people, events, or objects.
- Dependent upon language—symbolic, human-human-animal communication.
- Take them with you . . . therefore, implied presence of others is relevant.

➜ Core controversy: Is there something fundamentally different about an individual or group or not?

Early: LeBon and crowd behavior/Freud and the idea that crowds strip away the thin veneer and lay bare our base, human instincts
VERSUS

McDougall: Group mind—separate and unique from individual mind (e.g., Sherif, 1936 and norm development)
Allport: No group mind . . . just collection of individuals
    ➜ Reductionism: Explains the group in terms of individual properties

Problem: Too much reductionism makes it impossible to answer the important questions posed at the higher level.

We're left studying the interaction between individuals and not the social group.

e.g., arm and car window with the intention to turn can't be explained in terms of muscle contractions and nerve impulses.

Social Identity: Intellectual Pedigree
- Individuals are born into particular social groups/categories.

Sociological Influences
- Consensus Structuralists: Characterize society as a structured whole; no ideological divisions; "rules of the game" (e.g., Comte, Durkheim, Parsons, Spencer, Merton)
- Conflict Structuralists: There are profound differences in ideology, values, beliefs, etc. that can characterize society (e.g., Marx; Weber)
  - Raises issues of power, status quo, and its maintenance
  - Collective consciousness (Durkheim), Group Mind (McDougall)
→ Sociology and early, nonexperimental social psych. Leave unanswered the questions of how and why this happens to our minds.

Freud tries to answer this with psychodynamics—i.e., conflict with same-sex parent thus resolved by internalizing all the values/norms of the parent.

Mead and symbolic interactionism: Society's influence is mediated through self-concept born out of interaction.
- Interaction is symbolic as it's both functional but overwhelmingly expressive.
- Symbols are consensual and shared . . . therefore we construct ourselves as social objects.
- Language

Marx: There's a difference between demographics and social class.
- Groups form and become psychological out of a common plight.

Social identity is sympathetic with Marx and Mead but goes further: It explores the psychological processes involved in translating social categories into human groups.

Social identity approach is also functional: Group formation is adaptive; simplifying social stimuli (stereotyping) is adaptive.

Social Identity Theory
CATEGORIZATION
- We accentuate similarities between objects within the same category (you White guys are all alike) and differences between stimuli in different categories—the accentuation effect.
- Evidence: Tajfel and line judgments; judging degree of "negroness."
- Accentuation only happens when the dimensions are believed to be associated to the category (e.g., UofA students are unruly . . . look at how unruly they are!").

- More likely if it's relevant, salient, important, etc.
- We always categorize with reference to our self—in-group similarity and out-group dissimilarity
    - → 1. Categorization causes us to place our self in a group and
    - 2. It generates category-congruent behaviors that are stereotypic of the category.

    - → Self-categorization is the process that transforms individuals into groups.

SOCIAL COMPARISON
To help us understand the degree of accentuation or stereotyping.
- All knowledge is socially derived through social comparisons.

→ CATEGORIZATION AND SOCIAL COMPARISON work together to generate group behavior (e.g., discrimination, in-group favoritism, evaluative superiority over ou-tgroup, . . .)
- CATEGORIZATION → Stereotypic perceptions of self, in-group and out-group and degree of accentuation on intergroup differences.
- SOCIAL COMPARISON → Accounts for the selectivity of the accentuation effect (self-esteem enhancement) and the magnitude of the exaggeration of intergroup differences and intragroup similarities.

Social Identity and the Self-Concept
"I" = Cognitive Process
"Me" = Cognitive Structure, i.e., self-concept

Self-concept = Totality of self-descriptions and self-evaluations subjectively available including:
1) Social identifications: Derived from group memberships (nationality, sex, etc.)
2) Personal identifications: Your specific attributes

→ SIT assumes that social ids can be more salient than personal ids, and when this is so, you have qualitatively different behavior: group behavior.

Social categorizations will "fit" the data to the degree that they maximize the contrast between intercategory differences and intracategory differences.

e.g.: Four-person discussion; two males in agreement, two females in agreement but disagree with the males. Self-conceptualization is likely to be based on sex-category membership (sex becomes salient). If disagreements are based on race, race becomes salient, etc.

What if one is race conscious? He/she might present arguments in a way that render race irrelevant.

Social Identity and Social Structure
Basically, SIT addresses the relationship between society and the individual mediated by social identity.

Large-scale social categories (race, sex, religion, class, occupation, etc.) stand in power, status, and prestige relations to one another.

Dominant groups: Impose the dominant value system, maintain themselves.

Individuals are born into these structures by virtue of place of birth, skin color, parentage, etc. and are left out of others.

Subordinate group members are motivated to remedy negative consequences of group identity.

Subjective belief structures: Individual's beliefs concerning the nature of society and the relations between groups within it.
Two types:
1) Social Mobility: Boundaries between groups are permeable; one can "pass" from one to another.
   - Leaves status quo relatively unchanged
   - Therefore, it's in the interest of the dominant to promulgate the ideology of social mobility—"Just work hard, our society is color-blind."
   - Mythical: Mythical because of the difficulty; you can't just "individualize" everything; you can't ignore social identities and their intrinsic relationship to individual self.

2) Social Change: Boundaries between groups are rigid, fixed, and impermeable.
   - These are group strategies, not individual strategies.
   1) Social Creativity: Change the reference or dimensions that result in positive evaluation ("Sure the UofA might have more prestige, but not in Psychology!").
   2) Redefine ("Black is Beautiful").
   3) Don't compare with dominant ("Aryans with no real power and compare with and/or denigrate other low status groups").

Reaction by Dominant
   - Depends on strategy of subordinate
     - Lateral comparisons ➔ No reaction as this is simply divide and rule and maintains power.
     - Different dimensions ➔ Don't go too far; it must challenge/repudiate the attempts or legitimate other dimensions of intergroup comparisons that maintain power (e.g., "gay marriage").

       4) Compete: Only when there are no other cognitive alternatives
       - Constitutional change (Black civil rights)

       - Violent terrorism (Al Quaeda)
       - Civil War (Northern Ireland)
       - Revolution (Iran)
       - Passive resistance (Ghandi).

Glossary

Acceptance When both actions and beliefs are in line with the social norm.

Affect heuristic A shortcut in making judgments that involves the use of automatic (gut level) emotional reactions to make decisions.

Aggression Intentionally harming someone who is motivated to avoid that harm.

Altruistic Helping is altruistic when the action is engaged in with the ultimate goal of increasing the welfare of the other. Any self-benefit is an unintended consequence. Contrast with egoistic.

Attitudes Evaluations based on reactions, in terms of how we feel and what we think, toward some attitude object. The evaluations we have involve two aspects, strength and valence. Valence is how positive or negative that attitude may be.

Attribution An explanation of the behavior of others or the self.

Audience inhibition Inhibition of action (helping) that occurs because of embarrassment or self-consciousness in the presence of other people.

Automatic system The part of the cognitive system that processes information outside of consciousness. Processing occurs quickly, is relatively effortless, has a large capacity, and allows us to do many things at once.

Availability heuristic A shortcut in making judgments that involves assessing the frequency of something or the likelihood of an event occurring by how available it is in memory. Instances that come more easily to mind, and thus are more available, are judged to be more likely.

Base rate fallacy The error we make when we ignore the number of instances of an event in the population and base a judgment on other characteristics of the situation such as representativeness.

Brainstorming A strategy for coming up with ideas as a group involving generating as many ideas as possible, with encouragement to combine, improve, or expand on previous ideas.

Bystander effect The tendency for individuals to be less likely to help in an emergency situation when others are present, due to a combination of factors including pluralistic ignorance, diffusion of responsibility, and audience inhibition.

Catharsis   The idea that by engaging in aggressive actions, one reduces aggression. In fact, catharsis does not actually reduce aggression and may increase it.

Central route to persuasion   According to the elaboration likelihood model, the route taken when individuals have the time and energy to process a message deeply, evaluating the strength of the persuasive arguments.

Cognitive dissonance   A gap between attitudes or between attitudes and actions that creates tension or dissonance. We often change our attitudes when faced with a high level of dissonance.

Communal relationships   Relationships where partners respond to the needs of the other person, not worrying about when or how their contributions will be repaid. Contrast with exchange relationships.

Companionate love   The type of love characterized by deep caring for another person, comfort and trust, and enjoyment of shared experiences.

Comparison level   In interdependence theory, the expectations individuals have for the level of costs and rewards in a relationship. Helps determine satisfaction with a relationship.

Comparison level of alternatives   In interdependence theory, the outcomes we expect to receive if we were in an alternate relationship. Helps determine dependency on a relationship.

Compassionate love   A type of love characterized as a self-giving and caregiving.

Compliance   When actions are in line with the social norm, but belief remains distinct.

Confederate   A person working with an experimenter who appears to the participant to be another participant or part of the situation.

Conformity   Going along with a group in actions or beliefs.

Conjunction fallacy   The error of believing that two events occurring together is more likely than one of the events occurring alone.

Conscious system   The part of the cognitive system that we are consciously aware of and can direct. Processing occurs slowly and is effortful. The conscious system has a limited capacity, but allows for nuanced responses.

Contact hypothesis   The idea that contact between groups will lessen conflict.

Coordination loss   The loss of production that occurs in groups because of difficulty in coordinating efforts.

Correlation   A relationship between two variables. A correlation coefficient is a number that describes a relationship between two variables.

Correlational method   A research method that allows researchers to predict the value of one variable if provided with information about a second variable.

Credibility   Believability; a factor in whether a message is persuasive. Its two aspects are expertise and trustworthiness.

Debriefing   Explanation at the end of a research study of the true purpose of the study. If deception was used or a stressful situation was encountered during the study, the researcher uses the debriefing to identify and address the issues.

Decision/commitment   In Sternberg's triangular theory of love, the component that includes a short-term commitment, the decision to love a particular other person, or long-term commitment, the decision to stay with someone over the long term.

Deindividuation   The tendency to engage in behaviors with a group that one would not engage in alone because of a loss of individual accountability.

Dependent variable   The variable we measure in an experiment.

Descriptive norms   Norms describing what most people do. Contrasted with injunctive norms.

Diffusion of responsibility   The parceling out of responsibility to help in a large group, with the result of less helping in an emergency situation when a number of people are present.

Discrimination   Negative behavior toward individuals or groups based on beliefs and feelings about those groups.

Displaced aggression   The targeting of aggression toward a person or entity that is not the true target.

Distinctiveness   One thing that gives minorities power despite their minority status. When one point of differences from the group is held by a minority, but the minority agrees with the majority on other points.

Door-in-the-face technique   Persuasion technique that involves beginning with a large request, which is refused, and following with a smaller request, the target request.

Ego depletion   The diminished capacity for volitional action after engaging in some other volitional action.

Egoistic   Helping is egoistic when the action is engaged in with the ultimate goal of self-benefit. Improvement in the welfare of the other is an instrumental goal. Contrast with altruistic.

Elaboration likelihood model   A model that proposes two routes to persuasion: the central route, used when individuals have time and energy to engage with the message, and the peripheral route, used when individuals are lacking in time and energy and rely on other cues to help them make decisions.

Empathy-altruism hypothesis   The idea that adopting another person's perspective, feeling empathy, leads to altruistic responding.

Equity   A balance of inputs and outputs.

Exchange relationships   Relationships where contributions and rewards are counted and immediate repayment is expected. Contrasted with communal relationships.

Experimental method   A research method involving manipulation of one variable to investigate whether the manipulated variable causes change in a second, measured, variable.

Expertise   One aspect of credibility, along with trustworthiness. Describes a communicator who appears to have knowledge and is able to communicate it.

Explanatory style   The way a person explains events. Explanations include whether the event is explained as internal or external, stable or unstable, and global or specific.

Explicit attitudes   Attitudes we are conscious of and can report on. Contrasted with implicit attitudes.

External attribution   Attribution of an action that involves something external to the person, such as an unforeseen circumstance.

Extraneous variables   Variables that are outside of our interest but may affect the results of a study.

Foot-in-the-door technique   Persuasion technique that involves making a small request followed by a larger request, the target request.

Frustration   Emotion that results from the blocking of behavior that would have moved the person toward a particular goal.

Fundamental attribution error   Attributing behavior to dispositional factors when there are clear situational factors at work. Also known as correspondence bias.

Gain framed   A message that focuses on the benefits of a behavior.

Generalizability   A research study is high in this if what the participants do in the study is similar and can be applied to what people tend to do in the world. A study that is generalizable is one whose results can be applied in a variety of situations.

Group   Two or more people who are interacting and forming some kind of coherent unit.

Groupthink   A decision-making process that occurs when a desire for harmony and consensus within the group interferes with appropriate information seeking and leads to bad decision making.

Hard to get   Selective in one's social choices.

Heuristics   The shortcuts we use in making judgments.

Hindsight bias   Our tendency to believe, after the fact, that something was obvious. Also known as the I-knew-it-all-along phenomenon.

Hostile aggression   Aggression that is intended to harm another, with no other goal or motive.

Hostile attribution of intent   A way of attributing of the actions of others as having the intent of harm, even when those actions are friendly or ambiguous. Also known as hostile attribution bias.

Hypothesis   A testable prediction.

Implicit attitudes   Attitudes that are based in the automatic, unconscious reactions we have toward an attitude object. Contrasted with explicit attitudes.

Independent cultures   Cultures where people are viewed as separate, unique individuals whose qualities are independent of their social connections.

Independent variable   The variable we manipulate in an experiment.

Informational influence   A type of social influence toward conformity that occurs when the individual believes the crowd possesses knowledge the individual does not. Contrasted with normative influence.

Informed consent   Obtained from research participants. Within informed consent researchers tell the participants what they can expect within their participation and about their rights as participants, including the right to discontinue participation.

Ingratiation   Impression management strategy involving flattery.

Ingroup   The group to which one belongs.

Ingroup favoritism   The tendency to show preferential treatment toward members of one's own group.

Injunctive norms   Norms for what is approved or disapproved of. Contrasted with descriptive norms.

Institutional Review Board   A committee at a university, college, or other organization where research is done that evaluates the ethics of a research study.

Instrumental aggression   Aggression as a means to an end.

Instrumental goals   Goals an individual strives for in order to obtain an ultimate goal.

Insufficient justification   When our attitudes and behaviors are in conflict and we have no adequate explanation for why. Important for cognitive dissonance theory.

Interdependence theory   The theory that satisfaction and dependency in a relationship can be determined by investigating costs, rewards, and comparison level for satisfaction and costs, rewards, and comparison level of alternatives for dependency.

Interdependent cultures   Cultures where people are viewed as enmeshed within social connections such that the person cannot be described adequately without social context and connections. Also referred to as collectivistic cultures.

Internal attribution   Attribution for an action that involves something internal to the person, such as personality or attitude.

Intimacy   In Sternberg's triangular theory of love, the component that includes feelings of closeness or bonds to another person.

Intimacy group   Type of group. Intimacy groups are made up of relatives or friends, that is, those we are related to or those whose company we enjoy. Intimacy groups are viewed as small, long lived, having great deal of interaction, and being relatively impermeable to outsiders.

Investment   Within the investment model, investment may take the form of intrinsic investments like time and emotional energy or extrinsic investments like shared possessions or even mutual friends that might be lost if one were to leave the relationship. High investment tends to be related to higher commitment.

Investment model   Model that proposes that commitment is a function of satisfaction with the relationship, quality of alternatives, and investment.

Kin selection   The tendency for greater helping of those with whom we share the most genetic material.

Köhler effect   The tendency for individuals who are less capable than their group to work harder in a group context than they would if they were working alone.

Laissez-faire leadership   Characterized by a hands-off approach, with the leader simply allowing the followers to do what they would like without substantial input from the leader.

Leadership   Influencing a group and its members to contribute to the goals of the group and coordinating and guiding those efforts.

Legitimization-of-paltry-favors technique   A persuasion technique that involves making a very small contribution acceptable. It is difficult to not give when even a very small amount is described as legitimate.

Loneliness   The feeling that one is without desired social connections.

Loose association   Type of group. Loose associations are made up of those who are connected by common attitudes, experiences, or appreciations (such as an affinity for dogs). Loose associations are viewed as large, potentially short lived, having little interaction, and being very open to outsiders.

Loss framed   A message that focuses on what might be lost if a behavior is not done.

Low-ball technique   A persuasion technique involving an initial, reasonable request to which additional things are added that make the overall request less reasonable. People tend to maintain commitment to the request, despite the fact they would likely have refused if they had known all the costs initially.

Matching hypothesis   A tendency to have relationships with those who match us in physical attractiveness.

Mere-exposure effect   The tendency to have greater liking for people or things we see often.

Mindguards   With groupthink, the individuals who protect the leader from hearing a viewpoint contrary to his/her own resulting in the leader never hearing about dissenting opinions.

Need for cognition   An individual difference in how much people enjoy thinking.

Need to belong   A fundamental human need involving a need for frequent interactions with others and the presence of affective bonds.

Negative correlation   A relationship between two correlated variables in which one variable increases as the other variable decreases.

Normative influence   A type of social influence toward conformity that occurs when the individual conforms to avoid social rejection and to be liked or accepted by the group. Contrasted with informational influence.

Norms   Beliefs about what the group is thinking or doing.

Observational method   A research method that involves observing participants and not manipulating any variables within the situation. This method answers questions about what is happening.

Optimistic explanatory style   Someone with an optimistic explanatory style will explain positive events as internal, stable, and global, and negative events as external, unstable, and specific.

Outgroup   The group to which one does not belong.

Outgroup homogeneity effect   Members of outgroups, groups an individual is not a part of, are viewed as more similar, or homogeneous. Individuals tend to view members of their own group as more varied.

Overbenefited   Within equity theory, receiving more from a relationship than one puts into it.

Passion   In Sternberg's triangular theory of love, the component that includes the physical attraction to another person and/or expression of desires and needs.

Passionate love   The love we have for romantic partners; a more sexually based love.

Perceived behavior control   The belief that one can engage in the behavior. Part of the theory of planned behavior.

Peripheral route to persuasion   According to the elaboration likelihood model, the route taken when people do not have the time or energy to process a message. With this route individuals use other cues to evaluate the persuasive arguments.

Pessimistic explanatory style   Someone with a pessimistic explanatory style will explain positive events as external, unstable, and specific, and negative events as internal, stable, and global.

Pluralistic ignorance   The tendency to collectively misinterpret situations when a number of individuals are present.

Polarization   If we think of opinions on a continuum, with strong agreement on one pole and strong disagreement on the other pole, people tend to polarize. Involves a shift closer to whichever pole they were initially leaning.

Positive correlation   A relationship between two correlated variables in which one variable increases as the other variable increases.

Prejudice   Negative attitudes toward individuals based on their membership in a particular group.

Prisoner's dilemma   A social dilemma involving two individuals. If both compete, both lose. If both cooperate, they have the best collective outcome. The best individual outcome comes when one competes and the partner cooperates.

Private self-awareness   Your awareness of your internal states, for example your thoughts, feelings, or desires.

Public self-awareness   Awareness of how you appear to others.

Random assignment   Within an experiment, each individual in the sample has an equal chance of being in each of the groups (levels of the independent variable).

Reactance   The behavior one undertakes when one's freedom is threatened, such as when an item is available for a limited time.

Reciprocity   When others do something for us, we feel an obligation to do something for them.

Relational aggression   Aggression that is focused on the destruction of relationships or social status.

Representativeness heuristic   A shortcut in making judgments that involves making decisions based on how similar someone or something is to the typical, or representative, person, thing, or situation.

Resource dilemma   A social dilemma in which the individual can gain the best outcome by taking advantage of a collective resource without contributing but the collective does best if everyone contributes.

Scarcity technique   A persuasion technique where a product or option appears to only be available for a limited time or in a limited number.

Schemas   Knowledge structures that organize what we know and may affect how we process information.

Scripts   Knowledge structures that allow us to predict what is likely to occur in a situation (e.g., first date) and therefore engage in expected and appropriate behavior.

Self-concept   The collection of things you know about yourself.

Self-efficacy   Your evaluation of your ability to perform particular tasks.

Self-esteem   Your overall evaluation of the qualities you associate with yourself.

Self-fulfilling prophecy   Prophecies individuals make about the behaviors of others that become self-fulfilling when the individual who has the belief acts in a way that leads the other to act in the expected manner.

Self-handicapping   Creating an excuse for a later failure by doing something that is likely to hinder one's success.

Self-perception theory   The idea that attitudes can be determined by looking at one's behavior.

Self-reference effect   The tendency to better remember those things related to the self.

Self-schemas   Knowledge structures about the self.

Self-serving bias   A bias toward viewing successes as something we can attribute to our selves and blaming failures as something outside of the self. Overall, this bias allows for people to maintain a positive view of themselves.

Sleeper effect   Occurs when a message become more persuasive with time.

Social categorization   Type of group. Group made up of those with similar characteristics (such as Army veterans). Social categorization is characterized as large, long lived, potentially having little interaction, and being relatively impermeable to outsiders.

Social facilitation   The tendency for the presence of others to increase the dominant response tendency. For an easy or well-learned task the dominant response tendency is to do well. For a difficult or new task the dominant response tendency is to do poorly.

Social identity model   Model for deindividuation that proposes that as people lose their individual identity they take on the identity of the group around them.

Social loafing   The tendency for individuals to produce less or not work as hard when working with others.

Social psychology   The scientific study of human thoughts, feelings, and behavior as they relate to and are influenced by others.

Stereotype threat   The risk of confirming a negative stereotype about one's group. The stereotype predicts poor performance, so the person has to deal with the possibility of confirming that stereotype. Awareness that one is being evaluated based on membership in a stereotyped group can, therefore, interfere with performance.

Stereotypes   Beliefs about the characteristics of particular groups or members of those groups.

Subjective norms   Beliefs of important people in one's environment. Important aspect of the theory of planned behavior.

Superordinate goals   Goals held by both groups in a conflict that transcend the conflict and provide a common aim.

Task group   Type of group. Group that engages in a task together. Task groups are normally small and short lived and have a great deal of interaction.

That's-not-all technique   A persuasion technique involving making an offer and, before the customer can respond, lowering the price or offering additional products.

Theory   A set of principles or a framework for a set of observations and research findings.

Theory of planned behavior   A theory predicting behavior from (1) attitude toward that behavior, (2) subjective norms related to that behavior, and (3) perceived behavioral control.

Tit-for-tat strategy   Strategy used in playing the iterated prisoner's dilemma game that involves using the strategy used by one's partner on the previous turn.

Tragedy of the commons   A social dilemma in which the individual can gain the best outcome by taking advantage of a collective resource but if too many in the group take advantage of the resource it will not be sustainable and will no longer be available. Also called the commons dilemma.

Transactional leadership   Leadership involving offering an exchange of rewards for effort from followers. Contrast with transformational leadership.

Transformational leadership   Leadership where the leader offers followers a common purpose and asks that individual interests be put aside so the group can work together toward that goal. Contrast with transactional leadership.

Transportation   The joining of feelings, attention, and thoughts in the context of a story. Transportation involves getting lost in a story.

Triangular theory of love   Sternberg's theory of love that uses three components, intimacy, passion, and commitment, to describe different types of love.

Triggered displaced aggression   Displaced aggression directed toward someone who is not the actual cause of the aggressive feelings but who has done something minor.

Trustworthy   One aspect of credibility, along with expertise. Describes a communicator who we believe is telling us accurate information.

Ultimate goal   The true goal, the end toward which one is aiming.

Underbenefited   Within equity theory, providing more to a relationship than one receives from it.

Variable   Something that varies or can vary; the factors assessed when performing an experiment.

Violence   Physical aggression that has the potential of severely harming someone.

Weapons priming effect   The tendency for the presence of weapons to increase aggression. Also called the weapons effect.

Win-stay, lose-shift strategy   Strategy used in playing the iterated prisoner's dilemma game that involves using whatever strategy is providing the best outcome. If cooperation is providing the best outcome, the individual stays with that and changes when that strategy is no longer helpful.

Credits

Chapter 12

p189: William Stevenson/SuperStock

Chapter 15

p227: APAimages/Rex Features/
Associated Press

p228: Antonio Perez/Associated Press

p229: Comstock Images/Thinkstock

p230: Image100/SuperStock

p232: Cultura Limited/SuperStock

p233: Darryl Dyck/Associated Press

p236: Francisco Cruz/SuperStock

p241: Pablo Martinez Monsivais/
Associated Press

p242: iStockphoto/Thinkstock

References

Abrahams, M. F., & Bell, R. A. (1994). Encouraging charitable contributions: An examination of three models of door-in-the-face compliance. *Communication Research, 21,* 131–153. doi: 10.1177/009365094021002001

Abramson, L. Y., & Alloy, L. B. (1981). Depression, nondepression, and cognitive illusions: Reply to Schwartz. *Journal of Experimental Psychology, 110,* 436–447. doi: 10.1037/0096-3445.110.3.436

Adams, G. R., Ryan, B. A., Ketsetzis, M., & Keating, L. (2000). Rule compliance and peer sociability: A study of family process, school-focused parent-child interactions, and children's classroom behavior. *Journal of Family Psychology, 14,* 237–250. doi: 10.1037/0893-3200.14.2.237

Adler, J. M., Kissel, E. C., & McAdams, D.P. (2006). Emerging from the CAVE: Attributional style and the narrative study of identity in midlife adults. *Cognitive Therapy and Research, 30,* 39–51. doi: 10.1007/s10608-006-9005-1

Ahlfinger, N. R., & Esser, J. K. (2001). Testing the groupthink model: Effects of promotional leadership and conformity predisposition. *Social Behavior and Personality, 29,* 31–41. doi: 10.2224/sbp.2001.29.1.31

Aiello, J. R., & Douthitt, E. A. (2001). Social facilitation from Triplett to electronic performance monitoring. *Group Dynamics: Theory, Research, and Practice, 5,* 163–180. doi: 110.1037//1089-2699.5.3.163

Ajzen, I. (1991). The theory of planned behavior. *Organizational Behavior and Human Decision Process, 50,* 179–211. doi: 10.1016/0749-5978(91)90020-T

Alberts, H. J. E. M., Martijn, C., Nievelstein, F., Jansen, A., & deVries, N. K. (2008). Distracting the self: Shifting attention prevents ego depletion. *Self and Identity, 7,* 322–334. doi: 10.1080/152988601987583

Allen, M. (1991). Meta-analysis comparing the persuasiveness of one-sided and two-sided messages. *Western Journal of Speech Communication, 55,* 390–404.

Allport, F. H. (1920). The influence of the group upon association and thought. *Journal of Experimental Psychology, 3,* 159–182. doi: 10.1037/h0067891

Allport, F. H. (1924). *Social psychology.* Boston, MA: Houghton-Mifflin.

Allport, F. H. (1924). *Social psychology.* Boston, MA: Riverside Editions, Houghton Mifflin.

Allport, G. W. (1935). Attitudes. In C. Murchison (Ed.), *Handbook of social psychology* (pp. 798–844). Worchester, MA: Clark University Press.

Allport, G. W. (1954). The historical background of modern social psychology. In G. Lindzey (Ed.), *Handbook of social psychology* (Vol. 1, pp. 3–56). Reading, MA: Addison-Wesley.

Allport, G. W. (1954). *The nature of prejudice.* Reading, MA: Addison-Wesley.

Alter, A. L., Oppenheimer, D. M., Epley, N., & Eyre, R. N. (2007). Overcoming intuition: Metacognitive difficulty activates analytical reasoning. *Journal of Experimental Psychology: General, 136*, 569–576. doi: 10.1037/0096-3445.136.4.569

Amato, P. R. (1986). Emotional arousal and helping behavior in a real-life emergency. *Journal of Applied Social Psychology, 16*, 633–641. doi: 10.1111/j.1559-1816.1986.tb01164.x

Amato, P. R., & Previti, D. (2003). People's reasons for divorcing: Gender, social class, the life course, and adjustment. *Journal of Family Issues, 24*, 602–626. doi: 10.1177/0192513X03254507

Amato, P. R., & Rogers, S. J. (1997). A longitudinal study of marital problems and subsequent divorce. *Journal of Marriage and the Family, 59*, 612–624. doi: 10.2307/353949

Amato, P. R., Ho, R., & Partridge, S. (1984). Responsibility attribution and helping behaviour in the Ash Wednesday bushfires. *Australian Journal of Psychology, 36*, 191–203. doi: 10.1080/00049538408255091

Amiraian, D. E., & Sobal, J. (2009). Dating and eating: Beliefs about dating foods among university students. *Appetite, 53*, 226–232. doi: 10.1016/j.appet.2009.06.012

Ancona, D. G., & Cadwell, D. F. (1992). Demography and design: Predictors of new product team performance. *Organization Science, 3*, 321–341.

Anderson, C. A. (1989). Temperature and aggression: Ubiquitous effects of heat on occurrence of human violence. *Psychological Bulletin, 106*, 74–96. doi: 10.1037/0033-2909.106.1.74

Anderson, C. A., Shibuya, A., Ihori, N., Swing, E. L., Bushman, B. J., Sakamoto, A., Rothstein, H. R., & Saleem, M. (2010). Violent video game effects on aggression, empathy, and prosocial behavior in Eastern and Western countries: A meta-analytic review. *Psychological Bulletin, 136*, 151–173. doi: 10.1037/a0018251

Anthony, D. B., Holmes, J. G., & Wood, J. V. (2007). Social acceptance and self-esteem: Tuning the sociometer to interpersonal value. *Journal of Personality and Social Psychology, 92*, 1024–1039. doi: 10.1037/0022-3514.92.6.1024

Appel, M., & Richter, T. (2007). Persuasive effects of fictional narratives increase over time. *Media Psychology, 10*, 113–134.

Appiah, K. A. (October 24, 2010). The art of social change. *New York Times Sunday Magazine*, MM22. Retrieved from http://www.nytimes.com/2010/10/24/magazine/24FOB-Footbinding-t.html?_r=1

Archer, J. (2006). Cross-cultural differences in physical aggression between partners: A social-role analysis. *Personality and Social Psychology Review, 10*, 133–153. doi: 10.1207/s15327957pspr1002_3

Armitage , C. J., & Conner, M. (2001). Efficacy of the theory of planned behavior: A meta-analytic review. *British Journal of Social Psychology, 40*, 471–499. doi: 10.1348/014466601164939

Armitage, C. J. & Conner, M. (2000). Attitudinal ambivalence: A test of three key hypotheses. *Personality and Social Psychology Bulletin, 26*, 1421–1432. doi: 10.1177/0146167200263009

Aronson, J., Lustina, M. J., Good, C., Keough, K., Steele, C. M., & Brown, J. (1999). When white men can't do math: Necessary and sufficient factors in stereotype threat. *Journal of Experimental Social Psychology, 35*, 29–46. doi: 10.1006/jesp.1998.1371

Asch, S. (1958). Effects of group pressure on the modification and distortion of judgments. In E. E. Maccoby, T. M. Newcomb, & E. L. Hartley (Eds.), *Readings in Social Psychology*. New York: Holt, Rinehart, & Winston.

Asch, S. E. (1956). Studies of interdependence and conformity: A minority of one against the unanimous majority. *Psychological Monographs, 70,* No. 9 (Whole No. 416).

Ash, M. G. (1992). Cultural contexts and scientific change in psychology. *American Psychologist, 47,* 198–207. doi: 10.1037/0003-066X.47.2.198

Avdeyeva, T. V., Burgetova, K., & Welch, I. D. (2006). To help or not to help? Factors that determined helping responses to Katrina victims. *Analyses of Social Issues and Public Policy, 6,* 159–173. doi: 10.1111/j.1530-2415.2006.00113.x

Averill, J. R. (1980). Emotion and anxiety: Sociocultural, biological, and psychological determinants. In A. O. Rorty (Ed.), *Explaining emotions* (pp. 37–72). Berkeley: University of California Press.

Axelrod, R. (1984). *The evolution of cooperation.* New York, NY: Basic Books.

Bachman, J. G., & O'Malley, P. M. (1986). Self-concepts, self-esteem, and educational experiences: The frog pond revisited (again). *Journal of Personality and Social Psychology, 50,* 35–46. doi: 10.1037/0022-3514.50.1.35

Back, M. D., Schmukle, S. C., & Egloff, B. (2008). Becoming friends by chance. *Psychological Science, 19,* 439–440. doi: 10.11/j.1467-9280.2008.02106.x

Bailis, D. S. (2001). Benefits of self-handicapping in sport: A field study of university athletes. *Canadian Journal of Behavioural Science, 33,* 213–223. doi: 10.1037/h0087143

Bandura, A. (1977). Self-efficacy: Toward a unifying theory of behavioral change. *Psychological Review, 84,* 191–215. doi: 10.1037/0033-295X.84.2.191

Bandura, A. (2000). Exercise of human agency through collective efficacy. *Current Directions in Psychological Science, 9,* 75–78. doi: 10.1111/1467-8721.00064

Bandura, A., Ross, D., & Ross, S. A. (1963). Imitation of film-mediated aggressive models. *Journal of Abnormal and Social Psychology, 66,* 3–11. doi: 10.1037/h0048687

Bar-Tal, D., Raviv, A., & Goldberg, M. (1982). Helping behavior among preschool children: An observational study. *Child Development, 53,* 396–402. doi: 10.2307/1128982

Bargal, D. (2008). Action research: A paradigm for achieving social change. *Small Group Research, 39,* 17–27. doi: 10.1177/1046496407313407

Barile, L. (2010, May 19). *The Biggest Loser: Players Tackle a Marathon.* From http://today .msnbc.msn.com/id/37229137

Baron, R. A., & Lawton, S. F. (1972). Environmental influences on aggression: The facilitation of modeling effects on high ambient temperatures. *Psychonomic Science, 26,* 80–82.

Baron, R. A., & Richardson, D. R. (1994). *Human aggression* (2nd ed.). New York, NY: Plenum Press.

Barrick, M. R., Shaffer, J. A., & DeGrassi, S. W. (2009). What you see may not be what you get: Relationships among self-presentation tactics and ratings of interview and job performance. *Journal of Applied Psychology, 94,* 1394–1411. doi: 10.1037/a0016532

Bartholow, B. D., & Heinz, A. (2006). Alcohol and aggression without consumption: Alcohol cues, aggressive thoughts, and hostile perception bias. *Psychological Science, 17,* 30–37. doi: 10.1111/j.1467-9280.2005.01661.x

Bartholow, B. D., Anderson, C. A., Carnagey, N. L., & Benjamin, A. J. (2005). Interactive effects of life experience and situational cues on aggression: The weapons priming effect in hunters and nonhunters. *Journal of Experimental Social Psychology, 41,* 48–60. doi: 10.1016/j.jesp.2004.05.005

Bass, B. M. (1985). Leadership and performance beyond expectation. New York, NY: Free Press.

Bass, B. M. (1997). Does the transactional-transformational leadership paradigm transcend organizational and national boundaries? *American Psychologist, 52,* 130–139. doi: 10.1037/0003-066X.52.2.130

Batson, C. D. (1990). How social an animal? The human capacity for caring. *American Psychologist, 45,* 336–346. doi: 10.1037/0003-066X.45.3.336

Batson, C. D. (2010). Empathy-induced altruistic motivation. In M. Mikulincer & P. R. Shaver (Eds.), *Prosocial motives, emotions, and behavior: The better angels of our nature* (pp. 15–34). Washington, D. C.: American Psychological Association. doi: 10.1037/12061-001

Batson, C. D., Batson, J. G., Griffitt, C. A., Barrientos, S., Brandt, J. R., Sprengelmeyer, P., & Bayly, M. J. (1989). Negative-state relief and the empathy-altruism hypothesis. *Journal of Personality and Social Psychology, 56,* 922–933. doi: 10.1037/0022-3514 .56.6.922

Batson, C. D., Batson, J. G., Slingsby, J. K., Harrell, K. L., Peekna, H. M., & Todd, R. M. (1991). Empathic joy and the empathy-altruism hypothesis. *Journal of Personality and Social Psychology, 61,* 413–426. doi: 10.1037/0022-3514.61.3.413

Batson, C. D., Batson, J. G., Todd, R. M., Brummett, B. H., Shaw, L. L., & Aldeguer, C. M. R. (1995). Empathy and the collective good: Caring for one of the others in a social dilemma. *Journal of Personality and Social Psychology, 68,* 619–631. doi: 10.1037/0022-3514.68.4.619

Batson, C. D., Duncan, B. D., Ackerman, P., Buckley, T., & Birch, K. (1981). Is empathic emotion a source of altruistic motivation? *Journal of Personality and Social Psychology, 40,* 290–302. doi: 10.1037/0022-3514.40.2.290

Batson, C. D., Dyck, J. L., Brandt, J. R., Batson, J. G., Powell, A. L., McMaster, M. R., & Griffitt, C. (1988). Five studies testing two new egoistic alternatives to the empathy-altruism hypothesis. *Journal of Personality and Social Psychology, 55,* 52–77. doi: 10.1037/0022-3514.55.1.52

Batson, C. D., Klein, T. R., Highberger, L., & Shaw, L. L. (1995). Immorality from empathy-induced altruism: When compassion and justice conflict. *Journal of Personality and Social Psychology, 68,* 1042–1054. doi: 10.1037/0022-3514.68.6.1042

Baumeister, R. F., & Leary, M. R. (1995). The need to belong: Desire for interpersonal attachments as a fundamental human motivation. *Psychological Bulletin, 117,* 495–529. doi: 10.1037/0033-2909.117.3.497

Baumeister, R. F., Bratslavsky, E., Muraven, M., & Tice, D. M. (1998). Ego depletion: Is the active self a limited resource? *Journal of Personality and Social Psychology, 74,* 1252–1265. doi: 10.1037/0022-3514.74.5.1252

Baumeister, R. F., Campbell, J. D., Krueger, J. I., & Vohs, K. D. (2003). Does high self-esteem cause better performance, interpersonal success, happiness, or healthier lifestyles? *Psychological Science in the Public Interest, 4,* 1–44. doi: 10.1111/1529-1006.01431

Baumrind, D. (1964). Some thoughts on ethics of research: After reading Milgram's "behavioral study of obedience." *American Psychologist, 19,* 421–423. doi: 10.1037/ h0040128

Baxter, L. A. (1982). Strategies for ending relationships: Two studies. *The Western Journal of Speech Communication, 46,* 223–241.

Baxter, L. A. (1984). Trajectories of relationship disengagement. *Journal of Social and Personal Relationships, 1,* 29–48. doi: 10.1177/0265407584011003

Beauvois, J. L. & Joule, R. V. (1999). A radical point of view on dissonance theory. In E. Harmon-Jones & J. Mills (Eds.), *Cognitive dissonance: Progress on a pivotal theory in social psychology* (pp. 43–70). Washington, DC: American Psychological Association.

Becker, B. J. (1986). Influence again: An examination of reviews and studies of gender differences in social influence. In J. S. Hyde & M. C. Linn (Eds.), *The psychology of gender: Advances through meta-analysis* (pp. 178–209). Baltimore, MD: Johns Hopkins University Press.

Beggs, J. J., Haines, V. A., & Hurlbert, J. S. (1996). Situational contingencies surrounding the receipt of informal support. *Social Forces, 75*, 202–222. doi: 10.2307/2580762

Bem, D. J., & McConnell, H. K. (1970). Testing the self-perception explanation of dissonance phenomena: On the salience of premanipulation attitudes. *Journal of Personality and Social Psychology, 14*, 23–31. doi: 10.1037/h0020916

Bem, D. J. (1967). Self-perception: An alternative interpretation of cognitive dissonance phenomenon. *Psychological Review, 74*, 183–200. doi: 10.1037/h0024835

Berg, J., Forsythe, R., Nelson, F., & Reitz, T. (2001) Results from a dozen years of election futures markets research. *Handbook of Experimental Economic Results, 1*, 742–751. doi: 10.1016/S1574-0722(07)00080-7

Berkman, L. F. (1995). The role of social relations in health promotion. *Psychosomatic Medicine, 57*, 245–254.

Berkman, L. F., & Syme, S. L. (1979). Social networks, host resistance, and mortality: A nine-year follow-up study of Alameda County residents. *American Journal of Epidemiology, 109*, 186–204.

Berkowitz, L. (1964). Aggressive cues in aggressive behavior and hostility catharsis. *Psychological Review, 71*, 104–122. doi: 10.1037/h0043520

Berkowitz, L., & LePage, A. (1967). Weapons as aggression-eliciting stimuli. *Journal of Personality and Social Psychology, 7*, 202–207. doi: 10.1037/h0025008

Berkowitz, L., & LePage, A. (1967). Weapons as aggression-eliciting stimuli. *Journal of Personality and Social Psychology, 7*, 202–207. doi: 10.1037/h0025008

Bernstein, D. M., Atance, C., Loftus, G. R., & Meltzoff, A. (2004). We saw it all along: Visual hindsight bias in children and adults. *Psychological Science, 15*, 264–267. doi: 10.1111/j.0963-7214.2004.00663.x

Berscheid, E. (2003) Lessons in "greatness" from Kurt Lewin's life and works. In R. J. Sternberg (Ed.), *The anatomy of impact: What makes the great works of psychology great* (pp. 109–123). Washington, D.C.: American Psychological Association. doi: 10.1037/10563-006

Berscheid, E. (2010). Love in the fourth dimension. *Annual Review of Psychology, 61*, 1–25. doi: 10.1146/annurev.psych.093008.100318

Berscheid, E., Dion, K., Walster, E., & Walster, G. W. (1971). Physical attractiveness and dating choice: A test of the matching hypothesis. *Journal of Experimental Social Psychology, 7*, 173–189. doi: 10.1016/0022-1031(71)90065-5

Bettencourt, B. A., & Kernahan, C. (1997). A meta-analysis of aggression in the presence of violent cues: Effect of gender differences and aversive provocation. *Aggressive Behavior, 23*, 447–456. doi: 10.1002/(SICI)1098-2337(1997)23:6, 447::AID-AB4.3.0.CO;2-D

Bettencourt, B. A., & Miller, N. (1996). Gender differences in aggression as a function of provocation: A meta-analysis. *Psychological Bulletin, 119*, 422–447. doi: 10.1037/0033-2909.119.3.422

Bickman, L. (1974). The social power of uniform. *Journal of Applied Social Psychology, 4*, 47–61.

Billig, M., & Tajfel, H. (1973). Social categorization and similarity in intergroup behavior. *European Journal of Social Psychology, 3*, 27–52. doi: 10.1002/ejsp.2420030103

Binning, K. R., & Sherman, D. K. (2011). Categorization and communication in the face of prejudice: When describing perceptions changes what is perceived. *Journal of Personality and Social Psychology, 101,* 321–336. doi: 10.1037/a0023153

Black, H. K., (1974). Physical attractiveness and similarity of attitude in interpersonal attraction. *Psychological Reports, 35,* 403–406.

Blackwell, D. L., & Lichter, D. T. (2004). Homogamy among dating, cohabiting, and married couples. *Sociological Quarterly, 45,* 719–737. doi: 10.1111/j.1533-8525.2004. th02311.x

Bloom, P. N., McBride, C. M., Pollak, K. I., Schwartz-Bloom, R. D., & Lipkus, I. M. (2006). Recruiting teen smokers in shopping malls to a smoking-cessation program using the foot-in-the-door technique. *Journal of Applied Social Psychology, 36,* 1129–1144. doi: 10.1111/j.0021-9029.2006.00034.x

Boelen, P. A., & Reijntjes, A. (2009). Negative cognitions in emotional problems following romantic relationship break-ups. *Stress and Health, 25,* 11–19. doi: 10.1002/ smi.1219

Bohner, G., Frank, E., & Erb, H. P. (1998). Heuristic processing of distinctiveness information in minority and majority influence. *European Journal of Social Psychology, 28,* 855–860. doi: 10.1002/(SICI)1099-0992(199809/10)28:5,855::AID-EJSP894.3.0.CO;2-P

Bohner, G., Ruder, M., & Erb, H. (2002). When expertise backfires: Contrast and assimilation effects in persuasion. *British Journal of Social Psychology, 41,* 495–519. doi: 10.1348/10446602321149858

Bond, M. H. (2004). Culture and aggression—From context to coercion. *Personality and Social Psychology Review, 8,* 62–78. doi: 10.1207/s15327957pspr0801_3

Bond, R., & Smith, P. B. (1996). Culture and conformity: A meta-analysis of studies using Asch's (1952b, 1956) line judgment task. *Psychological Bulletin, 119,* 111–137. doi: 10.1037/0033-2909.119.1.111

Borsari, B., & Carey, K. B. (2003). Descriptive and injunctive norms in college drinking: A meta-analytic integration. *Journal of Studies on Alcohol, 64,* 331–341.

Bowles, T. (1999). Focusing on time orientation to explain adolescent self concept and academic achievement: Part II: Testing a model. *Journal of Applied Health Behavior, 1,* 1–8.

Bramlett, M. D., & Mosher, W. D. (2002). Cohabitation, marriage, divorce, and remarriage in the United States. *Vital Health Statistics, 23,* 1–32.

Brannon, L. A., & Brock, T. C. (2001). Limiting time for responding enhances behavior corresponding to the merits of compliance appeals: Refutation of heuristic-cue theory in service and consumer settings. *Journal of Consumer Psychology, 10,* 135–146. doi: 10.1207/s15327663jcp1003_2

Bray, R. M., & Noble, A. M. (1978). Authoritarianism and decisions of mock juries: Evidence of jury bias and group polarization. *Journal of Personality and Social Psychology, 36,* 1424–1430. doi: 10.1037/0022-3514.36.12.1424

Breuer, J., & Freud, S. (1893–1895/1955). *Studies on hysteria* (Standard Ed. Vol. II). London: Hogarth.

Brickman, P., Redfield, J., Harrison, A. A., & Crandall, R. (1972). Drive and predisposition as factors in the attitudinal effects of mere exposure. *Journal of Experimental Social Psychology, 8,* 31–44. doi: 10.1016/0022-1031(72)90059-5

Broadhead, W. E., Kaplan, B. H., James, S. A., Wagner, E. H., Schoenbach, V. J., Grimson, R., Heyden, S., Tibblin, G., & Gehlbach, S. H. (1983). The epidemiological evidence for a relationship between social support and health. *American Journal of Epidemiology, 117,* 521–537.

Brown, D. J., Cober, R. T., Kane, K., Levy, P. E., & Shalhoop, J. (2006). Proactive personality and the successful job search: A field investigation with college graduates. *Journal of Applied Psychology, 91*, 717–726. doi: 10.1037/0021-9010.91.3.717

Brown, J. J., & Reingen, P. H. (1987). Social ties and word-of-mouth referral behavior. *Journal of Consumer Research, 14*, 350–362. doi: 10.1086/209118

Brown, R., & Hewstone, M. (2005). An integrative theory of intergroup contact. In M. P. Zanna (Ed.), *Advances in experimental social psychology* (Vol. 37; pp. 255–343). San Diego, CA: Elsevier Academic Press.

Brown, V. R., & Paulus, P. B. (2002). Making group brainstorming more effective: Recommendations from an associative memory perspective. *Current Directions in Psychological Science, 11*, 208–212. doi: 10.1111/1467-8721.00202

Brucks, W. M., & Van Lange, P. A. M. (2008). No control, no drive: How noise may undermine conservation behavior in a commons dilemma. *European Journal of Social Psychology, 38*, 810–822. doi: 10.1002/ejsp.478

Buehl, M. M., Alexander, P. A., Murphy, P. K., & Sperl, C. T. (2001). Profiling persuasion: The role of beliefs, knowledge, and interest in the processing of persuasive texts that vary by argument structure. *Journal of Literary Research, 33*, 269–301. doi: 10.1080/10862960109548112

Burger, J. M. (1986). Increasing compliance by improving the deal: The that's-not-all technique. *Journal of Personality and Social Psychology, 51*, 277–283. doi: 10.1037/0022-3514.51.2.277

Burger, J. M. (1999). The foot-in-the-door compliance procedure: A multiple-process analysis and review. *Personality and Social Psychology Review, 3*, 303–325. doi: 10.1207/s15327957/pspr0304_2

Burger, J. M. (2009). Replicating Milgram: Would people still obey today? *American Psychologist, 64*, 1–11. doi: 10.1037/a0010932

Burger, J. M., & Caldwell, D. F. (2003). The effects of monetary incentives and labeling on the foot-in-the-door effect: Evidence for a self-perception process. *Basic and Applied Social Psychology, 25*, 235–241. doi: 10.1207/S15324834BASP2503_06

Burger, J. M., & Petty, R. E. (1981). The low-ball compliance technique: Task or person commitment? *Journal of Personality and Social Psychology, 181*, 492–500. doi: 10.1037/0022-3514.40.3.492

Burger, J. M., Girgis, Z. M., and Manning, C. C. (2011). In their own words: Explaining obedience to authority through an examination of participants' comments. *Social Psychological and Personality Science, 2*, 460–466. doi: 10.1177/1948550610397632

Burger, J. M., Reed, M., DeCesare, K., Rauner, S., & Rozolis, J. (1999). The effects of initial request size on compliance: More about the that's-not-all technique. *Basic and Applied Social Psychology, 21*, 243–249. doi: 10.1207/15324839951036407

Burkley, E. (2008). The role of self-control in resistance to persuasion. *Personality and Social Psychology Bulletin, 34*, 419–431. doi: 10.1177/0146167207310458

Burnett, D. G. (2009). A juror's role. *eJournal USA: Anatomy of a Jury Trial, 14*, 7–10. www.american.gov/publications/ejournalusa.html

Burnstein, E., & Vinokur, A. (1977). Persuasive argumentation and social comparison as determinants of attitude polarization. *Journal of Experimental Social Psychology, 13*, 315–332. doi: 10.1016/0022-1031(77)90002-6

Bushman, B. J. (2002). Does venting anger feed or extinguish the flame? Catharsis, rumination, distraction, anger, and aggressive responding. *Personality and Social Psychology Bulletin, 28*, 724–731.

Bushman, B. J., Baumeister, R. F., & Phillips, C. M. (2001). Do people aggress to improve their mood? Catharsis beliefs, affect regulation opportunity, and aggressive responding. *Journal of Personality and Social Psychology, 81*, 17–32. doi: 10.1037//0022-3514.81.1.17

Bushman, B. J., Baumeister, R. F., & Stack, A. D. (1999). Catharsis, aggression, and persuasive influence: Self-fulfilling or self-defeating prophecies? *Journal of Personality and Social Psychology, 76*, 367–376. doi: 10.1037/0022-3514.76.3.367

Bushman, B. J., Bonacci, A. M., Pedersen, W. C., Vasquez, E. A., & Miller, N. (2005). Chewing on it can chew you up: Effects of rumination on triggered displaced aggression. *Journal of Personality and Social Psychology, 88*, 969–983. doi: 10.1037/0022-3514.88.6.969

Buss, A. H. (1966). Instrumentality of aggression, feedback, and frustration as determinants of physical aggression. *Journal of Personality and Social Psychology, 3*, 153–162. doi: 10.1037/h0022826

Buss, D. M., Larsen, R. J., Westen, D., & Semmelroth, J. (1992). Sex differences in jealousy: Evolution, physiology, and psychology. *Psychological Science, 3*, 251–255. doi: 10.1111/j.1467-9280.1992.tb00038.x

Buss, D. M., & Schmitt, D. P. (1993). Sexual strategies theory: An evolutionary perspective on human mating. *Psychological Review, 100*, 204–232. doi: 10.1037/0033-295X.100.2.204

Buss, D. M., & Shackelford, T. K. (1997). Human aggression in evolutionary psychological perspective. *Clinical Psychology Review, 17*, 605–619. doi: 10.1016/S0272-7358(97)00037-8

Byrne, D., London, O., & Reeves, K. (1967). The effects of physical attractiveness, sex, and attitude similarity on interpersonal attraction. *Journal of Personality, 36*, 259–271. doi: 10.1111/j.1467-6494.1968.tb01473.x

Cacioppo, J. T., & Petty, R. E. (1982). Need of cognition. *Journal of Personality and Social Psychology, 42*, 116–131. doi: 10.1037/0022-3514.42.1.116

Cacioppo, J. T., Hughes, M. E., Waite, L. J., Hawlkey, L. C., & Thisted, R. A. (2006). Loneliness as a specific risk factor for depressive symptoms: Cross-sectional and longitudinal analyses. *Psychology and Aging, 21*, 140–151. doi: 10.1037/0882-7974.21.1.140

Cacioppo, J. T., Petty, R. E., & Morris, K. J. (1983). Effects of need for cognition on message evaluation, recall, and persuasion. *Journal of Personality and Social Psychology, 45*, 805–818. doi: 10.1037/0022-3514.45.4.805

Cadiz Menne, J. M., & Sinnett, E. R. (1971). Proximity and social interaction in residence halls. *Journal of College Student Personnel, 12*, 26–31.

Camacho, L. M., & Paulus, P. B. (1995). The role of social anxiousness in group brainstorming. *Journal of Personality and Social Psychology, 68*, 1071–1080. doi: 10.1037/0022-3514.68.6.1071

Camp, D. E., Klesges, R. C., & Relyea, G. (1993). The relationship between body weight concerns and adolescent smoking. *Health Psychology, 12*, 24–32. doi: 10.1037/0278-6133.12.1.24

Campbell, M. C., & Kirmani, A. (2000). Consumers' use of persuasion knowledge: The effects of accessibility and cognitive capacity on perceptions of an influence agent. *Journal of Consumer Research, 27*, 69–83. doi: 10.1086/314309

Campbell, W. K., & Sedikides, C. (1999). Self-threat magnifies the self-serving bias: A meta-analytic integration. *Review of General Psychology, 3*, 23–43. doi: 10.1037/1089-2680.3.1.23

Cann, A., Sherman, S. J., & Elkes, R. (1975). Effects of initial request size and timing on a second request on compliance: The foot in the door and door in the face. *Journal of Personality and Social Psychology, 32*, 774–782. doi: 10.1037/0022-3514.32.5.774

Card, N. A., Stucky, B. D., Sawalani, G. M., & Little, T. D. (2008). Direct and indirect aggression during childhood and adolescence: A meta-analytic review of gender differences, intercorrelations, and relations to maladjustment. *Child Development, 79*, 1185–1229. doi: 10.1111/j.1467-8624.2008.01184.x

Carter-Sowell, A. R., Chen, Z., & Williams, K. D. (2008). Ostracism increases social susceptibility. *Social Influence, 3*, 143–153. doi: 10.1080/15534510802204868

Cartwright, D., & Zander, A. (1968). *Group dynamics* (3rd ed.). Oxford, England: Harper & Row.

Carvallo, M., & Pelham, B. W. (2006). When fiends become friends: The need to belong and perceptions of personal and group discrimination. *Journal of Personality and Social Psychology, 90*, 94–108. doi: 10.1037/0022-3514.90.1.94

Castelli, L., Vanzetto, K., Sherman, S. J., & Luciano, A. (2001). The explicit and implicit perception of in-group members who use stereotypes: Blatant rejection but subtle conformity. *Journal of Experimental Social Psychology, 37*, 419–426. doi: 10.1006/jesp.2000.1471

Cate, R. M., Lloyd, S. A., & Long, E. (1988). The role of rewards and fairness in developing premarital relationships. *Journal of Marriage and the Family, 50*, 443–452.

Cate, R. M., Lloyd, S. A., Henton, J. M., & Larson, J. H. (1982). Fairness and reward level as predictors of relationship satisfaction. *Social Psychology Quarterly, 45*, 177–181. doi: 10.2307/3033651

Center on Philanthropy (2006, February 20). *Gulf coast hurricane relief donations*. Retrieved from http://www.philanthropy.iupui.edu/Research/Giving/Hurricane_Katrina.aspx

Centers for Disease Control and Prevention (2010). *Fact sheets: Binge drinking*. Retrieved from http://www.cdc.gov/alcohol/fact-sheets/binge-drinking.htm

Chadwick Martin Bailey (2010). *Match.com and Chadwick Martin Bailey 2009–2010 studies: Recent trends in online dating*. Retrieved from http://cp.match.com/cppp/media/CMB_Study.pdf

Chaiken, S. (1979). Communicator physical attractiveness and persuasion. *Journal of Personality and Social Psychology, 37*, 1387–1397. doi: 10.1037/0022-3514.37.8.1387

Chebat, J. C., Charlebois, M., & Gelinas-Chebat, C. (2001). What makes open vs. closed conclusion advertisements more persuasive? The moderating role of prior knowledge and involvement. *Journal of Business Research, 53*, 93–102. doi: 10.1016/S0148-2963(99)0078-8

Chemers, M. M., Hu, L., & Garcia, B. F. (2001). Academic self-efficacy and first-year college student performance and adjustment. *Journal of Educational Psychology, 93*, 55–64. doi: 10.1037/0022-0663.93.1.55

Chen, Z & Mo, L. (2004). Schema induction in problem solving: A multidimensional analysis. *Journal of Experimental Psychology: Learning, Memory, and Cognition, 30*, 583–600. doi: 10.1037/0278-7393.30.3.583

Cherlin, A. J. (1992). *Marriage, divorce, remarriage* (Revised and enlarged edition). Cambridge, MA: Harvard University Press.

Cheung, S. K., & Sun, S. Y. K. (2000). Effect of self-efficacy and social support on the mental health conditions of mutual-aid and organization members. *Social Behavior and Personality, 28*, 413–422. doi: 10.2224/sbp.2000.28.5.413

Chiou, J., & Cheng, C. (2003). Should a company have message boards on its Web sites? *Journal of Interactive Marketing, 17*, 50–61. doi: 10.1002/dir.10059

Cho, H. (2006). Influences of norm proximity and norm type on binge and non-binge drinkers: Examining the under-examined aspects of social norm interventions on college campus. *Journal of Substance Use, 11*, 417–429. doi: 10.1080/14659890600738982

Choi, I., Nisbett, R. E., & Norenzayan, A. (1999). Causal attribution across cultures: Variation and universality. *Psychological Bulletin, 125*, 47–63. doi: 10.1037/0033-2909.125.1.47

Cialdini, R. B., & Schroeder, D. A. (1976). Increasing compliance by legitimizing paltry contributions: When even a penny helps. *Journal of Personality and Social Psychology, 34*, 599–604. doi: 10.1037/0022-3514.34.4.599

Cialdini, R. B., Cacioppo, Bassett, R., & Miller, J. A. (1978). Low-ball procedure for producing compliance: Commitment then cost. *Journal of Personality and Social Psychology, 36*, 463–476. doi: 10.1037/0022-3514.36.5.463

Cialdini, R. B., Kallgren, C. A., & Reno, R. R. (1991). A focus theory of normative conduct: A theoretical refinement and reevaluation of the role of norms in human behavior. *Advances in Experimental Social Psychology, 24*, 201–234. doi: 10.1016/S0065-2601(08)60330-5

Cialdini, R. B., Reno, R. R., & Kallgren, C. A. (1990). A focus theory of normative conduct: Recycling the concept of norms to reduce littering in public places. *Journal of Personality and Social Psychology, 58*, 1015–1026. doi: 10.1037/0022-3514.58.6.1015

Cialdini, R. B., Vincent, J. E., Lewis, S. K. Catalan, J., Wheeler, D., & Darby, B. L. (1975). Reciprocal concessions procedure for inducing compliance: The door-in-the-face technique. *Journal of Personality and Social Psychology, 31*, 206–215. doi: 10.1037/h0076284

Clark, M. S., & Mills, J. (1979). Interpersonal attraction in exchange and communal relationships. *Journal of Personality and Social Psychology, 37*, 12–24. doi: 10.103780022-3514.37.1.12

Clark, M. S., & Monin, J. K. (2006). Giving and receiving communal responsiveness as love. In R. J. Sternberg & K. Weis (Eds.), *The new psychology of love* (pp. 200–221). New Haven, CT: Yale University Press.

Clark, R. D. (2001). Effects of majority defection and multiple minority sources on minority influences. *Group Dynamics, 5*, 57–62. doi: 10.1037/1089-2699.5.1.57

Clarkson, J. J., Hirt, E. R., Jia, L., & Alexander, M. B. (2010). When perception is more than reality: The effects of perceived versus actual resource depletion on self-regulatory behavior. *Journal of Personality and Social Psychology, 98*, 29–46. doi: 10.1037/a0017539

Cohen, D., Nisbett, R. E., Bowdle, B. F., & Schwarz, N. (1996). Insult, aggression, and the southern culture of honor: An "experimental ethnography." *Journal of Personality and Social Psychology, 70*, 945–960. doi: 10.1037/0022-3514.70.5.945

Cohen, R. (1972). Altruism: Human, cultural, or what? *Journal of Social Issues, 28*, 39–57.

Correll, J., Spencer, S. J., & Zanna, M. P. (2004). An affirmed self and an open mind: Self-affirmation and sensitivity to argument strength. *Journal of Experimental Social Psychology, 40*, 350–356. doi: 10.1016/j.jesp.2003.07.001

Cottrell, N. B. (1972). Social facilitation. In C. G. McClintock (Ed.), *Experimental social psychology* (pp. 185–236). New York, NY: Holt.

Cottrell, N. B., Wack, D. L., Sekerak, G. J., & Rittle, R. H. (1968). Social facilitation of dominant responses by the presence of an audience and the mere presence of others. *Journal of Personality and Social Psychology, 9*, 245–250. doi: 10.1037/h0025902

Cousins, S. D. (1989). Culture and self-perception in Japan and the United States. *Journal of Personality and Social Psychology, 56,* 124–131. doi: 10.1037/0022-3514.56.1.124

Crandall, C. S., Eshleman, A., & O'Brien, L. (2002). Social norms and the expression and suppression of prejudice: The struggle for internalization. *Journal of Personality and Social Psychology, 82,* 359–378. doi: 10.1037///0022-3514.82.3.359-

Crano, W. D., & Prislin, R. (2006). Attitudes and persuasion. *Annual Review of Psychology, 57,* 345–374. doi: 10.1146/annurev.psych.57.102904.190034

Crick, N. R. (1996). The role of overt aggression, relational aggression and prosocial behavior in the prediction of children's future social adjustment. *Child Development, 67,* 2317–2327. doi: 10.2307/1131625

Crick, N. R., & Grotpeter, J. K. (1995). Relational aggression, gender, and social-psychological adjustment. *Child Development, 66,* 710–722. doi: 10.2307/1131945

Crick, N. R., & Werner, N. E. (1998). Response decision processes in relational and overt aggression. *Child Development, 69,* 1630–1639. doi: 10.2307/1132136

Cruz, M. G., Boster, F. J., & Rodriguez, J. I. (1997). The impact of group size and proportion of shared information on the exchange and integration of information in groups. *Communication Research, 24,* 291–313. doi: 10.1177/009365097024003004

Cummings, L. L., Huber, G. P., & Arendt, E. (1974). Effects of size and spatial arrangements on group decision making. *Academy of Management Journal, 17,* 460–475. doi: 10.2307/254650

Cutting, J. E. (2006). The mere exposure effect and aesthetic preference. In P. Locher, C. Martindale, & L. Dorfman (Eds.), *New directions in aesthetics, creativity, and the arts* (pp. 33–46). Amityville, NY: Baywood Publishing Company, Inc.

Dahlstrom, K. (2011, February 8). How to play hard to get with a guy. *eHow.com.* Retrieved from ehow.com/how_4469172_play-hard-guy.html

Dambrun, M., & Valentine, E. (2010). Reopening the study of extreme social behaviors: Obedience to authority within an immersive video environment. *European Journal of Social Psychology, 40,* 760–773.

Danziger, K. (2000). Making social psychology experimental: A conceptual history, 1920–1970. *Journal of the History of the Behavioral Sciences, 36,* 329–347. doi: 10.1002/1520-6696(200023)36:4,329::AID-JHBS3.3.0.CO;2-5

Darley, J. M., & Batson, C. D. (1973). "From Jerusalem to Jericho": A study of situational and dispositional variables in helping behavior. *Journal of Personality and Social Psychology, 27,* 100–108. doi: 10.1037/h0034449

Darley, J. M., & Latane, B. (1968). Bystander intervention in emergencies: Diffusion of responsibility. *Journal of Personality and Social Psychology, 8,* 377–383. doi: 10.1037/h0025589

Dasgupta, N., Banaji, M. R., & Ableson, R. P. (1999). Group entitativity and group perception: Associations between physical features and psychological judgment. *Journal of Personality and Social Psychology, 77,* 991–1003. doi: 10.1037/0022-3514.77.5.991

David, E. J. R., Okazaki, S., & Saw, A. (2009). Bicultural self-efficacy among college students: Initial scale development and mental health correlates. *Journal of Counseling Psychology, 56,* 211–226. doi: 10.1037/a0015419

Davis, J. H., Kerr, N. L., Atkin, R. S., Holt, R., & Meek, D. (1975). The decision processes of 6- and 12-person mock juries assigned unanimous and two-thirds majority rules. *Journal of Personality and Social Psychology, 32,* 1–14. doi: 10.1037/h0076849

Davis, S. N., Greenstein, T. N., & Marks, J. P. G. (2007). Effects of union type on division of household labor. *Journal of Family Issues, 28,* 1246–1272. doi: 10.1177/0192513X07300968

Dawes, R. M. (1980). Social dilemmas. *Annual Review of Psychology, 31*, 169–193. doi: 10.1146/annurev.ps.31.020180.001125

De Castro, B.O. Veerman, J. W., Koops, W., Bosch, J. D., & Monshouwer, H. J. (2002). Hostile attribution of intent and aggressive behavior: A meta-analysis. *Child Development, 73*, 916–934. doi: 10.1111/1467-8624.00447

De Oliveira, P., & Dambrun, M. (2007). Maintaining the status quo and social inequalities: Is stereotype endorsement related to support for system justification? *Current Research in Social Psychology, 13*, 101–121.

de Wit, J. B., Das, E., & Vet, R. (2008). What works best: Objective statistics or a personal testimonial? An assessment of the persuasive effects of different types of message evidence on risk perception. *Health Psychology, 27*, 110–115. doi: 10.1037/0278-6133.27.1.110

Debevec, K., Madden, T. J., & Kernan, J. B. (1986). Physical attractiveness, message evaluation, and compliance: A structural evaluation. *Psychological Reports, 58*, 503–508.

DeBono, K. G., & Harnish, R. J. (1988). Expertise, source attractiveness, and the processing of persuasive messages: A functional approach. *Journal of Personality and Social Psychology, 55*, 541–546. doi: 10.1037/0022-3514.55.4.541

DeBono, K. G., & Telesca, C. (1990). The influence of source attractiveness on advertising effectiveness: A functional perspective. *Journal of Applied Social Psychology, 20*, 1383–1395. doi: 10.1111/j.1559-1816.1990.tb01479.x

DeCarlo, T. E., Agarwal, S., & Vyas, S. B. (2007). Performance expectations of salespeople: The role of past performance and causal attribution in independent and interdependent cultures. *Journal of Personal Selling and Sales Management, 27*, 133–147. doi: 10.2753/PSS0885-3134270202

DeJong, W., & Oopik, A. J. (1992). Effect of legitimizing small contributions and labeling potential donors as "helpers" on responses to a direct mail solicitation for charity. *Psychological Reports, 17*, 923–928. doi: 10.2466PRO.71.7.923-928

Denson, T. F., Aviles, F. E., Pollock, V. E., Earleywine, M., Vasquez, E. A., & Miller, N. (2008). The effects of alcohol and the salience of aggressive cues on triggered displaced aggression. *Aggressive Behavior, 34*, 25–33. doi: 10.1002/ab.20177

DeSteno, D., Dasgupta, N., Bartlett, M. Y., & Cajdric, A. (2004). Prejudice from thin air: The effect of emotion on automatic intergroup attitudes. *Psychological Science, 15*, 319–324. doi: 10.1111/j.0956-7976.2004.00676.x

DeSteno, D., Petty, R. E., Rucker, D. D., Wegener, D. T., & Braverman, J. (2004). Discrete emotions and persuasion: The role of emotion-induced expectancies. *Journal of Personality and Social Psychology, 86*, 43–56. doi: 10.1037/0022-3514.86.1.43

Deutsch, M., & Gerard, H. B. (1955). A study of normative and informational social influence upon individual judgment. *Journal of Abnormal and Social Psychology, 51*, 629–536.

Deutsch, M., Epstein, Y., Canavan, D., & Gumpert, P. (1967). Strategies of inducing cooperation: An experimental study. *Journal of Conflict Resolution, 11*, 345–360.

DeWall, C. N., & Baumeister, R. F. (2006). Alone but feeling no pain: Effects of social exclusion on physical pain tolerance and pain threshold, affective forecasting, and interpersonal empathy. *Journal of Personality and Social Psychology 91*, 1–15. doi: 10.1037/0022-3514.91.1.1

DeWall, C. N., Baumeister, R. F., Mead, N. L., & Vohs, K. D. (2011). How leaders self-regulate their task performance: Evidence that power promotes diligence, depletion, and disdain. *Journal of Personality and Social Psychology, 100*, 47–65. doi: 10.1037/a0020932

Diehl, M., & Stroebe, W. (1987). Productivity loss in brainstorming groups: Toward the solution of a riddle. *Journal of Personality and Social Psychology, 53*, 497–509. doi: 10.1037/0022-3514.53.3.497

Diener, E., & Diener, M. (1995). Cross-cultural correlates of life satisfaction and self-esteem. *Journal of Personality and Social Psychology, 68*, 653–663. doi: 10.1037/0022-3514.68.4.653

Diener, E., Fraser, S. C. Beaman, A. L., & Kelem, R. T. (1976). Effects of deindividuation variables on stealing among Halloween trick-or-treaters. *Journal of Personality and Social Psychology, 33*, 178–183. doi: 10.1037/0022-3514.33.2.178

Dillard, J. P. (1991). The current status of research on sequential-request compliance techniques. *Personality and Social Psychology Bulletin, 17*, 283–288. doi: 10.1177/0146167291173008

Dixon, J., Durrheim, K., & Tredoux, C. (2005). Beyond the optimal contact strategy: A reality check for the contact hypothesis. *American Psychologist, 60*, 697–711. doi: 10.1037/0003-066X.60.7.697

Doh, S. J., & Hwang, J. S. (2009). How consumers evaluate eWOM (electronic word-of-mouth) messages. *CyberPsychology & Behavior, 12*, 193–1971. doi: 10.1089/cpb.2008.0109

Dollard, J., Miller, N. E., Doob, L. W., Mowrer, O. H., & Sears, R. R. (1939). *Frustration and aggression*. New Haven, CT: Yale University Press. doi: 10.1037/1002-000

Donaghue, N., & Fallon, B. J. (2003). Gender-role self-stereotyping and the relationship between equity and satisfaction in close relationships. *Sex Roles, 48*, 217–230. doi: 10.1023/A:1022869203900

Donnerstein, E., & Wilson, D. W. (1976). Effects of noise and perceived control on ongoing and subsequent aggressive behavior. *Journal of Personality and Social Psychology, 34*, 774–781. doi: 10.1037/0022-3514.34.5.774

Dotsch, R., Wigboldus, D. H. J., & van Knippenberg, A. (2011). Biased allocation of faces to social categories. *Journal of Personality and Social Psychology, 100*, 999–1014. doi: 10.1037/a0023026

Douglas, K. M., & Sutton, R. M. (2004). Right about others, wrong about ourselves? Actual and perceived self-other differences in resistance to persuasion. *British Journal of Social Psychology, 43*, 585–603. doi: 10.1348/0144666042565416

Dovidio, J. F., Kawakami, K., & Gaertner, S. L. (2002). Implicit and explicit prejudice and interracial interaction. *Journal of Personality and Social Psychology, 82*, 62–68. doi: 10.1037/0022-3514.82.1.62

Dowden, S., & Robinson, J. P. (1993). Age and cohort differences in American racial attitudes: The generational replacement hypothesis revisited. In P. M. Sniderman, P. E. Tetlock, & E. G. Carmines (Eds.), *Prejudice, politics, and the American dilemma* (pp. 86–103). Stanford, CA: Stanford University Press.

Downey, G., Freitas, A. L., Michaelis, B., & Khouri, H. (1998). The self-fulfilling prophecy in close relationships: Rejection sensitivity and rejection by romantic partners. *Journal of Personality and Social Psychology, 75*, 545–560. doi: 10.1037/0022-3514.75.2.545

Downing, J. W., Judd, C. M., & Brauer, M. (1992). Effects of repeated expressions on attitude extremity. *Journal of Personality and Social Psychology, 63*, 17–29. doi: 10.1037/0022-3514.63.1.17

Droba, D. D. (1933). The nature of attitude. *Journal of Social Psychology, 4*, 444–463.

Duck, S. W. (1982). A topography of relationship disengagement and dissolution. In S. Duck & R. Gilmour (Eds.), *Personal relationships 4: Dissolving personal relationships* (pp. 1–30). New York, NY: Academic Press.

Duntley, J. D., & Buss, D. M. (2008). Evolutionary psychology is a metatheory for psychology. *Psychological Inquiry, 19*, 30–34.

Duval, T. S., & Silvia, P. J. (2002). Self-awareness, probability of improvement, and the self-serving bias. *Journal of Personality and Social Psychology, 82*, 49–61. doi: 10.1037/0022-3514.82.1.49

Dykema, J., Bergbower, K., Doctora, J. D., & Peterson, C. (1996). An attributional style questionnaire for general use. *Journal of Psychoeducational Assessment, 14*, 100–108. doi: 10.1177/073428299601400201

Eagly, A. H., & Carli, L. L. (1981). Sex of researchers and sex-typed communications as determinants of sex differences in influenceability: A meta-analysis of social influence studies. *Psychological Bulletin, 90*, 1–20. doi: 10.1037/0033-2909.90.1.1

Eagly, A. H., & Chaiken, S. (1993). *Psychology of attitudes*. Orlando, FL: Harcourt Brace Jovanovich College Publishers.

Eagly, A. H., & Steffen, V. J. (1986). Gender and aggressive behavior: A meta-analytic review of the social-psychological literature. *Psychological Bulletin, 100*, 309–330. doi: 10.1037/0033-2909.100.3.309

Eagly, A. H., Wood, W., & Chaiken, S. (1978). Causal inferences about communicators and their effect on opinion change. *Journal of Personality and Social Psychology, 36*, 424–435. doi: 10.1037/0022-3514.36.4.424

Ebster, C., & Neumayr, B. (2008). Applying the door-in-the-face compliance technique to retailing. *International Review of Retail, Distribution, and Consumer Research, 18*, 121–128. doi: 10.1080/09593960701778226

Egan, L. C., Santos, L. R., & Bloom, P. (2007). The origins of cognitive dissonance: Evidence from children and monkeys. *Psychological Science, 18*, 978–983. doi: 10.1111/j.1467-9280.2007.0201.x

Eisenberg, N. (1986). *Altruistic emotion, cognition and behavior*. Hillsdale, NJ: Erlbaum.

Ellis, W. E., Crooks, C. V., & Wolfe, D. A. (2009). Relational aggression in peer and dating relationships: Links to psychological and behavioral adjustment. *Social Development, 18*, 253–269. doi: 10.1111/j.1467-9507.2008.00468.x

Ellison, N., Heino, R., & Gibbs, J. (2006). Managing impressions online: Self-presentation processes in the online dating environment. *Journal of Computer-Mediated Communication, 11*, 415–441. doi: 10.1111/j.1083-6101.2006.00020.x

Emery, R. E. (1994). *Renegotiating family relationships: Divorce, child custody, and mediation*. New York, NY: Guilford Press.

Epstein, S. (1994). Integration of the cognitive and the psychodynamic unconscious. *American Psychologist, 49*, 709–724. doi: 10.1037/0003-066X.49.8.709

Escalas, J. E. (2007). Self-referencing and persuasion: Narrative transportation versus analytical elaboration. *Journal of Consumer Research, 33*, 421–429. doi: 10.1086/510216

Esses, V. M., Dovidio, J. F., Jackson, L. M., & Armstrong, T. L. (2001). The immigration dilemma: The role of perceived group competition, ethnic prejudice, and national identity. *Journal of Social Issues, 57*, 389–412. doi: 10.1111/0022-4537.00220

Essock-Vitale, S. M., & McGuire, M. T. (1980). Predictions derived from the theories of kin selection and reciprocation assessed by anthropological data. *Ethology and Sociobiology, 1*, 233–243. doi: 10.1016/0162-3095(80)90010-2

Even-Chen, M., Yinon, Y., & Bizman, A. (1978). The door in the face technique: Effects of the size of the initial request. *European Journal of Social Psychology, 8*, 135–140. doi: 10.1002/ejsp.2420080113

Facebook. (2011). *Facebook statistics*. Retrieved from http://www.facebook.com/press/info.php?statistics

Farrington, D. P. (1991). Childhood aggression and adult violence: Early precursors and later life outcomes. In D. J. Pepler & K. H. Rubin (Eds.), *The development and treatment of childhood aggression* (pp. 5–29). Hillsdale, NJ: Lawrence Erlbaum Associates.

Fazio, R. H. (2000). Accessible attitudes as tools for object appraisal: Their costs and benefits. In G. R. Maio, & J. M. Olson (Eds.), *Why we evaluate: The function of attitudes* (pp. 1–36). Mahwah, NJ: Lawrence Erlbaum Associates Publishers.

Fehr, B. (1994). Prototype-based assessments of laypeople's views of love. *Personal Relationships, 1*, 309–331. doi: 10.1111/j.1475-6811.1994.tb00068.x

Fehr, B., & Russell, J. A. (1991). The concept of love viewed from a prototype perspective. *Journal of Personality and Social Psychology, 60*, 425–438. doi: 10.1037/0022-3514.60.3.425

Fehr, E., & Fischbacher, U. (2003). The nature of human altruism. *Nature, 425*, 785–791. doi:10.1038/nature02043

Fejfar, M.C. & Hoyle, R. H. (2000). Effect of private self-awareness on negative affect and self-referent attribution: A quantitative review. *Personality and Social Psychology Review, 4*, 132–142. doi: 10.1207/S15327957PSPR0402_02

Felson, R. B. (2002). A theory of instrumental aggression. In *Violence and gender reexamined* (pp. 11–28). Washington, D. C.: American Psychological Association.

Fennis, B. M., Janssen, L., & Vohs, K. D. (2009). Acts of benevolence: A limited-resource account of compliance with charitable requests. *Journal of Consumer Research, 35*, 906–924. doi: 10.1086/593291

Ferguson, C. J., & Rueda, S. M. (2010). The hitman study: Violent video game exposure effects on aggressive behavior, hostile feelings, and depression. *European Psychologist, 15*, 99–108. doi: 10.1027/1016-9040/a000010

Festinger, L. (1957). *A theory of cognitive dissonance*. New York, NY: Row, Peterson, and Co.

Festinger, L., & Carlsmith, J. M. (1959). Cognitive consequences of forced compliance. *Journal of Abnormal and Social Psychology, 58*, 203–210. doi: 10.1037/h0041593

Festinger, L., Schachter, S., & Back, K. (1950). *Social pressures in informal groups: A study of a housing community*. New York, NY: Harper.

Fischer, P., Greitemeyer, T., Pollozek, F., & Frey, D. (2006). The unresponsive bystander: Are bystanders more responsive in dangerous emergencies? *European Journal of Social Psychology, 36*, 267–278. doi: 10.1002/ejsp.297

Fiske, S. (2001). Effects of power on bias: Power explains and maintains individual, group, and societal disparities. In A. Y. Lee-Chai and J. A. Bargh (Eds.), *The use and abuse of power: Multiple perspectives on the causes of corruption* (pp.181–193). New York, NY: Psychology Press.

Fong, J., & Burton, S. (2008). A cross-cultural comparison of electronic word-of-mouth and country-of-origin effects. *Journal of Business Research, 61*, 233–242. doi: 10.1016/j.jbusres.2007.06.015

Fontaine, R. G. (2007). Disentangling the psychology and law of instrumental and reactive subtypes of aggression. *Psychology, Public Policy and Law, 13*, 143–165. doi: 1.1037/1076-8971.13.2.143

Foss, R. D. (1981). Structural effects in simulated jury decision making. *Journal of Personality and Social Psychology, 40*, 1055–1062. doi: 10.1037/0022-3514.40.6.1055

Frager, R. (1970). Conformity and anti-conformity in Japan. *Journal of Personality and Social Psychology, 15*, 203–210. doi: 10.1037/h0029434

Fraidin, S. N. (2004). When is one head better than two? Interdependent information in group decision making. *Organizational Behavior and Human Decision Processes, 93*, 102–113. doi: 10.1016/j.obhdp.2003.12.003

Freedman, J. L., & Fraser, S. C. (1966). Compliance without pressure: The foot-in-the-door technique. *Journal of Personality and Social Psychology, 4*, 195–202. doi: 10.1037/h0023552

Fritzsche, B. A., Finkelstein, M. A., & Penner, L. A. (2000). To help or not to help: Capturing individuals' decision policies. *Social Behavior and Personality, 28*, 561–578. doi: 10.2224/sbp.2000.28.6.561

Gabrenya, W. K., Wang, Y., & Latane, B. (1985). Social loafing on an optimizing task: Cross-cultural differences among Chinese and Americans. *Journal of Cross-Cultural Psychology, 16*, 223–242. doi: 10.1177/0022002185016002006

Gabriel, M. T., Critelli, J. W., & Ee, J. S. (1994). Narcissistic illusion in self-evaluations of intelligence and attractiveness. *Journal of Personality, 62*, 143–155. doi: 10.1111/j.1467-6494.1994.tb00798.x

Galli, N., & Reel, J. J. (2009). Adonis or Hephaestus? Exploring body image in male athletes. *Psychology of Men and Masculinity, 10*, 95–110. doi: 10.1037/a0014005

Gecas, V., & Nye, F. I. (1974). Sex and class differences in parent-child interaction: A test of Kohn's hypothesis. *Journal of Marriage and the Family, 36*, 742–749. doi: 10.2307/350357

Geen, R. G., & Quanty, M. B. (1977). The catharsis of aggression: An evaluation of a hypothesis. In L. Berkowitz (Ed.), *Advances in experimental social psychology* (Vol. 10, pp. 1–37). New York, NY: Academic Press.

Geiger, T. C., Zimmer-Gembeck, M. J., & Crick, N. R. (2004). The science of relational aggression: Can we guide intervention? In M. M. Moretti, C. L. Odgers, & M. A. Jackson (Eds.), *Girls and aggression: Contributing factors and intervention principles* (pp. 27–40). New York, NY: Kluwer Academic/Plenum Publishers.

Giancola, P. R. (2000). Executive functioning: A conceptual framework for alcohol-related aggression. *Experimental and Clinical Psychopharmacology, 8*, 576–597. doi: 10.1037/1064-1297.8.4.576

Gibbons, F. X. (1990). Self-evaluation and self-perception: The role of attention in the experience of anxiety. *Anxiety Research, 2*, 153–163.

Gibbs, J. L., Ellison, N. B., & Heino, R. D. (2006). Self-presentation in online personals: The role of anticipated future interaction, self-disclosure, and perceived success in internet dating. *Communication Research, 33*, 152–177. doi: 10.1177/0093650205285368

Gibbs, N., & Roche, T. (1999, December 20). The Columbine tapes. *Time Magazine*.

Gilbert, D. T., & Malone, P. S. (1995). The correspondence bias. *Psychological Bulletin, 117*, 21–38. doi: 10.1037/0033-2909.117.1.21

Gilbert, D. T., Pelham, B. W., & Krull, D. S. (1988). On cognitive busyness: When person perceivers meet persons perceived. *Journal of Personality and Social Psychology, 54*, 733–740. doi: 10.1037/0022-3514.54.5.733

Gino, F., Ayal, S., & Ariely, D. (2009). Contagion and differentiation in unethical behavior: The effect of one bad apple on the barrel. *Psychological Science, 20*, 393–398. doi: 10.1111/j.1467-9280.2009.02306.x

Gintis, H., Bowles, S., Boyd, R., & Fehr, E. (2008). Gene-culture coevolution and the emergence of altruistic behavior in humans. In C. Crawford & D. Krebs (Eds.), *Foundations of evolutionary psychology* (pp. 313–329). New York, NY: Taylor & Francis Group/Lawrence Erlbaum Associates.

Glick, P. C. (1984). Marriage, divorce, and living arrangements: Prospective changes. *Journal of Family Issues, 5*, 7–26. doi: 10.1177/019251384005001002

Glock, S., & Kneer, J. (2009). Game over? The impact of knowledge about violent digital games on the activation of aggression-related concepts. *Journal of Media Psychology, 21*, 151–160. doi: 10.1027/1864-1105.21.4.151

Goffman, E. (1959). *The presentation of self in everyday life.* New York: Doubleday Anchor.

Goldstein, N. J., Cialdini, R. B., & Griskevicius, V. (2008). Room with a viewpoint: Using social norms to motivate environmental conservation in hotels. *Journal of Consumer Research, 35*, 472–482. doi: 10.1086/586910

Gonzales, P. M., Blanton, H., & Williams, K. J. (2002). The effects of stereotype threat and double-minority status on the test performance of Latino women. *Personality and Social Psychology Bulletin, 28*, 659–670. doi: 10.1177/0146167202288010

Goren, D. E. (2008, June 11). Hartford hit-and-run victim needs permanent hospitalization. *Hartford Courant.* Retrieved from http://www.courant.com/news/local/hr/hc-arcetorres0611.artjun11,0,357846.story

Gottman, J. M. (1993). The roles of conflict engagement, escalation, or avoidance in marital interaction: A longitudinal view of five types of couples. *Journal of Consulting and Clinical Psychology, 61*, 6–51. doi: 10.1037/0022-006X.61.1.6

Gottman, J. M. (1994). *What predicts divorce?* Hillsdale, NJ: Lawrence Erlbaum Associates.

Gottman, J. M. (1998). Psychology and the study of marital processes. *Annual Review of Psychology, 49*, 169–197. doi: 10.1146/annurev.psych.49.1.169

Gottman, J. M. (1999). *The marriage clinic: A scientifically based marital therapy.* New York, NY: Norton.

Gottman, J. M., & Carrere, S. (1994). Why can't men and women get along? Developmental roots and marital inequities. In D. J. Canary & L. Stafford (Eds.), *Communication and relational maintenance* (pp. 203–229). San Diego, CA: Academic Press.

Gottman, J. M., & Levenson, R. W. (2002). A two-factor model for predicting when a couple will divorce: Exploratory analyses using 14-year longitudinal data. *Family Process, 41*, 83–96. doi: 10.1111/j.1545-5300.2002.40102000083.x

Gottman, J. M., Swanson, C., & Swanson, K. (2002). A general systems theory of marriage: Nonlinear difference equation modeling of marital interaction. *Personality and Social Psychology Review, 6*, 326–340.

Gouldner, A. W. (1960).The norm of reciprocity: A preliminary statement. *American Sociological Review, 25*, 161–178.

Graham, F. (2009). American juries. *eJournal USA: Anatomy of a jury trial, 14*, 4–6. www.america.gov/publications/ejournalusa.html

Graham, K., Bernards, S., Osgood, D. W., & Wells, S. (2006). Bad nights or bad bars? Multi-level analysis of environmental predictors of late-night large-capacity bars and clubs. *Addiction, 101*, 1569–1580. doi: 10.1111/j.1360-0443.2006.01608.x

Green, M. C., & Brock, T. C. (2000). The role of transportation in the persuasiveness of public narratives. *Journal of Personality and Social Psychology, 79*, 701–721. doi: 10.1037/0022-3514.79.5.701

Greenberg, J., Pyszczynski, T., Burling, J., & Tibbs, K. (1992). Depression, self-focused attention, and the self-serving attributional bias. *Personality and Individual Differences, 13*, 956–965. doi: 10.1016/0191-8869(92)90129-D

Greenwald, A. G., McGhee, D. E., & Schwartz, J. L. K. (1998). Measuring individual differences in implicit cognition: The Implicit Association Test. *Journal of Personality and Social Psychology, 74*, 1464–1480. doi: 10.1037/0022-3514.74.6.1464

Greve, W., Rothermund, K., & Wentura, D. (Eds.) (2005). *The adaptive self: Personal continuity and intentional self-development*. Ashland, OH: Hogrefe & Huber.

Griskevicius, V., Goldstein, N. J., Mortensen, C. R., Sundie, J. M., Cialdini, R. B., & Kenrick, D. T. (2009). Fear and loving in Las Vegas: Evolution, emotion, and persuasion. *Journal of Marketing Research, 46*, 384–395. doi: 10.1509/jmkr.46.3.384

Gritz, E. R., & Crane, L. A. (1991). Use of diet pills and amphetamines to lose weight among smoking and nonsmoking high school seniors. *Health Psychology, 10*, 330–335. doi: 10.1037/0278-6133.10.5.330

Grote, N. K., & Frieze, I. H. (1994). The measurement of friendship-based love in intimate relationships. *Personal Relationships, 1*, 275–300. doi: 10.1207/S15327957PSPR0604_07

Gruter, M., & Masters, R. D. (1986). Ostracism as a social and biological phenomenon: An introduction. *Ethology & Sociobiology, 7*, 149–158. doi: 10.1016/0162-3095(86)90043-9

Gueguen, N., & Jacob, C. (2001). Fund-raising on the web: The effect of an electronic foot-in-the-door on donation. *CyberPsychology & Behavior, 4*, 705–709. doi: 10.1089/109493101753376650

Gueguen, N., & Pascual, A. (2003). Reciprocity and compliance to a request: An experimental evaluation in a natural setting. *Psychology and Education: An Interdisciplinary Journal, 40*, 16–19.

Gueguen, N., Marchand, M., Pascual, A., & Lourel, M. (2008). Foot-in-the-door technique using a courtship request: A field experiment. *Psychological Reports, 103*, 529–534. doi: 10.2466/PRO.103.6.539-534

Gueguen, N., Pascual, A., & Dagot, L. (2002). Low-ball and compliance to a request: An application in a field setting. *Psychological Reports, 91*, 81–84. doi: 10.2466/PRO.91.5.81-84

Gurven, M., Zanolini, A., & Schniter, E. (2008). Culture sometimes matters: Intra-cultural variation in pro-social behavior among Tsimane Amerindians. *Journal of Economic Behavior and Organization. 67*, 587–607. doi: 10.1016/j.jebo.2007.09.005

Hagger, M. S., Chatzisarantis, N. L. D., Barkoukis, V., Wang, J. C. K., Hein, V., Pihu, M., Soos, I., & Karsai, I. (2007). Cross-cultural generalizability of the theory of planned behavior among people in a physical activity context. *Journal of Sport and Exercise Psychology, 29*, 1–20.

Hagger, M. S., Wood, C., Stiff, C., & Chatzisarantis, N. L. D. (2010). Ego depletion and the strength model of self-control: A meta-analysis. *Psychological Bulletin, 136*, 495–525. doi: 10.1037/a0019486

Haines, H., & Vaughan, G. M. (1979). Was 1898 a "great date" in the history of social psychology? *Journal of the History of the Behavioral Sciences, 15*, 323–332. doi: 10.1002/1520-6696(197910)15:4,323::AID-JHBS2300150405.3.0.CO;2-1

Halberstam, D. (1972). *The best and the brightest*. New York, NY: McGraw-Hill.

Han, S., & Shavitt, S. (1994). Persuasion and culture: Advertising appeals in individualistic and collectivistic societies. *Journal of Experimental Social Psychology, 30*, 326–350. doi: 10.1006/jesp.1994.1016

Hancock, J. T., & Dunham, P. J. (2001). Impression formation in communication-mediated communication revisited: An analysis of the breadth and intensity of impressions. *Communication Research, 28*, 325–347. doi: 10.1177/00936500102/003004

Haney, C., Banks, C., & Zimbardo, P. (1973). Interpersonal dynamics in a simulated prison. *International Journal of Criminology and Penology, 1,* 69–97.

Hardin, G. (1968). The tragedy of the commons. *Science, 162,* 1243–1248.

Harris, T. M., & Kalbfleisch, P. J. (2000). Interracial dating: The implications of race for initiating a romantic relationship. *Howard Journal of Communications, 11,* 49–64. doi: 10.1080/106461700246715

Hastie, R., Penrod, S. D., & Pennington, N. (1983). *Inside the jury.* Cambridge, MA: Harvard University Press.

Hatfield, E. (1983). Equity theory and research: An overview. In H. H. Blumberg, A. P. Hare, V. Kent, & M. Davies (Eds.), *Small groups and social interaction* (Vol. 2, pp. 401–412). Chichester, England: Wiley.

Hatfield, E., Pillemer, J. T. O'Brien, M. U., & Le, Y. L. (2008). The endurance of love: Passionate and companionate love in newlywed and long-term marriages. *Interpersona, 2,* 35–64

Haugtvedt, C. P., & Petty, R. E. (1992). Personality and persuasion: Need for cognition moderates the persistence and resistance of attitude changes. *Journal of Personality and Social Psychology, 63,* 308–319. doi: 10.1037/0022-3514.63.2.308

Heider, F. (1958). *The psychology of interpersonal relations.* New York, NY: Wiley.

Heider, F. (1976). A conversation with Fritz Heider. In J.H. Harvey, W. J. Ickes, & R. F. Kidd (Eds.), *New directions in attribution research* (Vol. 1, pp. 3–18). Hillsdale, NJ: Erlbaum.

Heino, R. D., Ellison, N. B., & Gibbs, J. L. (2010). Relationshopping: Investigating the market metaphor in online dating. *Journal of Social and Personal Relationships, 27,* 427–447. doi: 10.1177/0265407510361614

Hertel, G., Kerr, N. L., & Messe, L. A. (2000). Motivation gains in performance groups: Paradigmatic and theoretical developments on the Köhler effect. *Journal of Personality and Social Psychology, 79,* 580–601. doi: 10.1037/0022-3514.79.4.580

Hibbert, S., Smith, A., Davies, A., & Ireland, F. (2007). Guilt appeals: Persuasion knowledge and charitable giving. *Psychology and Marketing, 24,* 723–742. doi: 10.1002/mar.20181

Hill, C. T., Rubin, Z., & Peplau, L. A. (1976). Breakups before marriage: The end of 103 affairs. *Journal of Social Issues, 32,* 147–168.

Hines, D. A., & Saudino, K. J. (2009). How much variance in psychological and physical aggression is predicted by genetics? In K. D. O'Leary & E. M. Woodin (Eds.), *Psychological and physical aggression in couples: Causes and interventions* (pp. 141–162). Washington, D. C.: American Psychological Association.

Hirsch, J. K., Wolford, K., LaLonde, S. M., Brunk, L., & Parker-Morris, A. (2009). Optimistic explanatory style as a moderator of the association between negative life events and suicide ideation. *Journal of Crisis Intervention and Suicide Prevention, 30,* 48–53. doi: 10.1027/0227-5910.30.1.48

Hodson, G., & Olson, J. M. (2005). Testing the generality of the name letter effect: Name initials and everyday attitudes. *Personality and Social Psychology Bulletin, 31,* 1099–1111. doi: 10.1177/0146167205274895

Hodson, G., Rush, J., & MacInnis, C. C. (2010). A joke is just a joke (except when it isn't): Cavalier humor beliefs facilitate the expression of group dominance motives. *Journal of Personality and Social Psychology, 99,* 660–682. doi: 10.1037/a0019627

Hoeken, H., & Geurts, D. (2005). Influence of exemplars in fear appeals on the perception of self-efficacy and message acceptance. *Information Design Journal + Document Design, 13,* 238–248. doi: 10.1075/idjdd.13.3.09hoe

Hoffman, M. L. (1981). Is altruism part of human nature? *Journal of Personality and Social Psychology, 40,* 121–137. doi: 10.1037/0022-3514.40.1.121

Hofling, C. K., Brotzman, E., Dalrymple, S., Graves, N., & Pierce, C. M. (1966). An experimental study in nurse-physician relationships. *Journal of Nervous and Mental Disease, 143,* 177–180.

Holmberg, D., & MacKenzie, S. (2002). So far so good: Scripts for romantic relationship development as predictors of relational well-being. *Journal of Social and Personal Relationships, 19,* 777–796. doi: 10.1177/0265407502196003

Holmes, T. H., & Rahe, R. H. (1967). The social readjustment rating scale. *Journal of Psychosomatic Research, 11,* 213–218. doi: 10.1016/0022-3999(67)90010-4

Homan, A. C., van Knippenberg, D., Van Kleef, G. A., & De Dreu, C. K. W. (2007). Bridging faultlines by valuing diversity: Diversity beliefs, information elaboration, and performance in diverse work groups. *Journal of Applied Psychology, 92,* 1189–1199. doi: 10.1037/0021-9010.92.5.1189

Hoshino-Browne, E., Zanna, A. S., Spencer, S. J., Zanna, M. P., Kitayama, S. & Lackenbauer, S. (2005). On the cultural guises of cognitive dissonance: The case of Easterners and Westerners. *Journal of Personality and Social Psychology, 89,* 294–310. doi: 10.1037/0022-3514.89.3.294

House, J. S., Robbins, C., & Metzner, H. L. (1982). The association of social relationships and activities with mortality: Prospective evidence from the Tecumseh community health study. *American Journal of Epidemiology, 116,* 123–140.

Hovland, C. I., Janis, I. L., & Kelley, H. H. (1953). *Communication and persuasion.* New Haven, CT: Yale University Press.

Howard, D. J., & Kerin, R. A. (2004). The effects of personalized product recommendations on advertisement response rates: The "Try this. It works!" technique. *Journal of Consumer Psychology, 14,* 271–279. doi: 10.1207/s15327663jcp1403_8

Huang, C. H., & Min, J. C. H. (2007). A research note of online bidders' conformity. *Social Behavior and Personality, 35,* 1033–1034. doi: 10.2224/sbp.2007.35.8.1033

Huang, I. C. (1998). Self-esteem, reaction to uncertainty, and physician practice variation: A study of resident physicians. *Social Behavior and Personality, 26,* 181–194. doi: 10.2224/sbp.1998.26.2.181

Huguet, P., & Regner, I. (2007). Stereotype threat among schoolgirls in quasi-ordinary classroom circumstances. *Journal of Educational Psychology, 99,* 545–560. doi: 10.1037/0022-0663.99.3.545,

Hunt, M. (1983). *The story of psychology.* New York: Anchor Books.

Hurlbert, J. S., Beggs, J. S., & Haines, V. S. (2006). Bridges over troubled waters: What are the optimal networks for Katrina's victims? *Understanding Katrina: Perspectives from the Social Sciences, the forum of the Social Science Research Council.* Retrieved from http://understandingkatrina.ssrc.org/Hurlbert_Beggs_Haines

Hutchings, B., & Mednick, S. A. (1977). Criminality in adoptees and their adoptive and biological parents: A pilot study. In S. A. Mednick & K. O. Christiansen (Eds.), *Biosocial bases of criminal behavior* (pp. 127–141). New York: Gardner Press.

Information Please Database (2010). *Time line of worldwide school shootings.* Pearson Education. Retrieved from http://www.infoplease.com/ipa/A0777958.html

Ingham, A. G., Levinger, G., Graves, J., & Peckham, V. (1974). The Ringelmann effect: Studies of group size and group performance. *Journal of Experimental Social Psychology, 10,* 371–384. doi: 10.1016/0022-1031(74)90033-X

Inzlicht, M., & Been-Zeev, T. (2003). Do high-achieving female students underperform in private? The implications of threatening environments on intellectual processing. *Journal of Educational Psychology, 95,* 795–805. doi: 10.1037/0022-0663.95.4.796

Jackson, J. W. (1993). Realistic group conflict theory: A review and evaluation of the theoretical and empirical literature. *Psychological Record, 43,* 395–413.

Jackson, S. E. (1991). Team composition in organizational settings: Issues in managing an increasingly diverse work force. In S. Worchel, W. Wood, & J. A. Simpson (Eds.), *Group process and productivity* (pp. 138–173). Thousand Oaks, CA: Sage.

James, W. (1890). *Principles of Psychology.* New York: Holt.

Janis, I. L. (1972). *Victims of groupthink.* Boston, MA: Houghton Mifflin.

Janis, I. L. (1982). *Groupthink: Psychological studies of policy decisions and fiascoes.* Boston, MA: Houghton Mifflin.

Janis, I., & Leventhal, H. (1968). Human reactions to stress. In E. F. Borgatta & W. W. Lambert (Eds.), *Handbook of personality theory and research.* Chicago, IL: Rand McNally.

Jellison, W. A., McConnell, A. R., & Gabriel, S. (2004). Implicit and explicit measures of sexual orientation attitudes: In-group preferences and related behaviors and beliefs among gay and straight men. *Personality and Social Psychology Bulletin, 30,* 629–642. doi: 10.1177/0146167203262076

Johnson, M. A. (1989). Variables associated with friendship in an adult population. *Journal of Social Psychology, 129,* 379–390. doi: 10.1037/a0014468

Johnson, R. D., & Downing, L. L. (1979). Deindividuation and valence of cues: Effects on prosocial and antisocial behavior. *Journal of Personality and Social Psychology, 37,* 1532–1538. doi: 10.1037/0022-3514.37.9.1532

Jones, E. E. (1998). Major developments in five decades of social psychology. In D. T. Gilbert, S. T. Fiske, & L. Gardner (Eds.), *Handbook of social psychology* (Vol. 1, 4th ed., pp. 3–57). New York, NY: McGraw-Hill.

Jones, E. E., & Harris, V. A. (1967). The attribution of attitudes. *Journal of Experimental Social Psychology, 3,* 1–24. doi: 10.1016/0022-1031(67)90034-0

Jones, E.E. (1998). Major developments in five decades of social psychology. In D. T. Gilbert, S. T. Fiske, & G. Lindzey (Eds.), *Handbook of social psychology* (4th ed., Vols. 1–2, pp. 3–57). New York, NY: McGraw-Hill.

Jost, J. T., Banaji, M. R., & Nosek, B. A. (2004). A decade of system justification theory: Accumulated evidence of conscious and unconscious bolstering of the status quo. *Political Psychology, 25,* 881–920. doi: 10.1111/j. 1467-9221.2004.00402.x

Joyce, W. F., Nohria, N., & Robertson, B. (2003). *What really works.* New York: Harper Business.

Judge, T. A., Piccolo, R. F., & Ilies, R. (2004). The forgotten ones? The validity of consideration and initiating structure in leadership research. *Journal of Applied Psychology, 89,* 36–51. doi: 10.1037/0021-9010.89.1.36

Jung, T., Shim, W., & Mantaro, T. (2010). Psychological reactance and effects of social norms messages among binge drinking college students. *Journal of Alcohol and Drug Education, 54,* 7–18.

Kahan, D., Polivy, J., & Herman, C. P. (2003). Conformity and dietary disinhibition: A test of the ego-strength model of self-regulation. *International Journal of Eating Disorders, 33,* 165–171. doi: 10.1002/eat.10132

Kahneman, D. (2003). A perspective on judgment and choice: Mapping bounded rationality. *American Psychologist, 58,* 697–720. doi: 10.1037/000.-066X58.9.697

Kahneman, D., & Tversky, A. (1973). On the psychology of prediction. *Psychological Review, 80,* 237–251. doi: 10.1037/h0034747

Kaighobadi, F., Shackelford, T. K., & Buss, D. M. (2010). Spousal mate retention in the newlywed year and three years later. *Personality and Individual Differences, 48,* 414–418. doi: 10.1016/j.paid.2009.11.008

Kaiser, F. G., Wolfing, S., & Fuhrer, U. (1999). Environmental attitude and eco-logical behavior. *Journal of Environmental Psychology, 19,* 1–19. doi: 10.1006/jevp.1998.0107

Kaiser, R. B., & Hogan, R. (2007). The dark side of discretion. In J. Hunt (Series Ed.) & R. Hooijbert, J. Hunt, J. Antonakis, K. Boal, & N. Lane (Vol. Eds.), *Monographs on leadership and management: Vol. 4. Being there even when you are not: Leading through strategy, systems and structure* (pp. 173–193). Oxford England: JAI Press. doi: 10.1016/S1479-3571(07)04009-6

Kaiser, R. B., Hogan, R., & Craig, S. B. (2008) Leadership and the fate of organizations. *American Psychologist, 63,* 96–110. doi: 10.1037/0003-066X.63.2.96

Kalven, H., & Zeisel, H. (1966). *The American jury.* Chicago, IL: University of Chicago Press.

Karau, S. J., & Hart, J. W. (1998). Group cohesiveness and social loafing: Effects of a social interaction manipulation on individual motivation within groups. *Group Dynamics: Theory, Research, and Practice, 2,* 185–191. doi: 10.1037/1089-2699.2.3.185

Karau, S. J., & Williams, K. D. (1993). Social loafing: A meta-analytic review and theo-retical integration. *Journal of Personality and Social Psychology, 65,* 681–706. doi: 10.1037/0022-3514.65.4.681

Katrina Facts Online. (2010, June 2). *11 Facts about Hurricane Katrina.* Retrieved from http://www.katrinanewsonline.com/11-facts-about-hurricane-katrina

Keller, P. A., Lipkus, I. M., & Rimer, B. K. (2003). Affect, framing and persuasion. *Journal of Marketing Research, 40,* 54–64. doi: 10.1509/jmkr.40.1.51.19133

Kelley, H. H., & Thibaut, J. W. (1978). *Interpersonal relations: A theory of interdependence.* New York, NY: Wiley.

Kelson, R. (2005). Hurricane Katrina Statistics. Institute for Crisis, Disaster, and Risk Management, *Crisis and Emergency Management Newsletter Website, 9.* Retrieved from http://www.seas.gwu.edu/~emse232/october200512.html

Kendzierski, D. (1990). Exercise self-schemata: Cognitive and behavioral correlates. *Health Psychology, 9,* 69–82. doi: 10.1037/0278-6133.9.1.69

Kenen, R., Ardern-Jones, A., & Eeles, R. (2003). Family stories and the use of heuristics: Women from suspected hereditary breast and ovarian cancer (HBOC) families. *Sociology of Health and Illness, 25,* 838–865. doi: 10.1046/j.1467-9566.2003.00372.x

Kennedy, J. L. (2008). *Job interviews for dummies* (3rd ed.). Indianapolis, IN: Wiley.

Kerr, N. L. Seok, D-H., Poulsen, J. R., Harris, D. W., & Messe, L. A. (2008). Social ostra-cism and group motivation gain. *European Journal of Social Psychology, 38,* 736–746. doi: 10.1002/ejsp.499

Kerr, N. L., Messe, L. A., Park, E. S., & Sambolec, E. J. (2005). Identifiably, performance feedback and the Kohler effect. *Group Processes and Intergroup Relations, 8,* 375–390. doi: 10.1177/1368430205056466

Kim, J., & Hatfield, E. (2004). Love types and subjective well-being: A cross-cultural study. *Social Behavior and Personality, 32,* 173–182. doi: 10.2224/sbp.2004.32.2.173

King, K., Steiner, B., & Breach, S. R. (2008). Violence in the supermax: A self-fulfilling prophecy. *The Prison Journal, 88,* 144–168. doi: 10.1177/0032885507311000

Kisielius, J., & Sternthal, B. (1984). Detecting and explaining vividness effects in attitudi-nal judgments. *Journal of Marketing Research, 21,* 54–64.

Kistner, J., Counts-Allan, C., Dunkel, S., Drew, C. H., David-Ferdon, C., & Lopez, C. (2010). Sex differences in relational and overt aggression in the late elementary school years. *Aggressive Behavior, 36,* 282–291.

Kitayama, S., Snibbe, A. C., Markus, H. R., & Suzuki, T. (2004). Is there any "free" choice? Self and dissonance in two cultures. *Psychological Science, 15*, 527–533. doi: 10.1111/j.0956-7976.2004.00714.x

Klehe, U., & Anderson, N. (2007). The moderating influence of personality and culture on social loafing in typical versus maximum performance situations. *International Journal of Selection and Assessment, 15*, 250–262. doi: 10.1111/j.1468-2389.2007.00385.x

Knafo, A., & Israel, S. (2010). Genetic and environmental influences on prosocial behavior. In M. Mikulincer & P. R. Shaver (Eds.), *Prosocial motives, emotions, and behavior: The better angels of our nature* (pp. 149–167). Washington, D. C.: American Psychological Association. doi: 10.1037/12061-008

Kocan, S. E., & Curtis, G. J. (2009). Close encounters of the initial kind: Implicit self-esteem, name-letter similarity, and social distance. *Basic and Applied Social Psychology, 31*, 17–23. doi: 10.1080/01973530802659752

Kooij-de Bode, H. J. M., van Knippenberg, D., & van Ginkel, W. P. (2008). Ethnic diversity and distributed information in group decision making: The importance of information elaboration. *Group Dynamics: Theory, Research, and Practice, 12*, 307–320. doi: 10.1037/1089-2699.12.4.307

Kosic, A., & Phalet, K. (2006). Ethnic categorization of immigrants: The role of prejudice, perceived acculturation strategies, and group size. *International Journal of Intercultural Relations, 30*, 769–782. doi: 10.1016/j.ijntrel.2006.06.003

Kravitz, D. A., & Martin, B. (1986). Ringelmann rediscovered: The original article. *Journal of Personality and Social Psychology, 50*, 936–941. doi: 10.1037/0022-3514.50.5.936

Krug, E. G., Dahlberg, L. L., Mercy, J. A., Zwi, A. B., & Lozano, R. (2002). *World report on violence and health*. World Health Organization.

Kugihara, N. (1999). Gender and social loafing in Japan. *Journal of Social Psychology, 139*, 516–526. doi: 10.1080/00224549909598410

Kuiper, N. A. (1978). Depression and causal attributions for success and failure. *Journal of Personality and Social Psychology, 36*, 236–246. doi: 10.1037/0022.3514.36.3.236

Kumkale, G. T., & Albarracin, D. (2004). The sleeper effect in persuasion: A meta-analytic review. *Psychological Bulletin, 130*, 143–172. doi: 10.1037/0033-2909.130.1 43

La Piere, R.T. (1934). Attitudes vs. actions. *Social Forces, 13*, 230–237.

Lampinen, J. M., Copeland, S. M., & Neuschatz, J. S. (2001). Recollections of things schematic: Room schemas revisited. *Journal of Experimental Psychology: Learning, Memory, and Cognition, 27*, 1211–1222. doi: 10.1037/0278-7393.27.5.1211

Laner, M. R., & Ventrone, N. A. (2000). Dating scripts revisited. *Journal of Family Issues, 21*, 488–500. doi: 10.1177/109251300021004004

Larson, J. R. Jr., Christensen, C., Franz, T. M., & Abbott, A. S. (1998). Diagnosing groups: The pooling, management, and impact of shared and unshared case information in team-based medical decision making. *Journal of Personality and Social Psychology, 75*, 93–108. doi: 10.1037/0022-3514.75.1.93

Latane, B., & Darley, J. M. (1968). Group inhibition of bystander intervention in emergencies. *Journal of Personality and Social Psychology, 10*, 215–221. doi: 10.1037/h0026570

Latane, B., & Darley, J. M. (1970). *The unresponsive bystander: Why doesn't he help?* New York, NY: Appleton-Century-Crofts.

Latane, B., & Rodin, J. A. (1969). A lady in distress: Inhibiting effects of friends and strangers on bystander intervention. *Journal of Experimental Social Psychology, 5*, 189–202. doi: 10.1016/0022-1031(69)90046-8

Lau, R. R., & Redlawsk, D. P. (2001). Advantages and disadvantages of cognitive heuristics in political decision making. *American Journal of Political Science, 45*, 951–971.

Leary, M. R. (1990). Responses to social exclusion: Social anxiety, jealously, loneliness, depression and low self-esteem. *Journal of Social and Clinical Psychology, 9,* 221–229.

Leary, M. R., & Downs, D. L. (1995). Interpersonal functions of the self-esteem motive: The self-esteem system as a sociometer. In M. H. Kernis (Ed.), *Efficacy, agency, and self-esteem.* New York, NY: Plenum Press.

Leary, M. R., Kowalski, R. M., Smith, L., & Phillips, S. (2003). Teaching, rejection, and violence: Case studies of the school shootings. *Aggressive Behavior, 29,* 202–214. doi: 10.1002/ab.10061

Leary, M. R., Tambor, E. S., Terdal, S. K., & Downs, D. L. (1995). Self-esteem as an interpersonal monitor: The sociometer hypothesis. *Journal of Personality and Social Psychology, 68,* 518–530. doi: 10.1037/0022-3514.68.3.518

Leary, M. R., Tchividjian, L. R., & Kraxberger, B. E. (1994). Self-presentation can be hazardous to your health: Impression management and health risk. *Health Psychology, 13,* 461–470. doi: 10.1037/0278-6133.13.6.461

Lee, C. M., Geisner, I. M., Lewis, M. A., Neighbors, C., & Larimer, M. E. (2007). Social motives and the interaction between descriptive and injunctive norms in college student drinking. *Journal of Studies on Alcohol and Drugs, 68,* 714–721.

Legrenzi, P., Butera, F., Mugny, G., & Perez, J. (1991). Majority and minority influence in inductive reasoning: A preliminary study. *European Journal of Social Psychology, 21,* 359–363. doi: 10.1002/ejsp.240210408

Levine, D. (2000). Virtual attraction: What rocks your boat. *Cyber Psychology and Behavior, 3,* 565–573. doi: 10.1089/109493100420179

Levine, J. M. (1999). Solomon Asch's legacy of group research. *Personality and Social Psychology Review, 3,* 358–364. doi: 10.1207/s15327957pspr0304_5

Levine, J. M., & Moreland, R. L. (1998). Small groups. In D. T. Gilbert, S. T. Fiske, & G. Lindzey (Eds.), *Handbook of social psychology* (4th ed., Vol. 2, pp. 415–469). New York, NY: McGraw-Hill.

Levine, M., & Crowther, S. (2008). The responsive bystander: How social group membership and group size can encourage as well as inhibit bystander intervention. *Journal of Personality and Social Psychology, 95,* 1429–1439. doi: 10.1037/a0012634

Lewin, K., Lippitt, R., & White, R. K. (1939). Patterns of aggressive behavior in experimentally created "social climates." *Journal of Social Psychology, 10,* 271–299.

Lickel, B., Hamilton, D. L., & Sherman, S. J. (2001). Elements of a lay theory of groups; Types of groups, relational styles, and the perception of group entitativity. *Personality and Social Psychology Review, 5,* 129–140. doi: 10.1207/S15327957PSPR0502_4

Lickel, B., Hamilton, D. L., Wieczorkowska, G., Lewis, A., Sherman, S. J., & Uhles, A. N. (2000). Varieties of groups and the perception of group entitativity. *Journal of Personality and Social Psychology, 78,* 223–246. doi: 10.1037/0022-3514.78.2.223

Lin, C. L., Lee, S. H., & Horng, D. J. (2011). The effects of online reviews on purchasing intention: The moderating role of need for cognition. *Social Behavior and Personality, 39,* 71–82. doi: 10.2224/sbp.2011.39.1.

Linville, P. W., Fischer, G. W., & Salovey, P. (1989). Perceived distributions of the characteristics of in-group and out-group members: Empirical evidence and a computer simulation. *Journal of Personality and Social Psychology, 57,* 165–188. doi:10.1037/0022.3514.57.2.165

Loeber, R., & Farrington, D. P. (Eds.). (1998). *Serious and violent juvenile offenders: Risk factors and successful interventions.* Thousand Oaks, CA: Sage.

Loeber, R., & Stouthamer-Loeber, M. (1998). Development of juvenile aggression and violence: Some common misconceptions and controversies. *American Psychologist, 53,* 242–259. doi: 10.1037/0003-0066X.53.2.242

Loeber, R., Farrington, D. P., Stouthamer-Loeber, M., Moffitt, T. E., & Caspi, A. (1998). The development of male offending: Key findings from the first decade of the Pittsburgh Youth Study. *Studies on Crime & Crime Prevention, 7,* 141–171.

London, P. (1970). The rescuers: Motivational hypothesis about Christians who saved Jews. In J. Macaulay and L. Berkowitz (Eds.), *Altruism and helping behavior: Social psychological studies of some antecedents and consequences* (pp. 241–250). New York, NY: Academic Press.

Loomis, J. M., Blascovich, J. J., & Beall, A. C. (1999). Immersive virtual environment technology as a basic research tool in psychology. *Behavior Research Methods, 31,* 557–564. doi: 10.3758/BF03200735

Luhtanen, R., & Crocker, J. (1991). Self-esteem and intergroup comparisons: Toward a theory of collective self-esteem. In J. Suls & T. A. Wills (Eds.), *Social comparison: Contemporary theory and research* (pp. 211–234). Hillsdale, NJ: Lawrence Erlbaum Associates.

Luo, S., & Zhang, G. (2009). What leads to romantic attraction: Similarity, reciprocity, security, or beauty? Evidence from a speed-dating study. *Journal of Personality, 77,* 933–963. doi: 10.1111/j.1467-6494.2009.00570.x

Lupien, S. P., Seery, M. D., & Almonte, J. L. (2010). Discrepant and congruent self-esteem: Behavioral self-handicapping as a preemptive defensive strategy. *Journal of Experimental Social Psychology, 46,* 1105–1108. doi: 10.1016/j.jesp.2010.05.022

Lynn, M. (1991). Scarcity effects on value: A quantitative review of the commodity theory literature. *Psychology and Marketing, 8,* 43–57.

Lynn, M., & McCall, M. (2000). Gratitude and gratuity: A meta-analysis of research on the service-tipping relationship. *Journal of Socio-Economics, 29,* 203–214. doi: 10.1016/S1053-5357(00)00062-7

MacCoun, R. J., & Kerr, N. L. (1988). Asymmetric influence in mock jury deliberation: Jurors' bias for leniency. *Journal of Personality and Social Psychology, 54,* 21–33. doi: 10.1037/0022-3514.54.1.21

Macintyre, S., & Homel, R. (1997). Danger on the dance floor: A study of interior design, crowding and aggression in nightclubs. In R. Homel (Ed.), *Policing for prevention: Reducing crime, public intoxication and injury* (Vol. 7, pp. 90–113). Monsey, NY: Criminal Justice Press.

Mackie, D., & Cooper, J. (1984). Attitude polarization: Effects of group membership. *Journal of Personality and Social Psychology, 46,* 575–585. doi: 10.1037/0022-3514.46.3.575

Macrae, C. N., Milne, A. B., & Bodenhausen, G. V. (1994). Stereotypes as energy-saving devices: A peek inside the cognitive toolbox. *Journal of Personality and Social Psychology, 66,* 37–47. doi: 10.1037/0022-3514.66.1.37

Madden, M., & Lenhart, A. (2006, March 6). Online Dating. *Pew Internet and American Life Project.* Retrieved from http://www.pewinternet.org/Reports/2006/Online-Dating.aspx

Madon, S., Guyll, M., Spoth, R. L., Cross, S. E., & Hilbert, S. J. (2003). The self-fulfilling influence of mother expectations on children's underage drinking. *Journal of Personality and Social Psychology, 84,* 1188–1205. doi: 10.1037/0022-3514.84.6.1188

Madon, S., Willard, J., Guyll, M., Trudeau, L., & Spoth, R. (2006). Self-fulfilling prophecy effects of mothers' beliefs on children's alcohol use: Accumulation, dissipation, and stability over time. *Journal of Personality and Social Psychology, 90,* 911–926. doi: 10.1037/0022-3514.90.6.911

Maheswaran, D., & Chaiken, S. (1991). Promoting systematic processing in low-motivation settings: Effect of incongruent information on processing and judgment. *Journal of Personality and Social Psychology, 61,* 13–25. doi: 10.1037/0022-3514.61.1.13

Majolo, B., Ames, K., Brumpton, R., Garratt, R., Hall, K., & Wilson, N. (2006). Human friendship favours cooperation in the iterated prisoner's dilemma. *Behaviour, 143,* 1383–1395. doi: 10.1163/156853906778987506

Malcolm, J., & Ng, S. H. (1989). Relationship of self-awareness to cheating on an external standard of competence. *Journal of Social Psychology, 129,* 391–395.

Mallick, S. K., & McCandless, B. R. (1966). A study of catharsis of aggression. *Journal of Personality and Social Psychology, 4,* 591–596.

Mantell, D. M. (1971). The potential for violence in Germany. *Journal of Social Issues, 27,* 101–112.

Marchetti, S., & Bunte, S. (2006). Retailers and banks leverage fundraising power, raising more than $130 million for hurricane relief. *Press Room: American Red Cross.* Retrieved from http://redcross.org/pressrelease/0,1077,0_314_5172,00.html

Marjanovic, Z., Greenglass, E. R., Struthers, C. W., & Faye, C. (2009). Helping following natural disasters: A social-motivational analysis. *Journal of Applied Social Psychology, 39,* 2604–2625. doi: 10.1111/j.1559-1816.2009.00540.x

Markey, P. M. (2000). Bystander intervention in computer-mediated communication. *Computers in Human Behavior, 16,* 183–188. doi: 10.1016/S0747-5632(99)00056-4

Markus, G. B. (1986). Stability and change in political attitudes: Observed, recalled and "explained." *Political Behavior, 8,* 21–44. doi: 10.1007/BF00987591

Markus, H. (1977). Self-schemata and processing information about the self. *Journal of Personality and Social Psychology, 35,* 63–78. doi: 10.1037/0022.3514.35.2.63

Markus, H. R., & Kitayama, S. (1991). Culture and the self: Implications for cognition, emotion, and motivation. *Psychological Review, 98,* 224–253. doi: 10.1037/0033-295X.98.2.224

Marrow, A. J. (1969). *The practical theorist: The life and work of Kurt Lewin.* New York, NY: Basic Books.

Martijn, C., Alberts, H. J. E. M., Merckelbach, H., Havermans, R., Huijts, A., & DeVries, N. K. (2007). Overcoming ego-depletion: The influence of exemplar priming on self-control performance. *European Journal of Social Psychology, 37,* 231–238. doi: 10.1002/ejsp.350

Martin, D. (1989, March 11). Kitty Genovese: Would New York still turn away? *New York Times.* Retrieved from http://www.nytimes.com/1989/03/11/nyregion/about-new-york-kitty-genovese-would-new-york-still-turn-away.html

Martin, K. A., & Leary, M. R. (1999). Would you drink after a stranger? The influence of self-presentational motives on willingness to take a health risk. *Personality and Social Psychology Bulletin, 25,* 1092–1100. doi: 10.1177/01461672992512003

Martin, R., Hewstone, M., & Martin, P. Y. (2008). Majority versus minority influence: The role of message processing in determining resistance to counter-persuasion. *European Journal of Social Psychology, 38,* 16–34. doi: 10.1002/ejsp.426

Martinez, E. (2009, October 27). Richmond high school gang-rape in California: Others watched and did nothing, say cops. *CBSNews.com.* Retrieved from http://www.cbsnews.com/8301-504083_162-5424131-504083.html

Masicampo, E. J., & Baumeister, R. F. (2008). Toward a physiology of dual-process reasoning and judgment: Lemonade, willpower, and expensive rule-based analysis. *Psychological Science, 19,* 255–260. doi: 10.1111/j.1467-9280.2008.02077.x

Matthews, K. A., Rosenfield, D., & Stephan, W. G. (1979). Playing hard-to-get: A two-determinant model. *Journal of Research in Personality, 13,* 234–244. doi: 10.1018/0092-6566(79)90033-3

McAllister, H. A., Baker, J. D., Mannes, C., Stewart, H., & Sutherland, A. (2002). The optimal margin of illusion hypothesis: Evidence from the self-serving bias and personality disorders. *Journal of Social and Clinical Psychology, 21,* 414–426. doi: 10.1521/jscp.21.4.414.22593

McCauley, C. (1989). The nature of social influence in groupthink: Compliance and internalization. *Journal of Personality and Social Psychology, 57,* 250–260. doi: 10.1037/0022-3514.57.2.250

McConnell, A. R., & Leibold, J. M. (2001). Relations among the Implicit Association Test, discriminatory behavior, and explicit measures of racial attitudes. *Journal of Experimental Social Psychology, 37,* 435–442. doi: 10.1006/jesp.2000.1470

McCord, J. (1983). A longitudinal study of aggression and antisocial behavior. In K. T. VanDusen & S. A. Mednick (Eds.), *Prospective studies in crime and delinquency* (pp. 269–275). Boston, MA: Kluwer-Nijhoff.

McCord, W., & McCord, J. (1960). *Origins of alcoholism.* Stanford, CA: Stanford University Press.

McGuire, W. J. (1968). Personality and susceptibility to social influence. In E. F. Borgatta & W. W. Lambert (Eds.), *Handbook of personality theory and research* (pp. 1130–1187). Chicago, IL: Rand McNally.

McNulty, J. K., Neff, L. A., & Karney, B. R. (2008). Beyond initial attraction: Physical attractiveness in newlywed marriage. *Journal of Family Psychology, 22,* 135–143. doi: 10.1037/0893-3200.22.1.135

Messick, D. M., Wilke, H., Brewer, M. B., Kramer, R. M., Zemke, P. E., & Lui, L. (1983). Individual adaptations and structural change as solutions to social dilemmas. *Journal of Personality and Social Psychology, 44,* 294–309. doi: 10.1037/0022-3514.44.2.294

Meyers, S. A., & Berscheid, E. (1997). The language of love: The difference a preposition makes. *Personality and Social Psychology Bulletin, 23,* 347–362. doi: 10.1177/0146167297234002

Mezulis, A. H., Abramson, L. Y., Hyde, J. S., & Hankin, B. L. (2004). Is there a universal positivity bias in attributions? A meta-analytic review of individual, developmental, and cultural differences in the self-serving attributional bias. *Psychological Bulletin, 130,* 711–747. doi: 10.1037/0033-2909-130.5.711

Michaels, J. W., Bloommel, J. M., Brocato, R. M., Linkous, R. A., & Rowe, J. S. (1982). Social facilitation and inhibition in a natural setting. *Replications in Social Psychology, 2,* 21–24.

Michaels, L., & Shimkin, T. (Producers), & Waters, M. (Director). (2004). *Mean Girls* [Motion picture]. U.S.: Paramount Pictures.

Michel, L. M. (2007). Personal responsibility and volunteering after a natural disaster: The case of hurricane Katrina. *Sociological Spectrum, 27,* 633–652. doi: 10.1080/02732170701533855

Milgram, S. (1963). Behavioral study of obedience. *Journal of Abnormal and Social Psychology, 67,* 371–378. doi: 10.1037/h0040525

Milgram, S. (1964). Issues in the study of obedience: A reply to Baumrind. *American Psychologist, 19,* 848–852. doi: 10.1037/h0044954

Milgram, S. (1965). Liberating effects of group pressure. *Journal of Personality and Social Psychology, 1*, 127–134. doi: 10.1037/h0021650

Milgram, S. (1974). *Obedience to authority*. New York, NY: Harper & Row, Publishers.

Millar, M. (2002). Effects of a guilt induction and guilt reduction on door in the face. *Communication Research, 29*, 666–680. doi: 10.1177/009365002237831

Miller, F. G., & Rowold, K. L. (1979). Halloween masks and deindividuation. *Psychological Reports, 44*, 422.

Miller, J. G., Bersoff, D. M., & Harwood, R. L. (1990). Perceptions of social responsibilities in India and in the United States: Moral imperatives or personal decisions? *Journal of Personality and Social Psychology, 58*, 33–47. doi: 10.1037/0022-3514.58.1.33

Miller, N. E., Sears, R. R., Mowrer, O. H., Doob, L. W., & Dollard, J. (1941). The frustration-aggression hypothesis. *Psychological Review, 48*, 337–342.

Mita, T. H., Dermer, M., & Knight, J. (1977). Reversed facial images and the mere-exposure hypothesis. *Journal of Personality and Social Psychology, 35*, 597–601. doi: 10.1037/0022-3514.35.8.597

Miyamoto, Y., & Kitayama, S. (2002). Cultural variation in correspondence bias: The critical role of diagnosticity of socially constrained behavior. *Journal of Personality and Social Psychology, 83*, 1239–1248. doi: 10.1037//0022-3514.83.5.1239

Monahan, J. L., Murphy, S. T., & Zajonc, R. B. (2000). Subliminal mere exposure: Specific, general, and diffuse effects. *Psychological Science, 11*, 462–466. doi: 10.1111/1467-9280.00289

Montoya, R. M. (2008). I'm hot, I'd say you're not: The influence of objective physical attractiveness on mate selection. *Personality and Social Psychology Bulletin, 34*, 1315–1331. doi: 10.1177/0146167208320387

Moreland, R. L., & Beach, S. R. (1992). Exposure effects in the classroom: The development of affinity among students. *Journal of Experimental Social Psychology, 28*, 255–276. doi: 10.1016/0022-1031(92)90055-O

Moreland, R. L., Argote, L., & Krishnan, R. (1996). Socially shared cognition at work: Transactive memory and group performance. In J. L. Nye & A. M. Brower (Eds.), *What's social about social cognition? Research on socially shared cognition in small groups* (pp. 57–84). Thousand Oaks, CA: Sage Publications.

Morgan, C. J. (1978). Bystander intervention: Experimental test of a formal model. *Journal of Personality and Social Psychology, 36*, 43–55. doi: 10.1037/0022-3514.36.1.43

Morris, M. W., & Peng, K. (1994). Culture and cause: American and Chinese attributions for social and physical events. *Journal of Personality and Social Psychology, 67*, 949–971. doi: 10.1037/0022-3514.67.6.949

Morrison, E. W. (1993). Longitudinal study of the effects of information seeking on newcomer socialization. *Journal of Applied Psychology, 78*, 173–183. doi: 10.1037/0021-9010.78.2.173

Morse, K. A., & Neuberg, S. L. (2004). How do holidays influence relationship processes and outcomes? Examining the instigating and catalytic effects of Valentine's Day. *Personal Relationships, 11*, 509–527. doi: 10.1111/j.1475-6811.2004.00095.x

Moscovici, S., & Lage, E. (1976). Studies in social influence III: Majority versus minority influence in a group. *European Journal of Social Psychology, 6*, 149–174. doi: 10.1002/ejsp.2420060202

Mullen, B., & Copper, C. (1994). The relation between group cohesiveness and performance: An integration. *Psychological Bulletin, 115*, 210–227. doi: 10.1037/0033.2909.115.2.210

Mullen, B., Johnson, C., & Salas, E. (1991). Productivity loss in brainstorming groups: A meta-analytic integration. *Basic and Applied Social Psychology, 12*, 3–23. doi: 10.1207/s15324634basp121_1

Munger, K., & Harris, S. J. (1989). Effects of an observer on handwashing in a public restroom. *Perceptual and Motor Skills, 69*, 733–734.

Munroe, R. L., Hulefeld, R., Rodgers, J. M., Tomeo, D. L., & Yamazaki, S. K. (2000). Aggression among children in four cultures. *Cross Cultural Research, 34*, 3–25. doi: 10.1177/106939710003400101

Myers, D. (1992). *The pursuit of happiness*. New York, NY: Morrow.

Myers, D. G., & Lamm, H. (1976). The group polarization phenomenon. *Psychological Bulletin, 83*, 602–627. doi: 10.1037/0033-2909.83.4.602

National Institute on Alcohol Abuse and Alcoholism (2011). *Statistical snapshot of college drinking*. Retrieved from http://www.niaaa.nih.gov/AboutNIAAA/NIAAA SponsoredPrograms/Documents/StatisticalSnapshotofCollegeDrinking.pdf

Neighbors, C., O'Connor, R. M., Lewis, M. A., Chawla, N., Lee, C. M., & Fossos, N. (2008). The relative impact of injunctive norms on college student drinking: The role of reference group. *Psychology of Addictive Behavior, 22*, 576–581. doi: 10.1037/a0013043

Nelson, G. (1989). Life strains, coping, and emotional well-being: A longitudinal study of recently separated and married women. *American Journal of Community Psychology, 17*, 459–483. doi: 10.4007/BF00931173

Nelson, G. (1994). Emotional well-being of separated and married women: Long-term follow-up study. *American Journal of Orthopsychiatry, 64*, 150–160. doi: 10.1037/h0079486

Nemeth, C. (1977). Interactions between jurors as a function of majority vs. unanimity decision rules. *Journal of Applied Social Psychology, 7*, 38–56. doi: 10.1111/j.1559-1816.1977.tb02416.x

Nemeth, C., Mayseless, O., Sherman, J., & Brown, Y. (1990). Exposure to dissent and recall of information. *Journal of Personality and Social Psychology, 58*, 429–437. doi: 10.1037/0022-3514.58.429

Ng, K., Ang, S., & Chan, K. (2008). Personality and leader effectiveness: A moderated mediation model of leadership self-efficacy, job demands, and job autonomy. *Journal of Applied Psychology, 93*, 733–743. doi: 10.1037/0021-9010.93.4.733

Nguyen, H. D., & Ryan, A. M. (2008). Does stereotype threat affect test performance of minorities and women? A meta-analysis of experimental evidence. *Journal of Applied Psychology, 93*, 1314–1334. doi: 10.1037/a0012702

Nolan, J. M., Schultz, P. W., Cialdini, R. B., Goldstein, N. J., & Griskevicius, V. (2008). Normative social influence is underdetected. *Personality and Social Psychology Bulletin, 34*, 913–923. doi: 10.1177/0146167208316691

Norman, P., Conner, M., & Bell, R. (1999). The theory of planned behavior and smoking cessation. *Health Psychology, 18*, 89–94. doi: 10.1037/0278-6133.18.1.89

Nosek, B. A., & Smyth, F. L. (2007). A multitrait-multimethod validation of the Implicit Association Test: Implicit and explicit attitudes are related but distinct constructs. *Experimental Psychology, 54*, 14–29. doi: 10.1027/1618-3169.54.1.14

Nowak, M., & Sigmund, K. (1993). A strategy of win-stay, lose-shift that outperforms tit-for-tat in the Prisoner's Dilemma game. *Nature, 364*, 56–58. doi: 10.1038/364056a0

O'Keefe, D. J. (2002). *Persuasion: Theory and research* (2nd ed.). Thousand Oaks, CA: Sage Publications.

O'Reilly, C., Cadwell, D. F., & Barnett, W. P. (1989). Work group demography, social integration, and turnover. *Administrative Science Quarterly, 34*, 21–37.

Oishi, S., & Diener, E. (2001). Goals, culture, and subjective well-being. *Personality and Social Psychology Bulletin, 27*, 1674–1682. doi: 10.1177/01461672012712010

Oliner, S. P., & Oliner, P. M. (1988). *The altruistic personality: Rescuers of Jews in Nazi Europe*. New York, NY: Free Press.

Olthof, T., & Goossens, F. A. (2008). Bullying and the need to belong: Early adolescents' bullying related behavior and the acceptance they desire and receive from particular classmates. *Social Development, 17*, 24–46. doi: 10.1111/j.1467-9507.2007.00413.x

Orbuch, T. L., Veroff, J., & Holmberg, D. (1993). Becoming a married couple: The emergence of meaning in the first years of marriage. *Journal of Marriage and the Family, 55*, 815–826. doi: 10.2307/352764

Orth, U., Robins, R. W., & Meier, L. L. (2009). Disentangling the effects of low self-esteem and stressful events on depression: Findings from three longitudinal studies. *Journal of Personality and Social Psychology, 97*, 307–321. doi: 10.1037/a0015645

Orth, U., Robins, R. W., Trzesniewski, K. H., Maes, J., & Schmitt, M. (2009). Low self-esteem is a risk factor for depressive symptoms from young adulthood to old age. *Journal of Abnormal Psychology, 118*, 472–478. doi: 10.1037/a0015922

Osborn, A. F. (1957). *Applied imagination*. New York, NY: Scribner.

Ostrov, J. M. (2006). Deception and subtypes of aggression during early childhood. *Journal of Experimental Child Psychology, 93*, 322–336. doi: 10.1016/j.jecp.2005.10.004

Ostrov, J. M., Gentile, D. A., & Crick, N. R. (2006). Media exposure, aggression, and prosocial behavior during early childhood: A longitudinal study. *Social Development, 15*, 612–627. doi: 10.1111/j.1467-9507.2006.00360.x

Packer, D. J. (2008). Identifying systematic disobedience in Milgram's obedience experiments: Meta-analytic review. *Perspectives on Psychological Science, 3*, 301–304.

Padawer-Singer, A. M., Singer, A. N., & Singer, R. L. J. (1977). An experimental study of twelve vs. six member juries under unanimous vs. nonunanimous decisions. In B. D. Sales (Ed.), *Psychology in the legal process* (pp. 77–86). New York, NY: Spectrum Publications.

Page, R. A. (1977). Noise and helping behavior. *Environment and Behavior, 9*, 311–334. doi: 10.1177/001391657700900302

Park, B., & Rothbart, M. (1982). Perception of out-group homogeneity and levels of social categorization: Memory for the subordinate attributes of in-group and out-group members. *Journal of Personality and Social Psychology, 42*, 1051–1068. doi: 10.1037/0022-3514.42.6.1051

Park, H. S., Klein, K. A., Smith, S., & Martell, D. (2009). Separating subjective norms, university descriptive and injunctive norms, and U.S. descriptive and injunctive norms for drinking behavior intentions. *Health Communication, 24*, 746–751. doi: 10.1080/10410230903265912

Pastore, N. (1952). The role of arbitrariness in the frustration-aggression hypothesis. *Journal of Abnormal and Social Psychology, 47*, 728–731. doi: 10.1037/h0060884

Paulus, P. B., Dzindolet, M. T., Poletes, G., & Camacho, L. M. (1993). Perception of performance in group brainstorming: The illusion of group productivity. *Personality and Social Psychology Bulletin, 19*, 78–89. doi: 10.1177/0146167293191009

Payne, B. K., Burkley, M. A., & Stokes, M. B. (2008). Why do implicit and explicit attitude tests diverge? The role of structural fit. *Journal of Personality and Social Psychology, 94*, 16–31. doi: 10.1037/0022-3514.94.1.16

Pelham, B. W., Mirenberg, M. C., & Jones, J.T (2002). Why Susie sells seashells by the seashore: Implicit egotism and major life decisions. *Journal of Personality and Social Psychology, 82*, 469–487. doi: 10.1037/0022-3514.82.4.469

Penner, L. A., Dovidio, J. F., Piliavin, J. A., & Schroeder, D. A. (2005). Prosocial behavior: Multilevel perspectives. *Annual Review of Psychology, 56*, 365–392. doi: 10.1146/annurev.psych.56.091103.070141

Pennock, D., Lawrence, S., Giles, C. L., & Nielsen, F. A. (2003). The real power of artificial markets. *Science, 291*, 987–988.

Perkins, H. W. (2007). Misperceptions of peer drinking norms in Canada: Another look at the "reign of error" and its consequences among college students. *Addictive Behaviors, 32*, 2645–2656. doi: 10.1016/j.addbeh.2007.07.007

Perkins, H. W., Haines, M. P., & Rice, R. (2005). Misperceiving the college drinking norm and related problems: A nationwide study of exposure to prevention information, perceived norms and student alcohol misuse. *Journal of Studies on Alcohol, 66*, 470–478.

Perkins, H. W., Linkenbach, J. W., Lewis, M. A., & Neighbors, C. (2010). Effectiveness of social norms media marketing in reducing drinking and driving: A statewide campaign. *Addictive Behaviors, 35*, 866–874. doi: 10.1016/j.addbeh.2010.05.004

Perloff, R. M. (1999). The third-person effect: A critical review and synthesis. *Media Psychology, 1*, 353–378. doi: 10.1207/s1532785xmep0104_4

Pessin, J. (1933). The comparative effects of social and mechanical stimulation on memorizing. *American Journal of Psychology, 45*, 263–270. doi: 10.2307/1414277

Peters, E., Hess, T. M., Vastfjall, D., & Auman, C. (2007). Adult age differences in dual information processes: Implications for the role of affective and deliberative processes in older adults' decision making. *Perspectives on Psychological Science, 2*, 1–23. doi: 10.1111/j.1745-6916.2007.00025.x

Peters, W. (1987). One Friday in April, 1968. In *A Class Divided: Then and Now*. New Haven, CT: Yale University Press. Retrieved from http://www.pbs.org/wgbh/pages/frontline/shows/divided/etc/friday.html#ixzz1ONy56kAu

Peterson, C. & Seligman, M. E. (1984). Causal explanations as a risk factor for depression: Theory and evidence. *Psychological Review, 91*, 347–374. doi: 10.1037/0033-295X.91.3.347

Peterson, C., & Barrett, L. C. (1987). Explanatory style and academic performance among university freshmen. *Journal of Personality and Social Psychology, 53*, 603–607. doi: 10.1037/0022-3514.53.3.603

Peterson, C., & Ulrey, L. M. (1994). Can explanatory style be scored from TAT protocols? *Personality and Social Psychology Bulletin, 20*, 102–106. doi: 10.1177/0146167294201010

Peterson, C., Semmel, A., von Baeyer, C., Abramson, L. Y., Metalsky, G. I., & Seligman, M. E. P. (1982). The attributional style questionnaire. *Cognitive Therapy and Research, 6*, 287–300.

Peterson, R. C., & Thurstone, L. L. (1933/1970). *Motion pictures and social attitudes of children*. Oxford, England: Macmillan.

Pettigrew, T. F., & Tropp, L. R. (2006). A meta-analytic test of intergroup contact theory. *Journal of Personality and Social Psychology, 90*, 751–783. doi: 10.1037/0022-3514.90.5.751

Petty, R. E., & Brock, T. C. (1981). Thought disruption and persuasion: Assessing the validity of attitude change experiments. In R. E. Petty, T. M. Ostrom, & T. C. Brock (Eds.), *Cognitive responses in persuasion* (pp. 55–79). Hillsdale, NJ: Lawrence Erlbaum Associates.

Petty, R. E., & Cacioppo, J. T. (1986). The elaboration likelihood model. In L. Berkowitz (Ed.), *Advances in experimental social psychology* (Vol. 19, pp. 123–205). San Diego, CA: Academic Press.

Petty, R. E., Cacioppo, J. T., & Goldman, R. (1981). Personal involvement as a determinant of argument-based persuasion. *Journal of Personality and Social Psychology, 41,* 847–855. doi: 10.1037/0022-3514.41.5.847

Petty, R. E., Cacioppo, J. T., & Schumann, D. (1983). Central and peripheral routes to advertising effectiveness: The moderating role of involvement. *Journal of Consumer Research, 10,* 135–146. doi: 10.1086/208954

Petty, R. E., Wells, G. L., & Brock, T. C. (1976). Distraction can enhance or reduce yielding to propaganda: Thought disruption versus effort justification. *Journal of Personality and Social Psychology, 34,* 874–884. doi: 10.1037/0022-3514.34.5.874

Petty, R. E., Williams, K. D., Harkins, S. G., & Latane, B. (1977). Social inhibition of helping yourself: Bystander response to a cheeseburger. *Personality and Social Psychology Bulletin, 3,* 575–578. doi: 10.1177/0146727700300405

Phillips, K. T., & Rosenberg, H. (2008). The development and evaluation of Harm Reduction Self-efficacy Questionnaire. *Psychology of Addictive Behavior, 22,* 36–46. doi: 10.1037/0893-164X.22.1.36

Piliavin, J. A., & Callero, P. L. (1990). *Giving the gift of life to unnamed strangers.* Baltimore, ME: Johns Hopkins University Press.

Piliavin, J. A., Dovidio, J. F., Gaertner, S. L., & Clark, R. D., III. (1981). *Emergency intervention.* New York, NY: Academic Press.

Pines, A. M., & Aronson, E. (1983). Antecedents, correlates, and consequences of sexual jealousy. *Journal of Personality, 51,* 108–136. doi: 10.1111/j.1467-6494.1983.tb00857.x

Pingdom. (2011). *Internet 2010 in numbers.* Retrieved from http://royal.pingdom.com/2011/01/12/internet-2010-in-numbers/

Piper. W., & Long, L. (2005). *The little engine that could.* New York: Philomen Books.

Platania, J., & Moran, G. P. (2001). Social facilitation as a function of mere presence of others. *Journal of Social Psychology, 141,* 190–197. doi: 10.1080/00224540109600546

Plaut, V. C., Adams, G., & Anderson, S. L. (2009). Does attractiveness buy happiness? "It depends on where you're from." *Personal Relationships, 16,* 619–630. doi: 10.1111/j.1475-6811.2009.01242.x

Pollock, C. L., Smith, S. D., Knowles, E. S., & Bruce, H. J. (1998). Mindfulness limits compliance with the that's-not-all technique. *Personality and Social Psychology Bulletin, 24,* 1153–1157. doi: 10.1177/01461672982411002

Postmes, T., & Spears, R. (1998). Deindividuation and antinormative behavior: A meta-analysis. *Psychological Bulletin, 123,* 238–259. doi: 10.1037/0033-2909.123.3.238

Postmes, T., Spears, R., & Cihangir, S. (2001). Quality of decision making and group norms. *Journal of Personality and Social Psychology, 80,* 918–930. doi: 10.1037//0022-3514.80.3.918

Powers, P. (2010). *Winning job interviews* (Rev. ed.). Franklin Lakes, NJ: Career Press.

Pratkanis, A. R., & Gliner, M. D. (2004). And when shall a little child lead them? Evidence for an altercasting theory of source credibility. *Current Psychology: A Journal for Diverse Perspectives on Diverse Psychological Issues, 23,* 279–304. doi: 10.1007/s12144-004-1002-5

Pratto, F., Liu, J. H., Levin, S., Sidanius, J., Shih, M., Bachrach, H., & Hegarty, P. (2000). Social dominance orientation and the legitimization of inequality across cultures. *Journal of Cross-Cultural Psychology, 31,* 396–409. doi: 10.1177/0022022100031003005

Pratto, F., Sidanius, J., Stallworth, L. M., & Malle, B. F. (1994). Social dominance orientation: A personality variable predicting social and political attitudes. *Journal of Personality and Social Psychology, 67,* 741–763. doi: 10.1037/0022-3514.67.4.741

Prentice-Dunn, S., & Rogers, R. W. (1982). Effects of public and private self-awareness on deindividuation and aggression. *Journal of Personality and Social Psychology, 43,* 503–513. doi: 10.1037/0022.3514.43.3.503

Priester, J. R., & Petty, R. E. (2003). The influence of spokesperson trustworthiness on message elaboration, attitude strength, and advertising effectiveness. *Journal of Consumer Psychology, 13,* 408–421. doi: 10.1207/S15327663JCP1304_08

Priester, J., Wegner, D., Petty, R., & Fabrigar, L. (1999). Examining the psychological process underlying the sleeper effect: The elaboration likelihood model explanation. *Media Psychology, 1,* 27–48. doi: 10.1207/s1532785xmep0101_3

Prislin, R., Limbert, W. M., & Bauer, E. (2000). From majority to minority and vice versa: The asymmetrical effects of losing and gaining majority position within a group. *Journal of Personality and Social Psychology, 79,* 385–397. doi: 10.1037/0022-3514.79.3.385

Rai, S. N., & Gupta, M. D. (1996). Donating behaviour as a function of age, culture, and outcome feedback conditions. *Psycho-Lingua, 26,* 105–110.

Ramirez, A., & Wang, Z. (2004). When online meets offline: An expectancy violations theory perspective on modality switching. *Journal of Communication, 58,* 20–39. doi: 10.1111/j.1460-2466.2007.00372.x

Ramirez, A., & Zhang, S. (2007). When on-line meets off-line: The effects of modality switching on relational communication. *Communication Monographs, 74,* 287–310. doi: 10.1080/03637750701543493

Read, S. (2009). A prosecutor's role. *eJournal USA: Anatomy of a jury trial, 14,* 24–27. www.american.gov/publications/ejournalusa.html

Regan, D. T. (1971). Effects of a favor and liking on compliance. *Journal of Experimental Social Psychology, 7,* 627–639. doi: 10.1016/0022-1031(71)90025-4

Regan, P. C. (1998). Of lust and love: Beliefs about the role of sexual desire in romantic relationships. *Personal Relationships, 5,* 139–157. doi: 10.1111/j.1475-6811.1998 .tb00164.x

Reifman, A. S., Larrick, R. P., & Fein, S. (1991). Temper and temperature on the diamond: The heat-aggression relationship in major league baseball. *Personality and Social Psychology Bulletin, 17,* 580–585. doi: 10.1177/0146167291175013

Reinhard, M., Messner, M., & Sporer, S. L. (2006). Explicit persuasive intent and its impact on success at persuasion: The determining roles of attractiveness and likeableness. *Journal of Consumer Psychology, 16,* 249–259. doi: 10.1080/15534510802045261

Remillard, A. M., & Lamb, S. (2005). Adolescent girls' coping with relational aggression. *Sex Roles, 53,* 221–229. doi: 10.1007/s11199-005-5680-8

Ren, J., Hu, L., Zhang, H., & Huang, Z. (2010). Implicit positive emotion counteracts ego depletion. *Social Behavior and Personality, 38,* 919–928. doi: 10.2224/sbp.2010.38.7.919

Reno, R. R., Cialdini, R. B., & Kallgren, C. A. (1993). The transsituational influence of social norms. *Journal of Personality and Social Psychology, 64,* 104–112. doi: 10.1037/0022-3514.64.1.104

Reyna, V. F. (2004). How people make decisions that involve risk: A dual-processes approach. *Current Directions in Psychological Science, 13,* 60–66. doi: 10.1111/j.0963-7214.2004.00275.x

Reynolds, B. M., & Repetti, R. L. (2010). Teenage girls' perceptions of the functions of relationally aggressive behaviors. *Psychology in the Schools, 47,* 282–296. doi: 10.1002/pits.20470

Rhodes, N., & Wood, W. (1992). Self-esteem and intelligence affect influenceability: The mediating role of message reception. *Psychological Bulletin, 111*, 156–171. doi: 10.1037/0033-2909.111.1.156

Rise, J., Astrom, A. N., & Sutton, S. (1998). Predicting intentions and use of dental floss among adolescents: An application of the theory of planned behavior. *Psychological Health, 13*, 223–236.

Rizley, R. (1978). Depression and distortion in the attribution of causality. *Journal of Abnormal Psychology, 87*, 32–48. doi: 10.1037/0021-843X.87.1.32

Rochat, F., & Modigliani, A. (1997). Authority: Obedience, defiance, and identification in experimental and historical contexts. In M. Gold & E. A. Malcolm (Eds.), *A new outline of social psychology* (pp. 235–246). Washington, D. C.: American Psychological Association. doi: 10.1037/10225-013

Rogers, S. J. (2004). Dollars, dependency, and divorce: Four perspectives on the role of wives' income. *Journal of Marriage and the Family, 66*, 59–74. doi: 10.1111/j.1741-3737.2004.00005.x

Rogers, T. B., Kuiper, N. A., & Kirker, W. S. (1977). Self-reference and the encoding of personal information. *Journal of Personality and Social Psychology, 35*, 677–688. doi: 10.1037/0022-3514.35.9.677

Rohsenow, D. J., & Bachorowski, J. (1984). Effects of alcohol and expectancies on verbal aggression in men and women. *Journal of Abnormal Psychology 93*, 418–432. doi:10.1037/0021-843X.93.4.418

Rokach, A. (2007). The effect of age and culture on the causes of loneliness. *Social Behavior and Personality, 35*, 169–186. doi: 10.2224/sbp.2007.35.2.169

Rose, S., & Frieze, I. H. (1989). Young singles' scripts for a first date. *Gender and Society, 3*, 258–268. doi: 10.1177/089124389003002006

Rosenhan, D. (1969). Some origins of concern for others. In P. Mussen, J. Langer, & M. Covington (Eds.), *Trends and issues in developmental psychology* (pp. 134–153). New York, NY: Holt, Rinehart & Winston.

Rosenhan, D. L. (1970). The natural socialization of altruistic autonomy. In J. Macaulay and L. Berkowitz (Eds.), *Altruism and helping behavior: Social psychological studies of some antecedents and consequences* (pp. 251–268). New York, NY: Academic Press.

Rosenthal, R., & Jacobson, L. (1966). Teachers' expectancies: Determinants of pupils' IQ gains. *Psychological Reports, 19*, 115–118.

Ross, L., Greene, D., & House, P. (1977). The false consensus effect: An egocentric bias in social perception and attribution processes. *Journal of Experimental Social Psychology, 13*, 279–301. doi: 10.1016/0022-1031(77)90049-X

Ross, L.D., Amabile, T. M., & Steinmetz, J. L. (1977). Social roles, social control, and biases in social-perception processes. *Journal of Personality and Social Psychology, 35*, 485–494. doi: 10.1037/0022-3514.35.7.485

Rowe, P. (2010, Feb. 1). Decision markets tap "wisdom of the crowd." *The San Diego Union-Tribune.* Retrieved from http://www.signonsandiego.com/news/2010/feb/01/1c01prediction/

Ruback, R. B., & Juieng, D. (1997). Territorial defense in parking lots: Retaliation against waiting drivers. *Journal of Applied Social Psychology, 27*, 821–834. doi: 10.1111/j.1559-1816.1997.tb00661.x

Ruiter, R. A. C., Abraham, C., & Kok, G. (2001). Scary warnings and rational precautions: A review of the psychology of fear appeals. *Psychology and Health, 16*, 613–630. doi: 10.1080/08870440108405863

Rusbult, C. E. (1983). A longitudinal test of the investment model: The development (and deterioration) of satisfaction and commitment in heterosexual involvements. *Journal of Personality and Social Psychology, 45,* 101–117. doi: 10.1037/0022-3514.45.1.101

Rusbult, C. E., Drigotas, S. M., & Verette, J. (1994). The investment model: An interdependence analysis of commitment processes and relationship maintenance phenomena. In D. J. Canary & L. Stafford (Eds.), *Communication and relational maintenance* (pp. 115–139). New York, NY: Academic Press.

Rusbult, C. E., Martz, J. M., & Agnew, C. R. (1998). The investment model scale: Measuring commitment level, satisfaction level, quality of alternatives, and investment size. *Personal Relationships, 5,* 357–391. doi: 10.1111/j.1475-6811.1998.tb00177.x

Rushton, J. P., Chrisjohn, R. D., & Fekken, G. C. (1981). The altruistic personality and the Self-Report Altruism Scale. *Personality and Individual Differences, 2,* 293–302. doi: 10.106/0191-8869(81)90047-7

Rydell, R. J., & McConnell, A. R. (2006). Understanding implicit and explicit attitude change: A systems of reasoning analysis. *Journal of Personality and Social Psychology, 91,* 995–1008. doi: 10.1037/0022-3514.91.6.995

Sagarin, B. J., Cialdini, R. B., Rice, W. E., & Serna, S. B. (2002). Dispelling the illusion of invulnerability: The motivations and mechanisms of resistance to persuasion. *Journal of Personality and Social Psychology, 83,* 526–541. doi: 10.1037/0022-3514.83.3.526

Saks, M. J., & Marti, M. W. (1997). A meta-analysis of the effects of jury size. *Law and Human Behavior, 21,* 451–467. doi: 10.1023/A:1024819605652

Samuelson, C. D., Messick, D. M., Rutte, C. G., & Wilke, H. (1984). Individual and structural solutions to resource dilemmas in two cultures. *Journal of Personality and Social Psychology, 47,* 94–104. doi: 10.1037/0022-3514.47.1.94

Sanaktekin, O. H., & Sunar, D. (2008). Persuasion and relational versus personal bases of self-esteem: Does the message need to be one- or two-sided? *Social Behavior and Personality, 36,* 1315–1332. doi: 10.2224/sbp.2008.36.10.1315

Sandys, M., & Dillehay, R. C. (1995). First-ballot votes, predeliberation dispositions, and final verdicts in jury trials. *Law and Human Behavior, 19,* 175–195. doi: 10.1007/BF01499324

SanJose-Cabezudo, R., Gutierrez-Arranz, A. M., & Gutierrez-Cillan, J. (2009). The combined influence of central and peripheral routes in the online persuasion process. *CyberPsychology & Behavior, 12,* 299–308. doi: 10.1089/cob.2008.0188

Sbarra, D. A., & Emery, R. E. (2005). The emotional sequelae of nonmarital relationship dissolution: Analysis of change and intraindividual variability over time. *Personal Relationship, 12,* 213–232. doi: 10.1111/j.1350-4126.2005.00112.x

Sbarra, D. A., & Ferrer, E. (2006). The structure and process of emotional experience following nonmarital relationship dissolution: Dynamic factor analyses of love, anger, and sadness. *Emotion, 6,* 224–238. doi: 10.1037/1528-3542.6.2.224

Schacter, S., & Singer, J. E. (1962). Cognitive, social, and physiological determinants of emotional state. *Psychological Review, 69,* 379–399.

Schmeichel, B. J., & Vohs, K. (2009). Self-affirmation and self-control; Affirming core values counteracts ego depletion. *Journal of Personality and Social Psychology, 96,* 770–782. doi: 10.1037/a0014635

Schmeichel, B. J., Vohs, K.D., & Baumeister, R. F. (2003). Intellectual performance and ego depletion: Role of the self in logical reasoning and other information processing. *Journal of Personality and Social Psychology, 85,* 33–46. doi: 10.1037/0022-3514.85.1.33

Schnabel, K., Asendorpf, J. B., & Greenwald, A. G. (2008). Assessment of individual differences in implicit cognition: Review of IAT measures. *European Journal of Psychological Assessment, 24,* 210–217. doi: 10.1027/1015-5759.24.4.4210

Schonfeld, E. (2010, June 8). *Constolo: Twitter now has 190 million users tweeting 65 million times a day.* Retrieved from http://techcrunch.com/2010/06/08/twitter-190-million-users/

Schug, J., Yuki, M., Horikawa, H., & Takemura, K. (2009). Similarity attraction and actually selecting similar others: How cross-societal differences in relational mobility affect interpersonal similarity in Japan and the USA. *Asian Journal of Social Psychology, 12,* 95–103. doi: 10.1111/j.1467-839X.2009.01277.x

Schultz, P. W., Nolan, J. M., Cialdini, R. B., Goldstein, N. J., & Griskevicius, V. (2007). The constructive, destructive, and reconstructive power of social norms. *Psychological Science, 18,* 429–434. doi: 10.1111/j.1467-9280.2007.01917.x

Schumacher, J. A. (2004). Attitudes and dating aggression: A cognitive dissonance approach. *Prevention Science, 5,* 231–243. doi: 10.1023/B:PREV.0000045357.19100.77

Schwartz, S. (1975). The justice of need and the activation of humanitarian norms. *Journal of Social Issues, 31,* 111–136. doi: 10.1111/j.1540-4560.1975.tb00999.x

Schwartz, S. H. (1973). Normative explanations of helping behavior: A critique, proposal, and empirical test. *Journal of Experimental Social Psychology, 9,* 349–364. doi: 10.1016/0022-1031(73)90071-1

Schwartz, S. H. (1974). Awareness of interpersonal consequences, responsibility denial, and volunteering. *Journal of Personality and Social Psychology, 30,* 57–63. doi: 10.1037/h0036644

Seepersad, S., Choi, M. K., & Shin, N. (2008). How does culture influence the degree of romantic loneliness and closeness? *Journal of Psychology: Interdisciplinary and Applied, 142,* 209–216. doi: 10.3200/JRLP.142.2.209-220

Seijts, G. H., & Latham, G. P. (2000). The effects of goal setting and group size on performance in a social dilemma. *Canadian Journal of Behavioural Science, 32,* 104–116. 10.1037/h0087105

Selfhout, M., Denissen, J., Branje, S., & Meeus, W. (2009). In the eye of the beholder: Perceived, actual, and peer-rated similarity in personality, communication, and friendship intensity during the acquaintanceship process. *Journal of Personality and Social Psychology, 96,* 1152–1165. doi: 10.1037/a0014468

Seligman, C., Bush, M., & Kirsch, K. (1976). Relationship between compliance in the foot-in-the-door paradigm and size of first request. *Journal of Personality and Social Psychology, 33,* 517–520. doi: 10.1037/0022-3514.33.5.517

Seligman, M. E. P., & Nolen-Hoeksema, S. (1987). Explanatory style and depression. In D. Magnusson & A. Ohman (Eds.) *Psychopathology: An interactional perspective* (pp. 125–139). San Diego, CA: Academic Press.

Seligman, M. E. P., & Schulman, P. (1986). Explanatory style as a predictor of productivity and quitting among life insurance sales agents. *Journal of Personality and Social Psychology, 50,* 832–838. doi: 10.1037/0022-3514.50.4.832

Shah, A. K., & Oppenheimer, D. M. (2008). Heuristics made easy: An effort-reduction framework. *Psychological Bulletin, 134,* 207–222. doi: 10.1037/0033-2909.134.2.207

Shanab, M. E., & Yahya, K. A. (1977). A behavior study of obedience in children. *Journal of Personality and Social Psychology, 35,* 530–536. doi: 10.1037/0022-3514.35.7.530

Shaw, J. L. (1976). Response-contingent payoffs and cooperative behavior in the prisoner's dilemma game. *Journal of Personality and Social Psychology, 34,* 1024–1033. doi: 10.1037/0022-3514.34.5.1024

Shepherd, H. (2011). The cultural context of cognition: What the Implicit Association Test tells us about how culture works. *Sociological Forum, 26,* 121–143. doi: 10.1111/j.1573-7861.2010.01227.x

Sher, P. J., & Lee, S. H. (2009). Consumer skepticism and online reviews: An Elaboration likelihood model perspective. *Social Behavior and Personality, 37,* 137–144. doi: 10.1224/sbp.2009.37.1.137

Sherif, M. (1936). *The psychology of social norms.* New York, NY: Harper.

Sherif, M. (1958). Superordinate goals in the reduction of intergroup conflict. *American Journal of Sociology, 63,* 349–356.

Sherif, M. (1966). *Group conflict and cooperation: Their social psychology.* London: Routledge & Kegan Paul.

Sherif, M., & Sherif, C. W. (1953). *Intergroup harmony and tension: An integration of studies of intergroup relations.* Oxford, U.K.: Harper and Brothers.

Sherif, M., Harvey, O. J., White, B. J., Hood, W. R., & Sherif, C. W. (1961). *The Robbers Cave experiment: Intergroup conflict and cooperation.* Hanover, NH: Wesleyan University Press, University Press of New England.

Shermer, M. (2007, July 15). Bad apples and bad barrels: Lessons in evil from Stanford to Abu Ghraib. *Scientific American Magazine.* Retrieved from http://www.scientific american.com/article.cfm?id=bad-apples-and-bad-barrels

Shotland, R. L., & Heinold, W. D. (1985). Bystander response to arterial bleeding: Helping skills, the decision-making process, and differentiating the helping response. *Journal of Personality and Social Psychology, 49,* 347–356. doi: 10.1037/0022-3514.49.2.347

Shotland, R. L., & Straw, M. K. (1976). Bystander response to an assault: When a man attacks a woman. *Journal of Personality and Social Psychology, 34,* 990–999. doi: 10.1037/0022-3514.34.5.990

Sidey, H. (2001, April 16). The lesson John Kennedy learned from the Bay of Pigs. *Time Magazine.* Retrieved from http://www.time.com/time/nation/article/ 0,8599,106537,00.html

Silvia, P. J. (2006). Reactance and the dynamics of disagreement: Multiple paths from threatened freedom to resistance to persuasion. *European Journal of Social Psychology, 36,* 673–685. doi: 10.1002/ejsp.309

Simpson, J. A. (1987). The dissolution of romantic relationships: Factors involved in relationship stability and emotional distress. *Journal of Personality and Social Psychology, 53,* 683–692. doi: 10.1037/0022-3514.53.4.683

Slovic, P., Monahan, J., & MacGregor, D. G. (2000). Violence risk assessment and risk communication: The effects of using actual cases, providing instruction, and employing probability versus frequency formats. *Law and Human Behavior, 24,* 271–296. doi: 10.1023/A:1005595519944

Slovic, P., Peters, E., Finucane, M. L., & MacGregor, D. G. (2005). Affect, risk, and decision making. *Health Psychology, 24,* S35–S40. doi: 10.1037/0278-6133.24.4.S35

Smith, B. N., Kerr, N. A., Markus, M. J., & Stasson, M. F. (2001). Individual differences in social loafing: Need for cognition as a motivator in collective performance. *Group Dynamics: Theory, Research, and Practice, 5,* 150–158. doi: 10.1037//1089-2699.5.2.150

Smith, R. L., Rose, A. J., & Schwartz-Mette, R. A. (2010). Relational and overt aggression in childhood and adolescence: Clarifying mean-level gender differences and associations with peer acceptance. *Social Development, 19,* 243–269. doi: 10.1111/j.1467-9507.2009.00541.x

Solomon, L. (1960). The influence of some types of power relationships and game strategies upon the development of interpersonal trust. *Journal of Abnormal and Social Psychology, 61*, 223–230. doi: 10.1037/h0047571

Sommer, K. L., Williams, K. D., Ciarocco, N. J., & Baumeister, R. F. (2001). When silence speaks louder than words: Explorations into the intrapsychic and interpersonal consequences of social ostracism. *Basic and Applied Social Psychology, 23*, 225–243. doi: 10.1207/153248301753225694

Sommer, R. (2009). Dissemination in action research. *Action Research, 7*, 227–236. doi: 10.1177/1476750308097028

Sommers, S. R. (2006). On racial diversity and group decision making: Identifying multiple effects of racial composition on jury deliberations. *Journal of Personality and Social Psychology, 90*, 597–612. doi: 10.1037/0022-3514.90.4.687

Sorenson, T. C. (1966). *Kennedy.* New York, NY: Bantam Books.

Sorlie, P. D., Backlund, E., & Keller, J. B. (1995). U.S. mortality by economic, demographic, and social characteristics: The national longitudinal mortality study. *American Journal of Public Health, 85*, 949–956.

Sprecher, S. (1986). The relation between inequity and emotions in close relationships. *Social Psychology Quarterly, 49*, 309–321. doi: 10.2307/2786770

Sprecher, S. (1992). How men and women expect to feel and behave in responses to inequity in close relationships. *Social Psychology Quarterly, 55*, 57–69. doi: 10.2307/2786686

Sprecher, S. (1994). Two sides to the breakup of dating relationships. *Personal Relationships, 1*, 199–222. doi: 10.1111/j.1475-6811.1994.tb00062.x

Sprecher, S., & Fehr, B. (1998). The dissolution of close relationships. In J. H. Harvey (Ed.), *Perspectives on loss: A sourcebook* (pp. 99–112). Washington, D. C.: Taylor & Francis.

Sprecher, S., & Fehr, B. (2005). Compassionate love for close others and humanity. *Journal of Social and Personal Relationships, 22*, 629–651. doi: 10.1177/0265407505056439

Sprecher, S., Felmlee, D., Metts, S., Fehr, B., & Vanni, D. (1998). Factors associated with distress following the breakup of a close relationship. *Journal of Social and Personal Relationships, 15*, 791–809. doi: 10.1177/0265407598156005

Sprecher, S., Zimmerman, C., & Abrahams, E. M. (2010). Choosing compassionate strategies to end a relationship: Effects of compassionate love for partner and the reason for the breakup. *Social Psychology, 41*, 66–75. doi: 10.1027/1864-9335/a000010

Stafford, L., & Canary, D. J. (2006). Equity and interdependence as predictors of relational maintenance strategies. *Journal of Family Communication, 6*, 227–254. doi: 10.1207/x15327698jfc0604_1

Stangor, C., Sechrist, G. B., & Jost, J. T. (2001). Changing racial beliefs by providing consensus information. *Personality and Social Psychology Bulletin, 27*, 486–496. doi: 10.1177/0146167201274009

Stasser, G. (2000). Information distribution, participation, and group decision: Exploration with DISCUSS and SPEAK models. In D. R. Ilgen & C. L. Hulin (Eds.), *Computational modeling of behavior in organizations: The third scientific discipline* (pp. 135–161). Washington, D. C.: American Psychological Association.

Stasser, G., & Titus, W. (1985). Pooling of unshared information in group decision making: Biased information sampling during discussion. *Journal of Personality and Social Psychology, 48*, 1467–1478. doi: 10.1037/0022-3514.48.6.1467

Staub, E. (1972). Instigation to goodness: The role of social norm and interpersonal influence. *Journal of Social Issues, 28*, 131–150. doi: 10.1111/j.1540-4560.1972.tb00036.x

Staub, E. (1978). *Positive social behavior and morality: Socialization and development* (Vol. 2). New York, NY: Academic Press.

Staub, E. (1999). The roots of evil: Social conditions, culture, personality, and basic human needs. *Personality and Social Psychology Review, 3*, 179–192. doi: 10.1207/s15327957pspr0303_2

Staude-Muller, F., Bliesener, T., & Luthman, S. (2008). Hostile and hardened? An experimental study on (de-)sensitization to violence and suffering through playing video games. *Swiss Journal of Psychology, 67*, 41–50. doi: 10.1024/1421-0185.67.1.41

Steele, C. M., & Aronson, J. (1995). Stereotype threat and the intellectual test performance of African Americans. *Journal of Personality and Social Psychology, 69*, 797–811. doi: 10.1037/0022-3514.69.5.797

Stephan, W. G., Boniecki, K. A., Ybarra, O., Bettencourt, A., Ervin, K. S., Jackson, L. A., et al. (2002). The role of threats in the racial attitudes of Blacks and White. *Personality and Social Psychology Bulletin, 28*, 1242–1254. doi: 10.1177/01461672022812009

Sternberg, R. J. (1986). The triangular theory of love. *Psychological Review, 93*, 119–135. doi: 10.1037/0033-295X.93.2.119

Stice, E., Rohde, P., Gau, J., & Shaw, H. (2009). An effectiveness trial of a dissonance-based eating disorder prevention program for high-risk adolescent girls. *Journal of Consulting and Clinical Psychology, 77*, 825–834. doi: 10.1037/a0016132

Stillman, T. F., Baumeister, R. F., Lambert, N. M., Crescioni, A. W., DeWall, C. N., & Fincham, F. D. (2009). Alone and without purpose: Life loses meaning following social exclusion. *Journal of Experimental Social Psychology, 45*, 686–694. doi: 10.1016/j.jesp.2009.03.007

Stone, J., Lynch, C. I., Sjomeling, M., & Darley, J. M. (1999). Stereotype threat effects on Black and White athletic performance. *Journal of Personality and Social Psychology, 77*, 1213–1227. doi: 10.1037/0022-3514.77.6.1213

Strack, F., & Deutsch, R. (2004). Reflective and impulsive determinants of social behavior. *Personality and Social Psychology Review, 8*, 220–247. doi: 10.1207/s15327957pspr0803_1

Stroebe, W., Diehl, M., & Abakoumkin, G. (1996). Social compensation and the Köhler effect: Toward a theoretical explanation of motivation gains in group productivity. In E. Witte & J. Davis (Eds.) *Understanding group behavior: Consensual action by small groups* (Vol. 2, pp. 37–65). Mahwah, NJ: Erlbaum.

Stucke, T. S., & Baumeister, R. F. (2006). Ego depletion and aggressive behavior: Is the inhibition of aggression a limited resource? *European Journal of Social Psychology, 36*, 1–13. doi: 10.1002/ejsp.285

Subra, B., Muller, D., Begue, L., Bushman, B. J., & Delmas, F., (2010). Automatic effects of alcohol and aggressive cues on aggressive thoughts and behaviors. *Personality and Social Psychology Bulletin, 36*, 1052–1057. doi: 10.1177/0146167210374725

Sundstrom, A. (2008). Construct validation and psychometric evaluation of the Self-Efficacy Scale for Driver Competence. *European Journal of Psychological Assessment, 24*, 198–206. doi: 10.1027/1015-5759.24.3.198

Surowiecki, J. (2004). *The wisdom of crowds: Why the many are smarter than the few and how collective wisdom shapes business, economics, societies and nations.* New York, NY: Doubleday.

Sweeney, J. C., Soutar, G. N., & Mazzarol, T. (2008). Factors influencing word of mouth effectiveness: Receiver perspectives. *European Journal of Marketing, 42*, 344–364. doi: 10.1108/03090560810652977

Sweeney, K. A., & Borden, A. L. (2009). Crossing the line online: Racial preferences of internet daters. *Marriage and Family Review, 45,* 740–760. doi: 10.1080/01494920903224335

Sweeney, P. D., Anderson, K., & Bailey, S. (1986). Attributional style in depression: A meta-analytic review. *Journal of Personality and Social Psychology, 50,* 974–991. doi: 10.1037/0022-3514.50.5.974

Symons, C. S., & Johnson, B. T. (1997). The self-reference effect in memory: A meta-analysis. *Psychological Bulletin, 121,* 371–394. doi: 10.1037/0033-2909.121.3.371

Tajfel, H. (1970). Experiments in intergroup discrimination. *Scientific American, 223,* 96–102.

Tam, K. Y., & Ho, S. Y. (2005). Web personalization as a persuasion strategy: An elaboration likelihood model perspective. *Information Systems Research, 16,* 271–291. doi: 10.1287/isre.1050.0058

Tashiro, T., & Frazier, P. (2003). "I'll never be in a relationship like that again": Personal growth following romantic relationship breakups. *Personal Relationships, 10,* 113–128. doi: 10.1111/1475-6811.00039

Tassava, S. H., & Ruderman, A. J. (1999). Application of escape theory to binge eating and suicidality in college women. *Journal of Social and Clinical Psychology, 18,* 450–466.

Tazelaar, M. J. A., Van Lange, P. A. M., & Ouwerker, J. W. (2004). How to cope with "noise" in social dilemmas: The benefits of communication. *Journal of Personality and Social Psychology, 87,* 845–859. doi: 10.1037/0022-3514.87.6.845

Tedeschi, J. P., & Melburg, V. (1984). Impression management and influence in the organization. *Research on the Sociology of Organizations, 3,* 31–58.

Tedeschi, J. T., & Felson, R. B. (1994). Frustration, aversiveness, and aggression. In J. T. Tedeschi & R. B. Felson, *Violence, aggression and coercive actions* (pp. 37–69). Washington, D. C.: American Psychological Association. doi: 10.1037/10160-002

Tesser, A. (1978). Self-generated attitude change. In L. Berkowitz (Ed.), *Advances in Experimental Social Psychology* (Vol. 11, pp. 289–338). New York, NY: Academic Press.

Tetlock, P. E., Peterson, R. S., McGuire, C., Chang, S., & Feld, P. (1992). Assessing political group dynamics: A test of the groupthink model. *Journal of Personality and Social Psychology, 63,* 403–425. doi: 10.1037/0022-3514.63.3.403

Thibaut, J. W., & Kelley, H. H. (1959). *The social psychology of groups.* New York, NY: Wiley.

Thoits, P. A. (1995). Stress, coping, and social support processes: Where are we? What next? *Journal of Health and Social Behavior, 35,* 53–79.

Thompson, L., & Spanier, G. B. (1983). The end of marriage and acceptance of termination. *Journal of Marriage and Family, 45,* 103–113. doi: 10.2307/351299

Tice, D. M. (1991). Esteem protection or enhancement? Self-handicapping motives and attributions differ by trait self-esteem. *Journal of Personality and Social Psychology, 60,* 711–725. doi: 10.1037/0022-3514.60.5.711

Timmers, R., & van der Wijst, P. (2007). Images as anti-smoking fear appeals: The effect of emotion on the persuasion process. *Information Design Journal, 15,* 21–36. doi: 10.1075/idj.15.1.04tim

Tolman, C. W. (1967). The effects of tapping sounds on feeding behavior of domestic chicks. *Animal Behavior, 15,* 145–148. doi: 10.1016/0003-3472(64)90008-9

Tomada, G., & Schneider, B. H. (1997). Relational aggression, gender, and peer acceptance: Invariance across culture, stability over time, and concordance across informants. *Developmental Psychology, 33,* 601–609. doi: 10.1037/0012-1649.33.4.601

Tong, E. M. W., Tan, C. R. M., Latheef, N. A., Selamat, M. F. B., & Tan, D. K. B. (2008). Conformity: Moods matter. *European Journal of Social Psychology, 38*, 601–611. doi: 10.1002/ejsp.485

Tormala, Z. L., & Petty, R. E. (2002). What doesn't kill me makes me stronger: The effects of resisting persuasion on attitude certainty. *Journal of Personality and Social Psychology, 83*, 1298–1313. doi: 1037/0022-3514.83.6.1298

Tormala, Z. L., & Petty, R. E. (2004a). Resistance to persuasion and attitude certainty: The moderating role of elaboration. *Personality and Social Psychology Bulletin, 30*, 1446–1457. doi: 10.1177/01461/20464251

Tormala, Z. L., & Petty, R. E. (2004b). Source credibility and attitude certainty: A meta-cognitive analysis of resistance to persuasion. *Journal of Consumer Psychology, 14*, 427–442. doi: 10.1207/s15327663jcp1404_11

Tormala, Z. L., Brinol, P., & Petty, R. E. (2006). When credibility attacks: The reverse impact of source credibility on persuasion. *Journal of Experimental Social Psychology, 42*, 684–691. doi: 10.1016/j.jesp.2005.10.005

Tormala, Z. L., Clarkson, J. J., & Petty, R. E. (2006). Resisting persuasion by the skin of one's teeth: The hidden success of resisted persuasive messages. *Journal of Personality and Social Psychology, 91*, 423–435. doi: 10.1037/0022-3514.91.3.423

Tremblay, R. E. (2000). The development of aggressive behaviour during childhood: What have we learned in the past century? *International Journal of Behavior Development, 24*, 129–141. doi: 10.1080/016502500383232

Triplett, N. (1898). The dynamogenic factors in pacemaking and competition. *American Journal of Psychology, 9*, 507–533.

TruckInfo.net. (2011). Trucking Statistics. Retrieved from www.truckinfo.net/trucking/stats.htm

Tsui, A. S. (1984). A role-set analysis of managerial reputation. *Organizational Behavior and Human Performance, 34*, 64–96. doi: 10.1016/0030-5073(84)90037-0

Tucker, P., & Aron, A. (1993). Passionate love and marital satisfaction at key transition point in the family life cycle. *Journal of Social and Clinical Psychology, 12*, 135–147.

Tuckey, M. R., & Brewer, N. (2003). The influence of schemas, stimulus ambiguity, and interview schedule on eyewitness memory over time. *Journal of Experimental Psychology: Applied, 9*, 101–118. doi: 10.1037/1076-898X.9.2.101

Turner, R. N., & Crisp, R. J. (2010). Imagined intergroup contact reduces implicit prejudice. *British Journal of Social Psychology, 49*, 129–142. doi: 10.1348/014466609X419901

Tversky, A., & Kahneman, D. (1973). Availability: A heuristic for judging frequency and probability. *Cognitive Psychology, 5*, 207–232. doi: 10.1016/0010-0285(73)90033-9

Tversky, A., & Kahneman, D. (1983). Extensional versus intuitive reasoning: The conjunction fallacy in probability judgment. *Psychological Review, 90*, 293–315. doi: 10.1037/0033-295X.90.4.293

Underwood, M. K., Beron, K. J., & Rosen, L. H. (2009). Continuity and change in social and physical aggression from middle childhood through early adolescence. *Aggressive Behavior, 35*, 357–375. doi: 10.1002/ab.20313

Valkenburg, P. M., & Peter, J. (2007). Who visits online dating sites? Exploring some characteristics of online daters. *CyberPsychology & Behavior, 10*, 849–852. doi:10.1089/cpb.2007.9941

Van Beest, I., & Williams, K. D. (2006). When inclusion costs and ostracism pays, ostracism still hurts. *Journal of Personality and Social Psychology, 91*, 918–928. doi: 10.1037/0022-3514.91.5.918

Van Boven, L., Kamada, A., & Gilovich, T. (1999). The perceiver as perceived: Everyday intuitions about the correspondence bias. *Journal of Personality and Social Psychology, 77*, 1188–1199. doi: 10.1037/0022-3514.77.6.1188

Van Boven, L., White, K., Kamada, A., & Gilovich, T. (2003). Intuitions about situational correction in self and others. *Journal of Personality and Social Psychology, 85*, 249–258. doi: 10.1037/0022-3514.85.2.249

Van de Kragt, A. J. C., Dawes, R. M., Orbell, J. M., Braver, S. R., & Wilson, L. A. (1986). Doing well and doing good as ways of resolving social dilemmas. In H. A. M. Wilke, D. M. Messick, & C. G. Rutte (Eds.), *Experimental social dilemmas* (pp. 205–234). New York, NY: Verlag Peter Lang.

Van Dijk, E., & Wilke, H. (1995). Coordination rules in asymmetric social dilemmas: A comparison between public good dilemmas and resource dilemmas. *Journal of Experimental Social Psychology, 31*, 1–27. doi: 10.1006/jesp.1995.1001

Van Eeden, R., Cilliers, F., van Deventer, V. (2008). Leadership styles and associated personality traits: Support for the conceptualisation of transactional and transformational leadership. *South African Journal of Psychology, 38*, 253–267.

Van Emmerik, I. J. H., & Stone, T. H. (2002). Engagement in high- and low-status volunteering. *Netherlands' Journal of Social Sciences, 38*, 239–251.

Van Harreveld, F., van der Plight, J., de Vries, N. K., Wenneker, C., & Verhue, D. (2004). Ambivalence and information integration in attitudinal judgment. *British Journal of Social Psychology, 43*, 431–447. doi: 10.1348/0144666042037971

Van Hooft, E. A. J., Born, M. P. H., Taris, T. W., & Van der Flier, H. (2006). Cross-cultural generalizability of the theory of planned behavior: A study on job seeking in the Netherlands. *Journal of Cross-Cultural Psychology, 37*, 127–135. doi: 10.1177/0022022105284491

Van Staden, W., & Coetzee, K. (2010). Conceptual relations between loneliness and culture. *Current Opinion in Psychiatry, 23*, 524–529. doi: 10.1097/YCO.0b013e32833f2ff9

Vaughn, D. (1986). *Uncoupling: Turning points in intimate relationships*. New York, NY: Oxford University Press.

Wagstaff, G. F., Wheatcroft, J., Cole, J. C., Brunas-Wagstaff, J., Blackmore, V., & Pilkington, A. (2008). Some cognitive and neuropsychological aspects of social inhibition and facilitation. *European Journal of Cognitive Psychology, 20*, 828–846. doi: 10.1080/09541440701469749

Wallace, D. S., Paulson, R. M., Lord, C. G., & Bond, C. F., Jr. (2005). Which behaviors do attitudes predict? Meta-analyzing the effects of social pressure and perceived difficulty. *Review of General Psychology, 9*, 214–227. doi: 10.1037/1089-2680.9.3.214

Walster, E., Aronson, V., Abrahams, D., & Rottman, L. (1966). Importance of physical attractiveness in dating behavior. *Journal of Personality and Social Psychology, 4*, 508–516. doi: 10.1037/h0021188

Walster, E., Walster, G. W., Piliavin, J., & Schmidt, L. (1973). "Playing hard to get": Understanding an elusive phenomenon. *Journal of Personality and Social Psychology, 26*, 113–121. doi: 10.1037/h0034234

Walton, G. M., & Cohen, G. L. (2003). Stereotype lift. *Journal of Experimental Social Psychology, 39*, 456–467. doi: 10.1016/S0022-1031(03)00019-2

Wang, S. S., Houshyar, S., & Prinstein, M. J. (2006). Adolescent girls' and boys' weight-related health behaviors and cognitions: Associations with reputation- and preference-based peer status. *Health Psychology, 25*, 658–663. doi: 10.1037/0278-6133.25.5.658

Warburton, W. A., Williams, K. D., & Cairns, D. R. (2006). When ostracism leads to aggression: The moderating effect of control deprivation. *Journal of Experimental Social Psychology, 42*, 213–220. doi: 10.1016/j.jesp.2005.03.005

Weber, M. J., & Murnighan, J. K. (2008). Suckers or saviors? Consistent contributors in social dilemmas. *Journal of Personality and Social Psychology, 95*, 1340–1353. doi: 10.1037/a0013326

Wedekind, C., & Milinski, M. (1996). Human cooperation in the simultaneous and the alternating Prisoner's Dilemma: Pavlov versus generous tit-for-tat. *Proceedings of the National Academy of Science, 93*, 2686–2689.

Weigel, R. H., & Newman, L. S. (1976). Increasing attitude-behavior correspondence by broadening the scope of the behavioral measure. *Journal of Personality and Social Psychology, 33*, 793–802. doi: 10.1037/0022-3514.33.6.793

Werner, C. M., Stoll, R., Birch, P., & White, P. H. (2002). Clinical validation and cognitive elaboration: Signs that encourage sustained recycling. *Basic and Applied Social Psychology, 24*, 185–203. doi: 10.1207/15324830276017911100

Werner, C. M., White, P. H., Byerly, S., & Stoll, R. (2009). Signs that encourage internalized recycling: Clinical validation, weak messages and creative elaboration. *Journal of Environmental Psychology, 29*, 193–202. doi: 10.1016/j.jenvp.2009.02.003

Werner, N. E., & Crick, N. R. (1999). Relational aggression and social-psychological adjustment in a college sample. *Journal of Abnormal Psychology, 108*, 615–623. doi: 10.1037/0021-843X.108.4.615

Werth, L., & Strack, F. (2003). An inferential approach to the knew-it-all-along phenomenon. *Memory, 11*, 411–419. doi: 10.1080/09658210244000586

West, D. J., & Farrington, D. P. (1977). *The delinquent way of life*. London, U.K.: Heinemann.

Whatley, M. A., Webster, J. M., Smith, R. H., & Rhodes, A. (1999). The effect of a favor on public and private compliance: How internalized is the norm of reciprocity? *Basic and Applied Social Psychology, 21*, 251–259. doi: 10.1207/S15324834BASP2103_8

Wheeler, L., & Davis, H. (1967). Social disruption of performance on a DRL schedule. *Psychonomic Science, 7*, 249–250.

Wheeler, S. C., Brinol, P., & Hermann, A. D. (2007). Resistance to persuasion as self-regulation: Ego-depletion and its effect on attitude change processes. *Journal of Experimental Social Psychology, 43*, 150–156. doi: 10.1016/j.jesp.2006.01.001

Whitty, M. T. (2008). Revealing the "real" me, searching for the "actual" you: Presentations of self on an internet dating site. *Computers in Human Behavior, 24*, 1707–1723. doi: 10.1016/j.chb.2007.07.002

Wicker, A. W. (1969). Attitudes versus actions: The relationship of verbal and overt behavioral responses to attitude objects. *Journal of Social Issues, 25*, 41–78.

Wicklund, R. A., & Brehm, J. W. (1976). *Perspectives on cognitive dissonance*. Oxford, UK: Lawrence Erlbaum.

Wiekens, C. J., & Stapel, D. A. (2010). Self-awareness and saliency of social versus individualistic behavioral standards. *Social Psychology, 41*, 10–19. doi: 10.1027/1864-9335/a00003

wikiHow.com (n.d.). How to play how to get. *wikiHow.com*. Retrieved from http://www.wikihow.com/Play-Hard-to-Get

Williams, K. D. (1997). Social ostracism. In R. M. Kowalski (Ed.), *Aversive interpersonal behaviors* (pp. 133–170). New York, NY: Plenum Press.

Williams, K. D. (2001). *Ostracism: The power of silence*. New York, NY: Guilford Publications.

Williams, K. D. (2007). Ostracism. *Annual Review of Psychology, 58*, 425–452. doi: 10.1146/annurev.psych.58.110405.085641

Williams, K. D. (2009). The effects of frustration, violence, and trait hostility after playing a video game. *Mass Communication and Society, 12,* 291–310. doi: 10.1080/15205430802461087

Williams, K., Harkins, S. G., & Latane, B. (1981). Identifiability as a deterrent to social loafing: Two cheering experiments. *Journal of Personality and Social Psychology, 40,* 303–311. doi: 10.1037/0022-3514.40.2.303

Williams, S., & Taormina, R. J. (1993). Unanimous versus majority influences on group polarization in business decision making. *Journal of Social Psychology, 133,* 199–205.

Williams, T. P., & Sogon, S. (1984). Group composition and conforming behavior in Japanese students. *Japanese Psychological Research, 26,* 231–234.

Wilmot, W. W., Carbaugh, D. A., & Baxter, L. A. (1985). Communication strategies. In H. T. Reis & S. Sprecher (Eds.), *Encyclopedia of human relationships* (pp. 434–435). Thousand Oaks, CA: Sage.

Wilson, B. J., Smith, S. L., Potter, W. J., Kunkel, D., Linz, D., Colvin, C. M., & Donnerstein, E. (2002). Violence in children's television programming: Assessing the risks. *Journal of Communication, 52,* 5–35. doi: 10.1111/j.1460-2466.202.tb02531.x

Wilson. T. D., Lindsey, S., & Schooler, T. Y. (2000). A model of dual attitudes. *Psychological Review, 107,* 101–126. doi: 10.1037/0033-295X.107.1.101

Witte, K. (1998). Fear as motivator, fear as inhibitor: Using the extended parallel model to explain fear appeal successes and failures. In P. A. Anderson & L. K. Guerrero (Eds.), *Handbook of communication and emotion; Research, theory, applications, and contexts* (pp. 423–450). San Diego, CA: Academic Press.

Wolfers, J., & Zitzewitz, E. (2004). Prediction markets. *National Bureau of Economic Research Working Paper, 10504.* Retrieved from http://www.nber.org/papers/w10504

Wood, W., & Kallgren, C. A. (1988). Communicator attributes and persuasion: Recipients' access to attitude-relevant information in memory. *Personality and Social Psychology Bulletin, 14,* 172–182. doi: 10.1177/0146467288141017

Wright, R. (1994). *The moral animal: The new science of evolutionary psychology.* New York, NY: Pantheon Books.

Wright, R. A., & Contrada, R. J. (1986). Dating selectivity and interpersonal attraction: Toward a better understanding of the "elusive phenomenon." *Journal of Social and Personal Relationships, 3,* 131–148. doi: 10.1177/0265407586032001

Wright, S. C., Aron, A., McLaughlin-Volpe, T., & Ropp, S. A. (1997). The extended contact effect: Knowledge of cross-group friendships and prejudice. *Journal of Personality and Social Psychology, 73,* 73–90. doi: 10.1037/0022-3514.73.1.73

Wu, C., & Shaffer, D. R. (1987). Susceptibility to persuasive appeals as a function of source credibility and prior experience with the attitude object. *Journal of Personality and Social Psychology, 52,* 677–688. doi: 10.1037/0022-3514.52.4.677

Wu, P. L., & Chiou, W. B. (2009). More options lead to more searching and worse choices in finding partners for romantic relationships online: An experimental study. *CyberPsychology, 12,* 315–318. doi: 10.1089/cpb.2008.0182

Xiao, H. (1999). Independence and obedience: An analysis of child socialization values in the United States and China. *Journal of Comparative Family Studies, 30,* 641–657.

Xiao, H. (2000). Class, gender, and parental values in the 1990s. *Gender and Society, 14,* 785–803. doi: 10.1177/089124300014006005

Yablo, P. D., & Field, N. P. (2007). The role of culture in altruism: Thailand and the United States. *Psychologia: An International Journal of Psychology in the Orient, 50,* 236–251. doi: 10.2117/psysoc.2007.236